do real men pray?

do

REAL MEN

pray?

✛ ✛ ✛

IMAGES OF THE CHRISTIAN MAN AND
MALE SPIRITUALITY IN WHITE PROTESTANT AMERICA

Charles H. Lippy

THE UNIVERSITY OF TENNESSEE PRESS / KNOXVILLE

Library of Congress Cataloging-in-Publication Data
Lippy, Charles H.
    Do real men pray? : images of the Christian man and male spirituality
in white Protestant America / Charles H. Lippy.
        p. cm.
    Includes bibliographical references and index.
    ISBN 1-57233-358-8 (hardcover : alk. paper)
    1. Protestant men—Religious life—United States—Case studies.   2. Men,
White—Religious life—United States—Case studies.   3. United States—
Religious life and customs—Case studies.   I. Title.
    BR517.L58 2004
    280′.4′0810973—dc22
                                                            2004010628

For Lucy, Winston, Truman, Kelley, Sydney, Meredith, and Jefferson

Contents

Foreword

CHARLES LIPPY CONFESSES THAT WHEN PLOTTING THIS BOOK HE had first wanted to "do it all," to tell it all, at least in sketch form. That would have meant the need to write concerning almost half of the church-goers in American history, and certainly the majority among the church leadership until the recent past. In other words, concerning the men. It would have meant canvassing the register of denominations, movements, and experiments from A through Z to locate the names that would eventually be indexed. More "would haves" come to mind: such a design would have meant Lippy's moving from the tangible institutions to the more elusive phenomena today clustered under the name "spirituality." We are only beginning. His original dream would have become a nightmare as he ranged through the phone books, *Who's Whos*, encyclopedias, and lists of donors and authors to determine who were most representative. Finally, he would have written, if not a library full, then at least many shelves full of books whose indexes would overwhelm even the persistent research scholar. The books would have been confusing, deadly dull, and out of print before anyone might have considered paper-backing them.

Disabused of his first vision, as he admits he was, he set out to write a book that will serve a very different purpose than a "do all" kind of treatise might have aimed to accomplish. And what he achieved will serve better than would encyclopedic volumes at revealing something of the character of American religionists through several centuries. Religionists? Should we not say only "the men among them"? Hardly, for what is now called "women's history" makes very clear, dealing with one gender or one class or one ideology informs the reader about others, if not all.

Lippy therefore faced a methodological problem. If a conventional book titled, say, *All about All the Men in American Religion* had emerged, you can be sure that scrupulous reviewers would find some favorite of theirs missing or another treated with too much reserve. This is not a conventional book, and reviewers can argue over issues other than those connected with the interests of the "can I find anyone who was left out?" school of critics.

What Professor Lippy chose to do, and he did it well, was to select six figures who, if they were representative, did not concern themselves too much about the question, of whom are they representative? Interesting people—I wish I could zero in on a more defining word than "interesting"—tend to impress us both by the way they relate to certain norms and traditions and by the way they ignore or violate them. Still, there must be some credible reason for finding six themes and then locating a person to match them, or finding six compelling persons whose stories help illumine time and place and context.

The method reminds me of what the great nineteenth-century cultural historian Jacob Burckhardt called choosing several *Durchschnitten*, "transverse sections of history," and having cut them, Lippy followed where they led. Another metaphor comes to mind: Lippy is taking soundings, the way ships entering or leaving harbors or encountering the unfamiliar do. Of course, finding a sounding does not assure safe passage: a hidden reef or an old shipwreck just under the surface a few yards away from the sounding could lead to confusion if not disaster. Still, transverse sections, to use the horizontal image, or soundings, based on the vertical, can be helpful to anyone who wants to grow in awareness of both a type, a model, an image of an age and a complex and revealing individual character, six times over.

Go through all the efforts of measuring and assessing that I have described and you could still fail to illumine the broader topic. The author has to bring provocative questions to his six characters in search of a plot. Lippy is particularly helpful here, because even when he is not explicit about a point, knowing that such explicitness can mean restricting a subject, he offers many apparent throwaway lines that in reality find him working away at themes that will be memorable and informative.

In many ways, this book is an essay on paradoxes of American religion, or at least of men in American religion. The paradox does not come in at the point of linkage between adjectives and nouns in the chapter headings and plots. Of course, patriarchs are expected to be dutiful, adventurers to be courageous, businessmen to be efficient, leaders to be faithful, and perhaps even entrepreneurs to be gentlemen and thinkers to be positive. There is no tension at this point. One could play around by breaking these linkages and fastening others together. There are efficient patriarchs, positive adventurers, efficient thinkers. But Lippy has something specific in mind in pointing to particular adjectives in nexus with particular nouns defining roles.

His paradoxes, subvert and overt, are of another character. So far as he and we can tell, in most religious movements in most corners of the nation, congregations were made up of more women than men, yet they were ruled by men. The women's names rarely appear in the history books, or rarely appeared until the "women's movement" in historical writing came along to knock old-school historians off balance. Why were the names not there? No one has to spend more than a few seconds coming up with an answer about power. The men had the power, the women did not.

Then questions like this come to mind: What do you mean by "power," and how did men come by their kind of power while women settled for and exerted their influence through a different kind? Did women willingly submit to the male minority and not mind being excluded from the records? Did a conspiracy of men keep their names out? How's this for a passageway into paradox: Did women choose to play apparently secondary roles? My colleague Martin Riesebrodt has written a book on Islamic and American Protestant "fundamentalist" women, who make up the majority of the membership in the movements. Yet they belong to such even as and perhaps because they "put women down." Did childbearing and other "womanly" roles confine most women so much that history passed them by? About the time these questions were becoming canonical, something happened in the writing of history. It occurred to writers who worked through and played with "women's history" in religion that there had been few histories of men in American religion. To push paradoxes further, if men were to be manly leaders, why did so many foreign observers note that many of the clerical leaders were feminized, not "muscular Christians," male style? Another question: If men are the main subjects of most histories of religion because they were seen as the history makers and because, as winners, they left the records and wrote the histories, why did not their being men, their maleness, their masculinity, become the subject matter of more than a few books that appeared at only a few moments in American religious history?

Perhaps Jacob Burckhardt is of help here, too. He wrote that many of the most important things in history do not get recorded because they are so taken for granted, so close up, that one can overlook them. They may be a big element in the "truth about life," but their truth is so manifest that no one bothers to explore what that truth is. So men ran the show, at least in the public zones of religious expression. We take for granted that women were imparting the truth about life to children, in the home, in restricted congregational circles, in auxiliaries and support movements. So why write them down? We have to notice the idiosyncratic, the offbeat, the men who get typed as leaders. While all this questioning goes on, we notice that isolating women and themes associated with the record of women in history was growing sophisticated. Schools, conferences, programs, curriculums, and books featured women in religion, and men as men, with men's interests as opposed to the interests of undifferentiated humanity, were on the sidelines and in the shadows.

So Charles Lippy comes along to bring some characters and characteristics onto the main stage and under the bright lights, as if to see what might happen. And what happened here is the emergence, out of mini-biographies, of some revealing strains and strands, some informative types and typologies. Yes, American religion, lay and clerical, naturally included patriarchs and entrepreneurs, adventurers and business people, thinkers and leaders. But shining the light on particular men in these roles moves beyond the "natural inclusion" to the brilliant paradigm, the exception that helps define the rule, or what passes for the rule in the chaos of America.

The reader need not worry about the representativeness of Lippy's elect few, since the stories he tells about them are sufficiently rewarding to hold attention and inspire enjoyment among even casual readers. Yet he shows how many tentacles and nexuses are related to the adjectives describing the nouns, which means the roles, and which means, in the end, the human agents. In following up on them, it is possible after the reading to have gained some new grasp of more than gender, more than religion, more than America, something fresh about the bewildering ways of being human.

Martin E. Marty
EMERITUS, THE UNIVERSITY OF CHICAGO

Preface

I AM NOT CERTAIN WHEN WRITING A BOOK ABOUT MALE SPIRITU-
ality and images of the Christian man in white Protestant America began
to take shape in my mind. As a student of American religious life, I have
long been sensitive to the growing literature that came from second-wave
feminists who made connections between the personal experience of
women as women and distinctive approaches to piety and spirituality. I
watched and applauded the movement for ordination of women to professional ministry. For many years, I addressed some of those developments
and included writing by women religious and theological authors in courses
I taught on American religion, modern Christian thought, and current religious issues.

Along the way, I realized that at the annual meetings of the American
Academy of Religion, I was drawn more and more to sessions offered both
in feminist studies and in men's studies; the topics under scrutiny there
required looking at what was familiar and assumed from very different
angles of vision. My friends Michael Clark and Bob McNeir spoke often of
their involvement with the American Men's Studies Association, prodding
me finally to become a member when I realized that the association's journal often carried articles that centered on religion and spirituality.

Frequently I recalled a conversation in the summer of 1988 when I was
privileged to be part of a Fulbright study program in India. While in the
home of a prosperous, upper-caste family, I asked about the ways in which
the family was religious. They had already showed me a rather elaborate
room in their spacious apartment for *puja* or daily devotion. I was struck by
the observation of the husband and father when he said, "I really leave religion to the women. I'm not very religious at all. I pray only two hours a day."
I wondered how many U.S. Christian pastors would classify male congregants who prayed only two hours a day as "not very religious at all." But I
understood that what this man meant was simply that he did not frequent a
Hindu temple with any regularity to make an offering or receive a blessing;

such public expressions of spiritual identity were, in his mind, more appropriate to women. His spirituality would find expression in more personal and private ways.

At some point, I also realized that issues of gender were having a profound impact on my teaching. Most telling were responses to an openended question on a final exam in my Religion in American Life class. I invited students to suggest three themes that they thought would best illuminate the overall story; every student in the class identified the role of women as one of those themes. That stunning reaction nudged me to think about offering a course devoted to Women and Religion in America, a course that spurred an enormous amount of reading and reflection on my part and one that finally made its debut at the University of Tennessee at Chattanooga in the spring of 2001. Indeed, the title for this book came from a question posed by one female student in that class. We had been discussing the disparity in membership figures and levels of participation in organized religious activities between white Protestant men and women in the United States when one student observed that, while driving to the university that morning, she had seen a bumper sticker on an automobile that read "Real Men Love Jesus." That comment prompted another to ask, "If men don't go to church but they love Jesus, do real men pray?"

By then, my roaming around in gender studies in religion, feminist theology, men's studies, and a host of cognate areas had convinced me that the story of American religion was far more complex than a tale of patriarchy and male-dominated institutions. After all, those of us who worked in the field knew that women, not men, had long filled the pews of American churches and provided the labor to sustain church activities, from those of local congregations to the work of national denominations. Then when the media began giving attention to the Promise Keepers movement in the mid-1990s, I was struck as well by how often commentators assumed that this ministry appeared out of the blue, that there was nothing in American religious history of a similar orientation, that never before had there been a concerted effort to draw men toward the spiritual life. As a historian, I knew better. I knew there was a story to be told. Not one of the old patriarchal triumphalism, but one that looked at what signals white Protestant American men had received from the religious and cultural worlds around them when they sought to cultivate their own spirituality and see themselves as Christian men.

My concern is not directly with the social construction of masculinity, although some work done in that area clearly informs my perspective. I am willing to leave to social scientists, especially psychologists and sociologists, the task of furthering our understanding of how gender is more than simply a biological matter, but one that profoundly reflects societal influence. Nor do I intend to address every movement in white American Protestantism that may have had an impact on Christian understanding of gender roles. For example, more than a decade ago Betty DeBerg called attention to the ways early-twentieth-century fundamentalism expressed apprehension about the changing roles of women in American society by attacking certain stereotypes of female behavior and ranting about the proper but submissive stance that was a mark of the white Protestant Christian woman.[1] Less was said directly about white Protestant Christian men, other than by implication. Hence, even though some of the ideas planted by early fundamentalists weave into the story that follows, I will not address every feature of the convoluted tale of links between this first wave of fundamentalism and white male Protestant spirituality.

This book is the first step in telling that story, but it is only the first step. When I first talked with colleagues about a book on male spirituality in America in historical perspective, I had ideas far grander than what unfolds in the following chapters. Always eager to tell the whole story, I wanted to look at everyone—Protestants, Catholics, Jews, Native Americans, Euro-Americans, African Americans, and more. Somehow I thought one book could do it all. Those who commented on the prospectus I submitted to the University of Tennessee Press quickly disabused me of such delusions of grandeur. Now, in retrospect, I am keenly aware that I have only scratched the surface by looking at six clusters of images that have dominated white American mainline and/or evangelical Protestant approaches to male spirituality and models of the ideal Christian man. For the most part, then, the emphasis falls on white men of social and economic privilege whose influence dominated public perceptions. There remain many more rich stories to be told and to be analyzed.

The opening chapter will lead us into some consideration of links between gender and spirituality, between gender and what it means for a male to identify himself as a Christian man. Each of the six clusters of images then receives its own chapter, followed by a biographical profile of a selected individual whose life exemplifies the particular image under scrutiny. There is a rough chronology here, for I look at these notions of the Protestant Christian man and male spirituality as they developed one on top of the other, from the time of Puritan arrival in the New World through the closing decades of the twentieth century. The final chapter returns to the more theoretical considerations posed at the outset. There I become a bit more speculative than is usually the case for a historian, but a good historian also struggles to listen to the evidence and let the evidence tell its own story. In this case, the evidence seemed to me to warrant that more speculative conclusion. However, I realize that I never resolve the dilemma of biology versus socialization, in part because I believe that the issue remains open-ended.

After I completed the draft of this book, I came upon Donald Capps's *Men and Their Religion,* an important cognate study. Capps is also convinced that white Protestant men are spiritual and religious, albeit in ways different from women.[2] Although he draws much more than I on a psychologically informed theological vocabulary in his discussion of the melancholy male, his insistence that there is a vibrant spirituality that buttresses white male Protestants, but one that is often "invisible" to both casual observers and men themselves, reflects some of my own understanding.

No book ever comes into being without the support of colleagues and institutions. Much of the reading for this study came during a year when I was honored to be designated a Visiting Research Scholar at Emory University. I am grateful to Profs. Laurie Patton and Paul Courtright for making that possible. I also relied heavily on the Interlibrary Loan services of the Lupton Library at the University of Tennessee at Chattanooga as well as the collections of the Chattanooga–Hamilton County Bicentennial Library, the Squires Library at Lee University, and the Dixon Pentecostal Research Center and Archive in Cleveland, Tennessee. I appreciate especially the way Don Smeeton and David Roebuck facilitated my use of materials at Lee University and the Dixon Pentecostal Research Center. Profs. Stephen Boyd, Nancy Hardesty, Merrill Hawkins, and Colleen McDannell read an early prospectus for this project; I have benefited from their wise suggestions. The end result is indeed rather different from what I first proposed, thanks to their astute critiques.

Just when some of the initial thinking about this book was underway, two program units of the American Academy of Religion at one annual meeting devoted sessions to scrutinizing the Promise Keepers movement. Responding to presentations in both sessions was Prof. Mary Stewart Van Leeuwen of Eastern University. Subsequently, I had further communication with her, for I found her observations unusually perceptive. She then extended me the privilege of reading her own next book in draft; there she offers a challenging understanding of masculinity from an evangelical Reformed perspective.

At the University of Tennessee at Chattanooga, Herbert Burhenn, dean of the College of Arts and Sciences, and William Harman, head of the Department of Philosophy and Religion, were instrumental in arranging for reductions in teaching loads that made the actual writing possible. Parts of chapter 1 formed the basis for a public lecture at the University of Tennessee at Chattanooga; observations, comments, and questions from those attending helped sharpen my thinking. As well, the course I mentioned on Women and Religion in America, which drew several students enrolled in the women's studies program and a few others, had an impact. Teaching that course turned out to be a joy; conversations with the women and men who took the class spurred me to rethink and refine all sorts of issues relating to gender and spirituality. Joyce Harrison, Scot Danforth, and others on the staff of the University of Tennessee Press have been a bulwark of support since the inception of this study. Thank you.

A great debt is also owed to those who read the complete manuscript and offered suggestions that have helped shape the pages that followed. I am deeply grateful to Prof. Nancy Hardesty (Clemson University), Prof. Stephen Boyd (Wake Forest University), Prof. Martin E. Marty (emeritus, University of Chicago), Prof. Wade Clark Roof (University of California at Santa Barbara), Dan Waterman (University of Alabama), and one anonymous reader for their diligent reading of an earlier draft, their wise counsel, and their judicious suggestions.

The dedication identifies those whose presence reminds me that there are other important things in life besides writing books.

CHAPTER I

✢ ✢ ✢

White Male Spirituality and the Christian Man

Do real men pray? When Promise Keepers burst onto the religious scene in the early 1990s, media coverage of the mass rallies held in athletic stadiums emphasized that these events were designed for men only. The media also trumpeted Promise Keepers' hopes of sparking a religious commitment among American men, for most commentators believed that such had never before been stirred. Promise Keepers emerged when a "men's movement" was moving into its adolescence, at least among scholars. That effort, in turn, owed much to the women's movement and the feminist consciousness that came to the fore in the last third of the twentieth century. Second-wave feminism in the religious sphere had articulated the ways experiences unique to women spurred a spirituality that was also unique and too often eclipsed by a religious world that tacitly made male experience normative. If there was a distinct and distinctive female spirituality, was there not also a distinct and distinctive male spirituality? For a white Protestant American male, what did it mean to be a Christian man?

To probe those issues adequately would require more than one volume. But to begin the process, I will focus on white Protestant men in the United States. They are, for the most part, men of social and economic privilege. Thus while they may not represent all American men, not even all American Christian men, they are indicative of those whose influence has long penetrated every niche of American life.

Problems of Terminology

Studies of baby boomers, those born in the two decades after the close of World War II, stress how that generation has spurned more institutional forms of religion in favor of spirituality.[1] By the dawn of the twenty-first century, it was fashionable in many circles to talk about spirituality as if it were something separate and distinct from religion and perhaps not even related to religion at all. For persons of this ilk, religion denoted institutions such as churches and temples, denominations and traditions, and professionals such as priests and pastors, theologians and denominational bureaucrats. For a variety of reasons, as boomers moved into adolescence and young adulthood, such religious institutions appeared increasingly bound to the culture around them, arid representatives of a status quo that was undone by social phenomena such as the civil rights movement and protests over American involvement in Vietnam. Whatever the reason, churches had lost their vitality.[2] Along with that erosion of institutional relevance went a decline in interest in religion. The easiest, albeit far from the best, way to document that erosion is by citing the steady drop in membership in those predominantly white Protestant denominations in the United States long dubbed "mainline," groups such as the Methodists, Congregationalists, Presbyterians, Episcopalians, and others whose heritage stretches back to the formative years of the nation.[3]

In opting for spirituality over religion, boomers were reaching for something personal that was not controlled by institutions or limited by traditions. But they also expected spirituality to provide the overarching meaning and sense of purpose for human life that religious traditions and institutions had once taken as their primary task. Yet even in earlier years, a sense of personal religious expression was not absent. Sociologists such as Wade Clark Roof and Robert Wuthnow have argued that the difference that came with boomers, male and female alike, was seeing spirituality as a quest or a journey, something that was always in process moving toward ultimate meaning but not fixed around a denomination or tradition or determined by one.[4] For those shaped by a Christian ethos, there remained ideas of the Christian man and the Christian woman, albeit ideas that were not confined to those advanced by religious organizations.

Even so, "spirituality" remains a slippery and elusive term. At one time, for example, it was a word used to describe something akin to mystical experience. Now, recent scientific studies suggest that mystical experience may have direct links to the structure of the brain in individuals who are prone to some direct apprehension of the Divine and sense of union with the transcendent.[5] Such is a far cry from the eclectic practices of boomers who draw on a host of resources to construct an understanding of reality that gives their lives meaning.

Before spirituality became a buzz word to denote that private, personal realm of belief and idiosyncratic practice, writers about religion often spoke of piety. At the most basic level, piety signals an abiding devotion to God, reflected in personal practices urged or mandated by particular religious institutions. Regular attendance at public worship might be the most obvious example of a practice associated with piety. Within Roman Catholicism the saying of the rosary illustrates the practice of piety. For many Christians, piety might include regular reading of Scripture, often with the aid of a devotional guide prepared under the auspices of a denominational or ecumenical agency.

Over the years, though, piety acquired a lot of negative baggage in popular perception. For many, it came to denote an excessive religious zeal that was too often condemnatory of those who did not share a firm commitment to orthodoxy. Most likely, the misunderstanding of Puritanism as a religious system that fostered a narrow and rigid way of being religious, which remained part of popular American thinking until well into the twentieth century, made piety the antithesis of pleasure and enthusiasm for things religious an anachronism in a scientific and technologically oriented world. Piety meant irrelevance, something removed from the perplexities of modern life. Spirituality, at least, lacked both the sense of being outmoded that went with piety and the sense of being wedded to the cultural status quo that went with organized religion.

Another term that carries mixed messages is "religiosity," which refers simply to the varied ways individuals go about being religious, pursuing and finding meaning in life, having some sort of lens through which to filter all human experience. In this sense, religiosity is really a synonym for piety, if not for spirituality. Yet religiosity, too, has acquired a host of negative connotations, so much so that most dictionary definitions link religiosity to excessive, overly zealous, and exaggerated devotion. Hidden in these designations is a dimension of hypocrisy, for zealots who tout their religiosity are thought to mask their true motives and thereby conceal their intent to deceive the unsuspecting.

Spirituality may be the most useful word at this juncture only because it has fewer negative associations than piety and religiosity. At the same time, it is not devoid of problems, for in popular parlance it does minimize explicit association with religious institutions and traditions. In an earlier age, piety clearly had links to institutions and traditions, and persons often drew on resources from these institutions and traditions in constructing a personal religiosity. If we adopt spirituality as the most inclusive term and the one with the fewest difficulties, then, we must remember that for many generations of American Protestants, spirituality was informed and shaped by the churches and denominations. Protestant preachers, pastors, and theologians provided some of the images of what spirituality entailed, although not always, as we shall see, in the detail that later students of American religion would like.

So too in the nineteenth century did those who penned handbooks for young men, guides for conduct for those leaving a rural America to make their way in the developing factory towns and cities, sketch verbal pictures of the model white Christian male. Those visions of the ideal spiritual man often came laden with socioeconomic nuances for those who were reaping the benefits of the American version of free enterprise. Sometimes, too, clues for spirituality would come in novels and other literature designed for a mass audience; sometimes they would come as popular writers offered written portraits of the figure of Jesus, always the primary exemplar of religiosity for men within American Protestantism. Hence, the understanding of white male spirituality is intertwined with ideas of what it meant to be a Christian man in Protestant America.

Spirituality is thus never completely divorced from organized religion but operates in a symbiotic relationship with it. Indeed, many of the beliefs and practices that go into a personal spirituality echo what the churches have taught and tried to inculcate in the faithful for centuries. Others may emerge from the culture at large. These cultural patterns often at first glance are not obviously religious until we look at them from a scholarly perspective and see that they operate to create and sustain a larger framework of meaning; in other words, they serve the purpose of religion and function as religious constructs.

In this study, I shall use all three terms—spirituality, piety, and religiosity—but without asserting that any one term reflects an exaggerated, unauthentic way of going about the business of finding meaning in life. Spirituality is thus not something discovered and first appropriated by the baby boomer generation, but, rather, a personal way of being religious reflected in human experience, frequently in conjunction with some sense of a transcendent reality. So too with piety and religiosity: both point to the human activity of trying to carry on in the world in ways that reflect personal ethics and values, link one to a larger transcendent reality, and, in the process, create a realm of meaning for all of human experience. But all these designations point to models of the Christian man for white American Protestants.

Spirituality's Links to Gender

To talk of a specifically male spirituality in American Protestant culture over the generations is thus to explore how men—not a generic term here, but one referring to persons who are by gender male—have looked to models of what it meant to be spiritual or religious and to appropriate them as ideals to emulate in their own lives. Consequently, it also opens up the issue of how spirituality is tied to gender or, more specifically, whether men and women express spirituality in different ways. Are the characteristics of the Christian woman different from those of the Christian man in white Protestant experience?

Such issues come to the fore for several reasons. First, if one presumes that much of Western culture historically has been patriarchal in character and that Christianity itself, with a scriptural heritage dominated by male referents for Deity (especially Father) and a savior figure—Jesus the Christ— who was biologically male, is also skewed to favor men, it would seem to follow that however men express spirituality would be construed as the normative ways of being religious for Protestant Christianity.

There is an implicit danger in presuming that any one expression of spirituality is normative or prescriptive. Once a particular approach achieves that designation, all others are automatically deemed inadequate or inferior. Here the flawed cultural assumptions that men were superior and women inferior easily get transferred to the arena of spirituality, leading to the erroneous conclusion that whenever persons write about spirituality or talk about what it means to be religious, they are operating from a male perspective or presuming only male experience.

What gets lost in making normative claims about forms of spirituality is the simple notion of difference. Difference in and of itself does not imply that one is superior and one is inferior. Rather, difference is just difference; it is value neutral. To assert that men may express spirituality in ways different from women is not to assert that male expressions are normative for all humans or in any way superior to those emerging from female experience. It is simply to assert that men may have expressed their quest for meaning and relation to the transcendent in white American Protestantism in some particular ways that are linked to their being biologically male and to their life experiences as males. There are models for Protestant men that pointed them to what a Christian male should be if he sought to lead a spiritual life.[6]

Thanks to the women's movement from the 1970s on and to the emergence of a significant body of feminist scholarship in religion shaped by the questions and concerns unique to women, it is clear that there are a range of spiritual concerns and a number of approaches to pursuing meaning in life that resonate with the experience of women as women, but not with the experience of men as men. For example, it is commonplace to note how numerous ancient cultures were oriented around fertility and elevated the goddess in ways that reflected the simple facts that women gave birth not only to children but probably to the cosmos as a whole. Men, after all, cannot give physical birth to children; they cannot get pregnant and thus cannot understand and perhaps cannot even appreciate what happens not just to a woman's body but also to her mind and to her spirit in the process of nurturing a child in the womb and then giving physical birth to another human being. Celebrating the cycle of birth and rebirth in the movement of the seasons affirms and validates experiences open to women, who themselves are capable of giving birth, not experiences open to men, who are biologically incapable of giving birth. Little wonder, then, that the women's movement fostered renewed interest in religious rituals and ceremonies that marked events unique to the biological experience of women.[7]

Ignoring the distinctive experience of women in white American Protestantism historically may not mean that patterns of male spirituality have actually dominated, but simply that men exercised control over the institutions and agencies that sustained Protestantism. But if there are spiritual approaches and images that do come directly from the experience of women, then there may well be approaches and images that stem from the experience of being male. Again, to assert such an argument is not to claim that one is better than the other, more important than the other, or more authentic than the other. It is simply to assert that gender makes a difference when it comes to images of spirituality and how people go about being religious. Images of the Christian man and the Christian woman might be different for American Protestants, while at the same time representing a common goal, namely, the shaping of life around a constellation of beliefs, values, and practices rooted in Protestant Christianity.

Is how one expresses spirituality determined by one's gender? Given human knowledge at present, a single, categorical answer is impossible. But it does seem clear that gender influences expressions of spirituality and the images that resonate with one's efforts to relate to the transcendent. After all, gender is one of the key ingredients in determining self-identity and constructing a place for oneself in the world. Given how fundamental gender is to who we are, it would be foolish to divorce gender from spirituality.

Perceptions of Gendered Spirituality

Part of the impetus for the Promise Keepers movement was, as I noted, the conviction that men were less religious than women in the American context, if not globally. There are countless problems with that supposition. On one level, determining how to measure spirituality or religiosity poses a challenge. Even then, measurement presumes that spirituality is something that is discernible in the public arena; if spirituality is most frequently expressed in the private realms of life, then it would be difficult to measure its presence and impact accurately. The same holds for those religious traditions in which what one does in the home, the private sphere, is more vital than what one does in public. In the Jewish tradition, for example, one mark of a Jewish identity is the religious observance centered in the home, particularly that which begins when the candles are lit to signal the arrival of the Sabbath. Unlike Christians, who have put a premium on public manifestations of religious identity particularly through the practice of regular attendance at corporate worship services, Jews have never earmarked attendance at synagogue services as the key barometer in determining whether one is faithful to the commandments. The growing Hindu population in the United States offers another example of a tradition in which historically what transpires in the private sphere of the home is more vital to nurturing a religious identity and promoting spirituality than visits to the temple, although in the American context temple activities have taken on an importance they do not have in India. The reason is patent: Hindus are a definite minority in the United States, whereas they constitute an overwhelming majority of the Indian population. Hence, the temple has taken on a different role as a means of sustaining the Hindu tradition in the United States than it historically has had in India.

In the colonial era in the United States, attendance at public worship in the areas controlled by England tended to be required by law, although authorities were never able to coerce all the people to attend. Thus, if one looks at colonial New England, one finds families regularly attending meeting, much of the time in seats designated by social rank in the community. But attendance, even in Puritan New England, and actual membership in the church body were never identical.[8] In colonial New England, for example, one was expected to testify to one's experience of election to salvation by God before owning the church covenant, that is before assuming the responsibilities and privileges that went with being a church member. Yet the lists of church members that have survived from the colonial era—and there are many of them—indicate that women were far more likely than men to testify to their religious experience and own the church covenant. Although there were exceptions, in most cases women out-numbered men roughly by a ratio of two to one as full-fledged members of the churches.[9] In New England there is a curious twist to that imbalance, for one of the privileges that accompanied church membership was being able to vote at town meetings and in local elections. For a man to vote and to be eligible for public office, then, he would need to be a church member. At the same time, women—the majority of the church members—were not regarded as eligible to vote and hold public office. When laws no longer mandated attendance at worship, men were far more likely than women to absent themselves from weekly preaching.

The same ratio prevailing in the colonial era has continued to the pres-ent. Periodically those who bemoan the presumed decline of religion's in-fluence in American life or the absence of men in the churches have mar-shaled as evidence this imbalance between women and men on Protestant congregational membership rolls. Hence, if one uses church membership as the key measure of whether one is truly religious, whether one's spirituality reflects a deep commitment to the ways of God, then clearly women are more religious in their public behavior than men.[10] But one can turn this point upside down.

Did women seek membership in a church body in part because of their unique experiences as women? If so—and I know of no studies that pose the question this way—one would expect women to outnumber men on membership rosters. If it is the case that formal church membership has just been far less important to men as a way to express their spiritual or religious identity, then one would not expect to find as many men as women listed as church members in the record books.[11] Such would follow because the two-to-one ratio has held constant across the centuries of the American enterprise. Even when various eras of significant religious revival, such as the time of the Great Awakening of the eighteenth century, have led to spurts of membership growth among men, the increase has been tempo-rary. Once the religious enthusiasm that sparked renewed interest has waned, the old patterns reassert themselves. But the haunting question remains: Are such measurements accurate reflectors of male experience of what it means to be religious? If not, then we need to decrease the empha-sis placed on church membership as an indicator of the strength and health of male spirituality in American culture.

Much of the public debate that marked second-wave feminism in the later twentieth century had to do with gender stereotypes and how such stereotypes were culturally determined rather than based on actual differences. Among those stereotypes was the claim that women were *by nature* more religious and therefore more spiritual than men. We can account for that image in a variety of ways. A sense that women were naturally inclined to things religious and should therefore be responsible for the religious nurture of children began developing in the antebellum period, when significant changes in family structure and work patterns were taking root in American life. Historian Barbara Welter was among the first to argue that in antebellum America, religion itself became feminized.[12]

What happened was actually the interworking of several parallel social forces. In the colonial era, the majority of white American families were functioning economic units; both parents and children were expected to work together, most often in an agriculturally based economy, to support family life. Everyone had roles to play in keeping this economic unit functioning, with none necessarily worth more than any other. Even male craftsmen and artisans usually worked out of their homes, so that the home was not a sphere separate from work but one integrally related to the world of work. However much child-rearing in the colonial period differs from what prevails in the United States today, both parents were actively involved in the process of raising children, since both were likely to be present in the home environment.[13] Given the much higher death rate of women in childbirth then, many men anticipated spending some time as a single parent, often with several children and perhaps some apprentices or other folks to provide for, although many men did remarry a second or third time, sometimes relatively quickly after the death of a spouse.

The nascent industrial economy that began developing in the antebellum period started to create separate spheres for work and home, transforming the home into a refuge from work for white American Protestant males. As more and more men sought employment outside the home, the family ceased to be a functioning economic unit. Work outside the home became the domain of men, for until the later nineteenth century, few employment opportunities were open to women in the businesses and factories that transformed the nation from an agrarian country to an industrial one. Even before the Civil War, young men began leaving their rural homes for life and jobs in the factory villages, leaving behind the religious culture of the evangelical Protestant home. The Young Men's Christian Association (YMCA) owes its genesis in part to efforts to take those values inculcated at home and use them as a base for shared living arrangements. As a result of this movement of young men from rural farms to factory villages, the home gradually became the sphere and domain of women, if for no other reason than men were absent so much of the time during the week.

Consequently, responsibility for what transpired in the home shifted from burdens shared by men and women, by husbands and wives, to women alone. Some of the shift reflected women's biological role as child bearers, for care and nurture of children were still a mainstay of the Protestant home and thus central to the work of women. Integral to that scheme was cultivating the religious sensibilities of children, both male and female.[14] Hence, one unwitting result of this trend was that American Protestants began to see religiosity or piety as likewise more germane to the sphere of women than men and to assume that women were not only by behavior but also by nature more spiritual.

Reinforcing this perception was another cultural trend of the nineteenth century that is more elusive to capture, namely, the sentimentality and romanticism that became attached to women in Victorian understanding. Portrayals of women as more emotional than men, motivated less by rational thinking than men and thus to be sheltered from the harsh realities of life, come from this Victorian understanding. There are important links to white Protestant spirituality that parallel and may well emerge from this Victorian gender construction. During the Great Awakening of the middle third of the eighteenth century, the renowned Jonathan Edwards offered a compelling analysis of the nature of religious experience based on his labors as a pastor and preacher who witnessed astounding conversions of both men and women during the revivals. For Edwards, religion was primarily a matter of the affections, a term which for him embraced not just emotions but a complex intermingling of emotion, intellect, and behavior.[15] Yet for many who witnessed the cataclysmic conversions of family and friends, the emotional element seemed paramount.

As those Protestant bodies that regarded a discrete experience of conversion as the basic mode of entry into the Christian life, especially the Methodists and Baptists, grew at a rapid rate, it became easy to equate "real" religion, the base for spirituality, with emotion. Groups such as the Methodists and Baptists also attracted more women than men because they offered women a spiritual empowerment they were denied by the prevailing society. When the larger culture began to link emotional expression to women rather than to men, it was easy also to see spirituality as more characteristic of women than of men. For some, it was thus a given that women were by nature more religious than men, in part because they were thought to be more emotional.

Scholars such as Barbara Welter and Ann Douglas,[16] although in very different ways, have argued that the net result of the economic changes in family structure and the rise of Victorian sentimentality was the feminiza-

WHITE MALE SPIRITUALITY AND THE CHRISTIAN MAN   II

tion of white American Protestantism. Even though the ranks of the clergy remained closed to women, they consistently outnumbered men as members of American Protestant churches and consequently as participants in church-related activities, from worship services to mission and outreach endeavors. Hence, clergy spent more time in the company of women than of men. Thus clergy, even though male, were more likely to promote devotional and other spiritual activities attractive to women than they were to minister to the men in their parishes. In other words, the clergy also became feminized while remaining a profession dominated by men. They were perceived to be less masculine than other men simply because they engaged in religious work.

One sees this trend in popular literature of the Victorian era. Although not her best-known novel, Harriet Beecher Stowe's *The Minister's Wooing*, set in antebellum Connecticut, features a fictionalized Samuel Hopkins as a bachelor pastor who makes his home with a widow, Mrs. Katy Scudder, and her daughter Mary. Pastor Hopkins is so caught up in things of the spirit that he has no sense of what actually goes on in the daily lives of those around him. The real world of men, such as the dangerous seafaring of the daughter's beloved, James Marvyn, is an alien realm for this feminized pastor.[17] Women are those who associate with preachers and churches, pray for the conversion of men, and even reach out to those inclined to other religious persuasions.

Likewise, spurring men to seek conversion was thought to be a far greater challenge than stirring women to do the same. Men were seen to lack the emotional base that supported such religious experience just because they were men. Again, Stowe's novel illustrates the prevailing perspective. James Marvyn, a young merchant sailor, quite clearly lacks the certainty that he has experienced conversion because he cannot use the same vocabulary to talk about his religious experience as does Mary Scudder, the young woman he loves. When it is feared that he is lost at sea, the women grieve because they believe his immortal soul is lost for eternity. When he miraculously returns, he acknowledges a conversion in a way that is not at all in keeping with Stowe's portrayal of masculine spirituality, for he resorts to the vocabulary reserved for women.

Barbara Epstein studied conversion accounts from the era of the Second Great Awakening of the early nineteenth century, concluding that in contrast with earlier eras, especially that of the Great Awakening of the eighteenth century, men and women approached religious experience in very different ways. They drew on different language to describe their experience and exhibited different results in how conversion had effected some changes in their lives.[18] Although others have challenged Epstein's conclusions, suggesting that there were some common features shared by men and women in their recounting of personal conversion, she is on target in highlighting the conviction that has marked much of American Protestantism from the nineteenth century, namely, that women and men came to the religious or spiritual life in different ways. Indeed, in the so-called businessmen's revival of the late 1850s, many of the personal accounts of male conversion catalogued by those eager to claim that there was something fresh and new about businessmen coming together for prayer and testimony rhapsodized about a devout mother or wife whose longsuffering and constant prayers were integral in bringing about a son's or husband's conversion.[19]

In the early twentieth century, there was a movement that has come to be called "muscular Christianity," a concerted effort to cast the Protestant version of the Christian message in forms that were intentionally designed to appeal to men rather than to women. I shall discuss this movement in some detail later; here I want to emphasize simply that white Protestant church leaders believed that it was necessary to fashion programs geared to men. A single message simply would not suffice.[20] One form of that endeavor was called the Men and Religion Forward Movement, a series of rallies held in towns and cities across the country addressing subjects thought to be of interest to men. While no doubt some of the topics, such as service opportunities within church and community, were also relevant regardless of the gender of the audience, women were in some cases urged not to attend meetings so that men would be able to probe spiritual issues and questions on their own terms.

We could draw on other examples, some of which will illustrate other points in later chapters. But by now it should be evident that from the time of European colonial settlement in North America, white Protestants have tended to regard women as being more religious than men. Some have argued that a religious nature is innate to women, whereas it must be acquired by men. Economic changes, shifts in work patterns, and alterations in family life helped promote the idea that the spiritual realm was properly part of women's domain, although men could have access to it. Victorian romanticism further cemented such notions in Protestant consciousness, fortified by consistent, continuing statistics that showed women outnumbering men on the rolls of the nation's Protestant congregations.

Constructing an understanding of the links between gender and spirituality along these lines may obscure the key point. If the categories that are used to measure spirituality—church membership, participation in church activities, having an emotionally charged conversion experience, and the like—are categories thought to describe the religious life of women, then it would seem that men will always come across as less religious, less devout, less pious, less spiritual. If the goal of Protestant church leaders is to make everyone religious, devout, pious, and spiritual in ways that women seem inclined to be, then there will always be a sense that there must be a conscious effort to pitch a message to men that will appeal to them as men, even if such serves only to awaken a feminized spirituality perhaps dormant in their deepest selves. It may turn out that men are not less spiritual than women, but just that they are spiritual in different ways.[21] For white American Protestants, the Christian man and the Christian woman are different in ways that go beyond biological distinctions.

White Protestant Images of the Christian Man and Male Spirituality

Close examination of the history of white American Protestantism reveals a host of images oriented toward men that illuminate what it means to be religious, of how to be spiritual, of what a life of Christian devotion is all about. The images are not always such obvious ones as daily prayer and reading of Scripture. From the colonial period on, these images have sought to address the unique experiences and life situations of white American Protestant men as men, to provide guidelines for a spirituality that derives from and speaks to specifically white male experience. Hence, when Promise Keepers promoted stadium rallies in the 1990s, the group was really offering yet one more cluster of images on which American men might draw in developing a spirituality that reflected their lives as men. It had a distinctive vision of the ideal Christian man.

Not all those images are necessarily exclusively targeted to men, although all of them have at times been cast in a form intended to zero in on male experience. Many are intertwined with social constructions of gender so that they also reflect cultural expectations of the responsibilities and obligations thought to accrue primarily to those who are biologically male. During the centuries that Protestantism has flourished in the United States, such images have appeared in materials as diverse as colonial sermons to self-help books in the twentieth century. We cannot consider every one of them here. Rather, for purposes of discussion and analysis, I will examine six broad categories in which several cognate images come together. These categories are by no means all-inclusive; they are clusters of images with many nuances.

These categories do have some common features. Each tends to be more outer-directed than inner-directed. That is, images of white male spirituality and the Christian man, while emerging from a particular understanding of God and of a man's relationship with God, focus more on a man's associations with other persons, ranging from family to associates in the workplace, than they do on cultivating a more private, interior, almost quasimystical, sense of spirituality, a piety more often identified with women. Each also emphasizes action more than contemplation, although more traditional forms of devotion, those thought more illustrative of female spirituality, may undergird and sustain a particular image. All exhibit a practical dimension, emphasizing what results spirituality brings in the world of lived reality. Hence, all downplay the intricacies of theology and doctrine, not only because theological differences too often reap conflict but also because theological speculation itself deflects attention from achieving pragmatic results. Finally, none of the images I shall discuss precludes any of the others. In other words, there may be multiple images, multiple signals, accessible at any one time as American Protestant men endeavor to construct a spirituality that resonates with their experience as men. Some images have been more dominant at particular times. Since I am trained as a historian, I always think in terms of historical development. Thus, the clusters of images that we shall consider will be presented in rough chronological order, beginning with one that was most powerful during the decades when New England Puritanism held sway over much of white American Protestantism and concluding with one that came to prominence only in the closing years of the twentieth century.

When Europeans began their colonial endeavors in North America, notions of hierarchy in government, society, religion, and even family were assumed and usually unchallenged. The seventeenth and eighteenth centuries also unquestioningly gave prominence in every sector of life to men. It was an age of patriarchy, and patriarchy carried with it an emphasis on deference to those who held higher status or exercised greater authority.[22] For most Puritans, who for this period will be taken as representative of white American Protestants, the primary cluster of images for male spirituality reflects that mix of patriarchy, deference, and authority. I label this cluster that of the *dutiful patriarch*. The Protestant male as husband and father was assumed to hold primary authority within the household, which might include several persons who were unrelated to the family but living with the family as apprentices, indentured servants, or perhaps even slaves. For the devout Protestant male, authority was never arbitrary but always reflective of a higher will, that of God. Hence, the primary burden of the white Prot-

estant male was always to do his duty as one chosen by God to have authority within the larger family circle. The ideal Christian man was indeed a
dutiful patriarch.

After the era of the American war for independence undermined some,
but by no means all, of the hierarchical assumptions that sustained the
image of the dutiful patriarch, Protestant writers developed another cluster
of images to help the white Christian man cultivate his spiritual identity. As
some of the economic shifts that marked the early Republic began to transform religious ways of thinking, they also had an impact on Protestant
images of male spirituality. By and large, although the dutiful patriarch had
not completely disappeared, in antebellum white American Protestantism
the *gentleman entrepreneur* became the model for male spirituality and the
ideal Christian man. This image, as we shall see, brought together a certain
sense of civility in a man's relationships not just within the household but
also—and perhaps more important—with those with whom a man came
in contact in the course of making a living. Yet for many there was also a
sense that individual initiative was a key ingredient in both church and society; it was individual initiative, after all, that motivated men to leave the
homes where they were reared to seek their fortunes in the factory villages
and cities. In Protestant circles, the move toward emphasizing individual
initiative in the experience of salvation paralleled the decline of the Calvinism undergirding the Puritan style and the ascendancy of the Arminianism
that gave the individual a critical role in the process of salvation. One was
in charge of one's spiritual destiny, just as one was in charge of one's well-
being in the larger society. The image of the gentleman entrepreneur has
remained a vital part of white American Protestant male spirituality and a
central feature of the model of the Christian man ever since.

By the closing decades of the nineteenth century, non-Protestant immigrants swelled the population of the nation's cities and the ranks of the
laboring classes in American industry. Some white Protestants—male and
female alike—felt as if they were going to be shoved to the margins of economic and social life by those whose values and ways of life were seemingly
incompatible with Protestant mores. Doing one's religious duty was not
enough; nor was it enough to be a gentleman entrepreneur. Hence, another
set of images emerged to reflect the spiritual and social needs of white
American Protestant men, that of the *courageous adventurer*. Here the movement known as muscular Christianity plays into our story, for preachers and
popular writers all sought to demonstrate that men who were truly spiritual,
who tried to order their lives according to Scripture and religious precepts,
were truly masculine in the sense of having brute physical power, if not

social power. As well, those forces already described that increasingly consigned vital religion to the sphere of women made the dutiful patriarch seem increasingly anachronistic. After all, devotion was the domain primarily of women, not of men. But the Christian man was given to adventure that required a display of courage.

Various social forces, especially World War I, interrupted the massive immigration of Roman Catholics, Jews, and Eastern Orthodox Christians who made their way to the United States in the decades after the Civil War. But business and industry continued to boom, often under the leadership of white Protestant men. Hence, a cluster of images that mirrored the new situation of white American Protestant men came to the fore. In the opening decades of the twentieth century, down at least to the time of the Great Depression, the *efficient businessman* became the model for the white Protestant male and man of privilege who endeavored to nurture a spiritual life. In much of American Protestant life at the grass-roots level, the image of the efficient businessman went hand-in-hand with the image of the powerful athlete. The same discipline that made one a powerful athlete could also make one a successful businessman. In American Protestantism, the white Christian man might still reflect the models of the dutiful patriarch, the gentleman entrepreneur, and the courageous adventurer, but he was also an efficient businessman.

A good bit of unsettledness in American culture accompanied the decades after World War II, when the return to a peacetime economy and social structure was plagued by the threat of communism and the fear that cold war could lead to hot war all too quickly. There was also a sense in which return to peacetime life and the mushrooming of suburbia that accompanied it did not simply did not give men enough control over their own lives. Their destinies seemed beyond their control. They not only worked for someone else away from their homes but also dealt with employers who seemed to care little about the humanity of their workers. And at any moment, dreams and hopes could be shattered if war—perhaps even nuclear war—erupted. The malaise emerging from this perceived loss of control had a counterpart in an approach to white male Protestant spirituality that was layered on to those that went before. A growing number of best-selling authors, represented most compellingly by the Rev. Norman Vincent Peale, began to press for a spirituality based on a fusion of popular psychology and religious faith. The result was the cluster of images that made up the spirituality of the *positive thinker*. A man could chart his destiny after all and thereby assure that life had meaning if he mustered the mental force to construct a world where he had a picture in the mind of

his destiny. It was an easy step to take that picture and make it reality. Whatever else he did, the Protestant Christian man epitomized positive thinking.

Beneath the surface of that purportedly more peaceful era that came in
the 1950s, there emerged a passion for human rights that erupted before the
decade's end and continued as a major social force throughout of the 1960s.
The civil rights movement transformed American society, even as it drasti-
cally altered the way Americans went about the business of finding meaning in life, for ideas rooted in the civil rights movement carried over into
other cognate phenomena such as the women's movement. Change swept
through the religious sector as well. With women calling for ordination, the
ranks of the Protestant clergy ceased to be as overwhelmingly male as they
long had been. The courageous adventurer could just as easily be a symbol
of oppression of the weak as a demonstration of spiritual maturity, and the
efficient businessman looked too often like a racist and sexist acting only on
the basis of self-interest.

As well, in the second half of the twentieth century, significant transformation came once again to the family as a core element in the social structure. If an earlier age had undermined the family as a functioning economic
unit by making gainful employment outside the home normative, the family faced fresh challenges as women reacted to the ways cultural patterns
had undermined their own human development. Many writers began to
wonder exactly what role men should play in the family in an age of divorce,
an age when women joined the work force at all levels in unprecedented
numbers, and an age when gender identity seemed particularly malleable.
A new cluster of images emerged to speak to the changing social situation
of white American Protestant men, one that reflected some of the earlier
visions but offered something new. That new cluster centered around seeing the man as *faithful leader*, one whose power came through serving others, particularly his wife and children, not through sheer exercise of authority. But by the first decade of the twenty-first century, even that set of
images may have started to recede, but for many American Protestants, the
Christian man was one who was a faithful leader.

Numerous other images emerged over the years to signal to white American Protestant men what being religious was all about and how they could
affirm their identity as males and as Protestant Christians. Those highlighted here are by no means exhaustive. But if we wish to look more deeply
into links between gender and spirituality for white American Protestant
men, closely examining and appraising the six clusters of images presented
here offers a beginning. To keep the discussion from being too abstract,
each discussion will conclude with a brief biographical vignette of a white

American Protestant male whose life illuminates that cluster, one who represents what it meant to be a Christian man whose life was oriented around the dominant spiritual image of the times. If men have not always expressed spirituality in the same ways as women, they may still be in pursuit of a spiritual identity. To that extent, at least, real men pray.

CHAPTER 2

✢ ✢ ✢

The Dutiful Patriarch

FOR NEW ENGLAND PURITANS, IN THEORY, IF NOT ALWAYS IN reality, the world was an orderly place. The Puritans, after all, were a people who took the Bible seriously, and, although they were not plagued by debates of a later age over whether the Bible was scientifically accurate in every detail, they did find in the Genesis accounts of creation a basis for understanding the world as a realm where everything fit together in a neat fashion. From the darkness and void, God brought forth order; even the seven-day pattern of creation spoke of order. Order almost by definition requires authority and control. If there is order, then there must be some authority that holds the power to effect that order, some force that controls that power, and some energy that sustains that order lest chaos return and destroy creation altogether. God, if nothing else, was thus a God of order who acted to maintain a corresponding sense of order throughout the universe.

There was another implication in this sense of order. If order presumes power and authority, it also presumes subordination of all that depends on that order. In Puritan thinking, creation culminated in the appearance of humanity, and to humans God extended power and authority, but of a secondary sort. Human authority was always to be exercised on behalf of God, whose prior authority remained supreme. Thus, in the story found in the second chapter of Genesis, humans receive the authority to give names to the various phenomena, but they did not create that which they named. In the biblical world, the power to name was the power to control, to order. So humanity, in naming the components of creation, discharged a divinely ordained responsibility that reflected the prior and superior power of God. Thus the very idea of God in Puritan understanding contained a sense of hierarchy.

Another ramification of this abiding sense of order came in the conviction that God's order was systematic. It operated through what Scripture and tradition called laws that governed the world. So too human society echoed the divine order when it constructed communities and governments grounded in the rule of law. Yet law by its nature demanded obedience, almost an unquestioning acceptance of its justice and its necessity as the foundation for maintaining order. As part of creation, humanity was obligated to obey. That obedience was directed first to God, on whom all order depended. But by extension, obedience was due all those to whom God had granted subsidiary power and authority in assuring that the world remained an orderly dominion.

Puritans, however, never doubted the potential for disorder. Indeed, as historian Edmund S. Morgan argued more than half a century ago, for Puritans, disorder had its theological corollary in the notion of sin.[1] The story of the Fall, also recounted in Genesis, was a story not just of disobedience to divinely established precept, although it is surely that. It was a story as well of disorder intruding into the orderly world fashioned by God, of disorder infecting creation in such a way that its effects would endure until the end of time. The potential for disorder would always plague humans, unless God intervened to assure that order was maintained. The Genesis accounts also provided a clue about the consequences of disobedience and disorder: whenever disorder prevailed, there must be punishment, both to remind humanity of the dangers of violating God's ways and to assure that order was restored.

Because of humanity's lapse into disobedience almost from creation itself, no one could hope to live an orderly life, to be obedient to the ways of God, apart from divine action, apart from grace. For Puritans, the most potent symbol of that grace was God's action in Jesus Christ in electing some for salvation, despite their shortcomings. In so doing, God infused them with the strength to commit their lives to obedience, to subservience to higher authority, to subordination to the hierarchical order that led finally to the Almighty.

I have sketched this sense of order and hierarchy in some detail because women and men of the twenty-first century are likely to misconstrue its theological base and recoil at the sense of subordination that governs the

Puritan worldview. For Puritans, who lived in a social world where hierarchy was evident through monarchy and aristocracy, order and subordination were simply the ways of God and therefore beyond challenge. One
could even obey the civil law, to all appearances living an orderly life, and in
the final analysis still be destined for eternal damnation. Only those chosen
for salvation could truly obey and live properly ordered lives because God's
action in Christ communicated through the Holy Spirit disposed the elect
to do so.

The Puritan sense of order and hierarchy, authority and subordination,
also had much to do with gender. It reveals an understanding of male spirituality and a model of what it meant to be a Christian man. Puritans were
people of their times and readily absorbed the biblical records that favored
male pronouns for Deity and designating God as Father, with Jesus as the
Son. The use of the terms "Father" and "Son" cemented male-based language for the Puritans in their theological vocabulary, as it did for countless
others within the orbit of Christianity. Further confirmation came in the
biblical stories of creation. In the translations favored among Puritans and
their descendants, the Geneva Bible and the King James Version of 1611,
there are two creation narratives. As many others, the Puritans tended to
collapse them into one. The familiar account of God's fashioning woman
from the rib of the man (Genesis 2:18–24) eclipsed the more inclusive rendering in the first chapter of Genesis (1:26–27) when the stories got
conflated.

The male language of their translations and the divine Father-Son imagery that was etched into the Puritan subconscious, along with the belief that
God created the male before he (most appropriately a male pronoun in
Puritan thought) created the female, had a consequence in the natural order
of things: It gave precedence to male over female. God's intended order
within creation thus granted the male superiority over the female in the
sense that the male was to exercise a subsidiary authority, ordained by God,
over the female. I emphasize the subsidiary dimension here because, contrary to much later popular thinking, such authority was never deemed to
be arbitrary or capricious but an authority that carried responsibility and
obligation because it was an authority employed on behalf of God the
Father, whose power reigned over all.

One other component of the Puritan appropriation of what they
believed to be an authentic biblical worldview is vital to understanding the
cluster of images shaping notions of how men were religious and what they
did as spiritual beings. That is the conviction that the order of creation presumed the union of male and female in marriage in order to procreate and
continue the orderly creation designed by God. Puritans expected men to

marry, although there were no civil laws requiring them to do so.[2] Civil law
could, however, mandate penalties for the failure of married men to fulfill
what both God and society expected of them. The assumption was that
married men would become heads of households, a term encompassing
more than just a nuclear family, and as such would carry out the role within
the household that paralleled the role of God the Father in creation at large.
Failure at this level would bring disorder to the very heart of the human
commonwealth.

In broad contours, these assumptions cut through the various Puritan
colonial ventures. They undergirded the more religiously radical Separatists
at Plymouth, popularly known as the Pilgrims, and those who settled Massachusetts Bay, as well as many others who populated other areas throughout British North America that later became the United States. All were
serious in their commitment to manifest in empirical reality the ideals they
believed were rooted in Scripture. All were intent on constructing a society
that would reflect the order established by God in creation and desired by
God even now, despite the human flaws signaled by the Fall. All were convinced that their understanding of God's revelation first in the saga of the
Hebrew people and then in Jesus Christ had implications for how ordinary
folk were to order their personal lives. It structured how they were to go
about the business of being religious and how they were to construct a spirituality in harmony with the divine will. All were certain that God had
called the elect to particular stations in life that were linked to gender, with
men and women each having assigned roles to play within the social and
religious orders.

Given this understanding, what clusters of images came together for
Puritan men who were intent on demonstrating that they were among the
elect of God? How should a man be religious? What went into a spirituality appropriate to those ordained of God to be heads of households and
thus to be almost substitutes for the Almighty in the everyday life? What
did it mean for a male American Puritan to be a Christian man? There were
many individual images, but together they combined to create a portrait of
the Christian man as the dutiful patriarch and a male spirituality oriented
around obligations toward those who made up one's household and then
one's community.

Although there is a vast literature surviving from clergy and laity whose
lives were informed by Puritanism, little of what is directed specifically to
men centers on doctrine or belief. What one ought to believe if one was
bold enough to own the church covenant and be regarded as among the
elect was spelled out frequently enough in sermons and discourses that
made their way into print. But doctrine and belief were, in a sense, gender

neutral. The man who was elect of God to salvation and the woman who was elect of God to salvation would subscribe to the same doctrine in a formal sense. To be sure, there would be some nuances that differed, but that could be true among persons of the same gender. After all, the life experiences of no two people, whether male or female, were identical. Here the diaries and letters that survived often offer particular insight. Where there was greater difference and where the image of the dutiful patriarch comes into focus centered around responsibility for Christian practice, for actions that the household and the larger public could observe, more than it did around doctrine or belief.

Also curious is the way those who have written about the daily life of men in colonial New England have ignored the centrality of spirituality and religious understanding to the way men understood who they were and what their roles in life should be. One would think that few males were concerned with what it meant to be a Christian man. Historian Lisa Wilson, for example, in her detailed appraisal of the domestic life of colonial New England men, virtually dismisses the role of spirituality and religion, except in her discussion of the relationship of a father to his children. She notes repeatedly that her readers will find her subjects overly consumed by religion but tends to push discussion of spirituality and religious impulses aside, perhaps because they do not fit neatly into late-twentieth-century patterns of appraisal.[3] So too Judith Graham, whose study of Samuel Sewall will inform our discussion later, pays little heed to spirituality as a primary factor in determining how this prominent figure in Boston life structured his identity and gave meaning to his existence. Graham notes how Sewall prayed when his wife was in childbirth and when family members and others were ill, how he was active in church affairs, and how pleased he was when one son entered the professional ministry. But there is little clue that spirituality was central to Sewall's sense of self.[4] My contention, however, is that the image of the dutiful patriarch was vital to the self-understanding and identity of colonial men whose lives were shaped by Puritan ways of thinking. Everything they did and every relationship they entered reflected the spiritual sensibilities represented by the dutiful patriarch. Whatever else the Christian man might be, he was at least a patriarch committed to doing his prescribed duty.

The Well-Ordered Family

In 1712, prominent Puritan pastor Benjamin Wadsworth published an extended sermon on his vision of the ideal family that contained many clues about how religiously committed men were expected to live their faith. The title and subtitle capture the heart of Puritan understanding: *The Well-Ordered Family; or, Relative Duties.*[5] The primary theme for male spirituality was the responsibility to maintain order within the household, the order that reflected the work of God the Father in creating and sustaining the universe. For Cotton Mather, a well-ordered family was the key to producing and maintaining order in society.[6] It was also central to Puritan visions of the church as a covenanted community. As William Gouge, a seventeenth-century Englishman of Puritan persuasion, wrote, "A familie is a little Church, and a little common-wealth, at least a lively representation thereof, whereby triall may be made of such as are fit for any place of authoritie, or of subjection in Church or commonwealth."[7] In the family, as in church and society, the danger of disorder was always present, especially if one forgot one's duties in relation to others within the household. In virtually every instance, those duties involved deference to those who were superior in authority.

For Mather and Wadsworth, ideas of duty and patterns of deference emerged from their understanding of Christian truth. Historians are well aware, however, that English folkways reinforced this religious understanding and helped create the image of the dutiful patriarch as the ideal for Puritan male spirituality.[8] Historian Mary Beth Norton has reminded us that much of the Puritan construction of a realm of order based on hierarchy, family, and male authority had roots in the understanding of society advanced by Sir Robert Filmer, whose thinking was influential on both sides of the Atlantic when American culture was in its formative stages.[9] Hierarchy and order were simply how the world operated, not just how God worked.

Twenty-first-century women and men might recoil at the first of those relationships in the household where maintaining order was essential, for Puritans assumed without question that the husband held authority over the wife.[10] Indeed, the man who did not assert that authority would not be living a Christian life. But as already noted, the authority of husband over wife was not arbitrary; nor should it ever involve what a later age would call abuse. Wadsworth, in his tract on the family, based his explication of the authority of the husband on a passage in Paul's first letter to the Corinthians that clearly speaks of mutuality as the basis for authority: "The wife hath not power of her own body, but the husband; and likewise the husband hath not power of his own body, but the wife" (1 Cor. 7:4, KJV). The verse follows one where Paul urges husbands to exercise benevolence in dealing with wives. Wadsworth wrote that the way the husband exerted authority in his relationship with his wife should be both gentle and easy, noting that if things went awry in most cases the blame rested with the husband, not with the wife (who should, however, always be loving and obedient). That ease and gentleness came because men needed to acknowledge their own humility before God, their own deference to divine authority, and, too often, their own stubbornness in resisting God's authority.[11]

Historian Edmund Morgan reminds us that civil law assured that male authority over a wife entailed serious responsibility.[12] The husband was obligated, for example, to provide support for a wife. Such support was construed to embrace more than simply food, clothing, and shelter; it also included a concern for the health and physical well-being of the wife. Although Puritans later acquired a reputation for frowning on sexual activity, the reality was rather different. In Massachusetts Bay, as Morgan noted, civil law could require a husband to have conjugal relations with his wife; of course, the wife was also expected to have conjugal relations with her husband. Adultery was strictly prohibited; civil law consistently mandated that regardless of what else transpired between husband and wife, so long as they were married, the husband was expected to remain faithful to his wife (and she to him).

As well, civil law decreed that no husband should strike his wife; nor should a wife strike her husband. So too the dutiful patriarch as a spiritual being should refrain from striking or beating his wife. Wadsworth was clear on that point: "If therefore the Husband is bitter against his wife, beating her or striking her (as some vile wretches do), or in any unkind carriage, ill language, hard words, morose, peevish, surly behaviour; nay if he is not kind, loving, tender in his words and carriage to her; he then shames his profession of Christianity, he breaks the Divine Law, he dishonours God and himself, too, by this ill behaviour."[13] If a man wished his life to reflect God's ways, if he were to exemplify the spirituality nurtured by the Puritan ethos, then his authority would be tempered by his duty to love his wife and otherwise care for her. Love was integral to the idea of the Christian man who sought to do his divinely appointed duty.

Male authority was primary in dealing with children, although deference was also owed the mother simply because of her superior status as a parent.[14] Here the analogy with the divine is most obvious in the image of the dutiful patriarch, and Puritan thinkers, such as Cotton Mather, were insistent that the human father should, like God, exercise a "sweet authority" over children.[15] Just as God the Father looks after all humanity, even though out of compassion and love disciplining and chastising those who err, so the human father is charged with looking after his children if he would be

faithful to the ways of God. Part of the rationale for granting such authority to the father stemmed from the Puritan convictions that children, as
humans, were infected by sin at birth and that left to their own devices,
children would thus inevitably bring disorder on themselves and their
families.[16]

Part of the parental authority centered in the father was a precaution
against disorder; the dutiful patriarch would seek to keep his children from
sin and thus preserve the family as a place of divine order. Yet common
sense also played into the authority of the dutiful patriarch when it came to
matters of discipline. Corporal punishment of children was not forbidden,
although excess was frowned upon. Cotton Mather, for example, warned
against disciplining children in anger, although he was also insistent that it
was vital for the father to establish his authority over children early in their
lives.[17]

Decades ago, John Miller suggested another reason why Puritan fathers
and mothers took very seriously their authority over their children's behavior: "Puritan parents were haunted by the fear that the punishment
for their transgressions—and in New England thoughts could be fully as
sinful as deeds—might fall on their children."[18] In other words, those who
were themselves trained to be acutely consciousness of their own sinful
nature knew too well how easily they slipped from their intended devotion
to the way of holiness. How easy it was for that to be transmitted to children
almost by an unconscious process. Dutiful patriarchs were all familiar with
the Scriptures, where, in the giving of the law to Moses, God noted that the
sins of fathers had an effect that could last three to four generations (Exo-
dus 20:5) and, where in the Fourth Gospel, Jesus' disciples inquired whether
a man blind from birth owed his lack of physical sight to his own sin or to
that of his parents (John 9:2). Hence, the father needed to take care lest he
unwittingly cause his children to fall more deeply into sin.

But there was another dimension to the fear that the father's sins might
be passed on to his children, namely, that the child—again most likely a
son—whose behavior diverged too much from Puritan norms brought dis-
repute on the father. In other words, the son's sins became the father's sins;
or at least they served as an indication that a father had not done his Christian duty in properly training the son. Being derelict in one's God-given
duty was something of a sin in its own right. Cotton Mather again provides
an example, for as committed as he was to promoting the Puritan image of
the dutiful patriarch, he had a son, Increase or Creasy, who simply would
not conform to expected norms. In a diary entry for September 7, 1717,
Mather confessed that he considered his son's sins his own. After all, they
signaled his own shortcomings as a dutiful patriarch. Yet Mather knew he

was not truly guilty of gross negligence. He had tried to train his son. So the entry concludes with Mather's personal pledge to strengthen his efforts to reform his son's behavior.[19] Some, however, thought that fathers like Mather placed so much emphasis on how the piety of sons and family members reflected on their own character that concern for their spiritual welfare became a matter of egotism rather than a sincere theological conviction.[20]

Fatherly concern for children, however, was by no means restricted to stern warnings against sin and misbehaving. Just as the authority of the husband over the wife carried with it responsibility and obligation, so too did the authority to govern children within the household. The first sign that a father accepted his religious responsibility for his children came within days of a child's birth when the child would be brought for baptism, a practice made easier in Puritan New England after the Half-Way Covenant of 1662 eased the requirements regarding church membership for parents who wished to have children baptized. Baptism brought children under the authority of the church long before they themselves could consider offering the testimony of personal religious experience that might result in covenant membership.[21] Cotton Mather, after the death of his daughter Abigail, wrote about the religious responsibility parents had for their children, again emphasizing the role of fathers as he developed the analogy of children being on loan from God; dutiful fathers knew they received their children from God and at any time might be called upon to return them to God.[22]

When children were baptized, fathers publicly acknowledged their responsibility for providing basic religious education for their children. Even settlers of the more rigorous Plymouth colony recognized the duty of parents, but especially of fathers, to make sure children had an ability to read so that they could go to the Bible for themselves to learn the ways of God. Such rudimentary education was essential as well in providing a basis for understanding basic Christian doctrine. After all, how could children grow into mature adults—how could boys become dutiful patriarchs themselves—if they did not comprehend the core doctrines and laws of the Christian faith? For boys, education included a very practical dimension in their preparation for becoming dutiful patriarchs, namely, training in a job that would enable them in time to provide support for their own families.[23] Indeed, Cotton Mather devoted considerable attention in his treatise popularly known as the *Essays to Do Good* to the duty of a father to provide for the education of his children.[24] In one of his sermons, Mather was more blunt: if a male wanted to become a real man, he asserted, he needed basic learning.[25]

Puritan fathers in many cases also saw their God-given authority as granting them the prerogative of intervening in the lives of their children, especially the lives of their sons, in ways that people of the twenty-first century

would find unwarranted and intrusive. For example, proper exercise of patriarchal authority could easily include involvement in the choice of a spouse
for a child, though usually more by indirect guidance than coercion. Because
Puritans saw family order as mirroring the order established by God in the
universe, they sought to assure as much as possible that the relations between
husband and wife would reflect order and harmony. It was, therefore, the
religious duty of a good father to try to make sure that his children found
spouses with whom they were compatible.[26]

Notions of romantic love that marked a later age did not yet control the
choice of a marriage partner. Rather, what the dutiful patriarch sought for
a son was a wife who would be appropriately subservient so that the newly
established household would become a place of order. By law in the Plymouth colony, fathers were expected to provide sons with property at the
time of a son's marriage so that the new household would have a secure economic foundation; by law and custom elsewhere in settlements dominated
by the Puritans, fathers also sought to provide land for sons. The difficulties that developed when land became scarce as population density put
pressures on the availability of land lie beyond our concern, though they are
well-documented, and in time they undermined the authority of the dutiful patriarch.[27] For our purposes, it is enough simply to remember that part
of the image of the dutiful patriarch was seeing sons enter into good marriages and settled on their own land.

The well-ordered family frequently included persons who were not
blood relatives of the male head of the household. Some might be children
from a wife's earlier marriages who became her responsibility when her
husband(s) died and who remained in the household when, as was frequently the case, the mother herself later died. Others were indentured servants who owed the household a fixed period of labor before they were discharged. Some might be children, usually male children, of parents who
had arranged with the head of the household for the children to become
apprentices in order to learn a trade. Apprenticing his male children to
another was one way for the dutiful patriarch to carry out his obligation to
make sure that his own sons would be poised to support a family of their
own in time. Those who accepted apprentices into the household received
the benefit of the apprentices' work as they learned the trade, but were in
turn obligated to provide for them as they did for their own children, with
the exception of seeing that they had land on which to settle their own families. Apprentices, for example, would receive rudimentary education so
that they could read the Bible and understand the contours of Christian

belief. Men were not obligated, however, to provide instruction in reading for adults who joined the household as servants.

But dutiful patriarchs were expected to assure that everyone in the household—family, apprentices, servants, and any others—would insofar as possible refrain from behavior that would bring disorder to the household and, by implication, to the larger society. Seventeenth-century Puritan pastor Thomas Shepard, for example, lumped together children, servants, and even visitors to the household when he described the responsibility of the dutiful patriarch in promoting proper observance of the Sabbath and the potential for disruptive disorder if fathers neglected their duty:

> Our children, servants, and strangers who are within our gates, are apt to profane the Sabbath; we are therefore to improve our power over them for God, in restraining them from sin, and in constraining them (as far as we can) to the holy observance of the rest of the Sabbath, lest God impute their sins to us, who had power (as Eli in the like case) to restrain them and did not; and so our families and consciences be stained with their guilt and blood.[28]

Benjamin Wadsworth reminded Puritan men that if they provided for the support and comfort of servants, kept them diligently employed, and instructed them well in the Christian faith, then servants would more readily honor them just as they honored God. Hence, the male head of the household was not only a God-like figure to his children as their father; he was also a God-like figure to servants and others residing within the home.[29] The father was indeed a representative of the Father, and the dutiful patriarch had authority over all within the household as God the Father had authority over all humanity. But the authority of the dutiful patriarch entailed heavy responsibility to assure that the household operated as a well-ordered family.

Spirituality in the Well-Ordered Family

The image of the dutiful patriarch included specific religious responsibilities that illuminate male spirituality and the idea of the Christian man that flowed from it. The most important was presiding at family devotions twice each day. Every morning and evening, the dutiful patriarch would lead the household in prayer, Scripture reading, and the singing of a psalm.[30] On the Sabbath, in addition to attendance at public worship, there might be up to four times when the household came together for prayer and devotion. Seventeenth-century Massachusetts pastor John Cotton, for example, gathered the household early in the morning on the Sabbath for family worship. Then, after attending public worship at the meeting house, he and others of an age to do so spent time in private study. Later in the afternoon, they would return to the meeting house for an afternoon service. Before retiring, another time of private devotions was the norm, along with a second period of family worship.[31] In addition, men were expected to offer grace before every meal. Sometimes, individual families would set apart particular days to spend entirely in reflection on religious matters in a manner akin to that expected on days of humiliation and fasting and days of thanksgiving decreed for the larger society. Little wonder that centuries later a writer probing the character of merchant life in Puritan New England would be struck by how much of each day the men spent in religious endeavors rather than attending to business.[32]

Eminent Puritan divine Cotton Mather, for example, early in the eighteenth century addressed the matter of household worship in several tracts and sermons that were revised and then published: *A Family Sacrifice, Family Religion Excited and Assisted,* and *Family Religion Urged* (which repeats much of the material in the previous work).[33] He noted in his diary that he saw some of this material through to publication and had, for example, one thousand copies of *Family Religion Excited and Assisted* printed because many "pious men" had expressed a need for clear guidelines to show them their religious duty.[34] They needed some concrete images of male spirituality, of what it meant to be a Christian man. At the same time, families that did not pray, exhorted Mather, were nurseries of ignorance and wickedness.[35] Family worship was thus incumbent on all who would lead a spiritual life, and the dutiful patriarch must set an example in leading family worship not only to avoid such disaster, but also to assure that those within the household who would later have responsibilities themselves for other households could understand their own duty. No doubt Cotton Mather had learned from his own father, the venerable Increase Mather, that parents—fathers especially—had a duty to pray for their children.[36]

Cotton Mather reminded Puritan men who sought to fulfill their religious obligations that such devotions need not be elaborate; nor did the men themselves have to demonstrate great oratorical skill in offering family prayer. After all, most Christian men were laity, not those trained to preach; their efforts simply reflected the duty of all to glorify God and to seek the signs of divine election in their own lives. Thus it was assumed that the dutiful patriarch would use times of family devotion for basic religious instruction. Mather repeatedly urged fathers to employ the catechism as a framework for such instruction so that right doctrine would be considered by and inculcated in all members of the household. At one point, he resolved that every Monday he would have his children read a selection from Baxter's catechism as a basis for family instruction, planning to follow through on Saturdays with an individual, private conversation with each family member as a way to instill piety.[37] Elsewhere, he urged fathers to have "deep conversations" with their children, for even though all baptized children were in covenant with God, they had to be taught right doctrine.[38] Benjamin Wadsworth noted that such catechetical instruction by the father helped protect children from unorthodox belief.[39]

Sermons heard by the family on the Sabbath provided additional resources for family discussion, not just on Sundays but frequently throughout the week that followed. Wadsworth linked the duty of fatherly instruction to preaching. He reasoned quite simply that the more a father instructed the family in right doctrine, the more all members of the household would profit from the sermons heard at public worship.[40] Family discussion of the pastor's sermons might also include having the father quiz the children on what had been presented. Such provided a mechanism for the father to make sure that children and others in the household had grasped the religious truth conveyed.

As with other aspects of family worship, this conversation became another vehicle that enabled the dutiful patriarch to discharge his obligation to make sure that all those under his roof were exposed to Puritan piety, remembering that how children exemplified religious teachings in their own lives reflected on the spiritual state of their parents, especially their fathers. Cotton Mather, in an entry in his diary for November 7, 1697, noted how he had used family devotions to admonish his daughter because her piety was an indication of Mather's own character.[41] On another occasion, he noted behavioral problems with his son, stressing that he regarded the son's sins as his own and optimistically suggesting that he would exert his authority to make sure that his son changed his behavior.[42]

Such instruction also served a larger purpose. Not only did it train the young in the Puritan understanding of basic Christian belief, but it also sensitized them to recognize the signs of divine grace in their lives, the clues given by God that one indeed had been elected to salvation and might therefore give testimony to faith and own the church covenant. In other words, family worship, led by the dutiful patriarch, was a laboratory in miniature where one could begin to appreciate what it meant to be chosen of God for salvation and how one might know whether God had graciously intervened in one's own life to pluck one from the damnation all deserved. Puritan divines regularly prompted fathers as dutiful patriarchs to engage in serious discourse with their children about religious matters—Cotton Mather's "deep conversations."[43] These conversations would be most effective one-on-one, apart from household worship. They provided a venue for fathers to probe the spiritual status of a child, to nudge them toward Puritan piety and to prod them to seek evidence of their own conversions. But in addition to being useful occasions to make sure that children were gaining proficiency in doctrine, these more personal times enabled a dutiful father to rebuke improper behavior and discipline children in a context where parental love was most evident.

Dutiful patriarchs were also encouraged to discuss the reality of death with their children when they were quite young, indeed, at a much earlier age than most twenty-first-century parents would be so inclined. The reason was not, as some might have it, simply because children who died were doomed to eternal damnation because of original sin if they had not testified to an experience of divine grace. To the contrary, dutiful patriarchs presumed they had the well-being of their children at heart when they broached conversations about death. It was important for the dutiful patriarch to talk about death with his offspring because death was so much a part of everyday life. Infant mortality rates were considerably higher then than now; many children would witness the death of siblings in their infancy or early childhood. The risks attendant on childbirth also meant that many children had to confront the possibility that their mothers would die while giving birth. Few Puritan children would not have known households where such was the case, even if it was not the experience within their own family circle. The death of a mother might also result in cousins or other family relations becoming incorporated into the household; the remarriage of widowers likewise created what a later age would call a blended family, though all were aware that the death of a spouse had preceded whatever new happiness followed on remarriage. So discussing death was central to the duty of a father who would be faithful to God's ways.[44]

Edmund Morgan noted that in some Puritan households, dutiful patriarchs intentionally devoted an extended period at least once each week to catechize children, apprentices, and servants so that they would have the knowledge that led to salvation.[45] But there were also other opportunities for young men to nurture their own spiritual lives in the quest to determine the ultimate destiny of their souls. Cotton Mather in his diary, for example, makes numerous references to meetings held on week nights in private homes for young men (not young women and young men together). Such meetings were in addition to occasions when Mather, as a pastor, would hold formal classes for both young women and young men to offer more sustained explication of Christian doctrine and prepare them for salvation, sometimes as part of their regular education.

We do not know as much about what transpired at these meetings as we might like. Mather suggests at one point that they centered on various maxims for piety, considering a different one each time; Mather, as pastor often recorded his attendance, usually noting that he offered an exhortation on some aspect of piety to the young men present.[46] On other occasions, he indicates that at least part of the meeting was spent trying to identify projects in which participants could engage that would be of benefit to the whole community. A few times, Mather comments that attendance at such gatherings reached around a hundred or more, so that a private home could not accommodate the crowd.[47]

What is not clear from surviving materials is the extent to which men actually carried out their religious duty to lead family devotions, speak with their children about their salvation, and encourage involvement in other religious activities. Many of the descriptions of daily devotions, built around prayer, psalm singing, and perhaps discussion of a sermon, come in diaries kept by clergy, who might be more inclined to note their attention to such activities, and by others who were among the more well-to-do merchant families. In her exhaustive study of letters and diaries of Puritan men in seventeenth- and eighteenth-century Massachusetts and Connecticut, Lisa Wilson concluded that many were no doubt hard-pressed to adhere to a strict schedule of morning and evening devotions led by the father. She believes that the majority, whose pursuits were primarily agricultural and whose work thus took them from the family home very early in the day, would have had great difficulty keeping to a regular program of family devotions, even if they had been inclined to do so. Wilson also notes that among rank and file New England colonial men were those who questioned whether such pursuits were necessary.[48] It was easier for men to hold to the ideal in larger communities like Boston, where merchants and professionals were clustered, since their work patterns provided more opportunities for the household to come together in the morning and evening for family prayer.

Compounding the matter of how many men lived up to the spiritual ideal of the dutiful patriarch is also the question of the state of the soul of each individual man. In colonial New England, women were more likely than men to own the church covenant, to give the requisite testimony to an experience of election that brought them into full church membership.[49]

Once again, Cotton Mather proved an astute observer when he wrote, "I have seen it without going a Mile from Home, that in a Church of between three and four hundred Communicants, there are but few more than one hundred Men, all the rest are Women, of whom Charity will think no Evil."[50] This pattern of having more women than men as members, as noted earlier, has prevailed in American Protestantism ever since. The issue here is simply whether men who were uncertain whether God had elected them to salvation would be poised to preside at family devotions and to carry on repeated conversations with their offspring about the state of their children's souls. Would a man uncertain of his own salvation be able to guide others to see the work of grace in their lives? Obviously, speculation rather than hard evidence enters into any response. We do know that more men attended public worship than were church members, in part because attendance was expected by society and at times required by law (though Mather's observation quoted above would suggest that many men found ways to avoid attendance at worship). Yet even if those men who did attend worship at the meeting house each week were not formal church members, they would have been exposed to pastoral admonitions regarding the dutiful patriarch and encouraged to carry out their religious responsibilities as moral citizens who upheld public order.

In other words, the image of the dutiful patriarch would have been part of the mental and spiritual world of most Puritan men, even if circumstances did not always allow for careful exercise of the responsibilities that went with the image. All men were called to a Christian life, even if they fell short of the ideal. After all, as Cotton Mather put it in the funeral sermon he preached on the death of the Rev. Joseph Belcher, men of good character were called to pursue a life of sinless perfection, even if they did not expect to attain it.[51]

Reflections

Central to the images surrounding the dutiful patriarch were relationships, not doctrine or belief. If the model for the dutiful patriarch emerged from a man's relationship with God the Father, it was carried out in his relationships with fellow human beings, especially those who were part of his household. Hence, most of what we read about the dutiful patriarch concerns relationships between a man and his wife, a man and his children (especially his sons), and a man and those outside the family who lived in the home and were part of the household. The image of the dutiful patriarch thus signals a spirituality that is more external than internal. That is, it is oriented more to what is observable in human conduct than what lies within the inner self. Later ages would see spirituality as concerning primarily the inner self; not so the Puritans who gave us the image of the dutiful patriarch.

The matter is compounded when one reads through the diaries of the likes of Cotton Mather, Samuel Sewall, and others who were intent on embodying in their lives and in their relationships with their families the ideals they received in sermon and Scripture, theological exposition and practical exhortation. Rarely do those who keep diaries charting family events, business concerns, and even public events of the day turn to that sort of deep inner scrutiny that would reveal a soul searching for meaning and truth. To be sure, there are countless references to times of personal prayer and fasting. But such times are generally simply recorded without commentary on what men were actually thinking about when they engaged in prolonged prayer. Some was prompted, of course, by the sort of family crises that came to all—a wife experiencing a difficult childbirth, a child who was taken ill and might not survive, tension between a child and the child's spouse, and a host of other very real concerns. Real men did pray at times.

Missing is discussion of basic belief, of doctrine, of theological construction, of what convinces a man that he is among the elect (or, perhaps, among the reprobate). Many, including Cotton Mather, did frequently bemoan their own sense of personal sin, but again only in general terms. Few express their own anxiety over whether they were themselves among the elect, although perhaps only those who were certain of their salvation would have been inclined to include any religious musings at all in their diaries. Nor is there discussion of images that would challenge or counter that of the dutiful patriarch, the married man with responsibilities for household and family whose authority comes from God. While twenty-first-century analysts would be quick to remind us that there were gay men in Puritan America whose inclinations did not fit the mold, there are no images of masculine spirituality, whether of the dutiful patriarch or otherwise, that include them. Most Puritans no doubt knew that colonial law everywhere made sodomy punishable by death. Diarists and surviving records note a smattering of arrests for sodomy. But there is no counter-image of male spirituality or the Christian man provided for gay Puritan men, most likely because the ordered universe of the Puritans admitted only those whose lives conformed at least on the surface to the ideal.

Yet perhaps here we have a clue to the nature of male spirituality. Male spirituality, even among Puritan Protestants, was less oriented to a quest for inner peace, a search for truth within, a framework to give life's experiences a sense of meaning and purpose. Rather, it was outer-directed, something that was lived in the practical world of daily routines and existence. Thus it was more important to talk about the role of the father in leading family devotions than it was to talk about the father's own sense of wondering whether he had been chosen for eternal salvation. It was vital in a world where maintaining order was paramount to describe the spiritual authority of the father over wife, children, and others in the household. It was critical to do one's duty, especially one's spiritual duty, less order collapse and chaos prevail.

The spirituality enjoined by the dutiful patriarch echoed the hierarchy in the religious and social worlds in which men lived out their days. The pastor was the religious authority, whose power came from God, the ultimate authority. So too with those in positions of political and economic power. In countless sermons dealing with public life, many preached on election days or when the colonial legislatures convened, Puritan pastors sketched images of the good ruler that are remarkably similar to that of the male head of a household as a dutiful patriarch.[52] But as economic and political shifts challenged the hierarchy that prevailed in common life, leading to a struggle for American independence from British monarchy, changes also came to Protestant images of male spirituality. In time, the dutiful patriarch gave way to the Christian gentleman, although some of the concerns for order and responsibility remained just beneath the surface.

In Focus
Samuel Sewall: Judge and Dutiful Patriarch

A good man, Cotton Mather once wrote in a discourse on Proverbs 17:27, was a rare commodity.[53] Mather thought he had found one of those rare good men in Samuel Sewall. When Mather penned his reflections on the duties of good men at the time his own daughter Abigail died, he dedicated the work to Sewall.[54] By then, Mather knew Sewall well. He also understood that Sewall appreciated even the difficult duties that came to men who accepted God's ways as guides for their own spirituality and understanding of what it meant to be a Christian man, for Sewall had also had the sad experience of witnessing the death of children he had fathered.[55] Indeed, of his fourteen children, only six survived infancy.

Samuel Sewall was born on March 28, 1652, in Bishop Stoke, Hampshire, England. With his mother and four siblings, he migrated to the Massachusetts Bay colony in 1661, where his father had already settled. What we know of his childhood and adolescence suggests that he for some time gave serious consideration to entering the professional ministry. For example, he studied with the Rev. Thomas Parker of Newbury, where the family resided, in order to prepare for college work at Harvard. At that time the vast majority of persons who were graduated from Harvard sought pastoral calls to New England pulpits. So a future call to the ministry was no doubt weighing on Sewall's mind when he entered Harvard in 1667 at the age of fifteen. Whatever the reason, Sewall did not ultimately train for the ministry but instead embarked on a career in business, after spending a year as a tutor at Harvard in 1673. Nonetheless, he remained keenly interest in Harvard and in the preparation of men for the ministry. A longtime member of the Harvard Board of Overseers, he rarely missed attending a graduation celebration for several decades.

Central to the image of the dutiful patriarch was seeking a good marriage, and Sewall was no different when it came to finding a wife with whom he could establish a family. On February 28, 1676, he married Hannah Hull, the daughter of a prosperous silversmith and mint master. Sewall worked with his father-in-law, and, from 1681 to 1684, he managed the colony's printing press. Marriage to Hannah Hull brought Sewall into an elite circle of wealthy Bostonians and immediately put him in the public eye. All Boston would be aware if he faltered as a dutiful patriarch.

Although Sewall did not describe his married life with Hannah in great detail in the diary he began keeping in 1674, leading some later analysts to assume that the marriage was one that lacked deep feeling, he remained deeply committed to Hannah and acutely conscious of his duties as a husband until her death in 1717. Hannah never had an easy time with pregnancy and childbirth; whenever she went into labor, Sewall notes how he entered a time of prayer after summoning the midwife and women who would assist at the birth. Indeed, it would seem that Hannah was frequently sick and unable to take part in many family activities over the years. Nowhere in the diaries or letters does Sewall complain about this. Rather, he repeatedly notes prayer and concern, the proper response of a dutiful husband. Real men pray. He also records those happy occasions when the two—with or without children in tow—were able to take short trips to visit family and friends or even just to take a carriage ride together.

If Hannah brought financial stability to the marriage, Samuel Sewall in turn fulfilled his duty as a husband in providing for her and for maintaining the place of prestige and high social standing that Hannah knew while growing up. After their marriage, Sewall and his wife lived with her parents, thus remaining in the orbit of political, economic, and social influence. In time, to accommodate their own needs, they added on to the house, and, after the deaths of Hannah's parents, it truly became the Sewall household. But Samuel knew his duty to find a calling where the gifts he believed God had given him could be properly developed and a household supported. In his case, along with the mercantile interests he shared with his father-in-law, those gifts came through public service.

Sewall was first elected to the Court of Assistants in 1684 and named to the Governor's Council in 1686, continuing when the colony received a new charter in 1691 and serving until 1725. For many years, he served as a superior court justice, succeeding Wait Still Winthrop as chief justice in 1718. He retained that position until he resigned in 1728, shortly before his death. Thus, Sewall's career exemplified that sense of duty incumbent on the Puritan husband to provide well for his wife and family. If Hannah Hull's wealth had helped sustain the family's position in the early years of their marriage, Sewall's judicial status maintained and secured it.

Sewall's judicial responsibilities made his public reputation during his lifetime, not his commitment as a Christian man to the spirituality epitomized by the dutiful patriarch. His diary records many transactions that came his way as a judge, but the most famous episode, probably the only one of which later generations have any awareness, was his involvement in the Salem witch trials in 1692. We can appreciate the dilemma that the trials posed for Sewall if we remember that he accepted the Puritan ideology that the world should be a place of order. The furor caused by the accusations at Salem Village threatened the gravest sort of disorder.

Like most Protestants of his time, Sewall looked on the world as a place where supernatural powers were always operative, some working for the benefit of humanity and some to humanity's detriment.[56] His worldview was indeed prescientific; in theory, witches could be a part of that world. Later historians have recognized that the events at Salem were about much more than witchcraft even on a symbolic level. Sewall himself later understood that the accusations and the trial represented far more than trying to discern if a few were possessed by Satan. Although at the time, in order to advance the good order that in turn supported the dutiful patriarch, he had concurred in the judgment that the accusations of witchcraft were legitimate and proved, Sewall ultimately recanted his involvement in the episode. But in 1692, it manifested his commitment to preserving social order, precisely what would be expected of a dutiful patriarch.

Sewall as Head of the Household

Sewall also took very seriously his religious duties as the head of the household. After he owned the church covenant and became a member of South

(Third) Church in Boston in 1677, he never wavered in his commitment to fulfilling his religious duty. But deciding to become a church member was a very grave matter for Sewall, as it was for many other men. Numerous diary entries in February and March 1677 reveal that he was plagued by uncertainty before taking on formal membership. For example, in the entry for February 15, 1677, he remarked that he had often been discouraged from joining both because of his own weakness and because of the apparent hypocrisy of some who were members, though he refers to the latter as "the undesirableness in many of its members."[57]

Other reflections make it clear that Sewall was especially concerned about his unworthiness to participate in the sacrament of the Lord's Supper, something celebrated only occasionally but nevertheless at that time a rite open just to church members and one in which they would be expected to take part. Yet there is no indication at all in the diary or surviving correspondence that Sewall led anything but a conscientious, morally upright life. Indeed, later generations would remember him in part because of his moral objections to slavery and his having penned one of the first antislavery tracts in British North America. Nonetheless, Sewall agonized over his own sin and his own potential for being a hypocrite unable to live up to the responsibilities of membership. He sought to resolve these dilemmas through extensive times of private prayer, always a characteristic of the dutiful patriarch.[58] Real men pray.

As well, becoming a church member signaled to Sewall a public acceptance of all the familial religious obligations that went with being a dutiful patriarch. There was perhaps some personal urgency for Sewall as he contemplated the obligations of church membership and his personal state of worthiness or unworthiness in the late winter of 1677. Shortly after he took the step and owned the covenant, Hannah gave birth to the first of their fifteen children. For a father, being a dutiful patriarch brought ever more responsibilities. Membership was Sewall's way to demonstrate to the community at large and perhaps even to himself his willingness to train and instruct his children, to be a father to them after the way of God the Father.

Over and over again in his diary, Sewall, without additional comment, refers to having led family devotions on a particular day. David Hall reminds us that such daily rituals of singing, praying, and reading Scripture became a way to remain constantly prepared to deal with the vagaries of life.[59] After all, Sewall inhabited a spiritual world where supernatural forces were always at work, sometimes for weal and sometimes for woe.[60] Occasionally he notes that he rose early to read a psalm in private or perhaps in the presence of one of his children, especially if a child was sick. Often, having exercised his duty to make sure that his children learned to read, Sewall would have one of the children read aloud from the Scriptures during times of family devotions.

The sense of responsibility that went with being a dutiful patriarch always weighed heavily on Sewall. On a day he set aside for personal, private prayer and fasting in 1708, he confided in the diary his overwhelming concern for his duty to see that his children were converted and his ongoing fear that something lacking in his own faith might keep him from that noble duty.[61] The fatherly concern for an individual child began when parental choice of a name was announced at the time the child was presented for baptism. For Sewall, the baptism of one of his children always evoked a twinge of anxiety; perhaps he himself was unworthy of the duty now his as the father of a baptized child. His observation on the day in 1690 when he presented his daughter Judith for baptism is typical: "Lord grant that I who have thus solemnly and frequently named the name of the Lord Jesus, may depart from Iniquity; and that mine may be more His than Mine, or their own."[62] Other notations indicate that when the religious state of one of his children became a matter of special concern, he would often set apart a day of fasting, with much Scripture reading and perhaps even the singing of psalms, to pray for that child's conversion.[63]

As a good dutiful patriarch, Sewall drew on the sermons he heard for reflection with the household on the Sabbath. M. Halsey Thomas, who edited Sewall's diary, observed that Sewall kept full notes, including Scripture texts used, of all the sermons he had heard.[64] No doubt he went back to some of them on those many days of private fasting and prayer. And as a dutiful patriarch, Sewall recognized that he needed to draw into the circle of the faithful all who lived in the household, not just his wife and children. Apparently sometimes a servant went with Sewall when he made the judicial circuit as a superior court justice. Such trips provided occasions for one-on-one religious conversation. But there were lapses. On one occasion, Sewall in his diary expresses regret that while traveling and finding himself particularly tired, he had failed to have prayer with his servant on the Sabbath.[65] In another instance, Sewall was also alert to his religious duty; apparently in 1696 his ward Samuel Haugh, while indentured to Thomas Savage, was responsible for the pregnancy of Mrs. Savage's maid. Sewall was apparently not shocked at what a good Puritan would have regarded as among the worst of human weaknesses, but instead commented that he had urged Haugh to accept parental responsibility as his own Christian duty.[66]

Too many times in his diary, Sewall recorded moments of prayer with pastors and friends, as well as in private, when one of his children died and he prepared to join the sad procession to the family tomb. Charles Hambrick-Stowe called attention to the way personal and family rituals had a transformative quality for Samuel Sewall when he wrote about Sewall's response to the death of his infant son Henry in December 1685. Not only were there prayer and Scripture reading that would have been expected of all, but Sewall also became actively involved in preparing the body of his son for burial and then was part of the procession that accompanied the body for burial in the family tomb. All such practices went into a ritual of grief, argued Hambrick-Stowe, that allowed Sewall to come to terms with his son's death while he carried out his obligations as a dutiful patriarch. Nonetheless, like others of his contemporaries, the solace that came from devotion did not completely mitigate his sense of guilt, his inner conviction that somehow something he had done, some sin that lurked within, had played into Henry's death.[67]

Sewall had to face the death of a child within the household many times; the process was always the same. He followed the ritual forms that would provide comfort but always wondered whether some personal sin he had committed, some way in which he had not lived up to the obligations and responsibilities of being a dutiful patriarch, had not caused God to take the child from the household. In 1696, when Hannah had a stillborn son, his sense of personal unworthiness was especially poignant.[68]

As other dutiful patriarchs, Sewall would also discuss with his children their own impending deaths, largely because so often death visited the family circle and was thus part of daily life. But fathers could not always determine how their children would receive discussions about death and the divine judgment that followed. There are striking passages in diary entries beginning in January and February 1696 and continuing over the next several months when Sewall's daughter Elizabeth (or Betty), then fourteen, seemed preoccupied with a fear of hell should she herself die. A sense of her own unworthiness consumed her. From the vantage point of the twenty-first century, one might understand that she was experiencing in a vivid way some of the turmoil of moving from adolescence into early young adulthood, with its accompanying challenges of faith. But Sewall's response was to pray with her and seek to comfort her, finally sending her for an extended stay with his brother, Stephen, when nothing the dutiful patriarch did seemed to relieve her anxiety.[69]

The Dutiful Patriarch's Concern for Adult Children

Sewall also understood that embedded in the spirituality of the dutiful patriarch was a concern for children even after they were grown. In Sewall's case, one of his children who lived to adulthood provided many opportunities for the dutiful patriarch to express ongoing love. Samuel Sewall Jr., called Sam, would have been a challenge to any father, but in Sewall's response to the various situations in which Sam found himself, he reveals his continuing commitment to the ideal of the dutiful patriarch. The first cluster of challenges came with settling Sam into a career.[70] In November 1691, Sewall sent Sam to board and study with the Rev. Nehemiah Hobart in order to prepare for admission to Harvard. It soon became clear that the arrangement was less than ideal and that Sam was unlikely to benefit from a Harvard education even if he were admitted. Hence, as the dutiful patriarch, the elder Sewall arranged for his son to be apprenticed to William Perry, a bookseller in Boston. That arrangement likewise did not work out. Nor did at least three subsequent apprenticeships, including one with another bookseller and one with Capt. Samuel Checkley. In the midst of trying to carry out his duty to see Sam settled in a respectable career, Sewall took a day in January 1696 to fast and pray for his son's conversion.

Even after Sam opted for a career as a farmer, he presented his father—and his mother—with challenges. On August 19, 1702, Sewall recorded that he had filed the appropriate papers with the town clerk for the marriage of Sam to Rebeckah Dudley, daughter of the colony's governor, Joseph Dudley. The marriage proved anything but ideal, at least for several years.[71] Sam was far from the model patriarch, having a reputation for excessive consumption of alcohol and, according to Rebeckah, an eye for women who worked in their household. Rebeckah was likewise not the model wife, for she was possessed of a strong temper and perhaps too apt to accept attention from other men. Sewall spent much time in private prayer over the situation, particularly when Sam moved out of the home he shared with Rebeckah in January 1714. Rebeckah and Sam had five children together before they parted ways, although none survived infancy.

During the three years the couple remained separated, Rebeckah gave birth to a son, although Sewall did not mention the name of the suspected father in his diary.[72] Indeed, the identity of the father remains something of a mystery; even Governor Dudley commented, "No body knew whose twas."[73] Perhaps because of the prominent position in Massachusetts Bay of both the Sewall and Dudley families, Rebeckah managed to escape formal charges of and punishment for adultery. Yet while the son was less than a year old, Sam and Rebeckah began to negotiate a reconciliation, one that no doubt was seen as divine intervention on the part of dutiful patriarch Samuel Sewall, but also one that involved renegotiation of the marriage agreement between the Dudley and Sewall families. Apparently the reconciliation, aided by the pastor of the church in Roxbury, was successful, for

THE DUTIFUL PATRIARCH   43

two years after Sam returned to his home with Rebeckah, she gave birth to another son, Henry Sewall. Sam may have given his father many anxious moments, but in doing so, he also brought out the best of what it meant for the judge to be a dutiful patriarch, whose love and concern for his children extended well after their childhood.

Sewall the Patriarch as Church Member

Once a church member, Sewall also took an active role in public worship; apparently he had some vocal abilities, for in that day before musical instruments accompanied congregational singing, Sewall for decades was the one to set the pitch for the singing of the psalm. Notations in his diary indicate that he did the same from time to time when the faithful gathered in the homes of church members to pray for the sick and comfort those who were grieving. Samuel Sewall did not hesitate to pray with and for his own family; real men did pray. Nor did he hesitate to visit the sick and pray with and for them. As well, from time to time, as, for example, on October 2, 1688, Sewall hosted a day of prayer in his home when others of the community would gather to seek divine guidance. Sometimes such gatherings were more organized; Sewall commented that at one private meeting he hosted on April 24, 1706, one attended as well by members of his family, he read Scripture and a published sermon to those who attended.[74] Sometimes while holding court away from home, he would seek out other men with whom to meet and sing psalms in the evening.[75] Often, whether at home or on the road with official duties, he would rise early in the morning and go to the meeting house for a time of personal prayer and meditation. His passion for exemplifying the best in Puritan male spirituality, in being a Christian man, also led him to accept appointment in 1714 as an ad hoc agent to report on missionary endeavors among the Native Americans living on Martha's Vineyard, although there is a lacuna in his diary for the time he was serving in that capacity.[76]

Sewall did not discuss directly his personal religious beliefs in the diary to any extent, despite his commitment to being a dutiful patriarch. Yet the practice of family worship and other religious disciplines, such as private prayer and occasional days given to fasting, seem to have spurred a kind of personal transformation. His faithfulness in trying to become the dutiful patriarch in time resulted in his actually doing so in fact. But for Sewall the dutiful patriarch, as for other men of his day, what seemed to matter most were the relationships he had with others, not so much what transpired in his inner life.

It is also clear that the more Sewall came to epitomize the dutiful patriarch, the more he came to see the hand of God at work in human affairs and sought to bring his own actions in conformity with the grander actions of God the Father. Indeed, even when his beloved Hannah died in 1717, Sewall looked through his grief to discern what God was trying to teach him. Taken seriously ill on October 15, 1717, Hannah died four days later, after Samuel had summoned two eminent divines, Cotton Mather and Benjamin Wadsworth, to their home to pray with her. "God is teaching me a new Lesson," he wrote, "to live a Widower's Life. Lord help me to Learn; and be a Sun and Shield to me, now so much of my Comfort and Defense are taken away."[77] Even grief, however, did not keep the dutiful patriarch from attending worship, both morning and evening, the next day.

Sewall, as many men of his day, remarried. It was not easy for Sewall to enter into courtship, and some of his efforts met with rebuffs from the women in whom he was interested. He also pondered for some time whether to remain single but became convinced that God intended for him to remarry. He mused in his diary, "This morning wandering in my mind whether to live a Single or a Married Life; I had a sweet and very affectionate Meditation Concerning the Lord Jesus; Nothing was to be objected against his Person, Parentage, Relations, Estate, House, Home! Why did I not resolutely, presently close with Him! And I cry'd mightily to God that He would help me so to doe."[78] After a few unsuccessful courtships, he married the twice-widowed Abigail Melyen Woodmansey Tilley in 1719, although she died just a few months after their marriage. Then in 1722, Mary Shrimpton Gibbs, who had been a widow for many years, became the third Mrs. Sewall; concern over whether Sewall's children's inheritance might leave Mary destitute if she outlived Sewall led to a prenuptial agreement Sewall negotiated through her son. In his commitment to provide for Mary Sewall, should she become a widow once more, Sewall further evidenced his faithfulness to the image of the dutiful patriarch. It was a wise move, for Mary lived for sixteen years after Sewall's death.[79]

As husband and father, church member and judge, Samuel Sewall exemplified what it meant to be a dutiful patriarch. In his life he sought to mirror the love, compassion, and duty shown by God the Father of all.

✢ ✢ ✢

CHAPTER 3

The Gentleman Entrepreneur

IMAGES OF THE DUTIFUL PATRIARCH WERE NOT THE ONLY ONES presented to Protestant men in British North America in the years leading to independence. In the southern colonies, where the Church of England held a privileged position and a plantation economy was taking root, images of the Christian gentleman may have been more evident, although, to a large extent, the white southern Christian gentleman was also a dutiful patriarch. In areas like the Tidewater region of Virginia or Charleston in the Carolinas, a notion of faith undergirded how white men understood what it meant to be religious different from that which had informed the Puritan idea of the dutiful patriarch. The established Church of England represented the *via media* on both sides of the Atlantic, a church broadly Protestant where, it was thought, reason might direct individuals in matters of belief and where at least tacit consent to set practice was as much a badge of loyalty to the state as it was a matter of heartfelt devotion.

Although the Church of England in North America suffered throughout the colonial period from a shortage of ordained clergy, leaving control of parishes to laymen to a much greater extent than was the case in Britain, lack of all the accouterments of proper church order did not necessarily betoken lack of interest in theology or in discerning one's proper role as a man. Surviving lists of books in the personal libraries of men of even modest means reveal that works of theology, curiously often of a Puritan bent, were on the shelves and there for perusal.[1]

The image of the Christian gentleman, however, emerged as much from contrast with other ways of being religious as it did from intentional construction of an ideal. The introduction of chattel slavery in Virginia in 1619 was of signal importance to the spirituality of white British Americans as it was to those of African American heritage. Whites, even those sent by the Society for the Propagation of the Gospel to evangelize among the slaves, never really appreciated the richness of African spirituality that flourished among slaves, despite the efforts of slave traders and owners to crush the cultural life slaves brought with them. But as evangelicals made their way into the South and itinerants such as George Whitefield brought a more enthusiastic gospel to bear in the middle third of the eighteenth century, white Anglican men found that as a matter of course their spirituality was shaped as a reaction against the more emotional and frenzied style of evangelicals, African or white. Whatever else a white Protestant Christian gentleman might be, he surely was not subject to outbursts of hysteria when hearing the Word preached. Nor was he prone to seizures and the like when experiencing the presence of God within. As a white Protestant Christian gentleman, he was in control. He was a product of the Enlightenment who looked to reason, not exaggerated affective displays, to lead him to truth.

Thomas Jefferson—planter, statesman, architect, educational theorist, scientist, violinist, slaveholder, nominal Anglican, philosopher—epitomizes this construction of the Christian gentleman in many ways, even if his personal belief was less than orthodox.[2] Conscious of proper conduct, the hallmark of the gentleman, he sought to model his life on his own understanding of religious ethics. If he was not an orthodox Christian, he did find his thinking so profoundly shaped by the Christian heritage that he wrestled to create a version of the New Testament that would reflect what reason told him was acceptable. Later generations would question whether Jefferson's allegiance to high moral standards was flawed, both through his failure to take a strong and consistent stance against slavery and through his purported dalliance over the decades with the African American slave Sally Hemmings. But Jefferson personally believed that he followed his God-given reason in all that he did. A staunch proponent of religious liberty in the sense that he believed everyone had the natural right—indeed, obligation—to follow where reason led without coercion from the state, a church, or even another individual, he also thought that tolerance was a sign of the proper behavior of a gentleman in civil society.

Historians in recent decades have argued forcefully that the evangelical style held especial appeal to slaves and women because it offered a power denied them by a male-oriented and male-controlled culture.[3] Slowly but inexorably, evangelicalism penetrated the South, first along the eastern slopes of the Appalachians, then through the midlands, and finally into the heart of Anglican strength along the coast. By the time of the American Revolution, evangelicalism was well on the way to dominating southern religious life. The disarray and sometimes outright decimation that the American War for Independence brought to the Church of England helped bolster the standing of the evangelical churches. Then, too, Christian gentlemen took their time about rebuilding the apparatus that allowed Anglican congregations to function, perhaps to assure that laymen retained the firm control that had fallen to them in the colonial era because of the clergy shortage and the failure of the Church of England to name a bishop for the colonies.[4] But it was clear that it would be the men who would determine what happened in the life of the emerging Episcopal Church, not the women and certainly not those who were held as property. Patriarchy may have prevailed, but with the Christian gentleman, it was a patriarchy sustained by privilege as much as by an image of what was involved in male spirituality.

Colonial Anglicanism was something of a genteel faith, without the passion that stirred New England Puritanism or the zeal of Protestant evangelicalism when it made its way into the South. Yet the church did foster a rational spirituality, one based more on intellectual musing than a burning conviction to ferret out sin and mold life according to an ideal. Dutiful patriarchs who sought to conform their spiritual lives to the ideal were probably always in the minority even among men in Puritan New England. So too those males who were in a position to live as Christian gentlemen were also likely a minority among men in those areas where the Church of England held sway. In colonial politics and economics, the developing southern planter class may have been dominant, but for most men, thinking about proper conduct and reasoning through to personal truth were luxuries precluded by the hard work necessary merely to survive. Then, too, the notion of the Christian gentleman assumed something of a mythic quality in the decades after the Civil War, as white southerners struggled to create a past that sanctified those values that seemed discredited by defeat in the war, even as it romanticized them.[5]

There were, however, other ideas of how spirituality and gentlemanly behavior were linked besides those that prevailed among the colonial southern gentry. Some analysts, for example, prefer to use the label of the Christian gentleman to refer to a style of spirituality that developed in American Protestantism in the later Victorian era, when, under the influence of the Social Gospel movement, leaders of business appropriated that image to describe the wealthy industrial magnates, such as Andrew Carnegie, who were both involved in religious affairs and extraordinarily successful in business. I shall offer different labels to describe male spirituality in that epoch. In the context of the age of independence and the early Republic, however, we may find the roots of that particular Victorian image when Protestant writers held up an idea of the *gentleman entrepreneur* as the ideal of white male spirituality and the model for the white Protestant Christian man. Although they did not use that particular designation, Protestants who talked about men and their religious life from the opening years of the nineteenth century down through the time of the Civil War revamped the ideas of both the Christian gentleman and the dutiful patriarch to fit the emerging industrial order that was taking shape. The individualism touted as distinctively American in popular culture combined with the penchant for moral conduct to create the gentleman entrepreneur.

Social Change in the Early Republic

After the War for Independence succeeded in fashioning a new nation on the North American continent, the United States experienced tremendous social transformation as new lands were opened for Euro-American settlement, immigration brought thousands more to already crowded cities in the north, and the economic infrastructure of the nation moved steadily away from an agrarian base to an industrial one. All had an impact on images of male spirituality for white Protestants and challenged the sway of the dutiful patriarch wherever that conception had prevailed. The idea of doing one's duty to God and to one's fellow human beings and the idea that men held the dominant position in all facets of society, part of the spirituality of the dutiful patriarch, never completely disappeared. Within much of American Protestantism, the Christian man remained a dutiful patriarch, even if his authority was muted.

Some of the change was prompted by the simple fact of the stunning population growth in the new nation and the concomitant need to push further inland to find enough space to support the increased number of people. As in the colonial age, it mattered little that some of the land that was usurped had long ties to indigenous cultures; Euro-Americans continued to assume that the land was theirs for the taking. The movement into newer areas of settlement drew as much, if not more, from sectors of the population that had been in North America for several generations as it did from newer immigrants who were coming into the port cities, particularly of the northeast. Movement into new areas was one way to resolve the dilemma of the dutiful patriarch in providing land for his sons to have in their own right on reaching adulthood and starting their own families.

Mary P. Ryan has demonstrated how the first generation moving westward from New England into central New York, the area that later became the heart of the "burned-over district," attempted to replicate the agrarian culture they had left behind.[6] That culture, as we have seen, was hierarchical in nature, with the father as the dutiful patriarch who had responsibility for the entire household, including any bond servants. But within a generation or so, there were shifts that began to undermine such endeavors. The most far-reaching was the construction of the Erie Canal and the economic boom in the region that accompanied its opening in 1825. Agrarian life did not vanish, but the emergence of factory villages and towns along the canal route offered new possibilities for economic advancement that had hitherto been unimagined.

Farm families, as well as those in the towns, began to send their sons to work in the factories that seemed to appear everywhere. The arrangement had some parallels with patterns in early New England but also some differences. In many cases, the boys boarded with the owners of the factories, much as families had taken in apprentices in colonial New England, and men were assumed to have the same overall authority over such boarders that they exercised within the family. At first, too, the hopes of the young men were no doubt similar to those of earlier generations, namely, that they would not only learn a business but also be poised later on to go into the same line of work on their own. They, too, could become entrepreneurs in their own right. Even though the factory system ultimately worked against fulfillment of that dream, it did provide one source for a new understanding of white male spirituality in the image of the entrepreneur, the individual who succeeded on his own in business or industry. Indeed, sometimes it seemed that some sort of identification as a Christian man was integral to achieving economic success in the developing world of American business and industry.

At the same time, though, the pattern emerging in central New York served to keep the early factories modest in size compared with those that developed in the closing decades of the nineteenth century. After all, a factory owner could take in only so many boys and young men as boarders. Within a generation or two, other options developed, as boardinghouses and the like emerged to provide accommodations for a growing class of single young men who were living independently of their families and without the household supervision of a dutiful patriarch. The accompanying sense of being in charge of one's life, of having responsibility for one's destiny, also fed into images of white male spirituality and the Protestant Christian man, especially the idea of the independent entrepreneur.

A significant shift in family life went along with the development of factory villages and towns. The earlier pattern had been for the family, based in the home, to function as an economic unit in which everyone had work that contributed to the well-being of the whole. The emergence of the factory created a place of work that was distinct from the home, physically as well as psychologically. Men began to leave home to go to work, with the result that women assumed primary responsibility for whatever transpired in the home. Even those families who boarded boys and young men working in the factories would see the males leave the home for a place of employment each weekday morning, returning in the evening for supper and then bed. Many analysts have probed the ways in which these shifts in what went on in the home and who was responsible for activities within the home led to a redefining of gender roles, creating stereotypes of appropriate male and female behavior that would endure until the latter half of the twentieth century.

The separation of home and work undermined at least one role that the dutiful patriarch had taken on, namely, being in charge of the spiritual life of the household. While family devotions were still lifted up as the ideal, work patterns made it difficult to gather all within the household for morning and evening prayers. The father may have still been regarded as ultimately responsible for the welfare of the household. But more of the responsibility for spiritual life, especially that of children, shifted to women. Concomitant with that change came the growing perception, fed by the romanticism that buttressed much of the larger cultural life, that women were by nature more religious than men and therefore more suited to nurture children in their own nascent spirituality.

Many would see the emphasis on nurture as marking a decisive change in how American Protestantism by and large understood the spirituality of children especially. In an earlier day, those of the ilk of Cotton Mather and Samuel Sewall had anguished over the spiritual welfare of their children and set aside times to talk individually with children about the state of their souls. Now such duties shifted to women. Mothers would nurture their children, boys and girls alike, although families might still pay lip service to the notion that the father was the spiritual leader of the household. In the process, it was assumed that daughters were also being educated in the roles and responsibilities that would some day be theirs when they had their own homes to manage, even if they learned primarily through watching their mothers from day to day. But it was different with boys.

Part of the special challenge that came to women were the expectations that they would not only teach boys things of the spirit but also that they would equip their sons with the skills and personal traits requisite to success as entrepreneurs in a business world that was not part of the domestic sphere. In other words, mothers were expected to both provide sons with moral training and prepare them for mercantile careers or other jobs in the embryonic industrial world that was transforming the economic life of the nation.

For a time, however, the obligation of men to carry out their spiritual duty toward the boys and young men working for them, even those who did not necessarily reside in their households, remained a matter of much concern. How did the spiritual life of men who were factory owners or heads of businesses relate to the spiritual life of apprentices and clerks?[7] Was part of white male spirituality, of being a Christian man, having responsibility for the religious life of one's employees? If so, how could that best be exercised? It was perhaps easier to define such duty toward workers who resided in the home since they were part of the larger household. But what of others? As workers were increasingly seen as independent of family control, were not employers released from having spiritual oversight of those who worked for them? When did men who labored in the factories or worked in businesses become responsible for their own souls? Paul Johnson and others have shown that the revivals engineered by Charles Finney and others in the fast-growing towns of central New York were one response to providing for the religious conversion and spirituality of a developing class of workers, most of whom were male, taking over the responsibility that once went with the spiritual role of the dutiful patriarch.

Scholars disagree in their appraisals of how conversion experiences of men and women were similar or different in the evangelical revivals of the Second Great Awakening. Susan Juster has linked the experience of male conversion to a renewed sense of familial relations, something that was in danger of being lost as young men left home for jobs in the factory towns. At the same time, conversion empowered women to move beyond the gender roles sanctioned by society, drawing them into social reform activities in the antebellum period. In Juster's view, conversion for men entailed something of a reappropriation of the moral values long associated with Protestant Christianity, moral values that women already espoused. In other words, conversion drew women into a social realm where men were in control, while it drew men into a moral realm where women were in control.[8] However, some men were also drawn into social reform efforts, once they undertook to lead a Christian life, one shaped by the spirituality of the gentleman entrepreneur. The Christian man could indeed seek social reform in an effort to transform the larger culture into one molded by biblical ideals.

In contrast to Juster, Barbara Epstein interprets evangelical conversion during the Second Great Awakening as fostering an antagonism between genders that endured for generations. She sees the world of male work, outside the domestic sphere, as a world that was by nature fraught with evil from a woman's point of view, a world where women were devalued. It was a man's world with no place for women. Likewise, men who were drawn to spirituality knew they were moving into a feminine arena, but did so, in Epstein's perspective, largely for pragmatic reasons. Simply put, they believed they stood a better chance of succeeding in business and industry if they came across as trustworthy, and religious identifications was a badge of trustworthiness.[9] The reality, no doubt, is somewhere in between.

In retrospect, it is clear that spirituality took on an even more gendered quality in the antebellum period than had been the case earlier. That curious mix of social and cultural factors that accompanied the move from romanticism to Victorianism in one sense cemented in the popular mind the notion that women were by nature more religious or spiritual than men and thus by nature perhaps morally superior.[10] But there was a corresponding socially constructed image of men that had implications for white male spirituality and models of the Christian man. Adapting labels advanced by Charles Rosenberg, Anthony Rotundo argued that throughout the nineteenth century, one of the clusters of cultural traits presumed to describe what men were like by nature held that men were naturally active, devoted to self-advancement through hard work and persistence, and free from emotional dependence on others, including women. This "masculine achiever" was but one ideal of manhood; the "Christian gentleman" was another.[11] But the two come together in the concept of the gentleman entrepreneur that informed much of the writing about white Protestant male spirituality and what it meant to be a white Protestant Christian man in the antebellum period. Critical to that idea, as it is to those of the masculine achiever and Christian gentleman, is the emphasis on action, the turning outward toward the external world and the relationships there that would result in success.

There emerged a vast literature that stressed how moral qualities were tied to success in the world of developing business and industry, and how men acquired those qualities through the experience of an evangelical conversion. Such morality was not necessarily cast only in feminine terms or seen as the domain of women. For men, spirituality had more to do with what happened beyond the home and family and less with what transpired within an inner life, even if the spark that ignited those other relationships came from the deep recesses of the self and a personal relationship with God. Morality, as understood by men, concerned a wide array of public relationships, not only those with one's wife and family but also those with employers, business associates, and others. Spirituality had stronger ties to observable conduct than to matters of belief or devotion. Behavior was central to the ideal of the Christian man.

This focus on publicly observable behavior is what gave male spirituality an activist dimension, what Juster saw conversion doing for women. Thus, it was not only women who were drawn into social reform as a public expression of their spirituality, as Juster argued. John Gilkeson, in his study of developing middle-class life in Providence, Rhode Island, from 1820 to 1940, found ample evidence that in the antebellum period, it was those men who had some transformative religious experience who were more likely to be drawn to movements like abolitionism because they saw such activity in the social arena as the natural concomitant of personal spirituality.[12]

Men, however, were still not drawn to religious institutions to find outlets for their spirituality the way women were. Perhaps because clergy and churches were thought to deal more with belief and devotion than with the kind of activist morality germane to male experience, even women in the antebellum period saw churches more as extensions of the home than as places where men would cultivate a spiritual life. Clergy, too, were part of the world of women, not necessarily the best models for laity of what it meant to be a Christian man.

Well-known European observers of American life Harriet Martineau and Frances Trollope, both writing in the 1830s, reinforced this perception of religious institutions as belonging more to the realm of women than of men. Martineau, for example, in her *Society in America*, noted that ministers seemed to find their most responsive audience among women and among those who were superstitious, although she also castigated the clergy for failing to be more actively involved in the antebellum assault on slavery. Even so, she remarked that the nation suffered from a shortage of clergy, a shortage created in part because men could command better wages in the industry than in the pulpit.[13]

Clergy, then, were thought to have little knowledge of the world of business and politics, the world where most men found their work. Martineau cited an unidentified informant who commented that "the clergy are looked upon by all grown men as a sort of people between men and women."[14] This observation was not an assertion about androgyny but a sign that the kind of concerns that traditionally concerned clergy—doctrine, belief, devotion—were not those that were of most immediate concern to men who were trying to make a living in the world of business and industry in the decades before the Civil War. One might be a Christian man without being a church member.

Frances Trollope, traveling in the United States between 1827 and 1831, commented that she had never been in a nation where ministers had so much influence over women and so little over men, although she added that she did not mean "to assert that I met with no men of sincerely religious feelings, or with no women of no religious feelings at all."[15] It would also be easy here to see Trollope as readily buttressing the perception that most men simply were not religious or interested in spirituality. But the key in Trollope's observation is her use of the phrase "religious feelings." Antebellum white Protestant male spirituality that emphasized the image of the gentleman entrepreneur was not a spirituality that emphasized the sphere of what Jonathan Edwards in the eighteenth century had called the "religious affections" or what the romantic age called "feelings." It was a spirituality that was oriented to practical results in the external world. That was the realm of the Christian man.

Guidebooks for Young Men

Precisely what images shaped the constellation of ideas and moral values that comprised the spirituality of the gentleman entrepreneur and the way the gentleman entrepreneur became the model of the Protestant Christian man? In the antebellum period, the publishing industry expanded and began to provide a wider range of reading materials aimed at workers and their families, who, it was presumed, now had more leisure time. The genre that developed in many ways combined what later generations would call etiquette books and self-help manuals. Such books were intended as references for readers to use in discerning what sort of behavior was acceptable in the maturing world of the factory village and city, of business and industry.

While many scholars have probed the guidebooks that were directed to young women, fewer have looked at those targeting young men as their intended audience. The young men to whom these books were directed were those who had left the family farm and headed to towns like those that sprang up along the route of the Erie Canal. There they sought a more secure life in the factories and businesses that were transforming the economic base of the young Republic. Even for those who might have boarded for a time with the families of owners of small factories, the situation was

fundamentally different from that of apprentices who lived in the household of a master craftsman or artisan. In many cases, these were young men,
not boys learning a trade, and young men had rather different social interests than boys or adolescents.

For most, whatever formal education they were going to receive had
been secured before they left home for life in the towns and cities. Time not
spent working in business or a factory was not likely to be time spent in
educational pursuits. Hence, there was a different understanding of leisure
and of both the possibilities and dangers of leisure time for spiritual growth
and development. Although the Civil War for a time interrupted the movement of young men from rural areas to more urban ones, in the latter part
of the nineteenth century, the proportion of young men hoping to find
work and success in the nation's urban centers grew exponentially, as did
both the threats to spirituality and possibilities for success and spiritual
growth.

Guidebooks on how to succeed in the emerging middle-class world of
business and the city, while still fostering male spirituality, were a staple
of American publishing at least from the late 1820s until around the time
of World War I.[16] William A. Alcott noted in the introduction to his *Gift
Book for Young Men*, for example, that an earlier guidebook for men that he
had prepared sold some fifty thousand copies in the first fifteen years after
it was published.[17] If his estimate is accurate, then such manuals were major
sellers of the day. In some cases, the material compiled in these primers for
success appeared first in popular magazines, thus reaching an even wider
audience. Many of the thirty-four chapters in Alcott's work, for example,
had appeared as pieces in the *New York Observer* before he included them in
his handbook.

Typical of the antebellum handbooks is Timothy Shay Arthur's *Advice to
Young Men on Their Duties and Conduct in Life*, published in 1847.[18] Like
most others of this ilk, Arthur's handbook assumed a basic evangelical Protestant orientation on the part of its readers. Hence, like most, even those
written by Protestant clergy such as Sylvester Graham, the Presbyterian
clergyman and natural foods advocate, did not delve deeply, if they delved
at all, into the particulars of religious belief or doctrine.[19] Indeed, *The Young
Man's Counselor*, written by the Rev. Daniel Wise, assumed a religious base
but had no chapter devoted exclusively to spirituality, faith, or religious
beliefs.[20] All presumed some sort of religious orientation on the part of
those who read them, but none probed matters of religious belief. Nor did
they urge the cultivation of spiritual disciplines like prayer, reading of
Scripture, intense self-examination, or meditation. By and large, they were

concerned almost exclusively with the practical consequences of religious profession, not its details. It was almost as if such writers took for granted that their male readers already knew what it meant to be a Christian man.

Arthur, for example, began his work with a general understanding of human origins, based on the biblical notion of creation, but moved from there to the responsibilities that came to young men on reaching adulthood at the age of twenty-one.[21] He was certain, however, that religion was essential to man's happiness.[22] Yet even if some spiritual sensibility was necessary to success, Arthur observed, it was difficult to discuss it with any precision because of the multiplicity of Protestant denominations that competed with one another for young men's allegiance. Most entertained some idea of God that was buttressed by regularly attending worship—about the most specific statement Arthur made about anything having to do with spirituality—but for him, men would do better to stay home if their participation in worship was insincere.[23] Graham's work, in fact, exhibits a near obsession with nutrition and reproduction, raging against masturbation and urging a "spiritual chastity" that would shun lust and lascivious thoughts. For Graham, spirituality's advantage was in providing a base for morality, which in turn would assure that young men would not fall into sexual excess in their minds, let alone in their lives.[24] Wise made many direct religious comments, but they were woven into the his larger, rather romanticized discussion. He suggested early on, for example, that a saving faith in Jesus Christ was the cornerstone of a successful life, but he did not describe that faith. Rather, he simply noted that such faith should precede a rise to social eminence.[25]

Alcott's *Gift Book for Young Men* addressed specifically religious topics in only two of its thirty-four chapters, and those were at the close of the volume. In one of those chapters, Alcott argued that although young men were naturally inclined to skepticism, those who wished to succeed in the world should avoid lapsing into skepticism since no one trusted a skeptic. The implication was simply that a man who was not trusted could never be a success. Further, he added, religious faith—undefined in terms of content, although he presumed an evangelical, white male Protestant audience— was favorable to physical health, itself a plus for success, and to blood circulation. The following chapter urged young men to consider the Christian religion not because its doctrines were true, but because the virtues it promoted advanced health and happiness. His negative appraisal of the clergy crept into that discussion in an aside; he did not identify professional ministry with being a feminized vocation, but he did comment that it was unfortunate that so many sickly male children were pushed into clergy careers.[26]

This passion for the practical consequences of religion and morality led all these writers to emphasize the importance of self-discipline; Arthur claimed that self-discipline and self-reliance in no way precluded a concomitant dependence on God.[27] But it was the nurture of personal discipline that would make a man a successful entrepreneur in the evolving world of business. Equally important as a moral virtue was self-education; many writers stressed need for men to set up a regular program for self-education that was not limited by any means to formal schooling. Alcott even remarked that schools were only a part of a man's real education.[28] Schools, he noted, instructed pupils; they did not necessarily educate them.[29]

Most handbooks urged young men to spend their leisure time in reading but were equally concerned that what was read would be profitable for self-improvement. Curiously, few stressed the reading of Scripture or devotional literature.[30] Many, such as Alcott, lifted up biographies of successful men as valuable resources; such would provide models for nurturing the kind of personal character that would bring success. Alcott could not resist noting that Jesus Christ would be the best model, but he did not probe the character of Christ or show explicitly how the imitation of Christ would yield success.[31] Some did have particular gender concerns when it came to self-education, concerns based on premises that a later age would reject outright. For example, Arthur exhorted young men to pursue self-education because, he argued, the intellectual part of the male brain was more fully developed than the intellectual part of the female brain. What women lacked in intellectual capabilities, he asserted, they made up for by having the affective parts of the female brain more fully developed than the male counterpart.[32]

The gentleman entrepreneur should also improve his conversational skills. In doing so, he could court an appropriate woman to be his wife and so he could carry on the level of conversation with established business professionals necessary for his own eventual success.[33] For most, good conversation would signal that a young man eschewed those bad habits that would work against success, such as swearing, consuming alcoholic beverages, using tobacco, and enjoying idle amusements; some exhorted the diligent to avoid drinking tea and coffee, both stimulants, and to refrain from seasoning food with pepper.[34] Any stimulant could excite the passions and lead a man astray from a life of integrity. Religion, however undefined in these works, accompanied by moral behavior carried an assurance that men who possessed it were men of integrity.[35]

In retrospect, it may seem that writers of these manuals for young men devoted an extraordinary amount of their discussion to what things men should avoid, the kind of behavior that was not part of the deportment of the white Christian man. But most were convinced that the emerging world of business and industry, in taking young men away from the influence of farm and family, presented temptations that could readily lure those who let their guard down. Those who did not fortify their diligence with spirituality would lapse into a way of life that would destroy the possibility of success and happiness. Success might be there on the surface, but the happiness that should go with it would be lacking altogether. If history provided models for molding good character, it also provided examples of those who had given into the passions of the moment and, however successful in terms of riches and prestige, had no inner happiness that was part of the spirituality of the gentleman entrepreneur. Rev. Daniel Wise, for example, reminded his readers that even men who were blatantly evil could achieve a high degree of success but would not experience the contentment that went with the spiritual life. Voltaire and Lord Byron were two he singled out as representative of those who were successful but evil and therefore devoid of true happiness.[36]

Honesty, integrity, diligence, self-education, and improvement—all became hallmarks of the gentleman entrepreneur as the ideal of the white Protestant Christian man. And although at first glance there seems to be nothing distinctively religious, let alone Christian, about these characteristics, writers of guidebooks for young men in the antebellum period were quite sure that without some sort of base in the Christian religion, in an authentic spirituality, men would never be able to cultivate these trademarks and achieve success.

The Gentleman Entrepreneur and His Friends

Especially critical, however, for the young man who hoped to become a gentleman entrepreneur was his choice of associates, the male friends with whom he worked and spent leisure time during the years before he married and became the head of his own family. Those who gave advice to young men were of one mind in highlighting the dangers that men faced if they fell into the company of men whose own moral values would be corrupting. They would tempt even the most devout to abandon the ideals of male spirituality for a life given over to debauchery and depravity. The wrong companions, observed Daniel Wise, would lure men into such habits as gambling, drunkenness, and association with wanton women.[37]

In the antebellum period, the sheer numbers of men leaving home for life in the towns and cities made the problem more acute. The early pattern, carried over from the days of colonial apprenticeships, presumed that adolescent boys and young men would board in the households of small factory owners and businessmen, where there would still be some male authority and a familial environment to control conduct and behavior. But this arrangement was viable only so long as the numbers of unmarried men seeking employment and hoping to become gentlemen entrepreneurs in their own right were relatively small. After all, if a worker were a boarder in the household of an established gentleman entrepreneur, he would naturally continue to pursue a moral life and cultivate those virtues that would issue in his own success later on. As the number of young men aspiring for careers in business and industry increased, there was simply not enough room for them all to board with their employers. But without that force to steer young men in the right direction that such a boarding arrangement made possible, the peril of abandoning righteous living and thus jettisoning all hope of following the spiritual ideal of the gentleman entrepreneur was high.

In this context, organizations such as the Young Men's Christian Association played a vital role as surrogates to the religious household in the attempt to keep the image of the gentleman entrepreneur ever before young working men. Founded in London, England, in 1844, the YMCA began its first U.S. operation in Boston in 1851 and spread quickly to other cities. Similar agencies, though without the national and international affiliation that the YMCA offered, were found in many of the factory towns and villages in the Northeast and Midwest. Today, the YMCA is identified primarily with physical fitness and an array of programs promoting exercise and gymnastic activity. In its early decades, it was much more self-consciously religious. The YMCA offered young men not only an environment where they could pursue physical activity and athletics but also one where they could nurture their personal spiritual growth. It was, in the words of Allan Horlick, an "incubator of Christian character."[38] Alongside gymnasia were reading rooms filled with religious literature; alongside organized sports activities were Bible study and prayer groups, almost always of an evangelical Protestant, but conspicuously nondenominational, character. In other words, perhaps aware that men tended to avoid involvement in churches, the YMCA sought to do for young men in the cities what the churches were not doing by providing a practical approach to spirituality, a spirituality that would yield success in the burgeoning mercantile world.[39]

In the larger cities, especially in the later decades of the nineteenth century, the YMCA program often embraced a range of social service activities designed to reach out to those who had no religious affiliation. For young working men, the aspect of the YMCA that was perhaps even more significant was its offering dormitories and boarding facilities. In other words, the YMCA represented an institution designed to make sure young working men had the opportunity to use leisure time in pursuits consonant with the moral values associated with the gentleman entrepreneur and to associate with other young men who were likewise committed to the same spiritual ideals.[40]

The spiritual dimension of the YMCA was thus especially important in transmitting and keeping alive images of what it was like to be a white Protestant Christian man and how an individual could adhere to a way of life that reflected those images when he was no longer under the immediate influence of his own family. It was also critical that the YMCA lacked identification with any one Protestant denomination. If organized religion— the Protestant churches themselves—was increasingly consigned to the sphere of women, the YMCA offered another option. It was not that the YMCA intended to compete with the churches for the allegiance of young men, since in some areas membership in an evangelical Protestant congregation was expected of those who participated in any programs it offered. Rather, the YMCA presented a milieu where men could develop a spirituality in the company of other men, apart from the influence of women, without yielding the traditional male reluctance to be committed to formal religious institutions. Unwittingly, then, the YMCA functioned as an alternative to the churches, but not as a substitute for them in the minds of those who organized them and ran their programs. It was also an alternative to the nuclear family in terms of moral influence.

The greatest impact of the YMCA would come in the decades after the Civil War, when the combination of spiritual, family, athletic, and social service endeavors would seem especially critical as industrialization and urbanization grew at an even more rapid pace. But the structure was in place in the antebellum period, and the YMCA and cognate organizations were vital to sustaining the spiritual image of the gentleman entrepreneur. Countless young men lived in the YMCA facilities and found their friends and surrogate families in the circles of other men whose lives gravitated around the YMCA.[41] The YMCA could buttress images of appropriate Protestant spirituality for young men until such time as they married and established households of their own. It could sustain models for what it meant to be a Christian man.

Such associations, however, also enabled men to develop friendships with other men, even as they pursued mutual interests and cultivated those virtues that would prod them toward success in the world of business and industry. It is difficult to assess how much this living apart from family while beginning a career helped cement the increasing cultural sense that home and church were the sphere of women and the workplace outside the home was the sphere of men. The workplace required its own set of virtues, reinforced by a particular style of spirituality, for success.

After marriage, men did not readily return to the domestic realm, even if they left the boardinghouse or a room at an agency like the YMCA behind. Nor did they necessarily look to the churches to undergird the spirituality of the gentleman entrepreneur. Rather, they were beginning to turn to other institutions that inculcated such useful values as prudence, honesty, and integrity. Those institutions, which reached their zenith of appeal in the era between the end of the Civil War and the Great Depression, were fraternal orders or secret societies such as the Masons. Evangelical clergy routinely castigated such organizations because they shrouded their ritual gatherings with cloaks of secrecy; after all, the democratic spirit seemed to imply that whatever was secret was somehow evil or, in the minds of some evangelicals, blasphemous and akin to the grossly misunderstood Catholicism whose Latin Masses were also cloaked in mystery.[42] The white Protestant Christian man might not belong to a church, but he could belong to a fraternal organization.

In the Masons and other cognate societies, men were not only outside the control of women and their sphere, but they were also creating institutions where male friendship could flourish and where men could cultivate the moral values and ethical standards associated with the external world of business in a male environment.[43] To that extent, they offered a religious experience that helped sustain a distinctive male spirituality and an idea of the Christian man, though the religious focus may not have been the primary inducement to membership.[44] Indeed, the religious belief and devotion seen as central to religious institutions were present here only in the most vague and ambiguous form; practical morality, however, was paramount.[45]

Historians have noted that the steadily growing interest in Freemasonry and other secret, fraternal societies that were restricted to men did provoke some hostility on the part of women. Some of that hostility should no doubt be attributed to the larger context in which men were being drawn outside the home and family circle for employment. Participation in a fraternal society also took men away from the family. Home and family were thus changing as much as gender roles. Whatever took men away from home, whether work or pleasure, made the change from earlier days more obvious. The age when work centered in the home was gone. But fraternal organizations promoted moral values among men, a function increasingly given over to women. Consequently women saw secret fraternal orders as infringing on the arena where they still had control and influence.[46]

Even some of the social reform movements helped support male friendship and morality in ways that spoke to male experience and thus fostered the spirituality prompted by the image of the gentleman entrepreneur. In his study of male abolitionists, for example, Donald Yacovone pointed out that the language men used to describe their friendship was highly emotive;[47] indeed, it was perhaps more emotive than language used to talk about ties within the family to wife and children. Male abolitionists unabashedly spoke of their love for other men, although in context there was no indication that such love had physical expression in the way that the love a man expressed for his wife was assumed to have.

Some of the rituals developed in fraternal orders likewise spoke in more emotive terms than one found in ordinary discourse, indicative of the bonds that linked men together as they sought to exemplify common values shaped by the spirituality of the gentleman entrepreneur. Yacovone suggests that the "language of fraternal love" remained a part of men's relationships with other men with whom there was a bond of brotherhood until near the end of the nineteenth century, when Euro-American culture began to link such fraternal love with homosexuality and the physical relationships implied by homosexual conduct. It is important to remember, however, that even when this more emotive language came into play, it was a complement to the emphasis on action and achievement that were thought to be central to male identity and spirituality. Men used such language only in the context of fortifying those religious and moral values that were characteristic of the gentleman entrepreneur.

The Gentleman Entrepreneur and His Family

Much of the image of the dutiful patriarch in an earlier age revolved around the obligations men aligned with Protestant Christianity had for maintaining order in the household as the supreme authority under God within the family circle. In particular, the white Protestant Christian man as dutiful patriarch had religious obligations that pertained to his children and their spiritual development and, to a lesser degree, the religious life of all others who might dwell within the household. Did those responsibilities receive confirmation in the images of spirituality associated with the Christian man as gentleman entrepreneur within antebellum Protestant circles?

Many of the manuals for young men talked at least briefly about courtship and marriage, although few contained extended discussions of the father's role as a parent. Echoing the long-held Protestant belief that men were intended in the order of creation to marry a woman, William Alcott argued that men had a moral duty to marry, a duty that would cement their prosperity in the realm of business and industry.[48] He summarized arguments against marriage: the expense of supporting a family, the removal of the married man from male society, the responsibilities toward a wife and children, and the risk that one's marriage might not be a happy one. Then he insisted that the marriage relationship lifted a man to his true nature, for in marriage the purity Alcott thought innate in women would extend to their husbands. Here, too, there is a practical consequence, just as Alcott and others emphasized the practical results of spirituality. Female purity would make a man more trustworthy and therefore a more likely candidate for success, even if the man was intended to have dominion over the woman within the family circle.

Daniel Wise was more sober in his assessment of marriage, although he too regarded it as establishing a relationship that offered unknown and unanticipated positive results for the gentleman entrepreneur. For Wise, it was essential that a spiritual man exercise great care in the choice of a wife; left to his own devices, a man might be as easily deluded by the charms and accomplishments of a woman as he could be by worldly amusements. What was critical was to identify a woman whose virtues would buttress those required for male success in the world of business.[49] Even so, Wise cautioned, a virtuous young man would have already started to establish himself in business and thus have something of a secure financial base before entering into marriage.[50] By the time Wise and Alcott were writing, notions of romantic love were intertwined with the idea of what ingredients went into an ideal marriage. If the gentleman entrepreneur was still a patriarchal head of the household, he should also be certain that there was an emotional, affective attachment to the woman whom he would take as his wife before they entered into marriage. No longer would it do to assume that within the household headed by a male who sought to fashion his life after a spiritual ideal such love would blossom after marriage.[51]

Alcott amplified his understanding of the role of the gentleman entrepreneur as a husband in his *The Young Husband,* one of another genre of guidebooks, these for men embarking on marriage.[52] There he began by insisting that a Christian man had a religious duty to God to marry, as well as a duty to have a useful and successful occupation in keeping with the divine will. But this picture of the gentleman entrepreneur is as authoritarian as that of the dutiful patriarch. Within the family, the husband is to be the final decision maker. What Alcott does not do in the way that, for example, Cotton Mather and Benjamin Wadsworth did for an earlier age, is see the gentleman entrepreneur as an extension or representative of God the Father within the household. For Alcott, as for an increasing number of white Protestants in antebellum America, the husband had a responsibility to lead because of his natural superiority, not because of his being a substitute for God.

Yet if the style of authority exercised by the dutiful patriarch was one that prohibited spousal abuse and any maltreatment of the wife, so too the authority of the gentleman entrepreneur forbade the husband from inflicting pain on the wife, whether mental or physical. Even fault finding was scorned. The husband instead should be both confidant and friend to his wife. At one point, Alcott reminded young men that they had a spiritual responsibility for the salvation of their wives and their neighbors, although neither his work nor several others in the genre detailed the role of the husband and father in leading daily devotions and family prayers the way Puritan writers outlined such obligations in their description of the dutiful patriarch.[53] The gentleman entrepreneur, like the dutiful patriarch, should strive for compatibility, mutual respect, and patience.

There is a striking silence, however, in the writings sketching portraits of the ideal gentleman entrepreneur with regard to children. The culture that saw the spirituality of the gentleman entrepreneur coming to fruition outside the home and largely outside the religious institution of the church likewise saw the nurture of religious sensibility as something that was primarily accomplished in the home. Therefore, since the home was the domain of the woman, nourishing the spiritual lives of children was by default the responsibility of the wife and mother, not of the husband and father. Male work outside the home compressed the time the gentleman entrepreneur had for activities such as leading morning and evening devotions in the household. The father was still the authority par excellence, but relieved of direct spiritual oversight of children. The father's primary religious duty was to provide steady, regular, sufficient economic support for his children. Then there would be opportunity for the mother to provide spiritual guidance. The spiritual role of the mother with regard to children could extend well into the child's adult life, as we shall see in testimonies of conversion offered by gentleman entrepreneurs whose spirituality was prompted or launched by the so-called businessmen's revival of 1857.

The Revivals of 1857–1858

The decade before the nation entered a time of civil war saw a fresh stirring in spirituality as gentlemen entrepreneurs, white Protestant Christian men, in cities and towns in the more industrialized areas of the country gathered in churches for noontime prayer and testimony. At the same time, Protestant women, later joined by men (mostly clergy), became absorbed in the quest for holiness through such home gatherings as the Tuesday afternoon meetings for the promotion of holiness associated with Phoebe Palmer and her sister, Sarah Lankford, that had begun in the late 1830s. There was a marked difference between the two, however, a difference that highlights something of the gender distinctions in approaches to spirituality becoming etched into white American Protestant spirituality. Phoebe Palmer's pursuit of holiness and entire sanctification, the second blessing, in some ways represented the culmination of religious experience in a life engrossed in spirituality. To that extent, it capitalized on the presumed religious nature inherent in women and, by extension, in professional clergy who were increasingly seen as exhibiting a feminized spiritual sensibility.[54] The testimonies of personal religious experience at Palmer's gatherings come mostly from women who were already part of the churches, who were already cultivating a traditional life of devotion, but looking to augment that with a capstone experience of holiness. Male clergy who might attend often began the meetings by reading Scripture and calling for the singing of hymns and a time of prayer. Once such preliminaries were over, women were free to testify to their own spiritual growth or to ask questions, directed primarily to other women, about the nature of holiness and how to receive the second blessing of entire sanctification.

The businessmen's revival had a rather different focus, although personal testimony was also central to the noontime gatherings. Most accounts trace the revival to six businessmen, already successful gentlemen entrepreneurs, who gathered for half an hour of prayer on September 23, 1857, at the Fulton Street (Dutch Reformed) Church in the heart of what was then the business district of New York City.[55] Within a matter of months, the meetings were crowded, and businessmen were coming together for noontime prayer and testimony in other cities around the country. Leadership rested with laymen, gentlemen entrepreneurs who were committed to becoming models of the spirituality that brought success in the world of business.[56] Meetings were held in churches but were not associated with the denomination of the church where the men gathered. Rather, they crossed over lines and represented what a later age would call a parachurch movement by ignoring denominational distinctions. Church membership was neither required nor assumed among participants. Hence, particular doctrines were unimportant, and the single hour allotted to a meeting directed virtually no attention to matters of belief. The one spiritual discipline that did receive emphasis, of course, was prayer. Real men pray.

In the businessmen's revival we have an example of a spiritual endeavor engineered by men for men, by laity for laity, by those involved in business for others who either were or wanted to become involved in business. The revival mushroomed, not because of the leadership of the clergy but because of the leadership of businessmen, of gentlemen entrepreneurs. Pastors may have preached about the success of the revival in sermons at regular worship services; rarely did they exhort at the noontime meetings. Individual laymen rotated responsibility for offering prayer and inviting testimony from other laymen. All men were welcome, and all attending were given an opportunity to participate. The revival did have a broad Protestant base, helped by the fact that around the country most often Protestant churches opened their facilities for the men to meet. But occasionally non-Protestants attended, for there are reports of Roman Catholics who turned toward Protestant spirituality after coming to the meetings and seeing for themselves the vibrancy of the male spirituality participants exhibited.

Many later analysts have noted how the revivals began in the wake of a serious economic downturn in the nation, the financial panic and near collapse that had come in 1857. Even participants, such as Samuel Irenaeus Prime, recognized that the difficulties faced by those whose livelihoods depended on rapidly expanding world of business and industry, the gentlemen entrepreneurs, were drawn to spiritual concerns because of the challenge of the times.[57] For some, perhaps, reaching out to supernatural power offered some consolation for the economic turmoil. But the links between the revival and business go much more deeply, as do the ways in which the revivals enhanced the image of the gentleman entrepreneur as the model for white Protestant male spirituality and the epitome of the Christian man.

Much of the literature reflecting first-person accounts of the revivals consists of testimonies of conversion, which usually meant the abandonment of a life of presumed immorality characterized by excessive use of alcohol, gambling, and neglect of those virtues associated with the gentleman entrepreneur. Commentators also reflected that few of these turns to a life of cultivating male spirituality resulted from the ministrations of clergy; if there was extensive prayer for an individual prior to his religious experience, more often than not that prayer came from a devout mother or wife.[58] Rarely are prayers of fathers for the conversion of their sons acknowledged. So if real men prayed, they prayed more in thanks for what had happened to themselves in the process of conversion than in petitioning the Almighty to steer their sons toward conversion.

The testimonies evidence some remarkable similarities. Those who reported conversion often noted the depth of sin in their past. In most cases, the sin identified was a way of life exhibiting rather different values and behavior than one would expect to find in a successful businessmen.

Accounts abound of immoral living, gambling, neglect of family responsibilities, idleness, alcohol abuse, and the like. The transformation that followed on conversion was the adoption of those values and modes of behavior associated with success in business and industry. In other words, men
took on for themselves the burden of living as gentlemen entrepreneurs
who would exhibit honesty in all transactions and, especially, hard work in
efforts to become successful. Samuel Irenaeus Prime noted, for example,
that even those businessmen who were already inclined to a life of morality
and integrity in their careers became more principled as a result of the
revivals. They were now more committed to doing business based on
Christian principles in the assurance that success would ultimately ensue.[59]
He also noted that those already in business reaped benefits from encouraging their employees to attend and from having male employees convert.
The connection was obvious to Prime: employees who absorbed the values
promoted in the revival would be diligent, hard working, and honest. Not
only would the worker benefit from living according to the image of the
gentleman entrepreneur, but the employer would benefit from having a
more serious and committed employee whose effort was likely to spur
greater prosperity.[60] James Alexander emphasized how the revivals supported friendships among businessmen young and old, friendships that
presumably helped sustain commitment to the ideals of the gentleman
entrepreneur.[61] As historian Kathryn Long observed, "The businesslike
approach to revival piety appealed to the evangelically oriented merchants,
clerks, and aspiring entrepreneurs who populated the downtown business
districts alongside their non-evangelical colleagues. . . . the revival demonstrated the existence of significant numbers of urban men sympathetic to
evangelical piety."[62] It promoted an "entrepreneurial religious activism" and
thus strengthened a subculture of masculine evangelical piety.[63] In other
words, the revival was as good for business as it was for drawing men into
the spirituality of the gentleman entrepreneur.

The coming of the Civil War did not bring the revival completely to a halt,
although it became more scaled down in many localities as men volunteered
or were drafted into military service. No doubt for many, their thinking
included a sense that the hard work, integrity, and honesty that were part of
the business world would also carry over in military endeavors. But the
image of the gentleman entrepreneur endured certainly among those
involved in promoting the work of the United States Christian Commission,
an interfaith operation that distributed Bibles and tracts among the Union
forces and took over from the YMCA the responsibility for hosting meetings among the troops that centered on prayer, singing, and exhortation.

Such meetings were similar to those that were characteristic of the noontime gatherings of the gentlemen entrepreneurs.[64] If those Southern states that formed the Confederacy were less industrialized than those in the Union, they did experience a religious renewal that spawned a tract industry, witnessed conversion to a masculine piety that countered the unruly behavior that was inconsistent with the moral values of the gentleman entrepreneur, and perhaps helped challenge the notion that spirituality was effeminate because women were by nature more religious than men.[65]

Reflections

Almost as soon as it achieved political independence, the United States began the process of moving from an agrarian economy to one grounded in business and industry. The process spanned the nineteenth century and exploded in the last decades of the century. In the antebellum period, the transition had important consequences for images of white Protestant male spirituality and models of what it meant to be a white Protestant Christian man. The dutiful patriarch began to make way for the gentleman entrepreneur, the man whose life exemplified honesty, integrity, hard work, trustworthiness, and a host of other values that would ensure success in the mercantile world. Those values became the center of a spirituality that spoke to the lives of men who left home for the workplace each day and for the countless young men who left family farms for jobs in emerging factories and business enterprises.

Like the image of the dutiful patriarch, that of the gentleman entrepreneur minimized matters of doctrine and belief. What mattered were the practical consequences of belief in bringing success in the world of business and industry. Religious conversion fit in as a turning from those values that would impede success and the adoption of those that would spur achievement in the world of work. The image of the gentleman entrepreneur thus promoted a spirituality that was more concerned with relationships with others, especially with employers and business associates, than it was with cultivating the depths of an inner life of devotion and traditional piety. Those became increasingly consigned to the domain of women, as the home became a sphere for women's concerns and the world outside the home became a sphere for men's endeavors. Through agencies like the YMCA and the growing fraternal orders, men developed networks of association that became arenas where men could pursue the spiritual interests of the gentleman entrepreneur in company with other men. If anything, the spirituality of the gentleman entrepreneur served to keep church membership primarily an activity of women. Even the businessmen's revival of 1857–58 served to reinforce those values associated with the spirituality of the gentleman entrepreneur.

Home and family concerns did not disappear. In theory, males were still regarded as heads of households and white Protestant Christian men as dutiful patriarchs who had responsibility for the spiritual life of the family and others residing in the home, from daily devotions to attendance at worship. But in reality, more and more the religious life of the home became part of the realm of women as families became "little churches" in which children could be nurtured into those values that would bring success in later life.[66]

At the same time, the emphasis on values external to the inner life of devotion and oriented to the world of business and industry helped cement the notion that men were by nature less religious than women. Certainly they expressed their spirituality increasingly in different ways in white Protestant culture in antebellum America. The Civil War may have disrupted life as usual throughout the nation, but it did not eliminate the image of the gentleman entrepreneur as marking the ideal of male spirituality and the model for the white Protestant Christian man. Even after the war, the image flourished as industrialization developed at an even greater pace than before the war. But in the postbellum epoch, in later Victorian America, another cluster of images came into focus for Protestant men intent on pursuing the spiritual life. That cluster of images looked to the courageous adventurer as providing the model for men who wished to cultivate the spiritual life.

In Focus
William E. Dodge: Merchant Prince and Gentleman Entrepreneur

New York City's Union Theological Seminary, founded in 1836, retains a professorship in "applied Christianity" that carries the name of a layman who was one of the seminary's founders and early benefactors, William E. Dodge. Dodge was a Presbyterian most of his life; he was also an extraordinarily successful businessman, thanks not only to his mercantile associations with his wealthy and influential father-in-law, Anson Greene Phelps, but also to his own commitment to the virtues exemplified by the gentleman entrepreneur: discipline, hard work, honesty, determination, integrity, and loyalty to one's employer and then, in time, to one's own business enterprises.[67] That the professorship bearing Dodge's name is in applied Christianity reflects the very practical understanding of male spirituality captured in the image of the Christian man as a gentleman entrepreneur.

Born near Norwich, Connecticut, in the town of Bozrahville on September 4, 1805, to David Low Dodge and his wife, Sarah Cleveland Dodge, William E. Dodge was the fourth of what would be a family of seven children. The Dodge family traced its heritage in North America to the arrival of another William Dodge in Salem in 1629, early in the Puritan colonial venture in Massachusetts Bay. David Low Dodge was himself an enterprising businessman who was involved in building the first cotton mill in Connecticut, although for a time he moved his family to New York City, where he was engaged as a merchant, before returning to Connecticut a few years later.

Even as a child, Dodge was drawn to religious concerns to such an extent that, although he came to exemplify the gentleman entrepreneur, he may not be typical of adolescent males of his time. His son noted, for example, that even as a teenager, Dodge "had probably never neglected reading of the Bible or maintaining the habit of prayer."[68] He thus always understood himself to be a Christian but nevertheless underwent a conversion experience in 1821 that led to his joining the Congregational Church in 1822. After his family returned to New York City in 1825, he became a Presbyterian and remained so for the rest of his life, helping to start several new congregations in Manhattan and lending each his financial support. He was perhaps more active than most laymen, for despite extensive travels as his business career flourished, Dodge volunteered as a Sunday school teacher most of his adult life. He was also well known in denominational circles, serving several times as an official delegate to the Presbyterian general assembly.

The depth of Dodge's involvement in organized religion also sets him apart from many of his male peers. However, there is little in the material about Dodge that discusses his personal religious beliefs or his personal theological position. What seems likely is that Dodge's own Christianity was, like the seminary chair that bears his name, very much something that was to be applied to daily life. Church membership and involvement were means of reinforcing the values and virtues of the gentleman entrepreneur and of receiving confirmation that those values and virtues carried divine sanction.

Formal education for Dodge ended when he was thirteen; in this regard, he was perhaps more typical of the young men of the day. Following what was becoming standard convention, in 1818 Dodge went to work for another merchant, arriving very early in the morning to clean and do whatever had to be done to get the establishment ready to open for business. During the day, he did various "odd jobs" as needed, while picking up a thorough understanding of exactly what went into running a business and what kind of work was involved in virtually every phase of operation. In the process, he developed a keen sense of dedication to work and loyalty to his employer. Already exhibiting the characteristics of the gentleman entrepreneur while still an employee, Dodge helped start the New York Young Men's Bible Society in 1825. His practical spirituality even then could not be confined to one congregation, or even to one denomination, but had to cut across those lines in an effort to provide spiritual opportunities for other young men from a variety of religious backgrounds who were also on their own, trying to achieve some success in the world of business. In these endeavors, he also had the support of his parents, who opened their home (as Dodge would open his own home later) for prayer meetings attended by young men who were trying to succeed in the world of business.

Little wonder, then, that Dodge in 1827 went into business for himself, opening a wholesale dry-goods business in New York. That same year, again demonstrating one of the characteristics of the gentlemen entrepreneur, he furthered his commitment to social reform by becoming a founding director of the New York City Mission. In time, his involvement in benevolent societies would include serving as manager of the American Bible Society, active member of the American Tract Society, and then an outspoken supporter of the embryonic temperance movement.

In 1828, he married Melissa Phelps, daughter of a prominent churchman and businessman Anson Greene Phelps. Phelps had already established himself as a shrewd, successful, but honest importer of metals and encouraged his son-in-law to join him as a business partner. Phelps had immediately recognized Dodge's business acumen. Even more, he acknowledged Dodge's commitment to the virtues of male spirituality inherent in the image of the gentleman entrepreneur—hard work, honesty, integrity, discipline, self-motivation, and the like. Dodge always sought to live as a Christian man. Thus in 1833, Dodge sold his own business and embarked on a new career as a partner in Phelps, Dodge, and Company, an international venture that included not only the importing of metals (especially copper) into the United States but also the exporting of cotton to Britain, where it would be turned into manufactured goods. For many years, another Phelps son-in-law oversaw the British operations of the parent company.

Becoming a Gentleman Entrepreneur

Early on, however, Dodge came to believe that faithful adherence to the morality expected of the gentleman entrepreneur would result in his becoming a millionaire and that success would be a sign that God sanctioned his endeavors. So he quickly expanded his business interests, particularly by investing in railroads as they became the primary transportation link fueling unprecedented economic growth in the expanding Republic. But Dodge's spirituality, his sense of what it was to be a Christian man, came into play when he insisted that railroads with which he was involved refrain from business on the Sabbath. When the Erie Railroad, of which he had been a founding director, in 1857 went to operating seven days a week, he resigned as a director and sold his stock, for he would not "break God's law for a dividend."[69] He reportedly did the same with other railroads in which he had invested heavily, such as the Central Railroad of New Jersey, but was apparently instrumental in keeping the Delaware, Lackawanna, and Western Railroad from offering passenger service on Sundays for many years, although even that company did transport coal shipments on the Christian Sabbath.

By the 1850s, Dodge had also bought thousands of acres of timberland from Tioga County, Pennsylvania, to Georgia (where Dodge County was named for him) and ventured into the iron and coal business that would sustain vast industrial expansion as a founder and director of the Lackawanna Iron and Coal Company based in Scranton, Pennsylvania, in the heart of the northeastern Pennsylvania anthracite country. He had also purchased stock in several insurance companies and what became Western Union and saw his family and Phelps, Dodge and Company become one of the largest real estate owners in New York City. So diversified were his business interests that when financial collapse threatened the United States in 1856–57, Dodge and his family remained unusually prosperous.

Nonetheless, Dodge enthusiastically lent his support to the businessmen's revival that emerged in part as a response to the difficult economic times. He had supported other revival endeavors over the decades.[70] He believed that revivals offered the spirituality that could create and sustain moral workers, workers who were Christian men. He wanted honest employees and associates. In other words, even if he was personally committed to Christianity, Dodge also understood that if the values and virtues of the gentleman entrepreneur were inculcated in his own employees, he would have a trustworthy and reliable staff and thus be more likely to achieve success. His spiritual principles, his son noted later, were responsible for his business integrity.[71] Theodore Cuyler made the same point when he remarked that Dodge's Christian conscience lay behind everything he did.[72]

In keeping with the image of the gentleman entrepreneur, Dodge took an active interest in the society around him, especially in social reform activities. We have already noted his early involvement with the New York City Mission and the American Tract Society. But as Dodge amassed a considerable personal fortune, he became a philanthropist, giving financial support to numerous charitable, educational, and religious causes. In addition, he served on the boards of agencies like the American Board of Commissioners for Foreign Missions and the Evangelical Alliance, paralleling the way he served on boards of corporations and business in which he had monetary investments. On some of his business trips abroad, he also represented groups like the Evangelical Alliance in trying to open doors for Christian missionary endeavors in places where the local political situation created unusual challenges.

Particularly important to Dodge was the work of the YMCA, an organization that was from its inception central to inculcating the moral values associated with the gentleman entrepreneur in factory workers, business clerks, and other young men who were trying to make their way in the developing industrial economic world. When Dodge reflected back on the changes that had come to business and industrial life in New York City in his widely circulated lecture on "old" New York, he singled out the YMCA for special praise.[73] His commitment to mercantile ideals, consonant with the spirituality captured by the Christian man as gentleman entrepreneur, carried over in his long association with the Chamber of Commerce, which he joined in 1852 and then served as president of the New York branch from 1867 to 1875.

Theological education and individuals training for the professional ministry also benefited from Dodge's desire to use his wealth in a manner befitting the gentleman entrepreneur. He was a benefactor of such institutions as Union Theological Seminary, Princeton Theological Seminary, Yale Divinity School, Maryville College in Tennessee, Williams College, and a number of others. He endowed scholarships at Lafayette, Dartmouth, Amherst, Beloit, Marietta, and Hamilton Colleges. Several other schools also received his occasional support. Without fanfare, he also privately helped scores of men who were theological students pay for their education, regularly assisting at one point around twenty students per year.[74] His rationale was consistent with the spirituality of the gentleman entrepreneur: an educated clergy would help perpetuate the moral values that would make for honesty in business and thus in turn prepare individuals for success.

Dodge was keenly aware of social problems that stood in the way of creating a moral climate in which all persons were on an equal basis. In his letters home while traveling in the South on business, he commented frequently on the injustice of slavery, although his commitment to order and decorum meant that like so many others he would not call for an immediate end to slavery.[75] Here he reveals that the spirituality of the Christian man as gentleman entrepreneur had a conservative underpinning that was more assumed than openly articulated. Dodge, like other of his ilk, believed that the Almighty was providentially at work in all the affairs of history and that divine purposes would ultimately prevail—much the same as the man of honesty and integrity would ultimately prevail in business, even if for a time the situation seemed to work against him. His interest in social reform endeavors in this arena were for the most part limited to service with the American Colonization Society, one of the more conservative efforts to end slavery by returning African Americans to Africa.

Not until civil war broke out in 1861 did Dodge identify more directly with the abolitionist cause. Even then, he did so more out of intense loyalty to the Union, a loyalty akin to what he expected workers to have to their employers, than out of conviction that justice must prevail. Detractors might attribute his reluctance to take a more direct antislavery stand to the extensive business interests he had in what became the Confederacy; others noted that those interests allowed him to gain considerable information about the Confederacy during the war, information that he apparently shared with government officials.

After the war, more or less retired from business, Dodge served one term in the U.S. House of Representatives, running as a Republican. His political career was less distinguished than his business career, although his voting record was one that supported business interests by and large. That political involvement, however, led to his becoming an ardent supporter of the presidential candidacy of Ulysses S. Grant. Once in office, Grant in 1869 appointed Dodge to serve on the U.S. Commission on Indian Affairs. Once again, Dodge's position was consistent with the spiritual values of the gentleman entrepreneur and thus, in retrospect, relatively conservative. Occasionally appreciating the integrity of Native American culture apart from its assimilation into Euro-American ways, Dodge nonetheless endorsed proposals to turn over education and kindred activities on reservations to different religious bodies. He was convinced that the moral values the churches would teach in turn would best position Native Americans to improve their economic status. However, there were limits to Dodge's paternalism and to his willingness to tolerate corruption in the administration of Indian affairs, and he and several other commissioners resigned in 1874 to protest the administration of federal Indian policies.

The Gentleman Entrepreneur as Dutiful Patriarch

When possible, like many gentleman entrepreneurs, Dodge also continued some of the spiritual activities associated with the dutiful patriarch, particularly when his children were small. The family home was something of a religious center, as one might expect, with religious samplers and such for decoration; no doubt the appearance of the Dodge home reflected the feminization of the domestic sphere. Dodge was noted for taking half an hour each week day morning after rising for a time of personal prayer and Bible study and then leading the household in a time of family devotions before breakfast was served at 8:00 A.M. Real men did pray.

Dodge routinely offered prayers of thanks at all meals when he was at home. When the seven Dodge children who survived to adulthood were young, Dodge exhibited great interest in the spiritual life of each. For example, for an hour before the 6:00 evening meal, he would discuss with them tenets contained in the Westminster Catechism (especially on Sundays), along with leading in the singing of hymns and reading of Scripture. As well, the household gathered at 10:00 P.M. for prayers that signaled the close of the day.[76] The aura of the gentleman entrepreneur, in this case one shaped by the Calvinist heritage that sustained antebellum Presbyterianism, meant that family life was a serious business, just like work outside the home. So if the household was not noted for having an atmosphere of gaiety and glee, it did function as an extension of the institutional church in the dynamics of its internal life.

Dodge also brought together features of the dutiful patriarch and the gentleman entrepreneur in his relationship with his wife. By all accounts, Dodge and his wife were unusually close to each other, perhaps a reflection that romantic love had become a part of their marriage at its inception, more so than had been the case with many marriages in the colonial era. It seems clear that Dodge was the patriarchal head of the household but by no means a harsh authoritarian figure. When the children were small and business interests took Dodge on travels around the country, he regularly wrote long and detailed letters to his wife, many of which have survived. Later, Melissa Phelps Dodge frequently joined her husband on his business travels, particularly when trips required an extended stay in Europe. One biographer remarked on the total mutuality that characterized the marriage.[77]

Dodge's success as a gentleman entrepreneur allowed the family to maintain a large home in Manhattan as well as an estate, Cedar Cliff, at Tarrytown. This second home served as a summer residence but was also the site of a festive gathering of family and friends on June 24, 1878, when the Dodges celebrated their fiftieth wedding anniversary. While family gathered privately for prayer to mark that event, so many friends were invited that Dodge chartered a special train to bring a large number from New York City to Tarrytown for the occasion. Estimates are that the Dodges hosted around one thousand people that day.[78] For Dodge, the success of marriage was akin to success in business. Commitment to the same basic moral values that described the spirituality of the gentleman entrepreneur likewise described what undergirded his identity as a husband who was a Christian man: loyalty, hard work, honesty, and integrity. As he followed all the conventions in business, he did so in his married life.[79]

Dodge, the gentleman entrepreneur, exhibited little interest in the fine points of theology. Dogma and doctrine belonged to a different realm that was alien to the practical spirituality that sustained Dodge and others like him. Success in the world of business required attention to practical details, not abstract speculation. For many, including Dodge, a spirituality centered on doctrine was of little use in dealing with the realities of daily life. Rather, for Dodge the gentleman entrepreneur, to embrace faith was to live a life of integrity and honesty. To become involved in social reform and philanthropic activities was a means to demonstrate in very practical ways a spiritual gratitude for the way God operated in and through empirical events. Nothing suggests Dodge harbored any beliefs that were counter to the prevailing evangelical orthodoxy of the early nineteenth century. Indeed, he did more to seek the conversion of others, particularly young working men, than he talked about doctrine and creed. Dodge was reputed to stuff his suit coat pockets with religious tracts that he would hand out to employees and others he encountered during the business day.

Biographers record only one episode when Dodge's dedication to spiritual principles came into question. At one point, Dodge became involved in an allegation of charges of conflict of interest brought by the president of the Delaware, Lackawanna, and Western Railroad, of which he was a director and major stockholder.[80] Dodge was not the only director so accused. But he had been adamant that the railroad would reflect his moral convictions by refraining from offering passenger service on Sunday, although coal was transported on the Christian Sabbath. Railroad officials believed that this practice made the line less competitive. In addition, there was some question, that may have a factual basis, about whether Dodge had secured for his own companies more favorable rates to transport goods and products than offered to other businesses. Therein lay the presumed conflict of interest. Did Dodge the business owner put personal advantage above his duty as a railroad director?

The full board conducted an investigation, after which it vindicated Dodge and the other directors accused. The railroad president, however, pursued the matter by going to the New York Fourth Presbytery and ultimately to the Synod of New York and Jersey, where he wanted Dodge tried on charges of "falsehood, conspiracy, slander or defamation and hypocrisy or disingenuousness."[81] Had Dodge been found guilty, he would hardly have served as an exemplar of the integrity, trustworthiness, honesty, and dedication that were hallmarks of the gentleman entrepreneur. However, every judicatory that had to consider the charges vindicated him. The vindication perhaps did as much as Dodge's philanthropic and social service work to cement in the popular mind that he was a splendid representative of the spirituality of the Christian man as gentleman entrepreneur.

William E. Dodge, from the time he became a clerk in the developing mercantile industry as a young teenager until his death on February 8, 1883, at the age of seventy-seven, exemplified the values and virtues captured in the image of the gentleman entrepreneur. Little wonder, then, that friends and even casual acquaintances commonly referred to him as the Christian merchant.[82]

CHAPTER 4

✣ ✣ ✣

The Courageous Adventurer

For generations, the Civil War seemed a turning point in American life, representing in theory either the vindication of the principles of liberty and equality presumed to lay at the heart of the American enterprise or the destruction of a sentimentalized agrarian way of life unfortunately linked to the economics of slavery. Although both of these aspects are part of the story, a century and a half later the devastation that this war brought to American life seems in other cases more an interruption in patterns already underway, particularly in areas outside the South where urbanization and industrialization had begun to take hold. The war brought a temporary halt to immigration, but the decades after the war saw a surge in the numbers of those coming to American shores. Immigrants provided industry with a seemingly endless supply of cheap labor and swelled the urban population to the point that the 1920 census revealed that a majority of all U.S. residents lived in cities. The idealized agrarian life offered a framework of meaning for ever smaller numbers of Americans. More and more, men turned to the cities and to business and industry for gainful employment that would allow them to support families and, they hoped, improve the quality of life for their children and grandchildren.

These seismic shifts in the character of American life had significant implications for images of male spirituality promoted by Protestant preachers and writers, for the context in which religious commitment and personal spirituality could be fostered had also changed. What it meant to be a white Christian man had fresh nuance. In the antebellum period, when the image of the gentleman entrepreneur was at its zenith, underlying white male spirituality was the presupposition that Protestant ways still defined American religious life and were the dominant influences in shaping how American men thought of themselves in religious and spiritual terms. Concepts based in Protestantism still governed the ideal for the white Christian man. The burgeoning cities where men—and increasingly larger numbers of women—flocked to find jobs and where immigrants clamored to carve out a place for themselves had become places where it was simply no longer possible to assume the exclusive plausibility and viability of Protestant belief and practice. After all, the overwhelming majority of immigrants who entered the United States in the half century after the close of the Civil War were Roman Catholics, Jews, and Eastern Orthodox Christians who came from central, southern, and eastern Europe. They not only brought with them a wide range of unfamiliar ethnic heritages, but they also transformed the industrial cities, especially outside the South, from centers of Protestant strength to threats to Protestant hegemony.

Hence, one of the primary concerns of those who sought to promote images of white male spirituality and advance models of the Christian man in the postbellum decades was how to advance Protestant spirituality in an environment that was growing increasingly pluralistic. Those who left Protestant families for life in such urban centers confronted new temptations; not only were the familiar supports for moral life in question, but the diminished presence of Protestantism also made it more likely that men of a Protestant bent would abandon spirituality altogether when they saw the range of religious possibilities growing by leaps and bounds. If generations of Protestant voices had articulated concerns about the failure of men to take on the responsibilities of church membership as one means to cultivating the spiritual life, those who surveyed the possibilities of promoting male spirituality in the cities worried that men were staying away from things spiritual in increasing numbers. To be a white Christian man still did not mean that a man would join a church. Then, too, some feared that Protestant men, particularly those who lacked church affiliation, once in the cities would meet, court, and marry women of other religious persuasions or of no religious persuasion at all. Such intermarriage would further erode white male spirituality.

Accompanying the perception that white Protestant men were slipping away from organized religion were two others trends, each well underway before the Civil War intervened. The first was the continuing consignment in the popular mind of vital piety to the domestic sphere, to the home and thus to the domain of women. Notions that women were by nature more religious than men continued to fuel the sense that real men were not inclined toward things spiritual, even though by the dawn of the twentieth century increasing numbers of young women were also leaving family homes to seek employment in the nation's cities and were thus exposed to the same dazzling array of temptations that lured young men away from the evangelical Protestant fold.

The second was the growth and increasing appeal of organizations and activities that were oriented to men but generally excluded women. Between the close of the Civil War and the Great Depression of the 1930s, the lodge and fraternal movements, long seen as rivals to organized religion for the commitment of men, reached their peak in terms of membership. Protestant church leaders might continue to condemn such groups and urge the faithful to avoid them, but they also began to wonder whether the churches themselves might prove more attractive to men if they could offer male communicants whatever it was that drew them to the Masons or the Odd Fellows.

Before the end of the nineteenth century, church leaders had to look in another direction for clues about what might draw the attention of men, the realm of athletics. Since the days of the Puritans, when sport was seen to be almost dangerous if not demonic for enticing participants away from devotion and for consuming time that could better be used for prayer and other spiritual endeavors, evangelical Protestants in the United States had questioned the value of athletics. By the beginning of the twentieth century, the churches were embracing sports and the competitive ethos athletics engendered as strategies for drawing men into a life of commitment. Churches began to build gymnasia and organize sports teams. In the midst of it all, many spoke of a "muscular Christianity" that was pitched to men, to real men whose lives were devoid of any feminine characteristics and who scorned the emotional sentimentality they admired in their wives and mothers as symbols of beauty. A muscular Christianity could transform the churches from havens of faithful women into strongholds of spiritual men.

The urban, industrial world also gave new life to the hope that white Protestant expressions of Christianity would sweep the globe. The foreign missions movement, as so much else that reverberated through white Protestant at the dawn of the twentieth century, had earlier roots. Almost fifty years before Civil War divided the nation, a group of men, huddled together in a storm on what today is the campus of Williams College, felt the call to foreign missions. Their experience sparked an enduring interest in carrying the Protestant gospel across the planet and linked American endeavors to British missionary efforts that had begun roughly a decade earlier. Yet in the later nineteenth century, when economic growth resulting from industrial expansion made greater financial resources available, foreign missions offered a renewed challenge to both men and women. To women, missions may have provided opportunities for religious leadership denied them in Protestant churches and agencies that were still run by men (despite the preponderance of women in them). To men, the risks and dangers of life in a foreign milieu, like the competitive challenge of sports, reinforced popular conceptions of masculinity and helped generate new images of white male spirituality and models of the Christian man.

In the midst of these transformations and the emergence of new images of white male spirituality and the Christian man, those already in place did not disappear. In many circles, the image of the dutiful patriarch held sway. Indeed, some historians have argued that the patriarchal assumptions undergirding the role of men as husbands and fathers remained especially strong, particularly in the South, where the end of the Civil War brought considerable cultural dislocation. Ted Ownby, for example, has argued that among white southern Protestant men in the postbellum decades, the responsibilities that went with being a husband and father were construed in religious terms, despite there being a flourishing male culture outside the home that represented an arena where men abandoned religious sensibilities altogether.[1] The image of the dutiful patriarch likewise remained layered onto that of the gentleman entrepreneur in those areas of the country where the postbellum years saw such a frenzy of industrial growth and development. The honesty, loyalty, proper behavior, hard work and commitment to business that fused in the image of the gentleman entrepreneur continued to inform white Protestant male spirituality and shape ideas of what it was for a man to be a Christian. What was new came in the cluster of images that advanced the courageous adventurer as the epitome of the Protestant Christian man committed to a spirituality that governed his life.

Men and Masculinity in Later Victorian America

Central to the understanding of what it meant to be a Christian man in the later Victorian period was the notion of moral ideals. To be sure, a keen sense of morality undergirded earlier images of white male spirituality, and those that came to the fore in the closing decades of the nineteenth century and beginning of the twentieth century were consonant with ideas of

morality that informed images of both the dutiful patriarch and the gentleman entrepreneur. But there was some reformulation as well.

In a series of articles that appeared first in the *Saturday Evening Post* and
then published in collected form as *The Young Man and the World*, Albert
Beveridge emphasized the way in which religion made moral ideals vital to
a life that was fulfilling and satisfying. Beveridge's words carried an authority that probably exceeded that of the clergy, still popularly perceived as
feminized, for he was not only a well-known lawyer and historian but also
a U.S. senator from Ohio. Identified with the Progressive movement in politics at the time his advice was offered to American men, Beveridge urged
preachers to remember that men were not interested in flashy oratory or in
a ponderous explanation of doctrine. Doctrine was secondary for men.
Rather, men wanted to hear about what constituted Christian moral behavior, something practical rather than something intellectual.

For Beveridge, the Sermon on the Mount as set forth in the New Testament provided the core model for moral behavior, for it minced few words
in setting out a moral code for men of all ages. Beveridge was no doubt
aware that men were less likely than women to attend religious services, for
he did urge men to go to church and even to carry a Bible. To keep the
attention of men, however, preachers in his view should keep their sermons
short. They should also be as direct in their preaching as the biblical text.
That way, both sermon and Scripture became good reading for times of
relaxation. But giving lip service to a moral code, however noble, was inadequate in Beveridge's mind. For the man who was a Christian, morality
required action, particularly in the form of public service.[2] Such service
required courage, energy, and steadfastness if it were to yield permanent
results. Others who advanced images of the courageous adventurer would
echo his advice when it came to seeing spirituality in terms of action in the
public arena.

Josiah Strong, the indefatigable secretary of the Evangelical Alliance
from 1886 to 1898 and then the founder of the League for Social Service
(later the American Institute for Social Service), was one of those who
stressed the kind of public service Beveridge had endorsed. Strong wrote
many analyses of the religious situation of his day that showed he was
keenly sensitive to the impact of urbanization, immigration, and industrialization on the religious climate. But he also penned one work specifically
addressed to men and what it meant for Protestant men to conduct a life
grounded in Christian spirituality.

In *The Times and Young Men*, Strong argued that there were three timeless laws that shaped male spirituality and the ideal of the Christian man.

The first was the law of service. The Christian man, suggested Strong, should consciously choose to dedicate his life to the service of others. In so doing, men would come to appreciate the second timeless law, that self-giving in service to the point of real sacrifice was integral to the very nature of God. For a male to reflect the image of God or to have a vital spirituality, he needed to abandon any self-interest for the sake of sacrifice. Here Strong hints at the importance of motivation, which comes into focus in his third law, the law of love. If self-interest propels public action, however beneficial such action is to the common good, it is misdirected. Without sacrificial love as the motivating force, service becomes a form of slavery. The courage essential to sacrifice allows men to leave self-interest behind.[3]

Given how employment patterns were transforming American work life for men when Strong was promoting his views, it is little wonder that he urged Christian men to choose their occupation or careers based on the potential for active service to others. He dismissed both a spirituality and a career focus that emphasized asceticism as overlooking if not negating the centrality of such altruistic service.[4] For Strong, the particulars of religious belief took a back seat to the courageous adventure that accompanied a life of loving service. If white Protestant churches were to emphasize loving service rather than doctrine or empty ritualism, Strong argued, they would count more men in their ranks.

For many young men who moved to the cities, the YMCA took on increasing importance as a place where they could live in an environment that would foster the moral convictions issuing in selfless service. As we have seen, the YMCA movement began to take hold even before the Civil War, but it reached its zenith as an agency complementary to religious institutions, such as local Protestant congregations, in the later decades of the nineteenth century. Josiah Strong was a tireless supporter of the YMCA, for he regarded it as an incubator of the morals he believed essential to male spirituality and of the ideals of social service through which that morality found public expression for the Christian man. There were dangerous pitfalls that awaited men who ventured into the bustling urban centers to carve out careers for themselves in industry, especially those who were single. But life in the city was a constant adventure.

Frederick A. Atkins, who was also a staunch supporter of the YMCA enterprise, reminded men intent on the life of courageous adventure that one did not need to experience the seamy side of life in order to appreciate the struggle to remain morally pure. To be a Christian man was to win the fight to preserve high moral character and to manifest that character in service. Atkins referred to the spiritual quality marking such character as "moral muscle," a term that would echo in the constellation of images that muscular Christianity added to the courageous adventurer. But Atkins knew that struggle was involved in maintaining that moral muscle. "The victory, then," he wrote, "is to be won by the man who, in the strength of the risen Lord, is able to conquer self and lay down his life for the brethren."[5] Morality and service weaved together in the image of the courageous adventurer.

In theological circles, the idea of selfless service, of courageous adventure, figured prominently in the Social Gospel movement associated with persons such as Walter Rauschenbusch. Spurred in part by concerns for the quality of life in the nation's urban centers and the conditions of work fostered by the mushrooming industrial economy, the Social Gospel sought to relate the claims of Christianity to the lived reality of working life in the cities. Here the theological arguments advanced by Rauschenbusch and others are of less significance than the ways in which Social Gospel advocates linked their perspective to the spiritual lives of white Protestant men and articulated a way of being religious that spoke specifically to men. The portrait of a Jesus dedicated to courageous adventure through moral service countered the depictions found in many of the "biographies" of Jesus popular among American Protestants in the Gilded Age. There, as Susan Curtis has observed, "Jesus was neither fully masculine nor fully feminine." Described as wearing "long white gowns" and having "long, wavy locks and a soft brown beard," Jesus was both "madonna and man."[6] Such a Jesus would never provide a model for male spirituality in the teeming cities and busy factories central to the Social Gospel endeavor. Hence, Rauschenbusch talked of a Jesus who had "nothing mushy, nothing sweetly effeminate" about him but was a "man's man." Indeed, Jesus "plucked the beard of death when He went into the city and the temple to utter those withering woes against the dominant class."[7] Jesus acted on moral principle. He was a man of courage. His ministry was an adventure in social service.

In the first decade of the twentieth century, when many of the white Protestant denominations followed the lead of Northern Methodists and the fledgling Federal Council of Churches in adopting social creeds or statements of social principles, they recognized that the spiritual world of white men revolved around courageous adventure in the world of work and the call for service in cooperative relationships. Formal religion, often spurned by the working class, was too removed from the spiritual realities encountered by men who understood that many of the prevailing perceptions of the totally self-made individual had vanished with the coming of the industrial age. The workplace was now an arena of courageous adventure where morality and diligence, those longstanding male virtues lifted up as ideals for Protestant men, would reap success. Popular pulpiteer Henry Ward Beecher, although not a voice of the Social Gospel movement per se, echoed these sentiments in his *Advice to Young Men* when he warned those who saw themselves as Christian to avoid being seduced by everything from sensuality to idleness. Only the morality of the courageous adventurer could hope to yield success and wealth that were justly obtained.[8]

From the Home to the Lodge

If, even before the Civil War, the home had become the domain of women and the spirituality nurtured there one cultivated by Christian wives and mothers, in the later Victorian period impressions of gender roles that accompanied such domestication became more firmly entrenched. So too ways of being religious promoted through institutions like congregations and churches were also increasingly seen as part of the realm of women. Vital male spirituality continued to be much less directly linked to the formal apparatus of religion. The white Christian man did not need formal affiliation with a religious institution. The norm of having more women than men in the churches, a pattern fixed long before the American Revolution, was one measure. Josiah Strong, for example, remarked that women outnumbered men by the standard two-to-one ratio in both Protestant church membership and attendance at worship at the dawn of the twentieth century.[9] In his mind, there simply was not the same degree of struggle or courage required to be a church member as there was to be a spiritual man in the world of work and service. Male spirituality therefore had to find its locus outside the churches. The father of novelist Henry James and psychologist William James was more damning in his appraisal. Although himself something of a mystic who was drawn to Swedenborgianism, the elder Henry James regretted that "religion in the old virile sense," which he associated with Calvinism, had "disappeared, and been replaced by a feeble Unitarian sentimentality" or by the "cuddling up to God" of evangelicals.[10] There was nothing here to awaken and sustain male spirituality, nothing to buttress a model for being a Christian man.

Images of the dutiful patriarch prevailed, at least in so far as the man was still perceived to be superior to the woman in terms of authority within the home and family. Yet there was a sense in which the "moral muscle" required of the courageous adventurer had a softer nuance when it came to relationships with his wife. Albert Beveridge, for example, urged young men—whom he thought should marry by the age of twenty-one—to pamper their wives. Yet at the same time, it was the man who was the courageous adventurer, who gave of himself to public service, who would also have more respect for the character of the home as the place where spiritual sensibilities were bred, especially those sensibilities that enriched a desire for courageous adventure in men.[11]

Even for male children, it was important to keep a distance between the world of the home and the world of work and society where the mettle of the courageous adventurer would in time be tested. The home needed to remain a safe environment for introducing boys to those moral values, those spiritual values, that would enable them to take their places in the world outside the home. If the primary responsibility for such training fell to wives and mothers, for whom the male world of work was perceived an alien domain, then the dignity of women was likewise enhanced, albeit indirectly and obliquely, because this was a sacred trust. In this way, the courageous adventurer unwittingly exalted motherhood and elevated the status of women, even while giving mothers the nearly impossible task of raising boys to be men in an arena that women were thought neither to understand nor want to experience.[12]

Thus, as in the antebellum period, it seemed that more and more men did not find in the home a locus for developing a mature spirituality that reflected their particular experiences as men. The home was too much the realm where women held sway. Nor were white Protestant local churches necessarily the places where men looked for an ethos that would stimulate and sustain spirituality. The ongoing imbalance in the ratio of female to male church members gives ample testimony to the extent to which men did not look to churches for promoting male spirituality. But the lodges and fraternal orders that had begun attracting larger numbers of men before the era of the Civil War did provide one outlet where men were able to find spiritual as well as social sustenance in a milieu identified neither with the world of work nor with the realm of women.

Mark Carnes has offered various estimates of how many American men were attracted to lodges and fraternal orders. He claimed that in the mid-1890s, some five and a half million of the approximately nineteen million men in the United States belonged to at least one such organization, with many—perhaps as high as 20 percent—holding membership in more than one. By the dawn of the twentieth century, Carnes noted, the figure was even higher, with perhaps up to 40 percent of all adult American males belonging to at least one lodge.[13]

Carnes also suggests that many men were drawn to lodges because women had taken over control of the domestic sphere. What was missing in the Victorian home was a way for the adult courageous adventurer to affirm the morality and values associated with being a spiritual male, a morality and set of values that had practical utility in the world of business outside the home. Lodge initiation led one into that male world, a realm as competitive as the home was nurturing. But initiation also placed members on a plane of equality with one another. The laboring man might well experience a loss of identity or have questions about his status while working alongside hundreds of others in a factory, with employers and bosses seemingly siphoned into a superior group that exercised authority and amassed wealth. Lodge rituals collapsed that distinction by placing initiates on a plane of equality with one another. Lodge membership thus became a way of affirming the plausibility of the behavior and values associated with the courageous adventurer in an ethos that was removed from an arena of threat.

Church leaders, of course, continued to see the lodges as rivals for male commitment and stewardship, for they believed that men "converted to the religion of the lodge and then abandoned their church."[14] The secrecy of fraternal rituals also raised suspicion, seeming to some religious leaders to substitute lodge fathers and sponsors for biological fathers who had abrogated any position of real leadership in homes dominated by women. Also, much of what was in the rituals of the lodges their Protestant detractors classified as "false doctrine," which undermined the truth of orthodox Protestant belief, since many of the rituals built on commonly accepted Christian ideals but augmented them with a more elaborate mythology.

At the same time, female images and language in lodge rituals buttressed the distinctions between male and female sensibilities that undergirded Victorian culture. Women were placed on a pedestal where they could be both admired and feared, impulses captured in the notion of "true womanhood." But at the same time, by enclosing female imagery in this way, men were able symbolically to eliminate the feminine influence that had pervaded their upbringing in the home. Fraternal rituals, especially those that centered on initiation or the induction of individuals into membership, were adventures in their own right that brought men into a world of men and prepared them to survive in the competitive climate of the industrial workplace. To join a lodge was to start an adventure where men were men. The image of the courageous adventurer received tacit support through the popularity of fraternal orders and lodges.

Urban Revivalism's Appeals to Men

For much of the nineteenth century, evangelical Protestantism had looked to revivals and the dynamic preaching associated with them as key mechanisms for converting the lost, both men and women, and bringing them into the ranks of committed church members. The major evangelists of the late nineteenth and early twentieth centuries were clearly aware that women were generally perceived as being more religious or spiritual than men and hence that they needed to couch their message and appeal in forms that would attract men, especially to make a public religious commitment and, they hoped, become church members in greater numbers. Part of the challenge confronting these revivalists was the related popular perception that professional ministry, whether identified with the local church pastor or the itinerant evangelist, was an effeminate occupation, one avoided by "real" men.

What is striking about the urban revivals and some of the leading evangelists from the postbellum period through the first two decades or so of the twentieth century is the way the evangelists chose to present themselves as models of the courageous adventurer. In so doing they proclaimed a message that would attract other men to take up that same spiritual ideal as their own. Focusing on urban revivals in Chicago just in the years from 1893 to 1918, Thekla Ellen Joiner Caldwell argued that revivalism itself became transformed in this epoch, abandoning a highly feminized approach and style that was still apparent in the 1890s for a religion of masculinity that characterized urban revivalism by the 1920s.[15] The challenge was compounded by the way gender roles were developing, for, as Caldwell pointed out, the "heightened emphasis upon female moral authority increasingly distanced men from spirituality, a development that was verified and strengthened by the socio-economic changes of the Gilded Age" that took men from the home to the workplace, from the sphere of women to one where men could affirm their identity after the model of the courageous adventurer.[16]

The two best-known Protestant evangelists of this epoch, Dwight L. Moody and Billy Sunday, both demonstrate how revivalists sought to craft a message that would attract men and offer an understanding of spirituality that would make Christian commitment an adventure that required masculine courage. At the same time, they continued to regard women as by nature more innately spiritual than men. Moody would always have claimed that he was preaching to all who were lost, to all who would benefit from an evangelical conversion, not just to men. Yet his work with the YMCA and his ongoing support for urban rescue missions, especially the Pacific Garden Mission in Chicago, suggest that he retained a particular understanding for the temptations men faced when they left the home environment, characterized by a feminized spirituality, to seek employment in urban industry. After all, the clientele who came to urban rescue missions, at least in the later part of the nineteenth century, was overwhelmingly male. Men who were unsuccessful in fusing a Christian manliness with the challenges of trying to achieve success in the world of business and industry were those who often wound up needing the support offered by rescue missions.

Caldwell noted that—especially in the Chicago revival of 1893 that followed on the Columbian Exposition or World's Fair—the popular press emphasized the personal masculinity of Moody. Here was a man who was aggressive in fighting for the salvation of the heathen; one result was turning the revival into something akin to a military assault on male irreligiousness.[17] One of Moody's early biographers went to great length to emphasize that Moody was "anything but a woman's man." As a result, men flocked to Moody's revivals because Moody himself had "the secret of touching them by his infinite manliness."[18] Even in his physical appearance, the large-framed, portly Moody, boasting a mustache, gave the appearance of one who was physically brave, one for whom Christian commitment was an adventure that took great courage.[19]

At the same time, Moody's sermons suggest that like generations of preachers before him, he tended to downplay the specifics of Christian doctrine and belief. Male spirituality was not one based on particulars of belief but on the notion that the Christian man was one who possessed extraordinary strength and courage. Here, however, Moody also revealed that he nevertheless shared the cultural assumptions that women were by nature more inherently spiritual than men. Not only did he frequently express his respect and admiration for women, thus elevating them to the social pedestal that went with moral superiority, but he also tended to identify evil and sin with the male culture of the day. The link between male culture and sin came into sharp focus particularly when men abandoned their mothers' religious teachings and opted for the wayward urban life. This negative adventure became a type of pollution, threatening the spirituality of men and women alike.[20] Nonetheless, for Moody, male spirituality was built around images of courageous adventure and strength.

But it was Billy Sunday whose evangelistic ministry completed the masculinization of revivalism, to borrow Caldwell's phrase, that was already evident in the work of D. L. Moody.[21] Sunday was able to lift up the image of the courageous adventurer in part because of his early career in professional baseball that preceded his evangelical conversion under the auspices of the Pacific Garden Mission. Even though he gave up a modest but promising athletic career to become a crusading evangelist, Sunday knew firsthand the discipline and strength that went into athletic success, characteristics that also marked the spiritual image of the courageous adventurer. But he was also well aware that much of white Protestant America was suspicious of sports and of athletes. Individual athletes, however disciplined when performing professionally, were thought to live loose lives that were amoral at best and immoral at worst. Sports were thus perceived to be a danger to the spiritual life that the churches hoped to awaken in men. Such was true even as spectator sports were becoming a major leisure time activity drawing the interest of millions. Sunday's genius revealed itself in part in the way he took his athletic background and transformed it from a potential liability into a major asset in pitching a message toward men and demonstrating that spirituality was masculine through and through.

Sunday's conscious intent to reach men came through in many of the most widely known features of his evangelistic style. Critics in his own day dismissed Sunday for some of the unpolished and unsophisticated language that he used in his sermons. They also scorned many of the antics in which he engaged while preaching, such as breaking chairs, that struck many as theatrical flourishes more than spiritual illustrations. But Sunday knew exactly what he was doing as he ranted and raged across the platform in front of rapt audiences.

Spending part of his childhood in orphanages and lacking sustained formal education, Sunday believed that his own experience resonated with that of the ordinary working man. Although he amassed considerable wealth as an itinerant evangelist, and in so doing reaped additional criticism, and although he enjoyed his associations with persons of prestige and power, Sunday never lost his affinity for the majority of American men who struggled to support families, lacked advanced education, and never owned or managed huge corporations or businesses. For these ordinary working men, evangelical Protestantism seemed something reserved for the elite, something removed from the rhythms of the working world. Sunday was determined to make Christian faith something that was vital and real to ordinary men. Hence, his sermons contained slang and more than a few awkward grammatical constructions. But he spoke what he thought to be the vocabulary of the men he wanted to reach, even as he echoed his own rather humble midwestern roots.[22] Indeed, when Sunday fell in love with Helen Amelia Thompson, later known to scores of the evangelist's associates simply as Ma Sunday, Helen's parents frowned on the budding romance, in part because Sunday, then a professional baseball player, lacked the polish and refined manners that they respected, for they were a part of the white evangelical Protestant elite.

Sunday was also known for his attacks on the consumption of alcoholic beverages, as Moody had been before him. Abuse of alcohol was widely thought to be one of the most serious problems confronting working men who left behind their families of origin for life in the city. Throughout his evangelistic career, Sunday would see his audience swell in numbers when word leaked out that he would be preaching a well-known sermon, such as "Get on the Water Wagon," that was basically an assault on the sale and consumption of alcohol.[23] But in urging ordinary men to give up alcohol, to abandon the mores that seemed often to accompany working life, he was in his own way fostering the image of the courageous adventurer. Sunday knew that it took courage for a man to set himself apart from his fellow workers, walk the famed sawdust trail, and shake Sunday's hand as a sign of commitment to a life oriented to spirituality, to being a Christian man.

Sunday did find his brief career in professional baseball of value in crafting an evangelistic style directed toward men. He understood that men were drawn to sports, both as participants and spectators, as urban factory work provided a modicum of leisure time. In the factory as well as in the sports stadium, men were in the company of other men. Work and leisure alike reinforced the separation of the spheres where men and women found their primary identities. Prior to his own conversion, Sunday was not a stranger to the temptations that went with the mobile life of the professional athlete and knew too well the lure of the saloon. He also knew the reputation that athletes had for association with women of questionable moral character, another of the temptations that preyed on those whose professional life took them away from home and kept them on the road for weeks at a time. Yet Sunday also appreciated the way in which professional athletes were becoming what a later generation would call role models. Like Sunday, many rose from relatively obscure backgrounds to positions of prominence in the popular male culture of the day. Here were men who seemed to have achieved success, albeit of a different order than the patrician who headed a large business enterprise.

Sunday's genius in part lay in his uncanny ability to take the stuff of hero worship and transform it into a representation of male spirituality and a model for the white Christian man. The strength, discipline, hard work, and courage under stress that were marks of the successful athlete became in Sunday's hands marks of the man of faith, the characteristics of the courageous adventurer who could scorn the ways of the world for Christian affirmation. Sunday's ability to use the world of sports and the appeal of athletics for spiritual ends were critical parts of the process by which evangelical Protestantism shed its suspicion of sports as idle amusements and embraced athletics as a strategy for bringing men into the company of the faithful. Especially in his addresses at meetings advertised as intended for men Sunday drew heavily on his previous athletic background to present an image of courage and adventure that were hallmarks of Christian male spirituality.

One of Sunday's biographers, Roger Bruns, captured well the way this evangelist's preaching offered a Christian spirituality oriented toward men: "This was no dainty, sissified, lily-livered piety the crowd was hearing. This was hard-muscled, pick-axed religion, a religion from the gut, tough and resilient. Prayer here was a manly duty; faith was mountain-moving, galvanic. There was power in reverence, energy in belief. The tough guys were on the right side. This was not a place for weak-kneed, four-flushing boozers and sin-soaked infidels."[24] When Sunday drew his sermon examples from men prominent in the Hebrew Scriptures, he likewise emphasized their courage and strength. As Thekla Caldwell reminded her readers, in Sunday's view, the ancient King David certainly did not want his son Solomon to be a sissy, a term in Sunday's day that would have tended to denote a lack of courage and a lack of a sense of adventure. Sunday proposed a spirituality that countered the feminized Protestantism of his day, reportedly praying at one time, "Lord save us from off-handed, flabby-cheeked, brittle-boned, weak-kneed, ossified three-karat Christianity." His was a spirituality that focused on the working man, the one who knew hard work, labor, and courage. It was not a spirituality for those who would shy away from tough adventure. It was not a spirituality that drew from the feminized family but from the world where men worked and played.

Another commentator, quoting newspaper accounts of Sunday's preaching, noted that Sunday had "transformed himself into a strong, sinewy physical specimen whose boundless energy was injected into his rousing tent sermons. Sunday 'brought bleacher-crazy, frenzied aggression to religion.' . . . 'He stands up like a man in the pulpit and out of it. He speaks like a man. He works like a man. . . . He is manly with God and with everyone who comes to hear him. No matter how much you disagree with him, he treats you after a manly fashion. He is not an imitation, but a manly man giving all a square deal.'"[25] Thus Sunday set out to "strike the death blow at the idea that being a Christian takes a man out of the busy whirl of the world's life and activity and makes him a spineless effeminate proposition." In his mind, a Christian man was not "some sort of dishrag proposition, a wishy-washy, sissified sort of galoot, that lets everybody make a doormat out of him. Let me tell you," Sunday proclaimed, "the manliest man is the man who will acknowledge Jesus Christ."[26] To commit oneself to Christian spirituality was to follow the way of courageous adventure, not to take on some "dainty, sissified, lily-livered piety."

At the same time, Sunday maintained a rather ambivalent attitude toward women and the family. On the one hand, he accepted the long-standing notion associated with the spirituality of the Christian man as dutiful patriarch that the man was the head of the family, yet he was almost unable to function personally at times unless Ma Sunday was with him. He knew his duty as a father, yet he maintained a distance from his children that resulted, in the case of three sons, in their falling into patterns of behavior that were at odds with what Sunday himself espoused. Somehow he was never able to bring the courage and adventure of male spirituality into his relationships with his sons, even if he inspired courage, discipline, and moral strength in thousands of other men.

Sunday demonstrates what we have seen earlier, namely, that once the home became the sphere of women and a piety that was presumed to be feminized, images of white male spirituality tended to be oriented more to relationships external to the home. Perhaps from his days on the road as an athlete, Sunday was also quick to link the failure of men to take on the life of courageous adventure to women who used their femininity to entice men away from spirituality and faith. He was less likely to hold men accountable for their actions when it came to associations with women than he was to attribute to women an almost superior power to distract men from the way of faith. Female lure held more sway in Sunday's world than male lust.

Yet Sunday also recognized that female spirituality could be a boon for men who opted for the life of the courageous adventurer. His urban campaigns frequently included special meetings for women that were somewhat different in focus from those where he urged men to become courageous adventurers. Early on in his career, Sunday included Virginia Asher and Grace Saxe on his staff. Asher was to oversee specialized ministry to women, and Saxe directed programs of Bible study that supplemented the revival preaching services and usually drew many more women than men. Asher, who was estranged from her husband for most of the time she worked with Sunday, targeted the growing number of young women who, like their male counterparts, had left the family home for employment in the nation's urban centers.

Temptation was also a danger for young working women, although it was less the seduction of the saloon than the loss of presumed feminine modesty and moral purity that were the greatest threats to the spiritual health of white women. Ma Sunday was also involved in this ministry to women, speaking at some of the noontime gatherings, scheduled so women could spend their lunch hours in wholesome activity, and writing in her syndicated newspaper column ("Ma Sunday Speaks") about the purer spirituality of women realized in marriage and motherhood and promoted in the feminized home. For both Sundays, then, the epitome of female spirituality was that which was lived in the home within the context of the family, while the embodiment of male spirituality was that which was lived in the world of work, sports, and other male arenas by those who sought to be .

courageous adventurers as men of faith. The white Christian man lived in the real world, not the romanticized world of family and home.

The Men and Religion Forward Movement

As the twentieth century opened, some men who were active leaders in white evangelical Protestant congregations dreamed of a nationwide spiritual endeavor that would bring men into the churches. They were not thinking necessarily of revivals led by the likes of Moody or Sunday, although no doubt they recognized the ways Sunday's style especially could attract a male audience. Nor were they necessarily hoping to bring back an enterprise like the businessmen's revival of the late 1850s. Their hope was to boost significantly the number of men whose spirituality and understanding of what it meant to be Christian men included active membership in a local congregation, for these leaders were keenly aware of the imbalance between men and women in the pews and on the rolls of church members. In some ways, what became the Men and Religion Forward Movement represented an effort to link together traditional expressions of spirituality, such as prayer and Bible study, that had become identified primarily with women, with the action-oriented spirituality rooted in the image of the Christian man as gentleman entrepreneur and developed more fully in the image of the courageous adventurer.

Early in the twentieth century, Harry W. Arnold, a Protestant layman from Maine who was convinced that men were open to more vital expressions of spirituality, organized a series of meetings in his home state that targeted men who were unchurched. He hoped that the meetings would convince men who had not done so to become formal members of local congregations.[27] His endeavors did not go unrecognized, and when Arnold joined his vision with the organizational ability of Fred B. Smith, another Protestant layman, the basis for a national movement was laid. Smith put together a committee of ninety-seven men, some clergy and some lay, who would spearhead an endeavor to reach men, aware that there were "3,000,000 more girls and women in the [white Protestant] churches of America than men and boys."[28]

Some fifty-one urban centers, both moderate-sized and large, soon had their own organizing committees that reflected the endeavor's commitment to the image of the courageous adventure, for the intent was to place on these committees "the one hundred strongest men" of a Protestant background in each community.[29] From the one hundred came a smaller, fifteen-person executive committee and eleven other committees that would develop specific programs for the campaign geared to the needs and conditions of the individual communities. Towns that might have lacked the population base for this level of organization frequently had smaller, ad hoc committees of churchmen that tried to plan events for men in their areas, albeit on a less grand scale.

From the outset, the focus of the Men and Religion Forward Movement was on action and service in the public arena. Personal spirituality played a part, but it is clear in retrospect that the organizers understood male spirituality in terms of action, of adventure expressed in service. The white Christian man expressed his commitment through what he did in the world around him. Overall, five general areas of concern were established, each represented by one point in the movement's five-pointed star logo: social service, evangelism, boy's work, missions, and Bible study.

At the time, the social service component attracted considerable attention. Headed nationally by Charles Stelzle, then superintendent of the Presbyterian Home Missions Board's Department of Church and Labor, the social service dimension dovetailed with the Social Gospel theology that was still in vogue, leading Walter Rauschenbusch to write that the

> Men and Religion Forward Movement of 1911–1912 is another evidence of the ascendancy of social Christianity. . . . Its leaders were determined to win the men back to religion by meeting the distinctively masculine interests; therefore they had to be bold. . . . When the movement began to be tried out, it grew increasingly plain that it was the trumpet call of the social gospel which rallied the audiences and brought men under moral and religious conviction. . . . The movement has probably done more than any other single agency to lodge the social gospel in the common mind of the Church. It has made social Christianity orthodox.[30]

In many communities, committees responsible for the social service component, frequently drawing on techniques identified with the emerging academic discipline of sociology, probed everything from prisons to the public schools, garbage collection to water supplies, labor unions to homelessness and the need for public shelters.[31] With the slogan "More Men for Religion, More Religion for Men," the Men and Religion Forward Movement, with its emphasis on social service, elevated a spirituality of action and a model of the Christian man as one whose life was marked by courage and adventure.

The plan was to have a series of meetings in Protestant churches across the nation beginning on September 18, 1911, and concluding with a Christian Conservation Congress in New York City in April 1912. In nearly eighty cities, those meetings were scheduled daily for eight consecutive days. Estimates are that rallies of one or more days were held in another thousand or so smaller towns between the opening of the movement and the New York City congress. When the campaign ended, it was claimed that more than nine thousand addresses had been given at more than seven thousand meetings around the country, drawing around one and a half million men in audiences large and small, with more than six thousand men receiving direct personal interviews about their religious state and possible church membership.[32] Major addresses and reports of the national organizing committee of ninety-seven were later published in six volumes, one for each of the five target areas and one for the speeches given at the wrap-up gathering in New York.[33]

Traditional forms of spirituality that were then so often associated with women, as well as the presumed lack of a natural spirituality in men, did receive attention, but more by way of calling attention to them than anything else. In the third volume of "messages" from the Men and Religion Forward Movement, the presentations devoted to Bible study and evangelism, William Murray noted that too few men read the Bible for themselves although it was a "masculine book." He urged fathers and sons to read study the Bible together, a departure from the generations-old expectation that men as heads of households would lead the entire family in devotions.[34] The "natural antipathy" of men to spiritual things, claimed George W. Robinson in his address, was the major reason men neglected Scripture and their role as a kind of family priest.[35]

Most of the speakers and writers, however, simply catalogued the way men did not express spirituality in ways expected by church leaders, although some noted that if men introduced a Christian element into trade and business, the world itself could be converted to evangelical Protestant styles of Christianity.[36] If Protestant men would only take on the spiritual style of the courageous adventurer, the world would become Christian.

The Men and Religion Forward Movement gave some attention to missionary work outside the United States, but its primary focus was on trying to draw men into the nation's Protestant churches through local outreach and service. However, the conviction that men should follow a spirituality of courageous adventure also spurred interest in what that age called foreign missions. The international missionary movement had roots in both Britain and the United States in the late eighteenth and early nineteenth centuries, as European colonialism spread into Asia and Africa. Missionary societies, often interdenominational in character, and a host of papers and periodicals brought word back to those at home of life in foreign lands that seemed as enticing as it was dangerous. Language and cultural barriers fostered considerable misunderstanding, propelled by the evangelical sense of the absolute truth of Protestant Christianity that rendered other peoples heathens and other religions examples of an insidious and menacing paganism.

Improvements in communications and transportation that were part of the complex transforming the United States from an agrarian to an urban nation also made it possible for evangelicals to ponder how their dream of converting all peoples to Christian ways could become reality. So strong was the prevailing spirit of optimism that many looked to the twentieth century as the "Christian century" when the global triumph of evangelicalism would be secure.[37] For that hope to be transformed into reality, men especially would have to opt for a life of courageous adventure. They would have to minister in places where indigenous peoples were often suspicious of, if not hostile to, efforts to convert them (as well as to Westernize them) and where living conditions prevailed that were much less comfortable than those to which middle-class white evangelical Protestants were becoming accustomed.

The call for men was to sacrifice comfort and security for the life of courageous adventure that the foreign mission field required, although in time many mission boards also began to commission women.[38] Part of what evoked the spirituality of courageous adventure was the constant threat of diseases that could be far more devastating for Westerners who lacked the natural immunities of indigenous peoples. Such diseases would often be difficult to treat because of the lack of medical facilities, supplies, and equipment. In some cases, even if the identification of missionaries with colonial powers often provided some security, there was also the threat of hostile response on the part of those the missionaries sought to convert. Such "natives" might attack mission stations and, as the missionary press sensationalized, slaughter those who were doing God's work. If the parish ministry had become a feminized vocation as the nineteenth century progressed, foreign missions called for men who were committed to a spiritual life oriented to courageous adventure. Like Billy Sunday's gospel, the mission field was not a place for the weak or dainty.

Muscular Christianity and the Spirit of Courageous Adventure

The cluster of images that went into the spirituality of the Christian man as courageous adventurer came together in a particularly powerful way in the movement within both British and American Protestantism known as "muscular Christianity."[39] Often identified with the changing attitudes of evangelical Christians toward sports and the work of the YMCA, muscular Christianity represents another effort to cast the Christian message in terms that would appeal to men and to offer a spirituality that resonated with what was assumed to be stereotypical male experience. Those who have probed muscular Christianity have tended to demonstrate how the movement played into evolving notions of masculinity in American culture, giving them a religious imprimatur. Our interest here is less in the ideas of masculinity and its social construction that were associated with muscular Christianity, but, rather, in the way in which it strengthened the constellation of images represented by a white male spirituality oriented to the courageous adventurer.

Some of the impetus for muscular Christianity came from what Tony Ladd and James A. Mathisen have called the "integration of sport, education, and Christian ideals."[40] As American colleges began to add athletic activities to their extracurricular programs, sports began to lose some of the negative associations evangelical Protestants had attached to leisure endeavors as idle deflections from religious pursuits. Revivalist Dwight L. Moody used the summer conferences at his Northfield schools to attract college students, many of them athletically inclined, to ponder careers in mission and evangelism. Robert E. Speer, whose life will model the image of the courageous adventurer, was a Princeton football player when he first attended one of those conferences and began to ponder a career related to international missions. Then, too, when Billy Sunday, a baseball player, suddenly abandoned a potentially lucrative career to become an itinerant evangelist, sports made further inroads into the arena of acceptable activity for white Protestant men. Competition, once thought to breed hostility, now became a means to develop courage and character. In other words, sports became a mechanism to attract men to the model of the white Christian man as courageous adventurer.

In the nation's cities, the YMCA moved to the forefront of organizations promoting sports as a way to nurture the spiritual life. Gymnasia became part of the physical plant of larger YMCA centers in order to provide Christian men with a "safe" environment in which to pursue athletic ventures. If men were going to participate in sports, far better for them to do so in a venue committed to spiritual ideals than to fall into temptation by having recourse to athletic activities only outside evangelically acceptable surroundings. Team contests became events that trained men for the struggle between good and evil. They paralleled the battle between dedicating one's life to the way of faith and spirituality and falling into a life of sin and moral degradation. Good sportsmanship, fair play, and giving one's best, even when losing, all became part of a life of courageous adventure filled with spiritual nuance, giving fresh meaning to the New Testament injunctions to "fight the good fight," to "finish the race" (2 Tim. 4:7), and to "press toward the mark of the prize" (Phil. 3:14).

It was natural for organizations like the YMCA to include sports as part of the array of programs and activities offered to single young men, particularly those who were YMCA residents, presumably on a temporary basis prior to marriage and having a family, while working in the businesses and industries that were transforming the American economy. Part of the mission of the YMCA was to provide an environment oriented toward evangelical spirituality for just such men. But what of those who had families and what of the sons of those families?

By the end of the nineteenth century, what some called the "institutional" church had begun to offer programs that went well beyond worship, Bible study, and prayer, not only for members but also for those to whom the congregation was hoping to reach with the evangelical message. Programs for women might include classes in various domestic arts. Some churches, in cities where the immigrant population was mushrooming, promoted activities intended to help introduce immigrant women to American ways as much as to spur their devotional life. But for men, whether those who were objects of outreach or those who were already part of the congregation, athletic teams and other sporting events became part of the overall program of Christian nurture in many of the nation's larger urban Protestant congregations. Church gymnasia, like those of the YMCA, became "safe" places for men to develop the athletic prowess of muscular Christianity that would lead them along the spiritual path of courageous adventure. Development of the body was a spiritual exercise as much as prayer and Bible study.

The values that went with good sportsmanship were the values that went with being a Christian man, and some who sought to further professional sports saw them as promoting Christian ideals. James Naismith, whose career was central to the emergence of basketball as a recognized sport, was one who regarded athletic contests as opportunities to inculcate participants in the moral values advanced by Christianity.[41] Once sports had became acceptable activity for Christian men, athletics would never again be seen as dangerous to the spiritual life per se, and even Jesus began to be portrayed as a man whose physical strength was primary. Such strength allowed Jesus to be a viable role model for the courageous adventurer.

The idea of muscular Christianity and the spirit of the courageous adventurer received significant popular support in the person of Theodore

Roosevelt, who seemed to embrace the constellation of moral values dominant in Protestant circles within industrializing America in the years just prior to the outbreak of World War I. Roosevelt may not be remembered as a man of great piety and spirituality, but he did make vigorous physical activity one hallmark of masculine identity on a popular level. Struggling to overcome childhood sickness and the limitations of poor eyesight, Roosevelt as the archetypal "rough rider" brought together a host of images of the courageous adventurer. Whether leading the charge up San Juan Hill during the Spanish-American War, hunting in the Black Hills, or encouraging his children in exuberant play during his White House years, Roosevelt epitomized both courage and adventure. He gave political embodiment to muscular Christianity.

Alternative Visions within White Evangelical Protestantism

Somewhat different images prevailed in the postbellum South, where the domain of men was seen in terms of courage and adventure. But, especially in the rural South, courage and adventure were not as powerful signals for advancing images of male spirituality as they were in white evangelical Protestant circles elsewhere. There were some common features, however. As Ted Ownby has shown, southern Protestant men participated in formal religious activities at a far lower rate than women. Even those who did attend public worship tended to avoid Sunday school. In the smaller towns and rural areas that remained more prominent features of the South as rapid urbanization and industrialization came to the North, the men often remained outside the church building, socializing until after the service had started.[42] Where men engaged in sports, there was often a violent cast to the activities in question that lay behind what was at best a veneer of genteel religiosity. If in the South, as elsewhere, white evangelical Protestant men were expected to lead their families in daily Bible reading and prayer, probably most did not. Hence, among southern white evangelical Protestant men, whatever images of spirituality prevailed functioned apart from formal religious activity and the realm of institutions like churches even more than elsewhere. In the white evangelical South, as in much of the rest of the country, churches were the domain of women and traditional religious activity was seen as something more germane to female experience than to male experience. Yet being a husband and a father carried religious responsibilities, although the home was perceived more as the counter to male sinfulness than the counter to a world of business and industry.

Yet it may well be that the aggressive traits thought to identify the white southern male, the self-assertiveness and competitive spirit required by popular male culture and the sense of honor that developed to compensate for the keen sense of loss when the antebellum slave culture vanished, in their own way served as a constellation of images that made the courageous adventurer a plausible paradigm for male spirituality among white southern evangelicals. Church discipline, always applied in heavier doses to men than to women, may have endured longer in the South than elsewhere. But as communities and states began to regulate what was perceived as the worst of male behavior, from foul language to alcohol abuse, the courageous adventurer shifted from being one who flouted evangelical values in private, even if he gave lip service to them in public, to one who called for adherence to the law and civic order. Thus in a backhanded way, the evangelical culture of the rural South gave its own form of support to the courageous adventurer as a model for male spirituality, but explicit examples were more fluid and elusive. Wherever the courageous adventurer appeared, regardless of region, physical strength was a virtue that seemed almost a prerequisite for moral strength.

Reflections

Like the images that preceded it, the image of the courageous adventurer as a symbol for white Protestant male spirituality and for what it meant to be a Christian man reflected currents within the larger culture as the nineteenth century gave way to the twentieth. The rapid urbanization and industrialization of the postbellum years gave a new tone to American life, as men left the security and serenity of home, the sphere of women, for work in the nation's businesses and industries, the sphere where men were men. For a man to espouse a spiritual life required courage, for the cities were rife with temptation that would readily lure one away from the values and responsibilities associated with righteousness. Courage likewise involved strength, both strength of character to withstand the temptation that lurked everywhere and strength of body to be able to engage successfully in most areas of industrial employment where labor was arduous and often dangerous.

Urban life and work in the factory were therefore also adventures, and the man who would be a Christian, whose spirituality shaped his life, would have to be willing to embark on an adventure if he were to achieve any self-fulfillment. The courageous adventurer did not abandon the spiritual ideals associated with earlier images of white male religiosity. The virtues of the gentleman entrepreneur—honesty, integrity, truthfulness—were still spiritual values upheld by the courageous adventurer; what had changed to some degree was the venue in which that adventure was lived. The world of work was a world where the presence of women was minimal. If traditional piety was part of the domestic sphere where women reigned, then men needed to develop some spiritual understanding that spoke to their experience as men.

Urban revivalists like Dwight L. Moody and then, especially, Billy Sunday tried to craft their messages in distinctively masculine tones and make their own personas fit popular ideas of what a man should be like in order to demonstrate that affirming the Christian faith was an adventure worthy of any man. But it still took courage to walk the sawdust trail.

The Men and Religion Forward Movement, the calls for men to take up careers in foreign missions, and the emergence of a "muscular Christianity" that saw sports almost as religious enterprises all buttressed the notion that male spirituality was one that reflected a life of adventure in which courage was requisite to success. Even the growing interest in fraternal orders and lodges that peaked in the decades between the Civil War and the Great Depression reflected the need to create a venue where men of faith, courageous adventurers, could come together in a milieu where a feminized piety could be left behind and a vibrant male spirituality could be cultivated apart from the influence of women. What it meant to be a white Christian man was frequently worked out in a context that was almost exclusively male.

To be sure, the courageous adventurer also retained some of the characteristics of the dutiful patriarch. As head of the household and family, the man who took on the spiritual image of the courageous adventurer was still expected to have some clear responsibility for the religious nurture of children by leading family worship and prayer. It is evident, however, that fewer and fewer men actually exercised this prerogative in practice, even if Protestant pastors and preachers exalted it. The home, after all, was the sphere of women, and a feminized spirituality was not one that would allow men to interpret their own experience and endow it with meaning.

The industrial boom that swept at least the northern parts of the United States in the decades after the Civil War was interrupted only briefly by the vicissitudes of World War I. But the war did not diminish the power of the courageous adventurer as a symbol for male spirituality and ideal of the Christian man. To join the military, to fight in the war, was an action that actualized the courage and sense of adventure basic to white Protestant male spirituality. It mattered not whether one was fighting a declared national enemy on the battlefields of Europe or the temptations to fall into immoral or unethical behavior in the nation's cities. Both required courage and adventure. Hence, like earlier models of the dutiful patriarch and the gentleman entrepreneur, the image of the courageous adventurer was one that moved outside the boundaries of traditional forms of devotion. Realized more in action and relationships that did not require church membership and sustained more by other men than by a local congregation where women outnumbered men, the courageous adventurer epitomized the Christian man and Protestant male spirituality in the closing decades of the nineteenth century and early decades of the twentieth.

But the same economic forces that fueled industrial expansion were by the second and third decades of the twentieth century helping to nurture yet another cluster of images and ideas on which white Protestant men could draw for spiritual sustenance. Courage, adventure, and the virtues of the gentleman entrepreneur were not all that went into success in the new urban industrial order. If one wanted to succeed, if one wanted to keep a vital spirituality, then efficiency and organization were also required. By the 1920s, white Protestant males thus had another constellation of conceptions to shape their spirituality and paragons for being Christian men, those associated with the efficient businessman.

In Focus
Robert E. Speer: Missionary Executive and Courageous Adventurer

At the time of his birth on September 10, 1867, Robert Elliott Speer seemed destined to follow a career path already set by his father's example.[43] Robert Milton Speer had become a prominent lawyer in Huntingdon, Pennsylvania, and its environs, capping his achievements with election to the U.S. House of Representatives as a staunch Democrat. Within his home, the elder Speer exhibited many of the qualities of the dutiful patriarch, particularly when it came to the religious nurture of his children. His burden increased when his wife, Martha McMurtie Speer, died when the younger Robert was just nine years old. As a dutiful patriarch, the elder Speer made sure that the family gathered daily for both morning and evening prayers, said grace at meals, attended Sunday school and worship every Sunday morning (though not necessarily in the evening), and studied the standard catechisms of the Reformed tradition. Indeed, all five of his children, including Robert, memorized both the Longer and Shorter Westminster Catechisms, along with many psalms.

Speer thus had a rather "Puritanical upbringing," a description appropriate for the style of a father committed to the spirituality of the Christian man as dutiful patriarch.[44] But even though the family lacked a biological mother much of the time the children were growing up, the home was still the center for religious education and instruction, much more than the church. Robert E. Speer, for example, did not even present himself for church membership until he was a freshman at Princeton and the only young man in his group of friends who had not taken that step.

Since the Speer family was rather well off, the young Robert was sent to Phillips Academy, Andover, Massachusetts, in 1883, where he so quickly established a reputation for serious study and academic achievement that he was able to enter Princeton University, then a bastion of Presbyterianism, after two years and without formally being graduated from the preparatory school. Early in his college career, Speer began to exemplify some of the qualities that came to mark the spirituality of the Christian man as courageous adventurer. He was drawn to athletics, just as white evangelical Protestants were shedding their disdain for sports as fostering idleness and violence and instead looking to athletics to cultivate the discipline, cooperative endeavor, and valor that came together in the image of the courageous adventurer. In addition to his achievements on the football team, at one point declining to serve as its captain, Robert Speer also distinguished himself in campus journalism as managing editor of the *Princetonian* and in campus religious life as president of the student YMCA. Despite this array of extracurricular activities, at graduation, Speer was class valedictorian and one of just three to earn his degree magna cum laude.

The Adventure of Missions

During his sophomore year at Princeton, Speer was particularly moved by presentations made on campus by John Forman, a representative of the Student Volunteer Movement (SVM). Consequently, Speer felt called to the foreign mission field, assuming then that he would at some point attend theological school and become ordained, a route taken by many who offered themselves for service on the foreign mission field. After finishing at the university, he spent a year working for the Student Volunteer Movement before entering Princeton Theological Seminary in 1890. But during his year working for the SVM, Speer almost overwhelmed many church leaders with his powerful and persuasive speaking ability, as well as with his personal character as a man of unwavering moral and intellectual integrity.

During his second of a projected three years at the seminary, Speer confronted a rather unexpected turn of events. He was invited at the age of twenty-three to become one of the secretaries or principal administrative executive officers of the Presbyterian Board of Foreign Missions. Speer left the seminary to accept the post, probably not anticipating that he himself would never serve on the foreign mission field and surely not anticipating that he would remain an executive of the mission board until he reached the mandatory retirement age of seventy.[45]

The discipline that marked Speer's life from childhood on became a tremendous asset as he embarked on this career and devoted his life to embodying the spirituality of the courageous adventurer. The job required much travel, domestic and foreign, as well as commuting time from his first home in New Jersey. But travel time was not time to be squandered. It could be spent reading, and Speer was an avid reader. His friends estimated that Speer devoured at least seventy-five books each year while he was working for the foreign mission board and probably twice as many each year after he retired. In addition, he used what "vacation" time he took for writing books of a spiritual and biographical nature, designed to encourage others, especially men, to give their lives to a spiritual adventure. The daily discipline that had shaped his childhood carried over into Speer's adult life. After his marriage to Emma Bailey, whom he met at the Northfield schools (established by evangelist Dwight L. Moody) during a summer missions endeavor sponsored by the Student Volunteer Movement, he made family prayer before breakfast the start of each day. After all, real men pray.

Although he never actually served on the foreign mission field himself, Speer nevertheless knew from personal experience some of the sense of courageous adventure required of men (and women) who did. Visits to mission stations took him first to Mexico in 1894 and then, with Emma Bailey Speer joining him, in 1896–97 on a trip that traversed the globe. On that trip more than any of the ones that followed—and at least a dozen more took him to mission sites or international conferences before his retirement—he encountered situations that called forth his spiritual commitment to a life of courageous adventure.[46]

On that second trip, the Speers came to a fresh appreciation of the courage that accompanied the missionary life. Writing to her parents from Singed, Persia, in October 1896, Emma Bailey Speer commented that the community where they were staying was so remote that it would not be found on a map and that their accommodations, shared with two others who were accompanying them on this stage of the deputation venture, had a floor of "roughest mud, with a few shallow holes dug in it for closets. The door is a frame work of branches, with twigs woven through them, and mud plastered on the inside. The roof is something of the same sort, with a few holes in it for windows and chimney, and the sole furniture is a few rough implements for cooking and some huge clay receptacles for flour and wheat."[47] Those conditions were only a harbinger of challenges yet to come.

The following month, Speer and one of the Presbyterian missionaries stationed in Persia were stranded in a snowstorm for two days while on their way to Teheran. When Speer returned to the mission in Hamadan, he was diagnosed with typhoid fever. The depth of his commitment to being a Christian man whose spirituality was that of the courageous adventurer was surely tested, for, as his wife noted in a letter to her mother, they were "twenty-four days from the nearest railroad, sixteen days from the Persian Gulf and English steamers, and in a place where we cannot send cablegrams nor receive them, and from which it takes a letter six weeks to reach New York, with high mountains (14,000 ft.) all around us and the winter storms just beginning, with just eleven English-speaking people in a Persian City of 80,000 inhabitants, and Rob—Rob who had never been ill since I have known him, who hardly ever was tired even, has typhoid fever!" There is a touch of irony in a subsequent remark, for Emma Spear also commented on her "thankfulness that we were not in some little hole on the way to Baghdad."[48]

Later, through a third party who was traveling on to Teheran, Emma Speer arranged to send a cablegram indicating that she and Robert Speer had "full confidence in [the missionary] physician" who was treating him.[49] Speer recovered, although he suffered a relapse while convalescing. The Speers continued their arduous journey around the world. There is no evidence that Robert Speer ever doubted the wisdom of his religious commitment or the ideal of a male spirituality that demanded such courage and adventure. The experience enabled him to develop a deep appreciation for the presumed perils missionaries confronted in their daily routine.

Writing about a Spirituality and Faith for Men

The spiritual discipline of the courageous adventurer not only sustained Speer during experiences such as his bout with typhoid but also echoed in his writing, perhaps more than it did in his sermons and chapel talks. In *The Stuff of Manhood,* which appeared just as the United States was entering World War I, Speer argued that every American man who sought a vital faith needed to develop the austerity, discipline, and courage requisite of soldiers on the battlefield. The hardship that military personnel confronted was a model for a male spirituality based on such virtues.[50] A decade earlier, when he had published a series of lectures presented at Ohio Wesleyan University, he had spoken in more general terms, elevating truth, purity, service, and patience as "marks of a man" who possessed "Christian character."[51] But the last characteristic, patience, led Speer to talk about the life of faith as an adventure in which a man learned courage and determination from failure. He cautioned his listeners and readers to concentrate on acquiring strength from a vital faith that would lead to overcoming limitations and thus conquering apparent failure.

When Speer turned to writing about individuals who exemplified the spirituality that he so carefully cultivated in his own experience, without exception he turned to men who demonstrated extraordinary courage and accepted life as an adventure. These were authentic models of the Christian man. His Cole lectures at Vanderbilt University, published as *Some Great Leaders of the World Movement*, are typical.[52] The "world movement" in the title denoted foreign missions, so each of his models was a man who had connection with the challenges of life in the potentially hostile environment of a foreign culture.

William Carey, for example, served not only to illustrate the adventure that went with being a pioneer on the mission field, but the practical sense that went with being a man of faith, while George Bowen, an American who, like Carey, toiled on the mission fields of India, demonstrated how one could combine a life of personal devotion (since Bowen had a profound mystical experience) with courageous "duty to others."[53] John Lawrence, British viceroy in India, and Charles George Gordon, a British businessman involved in Indian, Chinese, and Egyptian ventures, were both paragons of the religious discipline that made for success in the world of politics and industry.

Even Speer's writing on more traditional Christian topics, such as his *Studies of the Man Christ Jesus*, emphasized courageous action over doctrinal minutiae as the model for a dynamic spirituality.[54] Speer's Jesus was one who lived his religion; indeed, he "was his religion."[55] The man Christ Jesus did not recoil from challenge or adventure but "just plunged in."[56] The personal traits of Jesus were also those buttressed by the spirituality of courageous adventure: sincerity, humility, calmness, balance, and unselfishness.[57] Speer made no bones about his own orthodox Christian belief, which comes through clearly in his *The Meaning of Christ to Me*, but like others who advocated a vital spirituality, he was not inclined to elevate doctrine and belief over action, the realm of courageous adventure.[58]

Speer's ecumenical involvement no doubt brought home to him the wide range of interpretation of traditional Christian doctrine and led him to see doctrine as less significant that embarking on a spiritual adventure in faith. Some fellow Presbyterians, in the wake of the fundamentalist-modernist controversy of the 1920s, suspected that Speer was too latitudinarian in his own personal theology and supported missionaries whose doctrinal perspectives and approach to mission work did not stick to a narrow, orthodox understanding. John Gresham Machen led the assault. After Princeton Theological Seminary underwent reorganization in 1929, Machen left its faculty to become a founder of the Westminster Theological Seminary, and in 1936 he ultimately broke from the main northern Presbyterian body to start the more conservative Presbyterian Church of America (after 1939 known as the Orthodox Presbyterian Church). But earlier in the 1930s, Machen questioned Speer's leadership at a meeting of the General Assembly, claiming that Speer had allowed several whose doctrinal views were unorthodox to take posts through the mission board.

Speer had clearly earned the respect and support of not only the denomination's leadership but also the rank-and-file lay delegates. His own sense of courageous decorum meant he never replied directly to Machen's challenge, and the assembly refused to move against Speer or his associates on the mission board. Machen began an independent Presbyterian mission board and then, after the General Assembly condemned that action in 1934 and then revoked his ordination in 1935, made plans to started his own denomination.

The attack on Speer is instructive in demonstrating how Speer, like others who promoted a distinctive male spirituality before him, downplayed the significance of doctrine. When conflict between fundamentalists and modernists for control of denominational machinery seemed about to lead to schism and Machen was raising questions about Speer's leadership of the foreign missions board, Speer addressed the General Assembly in 1927, when he was serving as the denomination's moderator: "It would be a false and silly thing to sing of the faith of the fathers and their dungeons and their chains and their martyrdoms and our happiness to share in their experiences and to walk in their steps, and then in the safety and comfort of our easy and indulgent lives to abandon the missionary enterprise . . . because of such a transient storm as this."[59] What was essential not only to the missionary effort but also to a vibrant spirituality was not so much agreement on fine points of doctrine as it was acceptance of a heroic challenge.

Speer was simply living out the spirituality that had informed his life as a Christian man at least since his undergraduate days at Princeton and that echoed most distinctly in talks he gave to preparatory and college students. In such addresses, his biographer noted, he "always appealed to the heroic in a man. Duty was central; a man should be honest and courageous. His duty was to do what he believed to be right, to be loyal to Christ." Belief was thus best demonstrated in courageous adventure.

Commenting after Speer's death, Galen Fisher recalled that he had never heard Speer "indulge in theological speculation or the preaching of abstract doctrine."[60] Or, as John Timothy Stone observed, Speer "never flaunted his piety."[61] He may have been a man of prayer, but he seldom spoke of what associates knew to be his "constant reliance" on prayer.[62] Real men pray. But to those who observed him, Speer "stood like a soldier, unmoved by the swirling currents of theological controversy and ecclesiastical strife" in part because he was a "strong, masterful man."[63] The cluster of images converging in the spirituality of the Christian man as courageous adventurer resonated throughout Speer's life and career. Action in the world, not abstract doctrine was at the heart of that spirituality.

The Courageous Adventure of Ecumenical Activity

Speer's willingness to overlook doctrinal particularity may well have received encouragement from his ecumenical labors. Although identified throughout American Protestantism with Presbyterian denominational foreign missions, Speer was also a key figure in interdenominational cooperative ventures for much of his adult life.[64] In 1910, he had attended the World Missionary Conference in Edinburgh that was spearheaded by John R. Mott, who became a close friend through their work together. The World Missionary Conference was one of the stepping stones that led ultimately to the formation of the World Council of Churches in 1948, the year after Speer's death. But the exposure to other Protestant leaders and a recognition that denominational leaders shared a host of common concerns that Speer picked up in Edinburgh remained with him, although he never endorsed ecumenical activity just for its own sake.

During the era of World War I, when denominations sought to coordinate activities that supported the military enterprise, Speer became chairman of the General Wartime Commission of the Churches. After the war, when the Federal Council of Churches began once again to focus on issues of injustice in the area of labor, Speer likewise lent his support. During Speer's tenure as president of the Federal Council of Churches in the early 1920s, the council called for an end to the twelve-hour work day in the nation's factories and its replacement with an eight-hour work day. Speer understood that this move required not only social vision but also courage, for the opposition included many wealthy industrialists on whom not only

Presbyterian but virtually all Protestant mission boards relied for monetary support. But courage was essential to the spirituality to which Robert Speer had dedicated himself, a spirituality marked by adventure.

That spirituality was evidenced in one tragedy that came to Speer as a father during the decade before he retired from the foreign mission board in 1937, when he reached the denomination's mandatory retirement age of seventy. The Northfield schools founded by Dwight L. Moody and home to summer conferences designed to attract college and university students to missionary careers, like the one Speer himself had attended when he first met Emma Bailey, included the Mount Hermon School, a preparatory academy of boys.

With some pride, Speer had watched his son Elliott serve in the U.S. military during World War I, where the younger Speer learned firsthand what the life of courageous adventure required. With pride, too, Speer celebrated Elliott's being designated headmaster of Mount Hermon, where he could influence young men as they prepared for college education. But tragedy came soon after, when Elliott was found murdered. The loss of a child is always a challenge to faith, but the loss of a son to murder was particularly challenging. Yet the courage that had sustained Robert Speer for decades provided strength during this tragedy, even though later he was to observe that committing oneself to God's purposes required great struggle, as well as courage.[65]

After his retirement, Speer and his wife gave up their New York City residence and made "Rockledge," their summer home on ten acres in Lakeville, Connecticut, their permanent home. But retirement for Speer was anything but leisurely. He remained active in Presbyterian and ecumenical affairs, most notably serving as president of the board of trustees of Princeton Theological Seminary.

It was as if Speer had come full circle, for it was as a young man more than half a century earlier while a student at Princeton Seminary that Speer had committed himself to missionary endeavors, to courageous adventure as a man of faith. And it was during his student years at the seminary that Speer was offered a post with the Presbyterian foreign mission board. Dropping out of the theological program that was designed to prepare him for ordination as a pastor, Speer wound up spending the rest of his active career in the employ of the Presbyterian foreign mission board. When he returned to the seminary as board president, he returned as a Christian man who had exemplified for two generations of Presbyterian missionaries what the spirituality of courageous adventure was all about.

In retirement, Speer rejected pressure from friends and associates to write his autobiography, although he continued to be a prolific writer. He also urged others not to try to write a biography that would look at his career and his faith. Until his death from leukemia on November 23, 1947, Speer remained convinced that what had mattered in his life was not anything that he had accomplished, but whether he had been loyal to the Christ who for him had been the paragon of the courageous adventurer. In *The Stuff of Manhood,* Speer had written that the appeal of Christ was to those who would find the heroic in sacrifice.[66] That same spirit governed his life as one for whom spirituality demanded courage and adventure.

✝ ✝ ✝

CHAPTER 5

The Efficient Businessman

THE DRAMATIC SHIFT IN AMERICAN LIFE FROM A RURAL, AGRAR-
ian orientation to one based on business and industry and centered in urban
areas was particularly evident in the years immediately after World War I.
The census of 1920, the first to show that a majority of the nation's population lived in urban areas, was also the first to count more than one hundred million residents in the forty-eight contiguous states, a figure just over
double that of the 1880 census, taken just as the country entered a time of
massive immigration and unprecedented movement to the cities. The white
Protestant male spirituality centered on earlier images of the Christian man
as gentleman entrepreneur and courageous adventurer had spurred development of those qualities and social values that brought success in the
emerging urban, industrial world. In turn that success had allowed many
Protestant families to make considerable gains in their standard of living,
especially as men moved into managerial and executive positions, leaving
the lower paying, laboring jobs to the new immigrants, most of whom were
not Protestant.

By the 1920s, when the economic surge of the years after the Civil War
reached its peak and then ultimately collapsed, another image had been
layered on to those that had already helped generations of Protestant
men find a spiritual identity and cultivate a life of faith. Reflecting the
enthusiasm for capitalist economics and the emphasis on organization that

permitted such amazing industrial growth, at least until the stock market crashed in 1929, this cluster of images centered on the efficient businessman as the exemplar of male spirituality and the embodiment of the Protestant Christian man. Like earlier sets of images, those associated with the efficient businessman did not require jettisoning earlier images. They had deep roots, some stretching back to the dutiful patriarch of the seventeenth and eighteenth centuries, and many strands that came together in the images of the gentleman entrepreneur and the courageous adventurer continued to manifest themselves in the cluster of characteristics and traits that comprised the spirituality of the white Christian male as efficient businessman.

The Gospel of Wealth

One of the earliest venues for endowing the efficient businessman with extraordinary spiritual status came in the movement that became known as the Gospel of Wealth. To understand the Gospel of Wealth, one must also be familiar with some of the intellectual currents that were transforming American ways of thinking in the later nineteenth and early twentieth centuries, for the Gospel of Wealth is inextricably tied to social Darwinism. That idea is obviously tied to the theories of natural selection advanced by Charles Darwin. It is also linked to theories promoted by scientists such as Sir Charles Lyell, who, in his *Principles of Geology,* used surviving fossils, preserved rocks, and the like to date the age of the earth. Both influenced Herbert Spencer, the most prominent advocate in both the United States and Great Britain of social Darwinism, and American Episcopal minister William Graham Sumner, who trumpeted Spencer's theories after he left the pastoral ministry for a teaching career at Yale, first as professor of political economy and then as professor of sociology. In the realm of business, the Gospel of Wealth became identified with Andrew Carnegie, the steel magnate, who rose from modest origins to become one of the most successful and wealthiest business leaders in the United States.

What Carnegie, Sumner, Spencer, and others sought to explain was why some persons achieved great success in business, amassing great personal fortunes as a result, but others did not. Carnegie was also concerned with understanding how vast wealth related to spirituality, for he regarded his wealth as a sign of divine approbation that brought considerable responsibility with it. Carnegie could look at his own life experience as a Christian man for clues about how God worked through the spirituality of the efficient businessman.[1]

Born in Scotland in 1835 the son of a weaver, Carnegie came with his family to the Pittsburgh area in 1848. Early on he absorbed the moral and religious values of the gentleman entrepreneur, although he had only a grade school education himself. His hard work led him from a menial factory job to a position of some responsibility with the Pennsylvania Railroad by the time he was eighteen years of age. Carnegie demonstrated one of the characteristics of the efficient businessman when he started his first company in 1865, for he brought into the circle of leadership a cadre of knowledgeable, well-organized men. This inner circle of corporate leaders, however, was dedicated to using whatever means an unrestrained capitalism allowed to further their own—and Carnegie's—prosperity.

Carnegie had little use for those who would not commit themselves to hard work and discipline, marks of the gentleman entrepreneur and the courageous adventurer. They were simply not as dedicated as he to rising to the top. Thus, as a business magnate he was known for his opposition to the efforts of factory workers to organize. He believed in principle that such organization stifled individual initiative, a spiritual gift in Carnegie's mind but also a quality basic to the spiritual image of the efficient businessman. Consequently, Carnegie endorsed the decision of his associates to use force to put down a strike against the Carnegie Steel Company in 1892. Known as the Homestead Strike, the episode resulted in violence that many thought unnecessary and unwarranted.[2] But by that time, Carnegie was also devoting himself to an array of philanthropic activities, largely also because of his religious convictions as a Protestant Christian man and what he understood as the spirituality requisite of one who wished to exemplify Christian conduct.

The basis for that philanthropy was articulated in an article that Carnegie wrote in 1889. Originally simply titled "Wealth" but known more popularly as "The Gospel of Wealth," the piece argued that those who achieved success did so because they possessed skills given to them by God. Of course, those skills were precisely the same as those Carnegie thought he himself manifested in his career in industry.[3] Not all men received the skills that resulted in their accumulating the kind of wealth that had come to Carnegie. Thus wealth itself was given to those whom God chose. Carnegie was less concerned with the morality of the means used to acquire that wealth. Echoes of social Darwinism, with its notion that only the fittest survive even in the economic sphere, resound in Carnegie's words.

Because wealth was a gift from God, it was to be used to improve the quality of human life. Carnegie would have differed with advocates of the Social Gospel, who saw such improvement coming through better wages, safer working conditions, and the like. For Carnegie, the way to enhance human life was to provide the means whereby others, who were as blessed as he with individual initiative and the values of the efficient business-men, would have the opportunity to exercise that initiative. So Carnegie endowed libraries in towns and cities across the nation, believing that others chosen by God could use their resources for self-improvement just as he had. And he gave millions for various educational endeavors, the two most well known of which may be the Carnegie Foundation for the Advancement of Teaching and what was known at its founding as the Carnegie Institute for Technology, now Carnegie-Mellon University, in Pittsburgh.

Those whom God granted the spiritual legacy of the efficient business-man thus had incumbent on them an obligation to be responsible stewards of their wealth. Obligation was central to the spirituality characteristic of the dutiful patriarch generations earlier, but then that obligation had to do primarily with the spiritual status of those within the family circle. Now it had to do with the welfare of humanity at large. In both cases, the stew-ardship that was tied to spirituality was directed away from the self and toward others. For the dutiful patriarch, stewardship was directed toward the household. For the efficient businessman, it was oriented to the com-munity as a whole. For both, stewardship was a spiritual quality seen in action, not in quiet contemplation. The white Christian man was indeed a man of action.

William Lawrence, a contemporary of Carnegie who had a distin-guished career within the Episcopal Church culminating in his service as a bishop in Massachusetts, summarized the Gospel of Wealth in a slightly different but compatible way. Like Carnegie, Lawrence imbibed the ideol-ogy of social Darwinism, insisting that the man to whom God gave strength could conquer Nature (by implication, rising above all the odds) and the one granted a superior morality would realize wealth.[4] The appropriate response to such divine benevolence was to follow Christian precept in becoming an effective steward of wealth, for the biblical record was full of examples, especially in the parables told by Jesus, of the privileges and rewards that went with faithful stewardship.

Virtually all advocates of the Gospel of Wealth were Protestants, and many equated the combination of morality, efficiency, hard work, wealth, and stewardship with a religious orientation that often barely masked anti-Catholic and anti-Semitic tendencies. Those blessed by God with leader-ship and success in business knew full well that the workers whose labors brought magnates their wealth were increasingly drawn from the ranks of Catholic and Jewish immigrants in the later years of the nineteenth century.

The Gospel of Wealth, while helping give shape to the cluster of images that went into the spirituality of the white Protestant Christian man as efficient businessman, also belongs to the story of nativism and religious prejudice that has never been far beneath the surface in the saga of American religious life. By identifying Protestant economic success with divine approbation, those like Carnegie wittingly or unwittingly transformed non-Protestants into an "other" who deserved their lower economic standing in the emerging industrial order because they did not exemplify the spirituality of the efficient businessman.

Popular Variations: From Rags to Riches

Carnegie and others who made much of the Gospel of Wealth were fond of recalling their own humble origins. They remained convinced that their dedication to Christian principles, filtered through the spirituality of the efficient businessman and exemplified in acts of benevolent stewardship, had allowed them to cast aside poverty and acquire great riches. There were other ways, however, by which this transmutation of the so-called Protestant work ethic was presented to American males, virtually from the time they were schoolboys. The motifs captured in the spirituality of the Christian man as efficient businessman cascaded through the popular writing of Horatio Alger, for example. Alger penned scores of adventure novels targeted to young boys and teens, all of which glorified the hard work, honesty, and personal integrity that had been central to white Protestant male spirituality and models of the white Protestant Christian man from the time the image of the gentleman entrepreneur had come to the fore long before industrialization had recast the national economy in a new mold.

A Harvard-educated Unitarian who had natural sympathies with the emerging industrial class, Alger followed a formula in his novels that demonstrated repeatedly how boys who led a moral life would, thanks to a guiding Providence, achieve respectability and success despite all the odds. Although Alger wrote most of his works for younger readers between the close of the Civil War and his death in 1899, he actually achieved greater success posthumously, when in the early twentieth century the Progressive Era's enthusiasm for business growth gave their message new vitality.

Alger's writing has often been dismissed because in retrospect it seems to offer a simplistic, didactic message, uncritically glorifying the wealth that accompanied success. Recent biographers and analysts point out, however, that Alger retained a skepticism about wealth for its own sake and challenged some of the practices associated with emerging big business. Like some of those who advocated a Gospel of Wealth, Alger preached the responsibility to use wealth for the common welfare, not just for personal aggrandizement. Nor were his tales hackneyed accounts of impoverished rural yokels who, usually with the aid of a patron, almost miraculously overcame the odds to achieve unimagined success in the urban world of business by managing to avoid the corrupting temptations of the city and maintaining high moral standards, although they have been described as such.[5]

On the contrary, in an age when the spiritual nurture of boys was increasingly relegated to the female sphere of the home, Alger sought to inculcate the spiritual values of the efficient, but morally upright, businessman indirectly. Such subtlety has often been the case with the presentation of images of male spirituality and ideals of the Christian man. Alger perfected it in a format that would appeal to boys as they developed into men who would spend much of their adult working life in a male world.

The way Alger talks about the use of time illustrates his indirect approach to teaching what are essentially spiritual values. His *Bound to Rise* and *Risen from the Ranks*, which tell the story of Harry Walton, emphasize how an industrious young man will make the best use even of leisure time, how he will cultivate what a later age would call time management skills.[6] A similar point is made in a somewhat more dramatic way in the two novels that feature Sam Barker, *Young Outlaw* and *Sam's Chance*. Prior to his personal reformation, Sam is noted for his ability to waste both time and money. The second novel traces his gradual reformation, as Sam acquires habits that lead him to devote his time not to idleness and frivolity but to study and helping others.[7] Study will bring both self-knowledge as well as practical knowledge helpful to success in the business world. It represents an efficient use of time, even for adolescent boys.

Repeatedly, images of white male spirituality have highlighted particular virtues or ethical qualities, rather than overtly emphasizing prayer, devotion, or other specific activities associated more with a feminized piety. The seemingly secular tales of Alger are no different. Alger's stories exude a quiet confidence that the morally upright man will always emerge on top, even if the process requires efficient use of time. Some of that time can be spent in church attendance, a virtue Alger also frequently extolled.[8] Alger simply assumed that a benevolent deity would work through human affairs to guide men to success if they had been frugal with their resources. Alger elevated hard work to the level of a "spiritual ordinance"[9] that by definition required adherence on man's part to God's ways and blessing on God's part to acknowledge men's obedience. It helped, too, that most of Alger's heroes were inclined to a quiet, masculine piety. The proof of genuine piety was in the ethical life one lived.

In the novel that initially brought Alger renown, *Ragged Dick*, the theme quite simply is that spirituality and morality issue directly in respectability and only as an ancillary effect bring the business success that encouraged acquisition of wealth.[10] Alger's novels for adolescents are thus far from being just devotional tracts for boys. Through the fictionalized lives of their heroes, they promoted the spirituality of the efficient businessman in emphasizing honesty, service to others, hard work, time management, loyalty, and morality. Indeed, Frederick Lewis Allen observed that Alger's adolescent fiction did more to shape the attitudes of American businessmen in the 1920s than all the theory advanced by university economic professors.[11]

Another way in which the spirituality of the efficient businessman reached the masses of American Protestant men was through the sermons, lectures, and writings of Russell Conwell (1843–1925).[12] Conwell had already achieved success in the emerging world of business and industry and also as a lawyer and editor when he entered the professional ministry in 1880. Even as a lay person, Conwell had evidenced considerable interest in religion, working with the YMCA in its ministry to men and teaching a men's Bible study class. His personal spiritual interest intensified during the Civil War, when he suffered serious wounds and was forced to spend nearly three years convalescing. In 1882, he became pastor of Philadelphia's Grace Baptist Church, later popularly known as Baptist Temple, a post he retained until his death.

What made Conwell renowned and what linked him inextricably to the spirituality of the efficient businessman was his address called "Acres of Diamonds." Presented on the lecture circuit more than six thousand times, leading historian Martin Marty to suggest that Conwell "had a high threshold of boredom,"[13] this speech, Conwell claimed, was based on a story told to Conwell by an Arab guide when he was traveling overseas. In the story, a young man, who becomes in Conwell's retelling emblematic of every young American white Protestant male, determines to travel the world until he finds his fortune. Alas, the wealth he seeks eludes him, and, in a fit of despair, the young man commits suicide. There is an ironic twist, however, that gives the popular lecture its title, for shortly after the young man set out on his quest, on the site where the home he left behind was located, a vast diamond mine was discovered. The moral of the story was simple and simplistic: Had the young man looked carefully in his own backyard and cultivated what was already given to him, he would have discovered "acres of diamonds" and the very wealth that he never found in his odyssey around the world.

Diligence, another mark of the spirituality of the efficient businessman, would have led the chief character in Conwell's story to find the success and riches that constantly eluded him when he looked in all the wrong places. Diligence, of course, represented hard work and honest endeavor, two other characteristics of the efficient businessman who reaped success that were likewise found in the spiritual image of the gentleman entrepreneur. At one point, Conwell was reported to have remarked that making money through hard work and honesty was the same as preaching the gospel.[14]

Like Gospel of Wealth advocates, Conwell tended to see poverty and perhaps even only moderate success and wealth as signs of sinfulness or a lack of authentic spiritual commitment. It was up to the individual to determine what would become of his life. Here again it is obvious that a spirituality for white American Protestant men in the early twentieth century was one that looked not to prayer and contemplation but to diligent labor in whatever circumstances one was given. As with other images of white Protestant male spirituality and models of the white Christian man, that of the efficient businessman was directed outside the self, to the world of economic endeavor, although the results could bring high status and presumably happiness and contentment to the individual man.

After a man reaped the "acres of diamonds," Conwell thought, he must be a responsible steward. Here, too, there are echoes of ideas found in the Gospel of Wealth. Conwell personally practiced what he preached. Although he himself accrued considerable income from his popular lectures, especially from "Acres of Diamonds," he did not keep that money solely for personal use. Early in his ministry in Philadelphia, Conwell started a program of tuition-free night classes at the church so that young men could acquire the education that would position them for better success in the world of business. In 1888, that program took more permanent shape in what became Temple University. At its inception, the university sought to attract young men (and women) who were trapped in relative poverty because they lacked the education that would have allowed them to secure higher paying jobs and started them on the road to success and wealth.

Much of the money Conwell earned on the lecture circuit, estimated to be at least $11 million, was given directly to young men to pay for their college education. Conwell sought out those who were willing to commit themselves to hard work, diligent labor, efficient use of time and resources, and all the other attributes that went with the spirituality of the efficient businessman, convinced that they, too, would reap the success that God intended for them. Efficiency would make the Christian man a success.

Conwell's approach, however, shared some of the same limitations in its fusing spirituality and economic success that went with the Gospel of Wealth. It, too, gave virtually unqualified endorsement to the laissez-faire capitalism that fueled the Gospel of Wealth. Even contemporary critics recognized that Conwell offered comfort to the already successful; his assurance that riches and the gospel were synonymous bred a smug self-righteousness that too easily led to the exploitation of others. But with the popular fiction of Horatio Alger, Conwell's understanding helped cement the spirituality of the efficient businessman in male understanding of what it meant to be a Christian man in Protestant America.

Others made similar connections between spiritual commitment and success in the world of business. Roger Babson, a Congregationalist layman whom Martin Marty castigated as "a man without evident guile,"[15] also reached millions of men through his books and newspaper columns in which he trumpeted the results of efficiency, hard work, time management, thrift, and the other virtues linked to the spirituality of the efficient businessman. Like Conwell, Babson was convinced that these practical virtues that poised one for success in business also reflected the thrust of biblical teaching, particularly the teaching of Jesus. The spirituality of the efficient businessman was a practical matter first and foremost. The Christian man was always concerned with that which was practical.

Babson's most widely known books, *Religion and Business* (1921) and *New Tasks for Old Churches* (1922), were essentially handbooks linking hope for business success to the spiritual principles Babson deduced from such things as the Golden Rule and the Sermon on the Mount.[16] Spirituality became in effect a resource to use in the world of business if one wanted practical results. Babson insisted that businessmen quite rightly had no interest in theology. Doctrines and their interpretation divided people and therefore wasted energy in conflict, energy that could be given instead to diligent labor.[17]

Although the enthusiasm of the Gospel of Wealth advocates and men such as Horatio Alger, Russell Conwell, and Roger Babson for equating wealth with the gospel and riches with spirituality suffered serious setbacks when the Great Depression undermined much of the economic base that they simply assumed would always support American capitalistic enterprise, the conviction that individual initiative was a spiritual value did not. It endured in part because of the continuing popularity of the adolescent fiction of Horatio Alger Jr., even though Alger's personal thinking did not absorb the ideology of unrestrained capitalism or even of the social Darwinism implicit in much of that approach. Then, in a later era, the emphasis on individual initiative as a spiritual value would play into another constellation of images shaping male spirituality, those associated with the "positive thinking" of Norman Vincent Peale or the "possibility thinking" of Robert H. Schuller that will come under scrutiny in the next chapter.

Fashioning the Life of a Masculine Jesus

The image of the efficient businessman as the epitome of the white Protestant Christian man came together with the image of the courageous adventurer in a spate of "biographies" of Jesus that were designed to attract a male readership. If the intellectual ethos of the later Victorian age provided the context for Protestants to meld features of Darwinian thinking into their images of male spirituality, it also supplied a broad framework for rethinking what Protestants knew about the figure of Jesus. By the later nineteenth century, the principles of biblical criticism had begun to penetrate Protestant thinking, as seminary professors used the techniques of historical, textual, and literary analysis to reexamine biblical texts and to offer fresh interpretations, for example, of what the Gospels and other known early Christian writing actually said about the life of Jesus.

In academic circles, there was already a long history of efforts to reconstruct the life of Jesus, but in the late nineteenth and early twentieth centuries, that academic effort began to spill over into a body of literature targeted for a lay audience. Ironically, the burst of popular interest in reconstructing the life of Jesus came when New Testament scholars were about to abandon the task as an exercise in futility.[18] It also came as more conservative Protestant theologians were beginning to launch an attack on the critical method that sustained efforts to write the life of Jesus, efforts that combined with a host of other theological concerns to give birth to Protestant fundamentalism in the United States.

To some extent, methods of biblical criticism themselves took hold because the idea of efficiency that was shaping images of white male spirituality and models of the Christian man was also influencing the academy. At the heart of critical method was an often unstated assumption that analysis of the biblical text required not only competency in the biblical languages but also a thorough understanding of textual transmission, various genres of literature, historical context, writing styles, and literary theory. In other words, mastering critical method and then applying it to the biblical documents required a systematic, comprehensive approach that was in principle the same systematic, comprehensive approach that an efficient businessman would use to gain and sustain success in the economic sphere. The same qualities that buttressed business acumen likewise supported scholarship—hard work, industry, integrity, and an efficient use of time.

Another cultural and religious trend also stimulated ventures in producing books about Jesus intended for a male audience and built on what authors believed were quintessential male concerns. If men, as fathers and therefore as heads of households, were still in theory charged with oversight of the spiritual environment of the family, echoing the spirituality of the Christian man as dutiful patriarch, by the end of the nineteenth century, as we have seen, women had gradually assumed practical responsibility for the spiritual nurture of children. Because men's work took them away from the home, women's duties absorbed the religious responsibilities once primarily assigned to men.

At the same time that maternal models increasingly superseded patriarchal ones, there was also a dramatic growth in the popular literature available for use in religious instruction in the home, particularly as religious periodicals became a common way for the mainline denominations to disseminate religious teaching. Although there might be pages in monthly magazines that supported the priestly role of the husband within the home, more attention and more space were given to materials that seemed increasingly feminized. Denominational publishers recognized that women were the primary readers of such periodicals.[19] Indeed, although painted in 1940, the immensely popular portrait of the face of Jesus by Warner Sallman, which now seems rather romanticized and, while clearly male, somewhat less than macho, was intended to portray a distinctively masculine Christ when its earlier form as a charcoal drawing first appeared in 1924. It graced the cover of the *Covenant Companion,* a family periodical of the Evangelical Covenant Church, a small denomination with roots in Swedish pietism.[20]

Among the best-selling novels of the later nineteenth century was *Ben-Hur.* Although surely not designed to appeal exclusively to a male readership, *Ben-Hur* did represent an immensely popular attempt to present an understanding of Jesus who was decidedly masculine and who had a lasting impact on other men. Lew Wallace, who wrote this stunning piece of historical fiction, was a lawyer by profession, one-time army general, and ultimately governor of the New Mexico territory. But he never had a formal affiliation with any Protestant denomination.

Wallace set out to craft a fictional portrait of Jesus in 1878 as an alternative to the attacks on Jesus and Christianity proffered by well-known free thinker Robert Ingersoll. Through the title character's personal experience, readers are also drawn to respect the sheer physical courage Jesus exhibited, not to mention his charismatic power and his insight. Such qualities were precisely those that were part of the spiritual images associated with the courageous adventurer and the efficient businessman, a man who could lead others because of his knowledge, his understanding of human nature, and his willingness to venture into new areas of opportunity.

Ben-Hur did not claim to present a Protestant or even a biblical under-standing of Jesus, but the response of the American public assured that its depiction of Jesus took deep root in Protestant spirituality. The novel sold an amazing half million copies its first year in print, and less than twenty years later the story line became the basis for a stage production that, in either its Broadway or touring versions, reached an audience estimated at more than twenty million. In the twentieth century, *Ben-Hur* provided the plot line for two film versions, a silent movie released in 1926 and a sound and color one released in 1959. What made *Ben-Hur* significant to white Protestant male spirituality was the way it sent signals about what it meant to be like Jesus, what it meant to be a Christian man. In turn, those signals reinforced the qualities that were part of the ethos of the world of big busi-ness that helped shape white mainline Protestantism especially in the first half of the twentieth century.[21]

Some analysts restrict the attempts to recast the popular understanding of Jesus in a more masculine fashion, such as that found in Warner Sallman's drawings and paintings of the face of Christ and Lew Wallace's *Ben-Hur*, to the muscular Christianity movement examined in the previous chapter. They link these efforts then to the cluster of images associated with the courageous adventurer.[22] However, they are better seen as bridges that join the spirituality of the courageous adventurer with that of the efficient busi-nessmen. So too the many popular biographies of Jesus fused qualities of the courageous adventurer with those linked to the efficient businessman in their depictions of Jesus as a model for the Protestant man intent on a spiri-tual life.

Harry Emerson Fosdick, whose thought was informed by the canons of biblical criticism, published a discussion of the personality of Jesus repre-sentative of this genre in his *The Manhood of the Master*, which appeared in 1913. Several decades later, after retiring as pastor of New York City's famed Riverside Church, Fosdick again turned to the personality of Jesus in a work that is less obviously intended to appeal to a male audience, his *The Man from Nazareth*.[23] The year after Fosdick's earlier book appeared, two cognate studies became available: *The Masculine Power of Christ; or, Christ*

Measured as a Man by Jason Noble Pierce and *Building the Young Man* by Kenneth Wayne.[24] Given the wording of these titles, it is easy to see how later historians linked them to the muscular Christianity movement.

There is more to these quasi-fictional, quasi-biographical portrayals of Jesus than a bold emphasis on the raw masculinity of Jesus. In *Building the Young Man,* for example, Kenneth Wayne stressed how the historical Jesus was a working man like most white American Protestant men but had gained an extraordinary knowledge of human life while laboring as a carpenter.[25] That knowledge of life and of human nature was one requisite for success in the world of business in the early twentieth century.

One book that almost falls into a class by itself, *The Call of the Carpenter* by Bouck White, also deserves attention. Among some writers taken with the tenets of the Social Gospel noted in the last chapter, there was also a fascination with emerging socialist thinking, although rarely in the form that Marxist ideology took following the revolution in Russia under Lenin. Michael Kimmel has noted that White recasts "Jesus' story as a socialist allegory."[26] The Roman empire, in White's view, sought to keep the masses under its control in a condition of servitude, which in turn meant that Roman authorities were akin to "effeminate parasites." In contrast, as a carpenter coming from the working class, Jesus was nothing less than an "agitator" who awakened the proletariat by using the wisdom provided by a superior intellect, coupled with a dedication that reflected a determined will.[27] Intellect represented something other than formal education. What a man needed if he wanted to become a leader in business, as was the case with this master carpenter who could lead the working class to both personal and social salvation, was the ability to see through a situation, to appraise various courses of action, and then to select that one most likely to issue in triumph. The intellect of Jesus, in White's portrayal, was the intellect of the efficient businessman. To become a follower of Jesus and therefore to forge a Christian spirituality that reflected white male experience was to have such an intellect and determination.

The epitome of linking an understanding of Jesus to the spirituality encapsulated in the image of the efficient businessman came in the best-selling work of advertising executive Bruce Barton. *The Man Nobody Knows* was so wildly successful that it went through twenty-two printings between its appearance in March 1925 and December 1927. In the opening pages, Barton recounts his personal dissatisfaction with the understanding of Jesus he had imbibed as a child, a Jesus "who was weak and unhappy, passive and resigned." He therefore set out to read the New Testament accounts as if he had no prior notions about Jesus. Then he decided to write a book detailing the results of his inquiry, since most of the material available perpetuated the rather dismal picture of Jesus that Barton formerly entertained.

As he explains in his introduction, Barton discovered that Jesus was not a "physical weakling":

> Where did they get that idea? Jesus pushed a plane and swung an adz; He was a good carpenter. He slept outdoors and spent His days walking around His favorite lake. His muscles were so strong that when He drove the money changers out, nobody dared to oppose Him!
>
> A kill-joy! He was the most popular dinner guest in Jerusalem! The criticism which proper people made was that He spent too much time with publicans and sinners (very good fellows, on the whole, the man thought) and enjoyed society too much. They called Him a "wine bibber and a gluttonous man."
>
> A failure! He picked up twelve humble men and created an organization that won the world.[28]

Barton then sets out to demonstrate precisely how Jesus demonstrated the qualities of the successful businessman, the man who built an organization that won the world. Jesus was a man possessed of that conviction that "begets loyalty and commands respect" such that even those who, in Barton's day, wondered whether they were in the "right jobs [or] making the right investments"[29] would instinctively accept Jesus' authority. Jesus himself had an uncanny ability to select associates whose skills at building an organization went unrecognized by most. Barton highlights here how the Gospels note that Jesus simply "called" men as diverse as fishermen and a tax collector who, like those of a later day pondering their investments, gave up all to follow this magnetic personality.[30] And Jesus had the patience to work with those whom he called until they recognized his identity and, even after betrayal, could take the reins of leadership on their own.[31]

In other words, the natural authority, insight into human ability, and patience characteristic of Jesus were exactly the qualities needed in the early twentieth century world of business if one were to succeed. No wonder that Barton commented that "Jesus' universal genius may perhaps be best understood by the psychologist and the businessman."[32] Like the successful salesman, Jesus knew how to pitch a product—the gospel—so that hearers would understand the message without realizing that they had received it from a master teacher.

For Barton, Jesus exemplified that teaching gift in the use of parable, a literary form that drew hearers into understanding, almost unaware of the

process that was taking place. Barton is quick to add that Jesus is not trick-
ing his audience into understanding the gospel; nor would the honest businessman trick a client. Rather, Jesus knew that the product being offered,
the gospel, was of great worth to those who listened and could transform
their lives. Jesus also knew how to communicate effectively and efficiently.
Barton lifts up the parables as examples of how Jesus used a minimum of
words (Barton called the parables "condensed"), simple language, sincerity
of expression, and repetitiveness to get across the message of the gospel.[33]

So too with the methods of modern business, not only did a minimum
of words, simple language, sincerity, and repetitiveness sell a product, but a
genuine concern for how a product could enrich life also outweighed the
profit motive in laying the groundwork for success. Barton's work in advertising convinced him that such concern had superseded the greedy desire
for profit in any successful business: "The evidence of this new attitude is
overwhelming. Manufacturers of building equipment, of clothes, of food;
presidents of railroads and steamship companies; the heads of banks and
investment houses—*all* of them tell the same story. They call it the 'spirit
of modern business'; they suppose, most of them, that it is something very
new. Jesus preached it more than nineteen hundred years ago."[34]

As a founder and one-time board chairman of the prominent advertising firm of Batten, Barton, Durstine and Osborne, Barton instinctively was
drawn to a masculine Jesus who evidenced such advertising skills. But in
Barton's hands, such skills became more than the "spirit of modern business." They became spiritual virtues, hallmarks of the faithful disciple of
Jesus Christ. One sees this in Barton's brief discussion of the impact of Jesus
on the twelve he had called as his most intimate followers. This number,
Barton notes, was smaller than the following of John the Baptist, which
collapsed once John was beheaded. By contrast, these twelve "untrained,
simple men, with elementary weakness and passions," because of Jesus'
"personal conviction, because of His marvelous instinct for discovering
their latent powers, and because of His unwavering faith and patience,"
became "molded into an organization that carried on victoriously" after the
death of Jesus.[35] The movement they spearheaded within a few generations
came to dominate the religious life of the Roman Empire.

Equally important in Barton's characterization of Jesus as a model for the
spirituality captured in the image of the white Protestant Christian male as
efficient businessman is the lack of emphasis on doctrine or theology. As
with other images fostering male spirituality, that of the efficient businessman is oriented more toward action than to theological speculation or the
fine points of particular creeds. Barton himself was convinced that formal

theology had diminished a vital understanding of the "real" Jesus, and he therefore urged his readers to "forget all creed for the time being." By looking at the qualities that distinguished Jesus, the qualities that went into the spirituality of the efficient businessman, one would find a freshness that doctrine had too often obscured. The story of Barton's Jesus and the spirituality inspired by that story, when "stripped of all dogma, . . . is the grandest achievement story of all!"[36]

If an enterprise such as the Men and Religion Forward Movement of 1911–12 endeavored to construct a Protestant Christianity that would appeal to men, reflecting the spiritual images of the courageous adventurer, men such as Lew Wallace and Warner Sallman, and popular biographers of Jesus from Harry Emerson Fosdick to Bruce Barton, developed a symbiotic relationship with the business ethos that reached its peak in the 1920s. They drew from that ethos a range of spiritual images that came together in the symbol of the efficient businessman. But, in turn, they invested the efficient businessman with an aura of sanctity. Like the Puritan dutiful patriarch whose role within the household echoed the role of the Almighty in the governance of the universe, so the efficient businessman became the spiritual paragon of the white Protestant male who sought to be a faithful follower of Jesus.

The Efficient Businessman and White Protestant Churches

There were other ways that ideas and principles associated with capitalist success in the world of business and industry influenced the spirituality of white American Protestant men in the opening decades of the twentieth century. Urban congregations with both substantial resources and members that imbibed from the wells of both muscular Christianity and the institutional church movement built increasingly larger physical plants. Their building complexes often included gymnasia, classrooms for a variety of educational activities, auditoriums in which to stage musical and theatrical productions, and other facilities to support leisure time programs, in addition to space for worship. Those with ties to immigrant communities sometimes added rooms or apartments to house new arrivals in the United States on a temporary basis as they sought employment opportunities and more permanent accommodations. Although religious leaders may have understood such expansion of program and facilities as providing evidence of the congregation's commitment to appeal to men and to expand the scope of the mission of the church, from another vantage point it is also evident that these congregations and their denominations were themselves becoming businesses.

The pace of national growth and perceptions that denominations needed to develop bureaucracies to sustain work on a national level helped fuel the interest in applying business methods to religious institutions.[37] Consistent with the cluster of images that shaped the spirituality of the efficient businessman, theology and doctrine played only very minor roles as Protestant denominations began to examine how religious institutions, from local churches to denominations, could be structured as businesses.[38] If those who constructed biographies of Jesus or interpretations like that of Bruce Barton sought to cast Jesus in a modern, masculine mold, church leaders argued that bringing business methods into the churches, making the churches models of efficient operation, would demonstrate that Protestant Christianity retained relevance for the modern world dominated by business and industry.

University of Chicago Divinity School theologian Shailer Mathews, who was committed to an understanding of Christianity shaped by both the Social Gospel and scientific method, endorsed bringing business procedures into the churches as early as 1912, when he published his *Scientific Management in the Churches*.[39] Those caught up in the Men and Religion Forward Movement also concluded that the churches had much to learn from how business operated. In an article reflecting on what the leaders of that movement had learned from their effort to bring men into the churches, William Ellis, who had spearheaded publicity for the Men and Religion Forward Movement, observed that successful Christian work among men now had to "meet the test of practical efficiency."[40]

In the opening decades of the twentieth century, virtually all of the nation's Protestant denominations organized conferences promoting efficiency in administration. Their periodicals carried a spate of articles advocating efficiency in the local churches, while a host of books appeared describing everything from how to organize efficient Sunday schools to how to be more efficient in the recruitment of missionaries.[41] But at base, the calls for efficiency were inextricably tied to the issue of what sort of spirituality was appropriate for white Protestant Christian men.

Episcopal layman Meredith Nicholson, perhaps better known at the time as a popular novelist than as an expert on church bureaucracy, made the connection explicit in an essay published in the *Atlantic*.[42] Nicholson described a typical Protestant male named Smith who pondered what went into a life of discipleship, what formed the basis for a spirituality that would guide the life of a twentieth-century white Protestant Christian man.

Nicholson noted that Smith would be drawn to the church only if he were convinced that the church was efficient. A similar point was made by Henry Frederick Cope, who devoted a book to discussing what a later age would call male spirituality, though his term was the "religious training," of Protestant men. Cope's title was simply *The Efficient Layman*.[43] Methodist writer Lynn Harold Hough indicated what would result for the man whose spiritual life was shaped by a congregation and denomination organized according to the latest principles of business management in a book that he subtitled *A Series of Studies in Christian Efficiency*. Christian efficiency, Hough claimed, would yield men of power—power to achieve material success and personal happiness as well as salvation.[44]

Even within the churches, however, there were some who questioned whether the intrigue with business methods and the efforts to make churches and ever-growing denominational bureaucracies more efficient deflected energies away from cultivating the spiritual life rather than enhancing a viable and vital spirituality. Harry Emerson Fosdick, who contributed to the cluster of images that elevated the efficient businessman as a model for white male spirituality in his own writing about the figure of Jesus, was one who ultimately came to criticize the way the passion for efficiency placed too much emphasis on external relations and measurable results. *Harper's* in June 1928 carried several pieces that examined the impact of appropriating images and techniques from business in American Protestantism. In his contribution, Fosdick looked at the consequences for preaching of approaching the church as a business. He concluded that most Protestant churches had become so caught up in matters of organization and administration that clergy even in their sermons had no time for their "chief business [which] lies inside individuals."[45] Like other images of white male spirituality, that of the efficient businessman had little room for the interior life because it focused on action in a wide range of associations with others.

The author of another article in the same issue wondered whether parish ministers had actually abandoned their pastoral roles altogether and had instead become business executives.[46] But in a culture where images of the efficient businessman were prominent, one should expect that they would also hold sway within Protestant churches that wanted to promote a spirituality for men that was relevant to daily life in the contemporary world. The net result was the perception, probably not matched by reality, that real men were at last taking their places in the Protestant churches and using them as a base to cultivate their spiritual lives.

Russell Niese, the news editor of the *Nashville Tennessean*, evidenced the optimism that prevailed when he observed in 1925:

The biggest men in the country today are found to proclaim their faith in the Nazarene—and they do so without a blush or a stammer.

Witness the great Bible classes of every Christian denomination where millions of big red-blooded men go every Sunday to learn more of the Word of God. Doubtless many of you readers, like I, remember when the Sunday school was looked upon as a place only for women and children. A business men's Bible class then was unheard of. Today, aside from the great Bible classes, we have weekly men's luncheon clubs composed exclusively of Bible class members who gather round the table and have an hour of fellowship where campaigns for building . . . Sunday schools are planned.[47]

With the spirituality of the efficient businessman the order of the day, men seemed to be taking a greater interest in spirituality than ever before in the story of white American Protestantism. It was a practical spirituality, not a contemplative one, and a spirituality measured by concrete results in the empirical world. The Christian man always looked at results.

Reflections

A spirituality centered on efficiency and business methods captured much of white mainline American Protestantism in the first half of the twentieth century. But the fascination with the efficient businessman had consequences that those who most stridently advocated the application of business approaches to things spiritual did not anticipate or even intend. Some later analysts have suggested that the move toward a spirituality of the efficient businessman and an ecclesiology emphasizing bureaucracy and administration contributed to an increasing secularization within American Protestantism over the course of several decades. Others have argued that seeing the church as a business and committed men as efficient above all else helped grant white American Protestantism new vitality in an epoch when participation in organized religious institutions was on the decline elsewhere, such as in Europe.[48]

What does seem clear is that the spirituality of the efficient businessman further cemented the ties between much of American Protestantism and capitalist economics. Whether they were active in churches and consciously intent on nurturing a spiritual identity, the bulk of the leaders of American business and industry until well into the twentieth century came disproportionately from white Protestant circles. At the same time, the rank and file whose labor enabled these men to achieve material success in business came disproportionately from religious communities outside the orbit of mainstream Protestantism. Although such discussion lies beyond the scope of this study, the spirituality of the efficient businessman does have ramifications for understanding the anti-Catholicism, anti-Semitism, and racism that remained strong undercurrents in American life in the first half of the twentieth century.

Few advocates of applying business methods to the churches and few who crafted portraits of Jesus such as those in Fosdick's *The Manhood of the Master* or Barton's *The Man Nobody Knows* would have intentionally promoted religious or racial prejudice. But there are links between the surge of industrial growth and enduring prejudice, as evidenced in the support provided by automobile magnate Henry Ford for the advancing the anti-Semitic ideology contained in the spurious *Protocols of the Elders of Zion* and using the newspaper that he bankrolled, the *Dearborn Independent,* to trumpet rumors of a purported Jewish conspiracy to seize control of American and then worldwide economic life.[49]

The spirituality of the efficient businessman had racist overtones, for it lifted up concepts of success that a culture wedded to racial segregation embodied in Jim Crow laws and ideas of "separate but equal" that reserved the best for white Protestant men alone. Little wonder that many of those who made their way into the ranks of the Ku Klux Klan were those whose religious life was shaped by a Protestantism that promoted the ideal of the efficient businessman as the epitome of white male spirituality and the model for the white Protestant Christian male.

Federal legislation regulating business and influenced to some degree by the Social Gospel was part of the Progressive vision that tried to join efficiency with justice. In some intellectual circles, more in Europe than in the United States, the Great War left deep disillusionment with presumed progress and human possibility. However, the mood of the nation after the end of World War I by and large once again turned to unbridled rejoicing in economic gain. The spirituality of the efficient businessman held sway in mainline Protestant circles, layered onto images of the courageous adventurer, the gentleman entrepreneur, and the dutiful patriarch. It would take economic depression and another world war to undermine the cultural buttresses for such an orientation to male spirituality. Once the nation was adjusting to a post-Depression, post–world war ethos, other images would come to the fore. Among the more prominent would be the image of the positive thinker. But even then, the business focus would never entirely disappear. Out of the Pentecostal resurgence that came in the postwar years, for example, emerged groups such as the Full Gospel Businessmen's Fellowship International (FGBMFI), founded by Demos Shakarian in 1953. Groups like FGBMFI in some ways operated in a fashion akin to the noonday prayer meetings of the businessmen's revival of the 1850s, for usually Christian (often both Protestant and Catholic) men who were already successful in business or who were committed to succeeding in the business world of the later twentieth century would come together for fellowship, usually over lunch, and offer testimony to how their faith in God had issued in their success.[50] To that extent, the approach typified by the efficient businessman overlapped with the emerging image of the positive thinker.

In Focus
Bruce Barton: The Efficient Businessman No One Knows

Generations of Americans have become familiar with Betty Crocker, the symbol of efficiency in the kitchen, through the host of food products bearing her name. Crocker's image has changed over the decades since it first appeared, shifting from the motherly but rather dowdy matron to the idealized suburban housewife, and then to the rather chic professional woman whose looks suggest that she retains a commitment to providing nourishing and healthy meals for her family while making her mark in the world. Betty Crocker was the creation of advertising genius Bruce Barton. Although identified with New York City and the Madison Avenue advertising ethos most of his adult life, Bruce Fairfield Barton was born in Robbins, Tennessee, on August 5, 1886, the son of Congregationalist minister William E. Barton and his wife, Esther Treat Bushnell Barton.[51] Bruce was the oldest of five children, and for a time, the family also provided a home for two African American children.

In his father, Bruce Barton found an example of what contemporaries called a "self-made man." After leaving home without any clear sense of vocation or direction, the elder Barton enrolled at Berea College in Kentucky. Then as now, Berea was distinguished among American institutions of higher education for its program requiring all students to work at jobs that would benefit the college community and thus help defray the costs of their studies. Berea's approach meant that many who otherwise would be unable to afford a college education would be able to obtain one. William Barton fit that category. After graduation, he accepted the pastorate in Tennessee where he was serving when Bruce Barton was born. But eager to gain the proper professional training, he soon moved with his family to Oberlin, Ohio, where he received his seminary education. Following a pastorate in

Boston, William accepted a call to a church in the Chicago suburb of Oak Park, Illinois, where Bruce spent his formative years.

The home environment that shaped Bruce Barton was one where spiritual nurture was central. By all accounts, the family engaged in serious conversation, some of it prompted by the pastor-father's own theological inquiry and writing. Committed to a stance that linked religious faith to the modern world, the father instilled in his son an abiding appreciation for progressive and contemporary ways of talking about spiritual matters, informed by the canons of scholarly criticism. For much of Barton's adolescence, it seemed likely that he would follow his father and enter the ministry himself. Indeed, Barton took a stab at preaching one summer during his student years, garnering much acclaim from those who heard his preaching, but was forced to stop when some congregants learned that he smoked a pipe. For them, use of tobacco was simply incompatible with the professional ministry, and whatever thoughts Barton entertained about a clergy career seem to have evaporated as a result.

Barton spent one year at Berea College, complying with his father's wishes, although his own desire was to study at all-male Amherst in Massachusetts. Since he was required to have a job that would benefit the college community while at Berea, Bruce Barton worked in a printing office, where he started to become intrigued with the more technical aspects of publishing and production. His father did consent to his transferring to Amherst after a year, where Barton demonstrated his own commitment to hard work and his own leadership capacities not only by being elected to Phi Beta Kappa prior to his graduation in 1907 but also by serving in official capacities in organizations ranging from a social fraternity to the YMCA.

Friends and associates at Amherst recognized that Barton had an ability to persuade and to express in words what others felt but could not articulate nearly as well. Hence, it was logical that classmates elected him "most likely to succeed" at graduation. At graduation, Barton had not yet settled on what direction his own life and commitment would take. Drawn to the ministry but doubting whether he would finally do well and be happy in the ranks of the clergy, and drawn to business but doubting whether he could remain faithful to his spiritual ideals without succumbing to the increasingly cutthroat nature of the working world, Barton took his first job at a railroad construction camp in Montana while he made up his mind about a future vocation.

His experience at Berea finally led him to look to journalism as an arena where he could bring together his deeply held spiritual values and his interest in business. Returning to the Chicago area, he began work with *Home*

Herald, soon becoming managing editor. In 1909, he was offered a post with a Presbyterian periodical, the *Continent.* This position required him to relocate to New York, which remained his home until his death. Barton seemed to move quickly from one magazine to another, but finally in 1914, the year after his marriage to Esther Randall, he took over the editorial reigns of a new mass circulation magazine, *Every Week,* where his breezy editorial writing style helped boost paid circulation rather quickly to more than half a million subscribers, in addition to counter sales. His columns became the basis for a collection of essays, *More Power to You,* published in 1917,[52] and several subsequent anthologies.

The economic uncertainties that accompanied World War I, however, had a deleterious impact on *Every Week,* which was forced to cease publication in 1918. The one designated "most likely to succeed" now seemed a failure. But the commitment to a work ethic and a conviction that one can learn from failure, the topic of one of his *Every Week* editorials, propelled Barton to shift gears and look to advertising for fresh opportunities. Some later observers have suggested that the pithy quality of much of his writing almost turned his editorials into advertising copy, making the vocational transition an easy one.

In 1919, with Roy Durstine and Alex Osborne, he founded an advertising agency that, with the addition of George Batten as a fourth partner nine years later, became popularly known as BBDO and ultimately one of the leading advertising agencies in the nation. In time, BBDO counted U.S. Steel, General Motors, General Electric, and Standard Oil among its clients. Barton also remained a free-lance writer, whose work appeared in such mass-circulation publications as *American Magazine* and *Red Book.* Before long, too, the man who created the familiar slogan for the Salvation Army—"A man may be down but he's never out"—turned his hand to writing religious books, ones targeted especially for businessmen who sought to affirm their own spirituality through a deep commitment to the Christian faith. The businessman provided Barton with a model for the ideal white Protestant Christian man.

Spirituality and the World of Business

Although Barton is associated with big business and promoting the world of business, from his early writings on he evidenced a concern that absorption in business deflected men away from spiritual concerns. In the editorial reprinted from *Every Week* that opened *More Power to You,* for example,

Barton urged his readers to beware lest they be consumed by business and lose a focus on what really mattered in life, qualities and interests such as having dreams, keeping a garden, reading for self-improvement, and listening to music, which he described as "medicine for the soul."[53] After all, he wrote, there were dimensions of life that mattered more than the accumulation of wealth or great material success. These more important aspects of life embraced maintaining one's health (a practice that included setting aside a reasonable amount of time for both sleep and recreation), keeping a home that was more than just a physical house, and upholding one's honor and integrity.[54]

Implied here as well are salient characteristics that pervaded images of white male spirituality and models of the white Protestant Christian man from those of the gentleman entrepreneur to those of the efficient businessman and beyond. In one essay, Barton insisted that no one needed to fail in business, although just a few pages later he argued that one could learn from failure.[55] What could thwart potential failure and even transform apparent failure into success came in the "law of compensation." That law, as Barton put it, was quite simply that hard work would always pay off.[56] After all, one did not get a better job without putting forth energy. To be a man of faith required work.

Work, for Barton, was a kind of positive action in the world, and Barton's understanding of spirituality was consonant with the tenor of what had been offered to white American Protestant men for generations, namely, that the interior life and matters of belief were of secondary importance when compared with what men actually did. That emphasis was manifest in Barton's portrait of Jesus as the consummate corporate executive. But it was a theme that pervaded virtually all of his writing in the area of religion, writing that was perforce addressed more to men than to women. The downplaying of doctrine in favor of an understanding of spirituality resonated even in one book whose title might suggest otherwise.

In 1927, Barton published a work called *What Can a Man Believe?*[57] He noted at the outset that he wrote this work in response to a letter he had received from an unidentified individual who inquired which of the world's religions was best suited to provide spiritual direction for a businessman. Barton began with a quick review of popular arguments that religion had on balance done more harm to humanity than good if one looked at accounts of massacres in the name of a particular religion, blood sacrifice, and the like. He readily dismissed them all. Then he went on to offer a cursory comparison of Buddhism, Confucianism, Christianity, and Islam, based on the assumption that all had some common ethical base. Not surprisingly, he thought Christianity superior because he found in the approach of Jesus an optimism lacking in the others.

Finally, he got to the heart of the matter. Men, Barton insisted, needed to abandon the notions of God inculcated in young boys, particularly ideas of God as one who was always on tap to help and always keeping an account of human shortcoming.[58] None of that was in keeping with a modern perspective buttressed by science; nor were such notions consistent with what men knew from the world of business. Barton admitted that men did not discuss religious beliefs with one another. Although he claimed that one of his goals was to make religion more public, he also urged men to forget about creeds, since creeds did not reflect a businesslike approach to spirituality. For men, behavior was more vital than doctrine.

"In other words," Barton wrote, "the way to know God is not to think too much about Him, certainly not to argue about Him, but to know and love your brother."[59] Part of Barton's rationale was simply that the intricacies of doctrine remained mysteries; men cannot picture heaven, for example, or explain why those who are good must endure seemingly unwarranted suffering. So they should just get about the business of leading moral lives.

For Barton, the work of the businessman was an expression of worship more than what happened on Sundays in the churches. He thought that here he reflected the approach taken by Jesus, who spurned hypocritical lip service to public and private devotion alike. Hence, the church as an institution could learn much from how business operated. It could learn honesty, the hallmark of success in business, and earn the respect of businessmen by being forthright in, for example, learning to emphasize the benefits of Christianity.

Barton regretted that twentieth-century Protestant churches did not even demonstrate the kind of faith that was essential to business. Businessmen knew that change was needed to keep pace with the times, but the church resisted change. Businessmen, if they were successful, had learned to adapt and be flexible. The Protestantism that Barton observed in the world around him, however, was rigid and resistant to adapting to new circumstances. More telling, business faced failure if it did not make sure that the quality of its leaders and workers remained of the highest order. Yet the church did not attract the "best men" because it was too caught up in the fine points of doctrine and creed and failed to remain oriented to its goal of offering forgiveness and uplift.

At one point Barton mused about the church of the future, assuming that the church remained viable and moved more toward success. There would be little emphasis on preaching, since such promoted doctrine and creed. Rather, the church of the future would focus only on spirituality. It went without saying that what Barton meant was the spirituality captured in the image of the white Protestant Christian man as efficient businessman.[60]

Upsetting the World

In religious circles, Barton was most well known for his portrayal of Jesus in *The Man Nobody Knows*, published in 1925. Cut from the same mold is his less well known study of the apostle Paul, *He Upset the World*, which appeared in 1931.[61] Barton's religious writings give evidence that he was familiar with the tools advanced by biblical scholars, although he still tended to take the biblical text at face value and then to filter his own interpretation through the lens of the efficient businessman.[62] In his appraisal of Paul, for example, Barton accepts without question the presumed biographical information about Paul provided in the Acts of the Apostles as well as the Pauline authorship of the pastoral epistles. By Barton's day, New Testament scholars had questioned such a reliance on the Acts of the Apostles and had generally concluded that the pastoral epistles reflected developments in early Christianity that could not have come until a generation or so after the time of Paul. Yet he also was familiar with some of the noncanonical literature about Paul, such as the Acts of Paul and Thecla, and accepted the prevailing scholarly cautions about the value of such literature in constructing an understanding of the apostle's life.

If the Jesus of *The Man Nobody Knows* had the skills and talents of the efficient businessman in drawing a group of followers and energizing them while he was present to guide them, Jesus did not craft a long-term business program. In the parlance of a later age, he lacked a strategic plan.[63] The net result was that, when Jesus was no longer physically present to inspire the disciples, most of them became inactive. Barton highlights the brief account of Matthias, the one chosen to replace Judas Iscariot as a disciple, rightly observing that Matthias vanished from the biblical record as soon as he had been designated one of the twelve. It was Paul who provided the leadership that transformed a faltering movement into an enormously successful religious enterprise. Barton suggests that the shaky status of early Christianity resulted at least in part from the disciples' self-limiting understanding of Christianity as an eschatological phenomenon and their increasing concern for doctrine and belief.[64]

What was critical to Christianity's survival was the practical nature of Paul's leadership, a quality essential to the spirituality of the efficient businessman. Paul, Barton notes with some satisfaction, was not very theological in most of his early sermons. For Barton, the practical was always more important. After all, he insisted, Jesus himself had never promoted dogma. So Paul used the language of the athletic field and Roman arena to demonstrate that authentic religion is "not form but life."[65] Like the efficient businessman, Paul never confused what was inessential (doctrine) with what was essential (the practical value of faith). If Paul was idealistic in his aims, he still was not bound by creed. As his sermon in Athens recorded in Acts 17 demonstrates, he had a working knowledge of practical psychology and a willingness to change his methods according to the audience with which he was working. Both were likewise vital to success in the world of business in Barton's day. Like the efficient businessman, Paul was interested in results and was open to adopting whatever means were necessary in order to achieve the desired results.[66]

There was one constant, however, and in describing that constant, Barton comes as close to making a theological affirmation as he does throughout his religious writing. That constant is Paul's reliance on and unflinching trust in a power beyond the human realm. That controlling power, or God, Barton insists, also undergirds scientific inquiry and thus sustains the progress that in his day was still associated with scientific and technological advance.[67] Real men might pray, but the test was in the results of faith, not in acts of piety.

In a more practical fashion, therefore, Paul becomes for Barton the model of the spirituality of the efficient businessman. Paul was not the founder but the leader of the next generation who was able not only to keep the vision alive but also to infuse it with fresh energy. Once again, it was action in the world, the willingness to change and adapt means to achieve one's goals, not a life of quiet contemplation removed from the realities of everyday existence, that allowed Paul to "upset the world." The same was true for men in Barton's day who were willing to jettison the primacy of doctrine and creed for a life of practical action that went with the spirituality of the efficient businessman.

The Businessman as Politician

When Barton's biographical sketch of St. Paul was published in 1931, his own life was already experiencing challenges that would undermine the plausibility of the spirituality of the efficient businessman and ultimately challenge the stature of Barton as one who was a model for the white Protestant Christian man. Some of those challenges were personal. Others reflected currents in the larger culture. The stock market crash of 1929 that drew the United States into the Great Depression that swept across much of the globe eroded much of the popular confidence in business and unfettered capitalism that had sustained Bruce Barton the advertising genius. For many, it also undercut the prevailing understanding of Christianity and its accompanying male spirituality.

Barton, however, seems to have retained his own confidence in business throughout the Depression years. He gave extraordinary energy to advertising campaigns promoting the products and businesses that were under the purview of Batten, Barton, Durstine, and Osborn. But it was clear even to Barton that, as the Depression dragged on, business alone could not solve the nation's economic dilemma. A genuine solution required a cooperative relationship with government. The sobering consequences of global economic depression tempered the enthusiasm that Barton exuded in his earlier writings.

More serious in testing the viability of the spirituality of the efficient businessman for Barton was a series of personal crises that began in the late 1920s. In the year before the stock market collapsed, Barton experienced a prolonged siege of personal depression that finally required professional treatment in a sanitarium. Soon after, in 1930, his father died, and with him died the symbol of religious nurture and encouragement that had for decades nudged Barton to excel as the efficient businessman in his professional life as well as in his personal life. A lifelong Republican, Barton also saw his world shattered when Herbert Hoover, with whom he had more than a casual acquaintance, lost reelection to the presidency in 1932 to Franklin Delano Roosevelt. Three years later, his daughter became permanently paralyzed. Her condition only added to the disarray that threatened to erode Barton's world of meaning.

The most shattering episode is one that still remains clouded in mystery. Apparently at some point in the late 1920s or early 1930s, Barton had an extramarital affair. Apparently, too, he sought to end the relationship, but so convoluted had circumstances become that, before the episode came to resolution, there was a trial for blackmail in 1932–33. Even though Barton was exonerated in the trial, he saw his reputation as the advocate for "the man nobody knows" destroyed and his family exposed to humiliating personal scrutiny.

Nothing suggests that Barton abandoned his Christian faith or jettisoned the spirituality of the efficient businessman that he had started to promote in magazine editorials decades earlier. He remained a Christian man. But he never again published a religious work and refrained from being a voice for expressions of white Protestant male spirituality. Yet he did not altogether abandon a public presence for the principles with which he had for so long been associated. Rather, he shifted from the arena of popular religious and spiritual writing to the world of politics.

His view of capitalism, although moderated by the Depression, kept him within the ranks of Republican politics, even if he was attracted to some of the economic initiatives associated with the early days of the New Deal. By the mid-1930s, however, Barton had become convinced that Franklin Roosevelt and his policies were undermining the very forces that had made the United States a haven for business and that rewarded competence, efficiency, adaptability, and all the other images that had both professional and spiritual associations in Barton's way of thinking. In 1936, Barton sought election to the U.S. House of Representatives from his home district in New York City. He was successful in his bid and served two terms. Had he run for reelection to Congress in 1940, he might well have won a third term, but Republican Party officials, who savored Barton's name recognition, urged him instead to run for the Senate, challenging a popular Democratic incumbent. His stunning defeat led to his withdrawal from political life and his return to BBDO, where he remained as president or board chairman until he suffered a debilitating stroke in 1957.

If Barton remained silent on religious matters in his later years, he retained an almost idealistic commitment to corporate capitalism. He remained convinced that business could bring prosperity and happiness when carried out with efficiency and with the welfare of the public as its aim. That commitment meant that he was not always silent, for example, about his reservations about the cold war and even American involvement in Korea. Such international rivalry and hostility, he believed, worked against the best interests of American business. Even so, he was able to sustain friendships and associations with Republican political figures, including President Dwight D. Eisenhower, whose policies otherwise Barton found more in keeping with his own vision of the efficient businessman. He died in New York City on July 5, 1967.

From advertising whiz to popular writer, Bruce Barton exemplified the spirituality captured in the image of the efficient businessman. Open to change, possessed of a dynamic personality, eager to offer leadership and direction, organized and productive, suspicious of doctrine and dogmatism in any form, Bruce Barton not only promoted the spirituality of the efficient businessman. He also exemplified it in his own life. If personal and cultural crises muted his religious voice, they also awakened a resiliency in his spirit. Adaptability to changing circumstances accounted both for the apostle

Paul's success as he upset the world by transforming a foundering Christian movement into a dynamic religious enterprise and for Barton's entrance into the world of politics. From his days as a student exploring the world of Berea College to his retirement as chairman of the board of one of the nation's leading advertising agencies, Bruce Barton persisted in his dedication to the spirituality that made the efficient businessman the paragon of the white Christian man.

CHAPTER 6

✛ ✛ ✛

The Positive Thinker

T HE STOCK MARKET CRASH OF 1929 CHALLENGED THE IMAGES OF Protestant male spirituality associated with the Christian man as efficient businessman that Bruce Barton epitomized. The economic growth of the 1920s, it became evident, was far from limitless. Little wonder then, that personal problems aside, Barton tempered his optimism as the nation moved into the Great Depression and refrained from penning other works of popular piety. The economic depression had a deep impact on mainline Protestantism. It was, as historian Robert T. Handy called the era, a time of "American religious depression" as well.[1] For some, the fascination with efficiency was itself the culprit, for it reflected the absorption of American culture, not just Protestant male spirituality, in unrestrained commercial growth and a consumerism that a later age would label "conspicuous consumption."

In *The Confessions of a Puzzled Parson*, published the year before the stock market crashed, Episcopal bishop Charles Fiske condemned the dominant style of mainline Protestantism when he noted, "Our conception of God is that he is sort of a Magnified Rotarian. Sometimes, indeed, one wonders whether the social movement and the uplift in general have not become, among Protestants a substitute for devotion." Even worse, he continued, the devotion to commercialism had made business prosperity "a substitute for real religion. Efficiency has become the greatest of Christian virtues."

The result, for Fiske, was that one could no longer "distinguish between what is offered to God and what is accomplished for the glory of America and the furtherance of business enterprise."[2] The image of God as a Rotarian is also an indirect appeal to male sensibilities, for when Fiske was bemoaning the state of American piety, the nation's Rotary Clubs were the exclusive domain of males. Later historians recognized the results of wedding spirituality to business. By the end of the 1920s, as Winthrop Hudson observed, the "contagious enthusiasm" for things religious and spiritual represented by such enterprises as the Men and Religion Forward Movement "had largely evaporated."[3] In its place was "spiritual depression."[4]

Economic recovery was slow in coming, nudged by the New Deal programs promoted by President Franklin D. Roosevelt and then by the need for rapid and large-scale production of a wide range of items needed to sustain American involvement in World War II. It is hardly an exaggeration to say that from the time of the stock market crash in 1929 until after the defeat of the Axis powers in 1945, economic and military concerns superseded spiritual concerns for the vast majority of white American Protestant men. But the religious and cultural world of post-Depression, postwar America was rather different in substance and style from the world that had sustained the spirituality of the efficient businessman among white Protestant men. The cultural transformations of the first decades after the war are legion and here can receive only cursory treatment.

During the war years, as men were drafted into the military by the thousands, increasing numbers of women joined the labor force outside the home. If "Rosie the Riveter" became a popular symbol of American women's support for the war effort, she also cemented into American life the notion of women having careers outside the home. As the economy struggled to absorb millions of men into the civilian labor force after the war, women did not heed much of the popular advertising that extolled the virtues of the female as homemaker and rush back to the domestic sphere; rather, women continued to enter the paid work force, propelling a trend that continued into the twenty-first century. One consequence was the gradually diminished role of the home as the sphere of women and the incubator of spirituality for young men and young women alike. Another was the declining influence of the layers of spiritual images for white Protestant men that drew together strands associated with the gentleman entrepreneur, the courageous adventurer, and the efficient businessman.

The years after the war also witnessed a surge in mobility among the American population, as families relocated to areas where employment opportunities were plentiful. For mainline Protestants, with that mobility came a gradual, but steady erosion in loyalty to the denominations of birth and ancestry, as persons switched membership from one group to another in increasing numbers. Often the proximity of a congregation—regardless of denomination—to the new suburban development where one acquired a home determined a family's formal affiliation. Added to the mix was the swift expansion in the proportion of Americans earning college and university degrees as war veterans took advantage of the GI Bill to defray the cost of higher education. From fighting in the trenches to sitting in college classes with persons of other faiths, American men began to expand their religious horizons. The rapid increase in intermarriage not only across denominational lines but also across religious traditions added to the sense of rootlessness fostered by mobility and the frequency of denominational switching.[5]

To casual observers, however, the 1950s seemed like an age of religious revival, with millions of dollars being spent on construction of facilities to house religious institutions, evangelistic crusades conducted by revivalists such as Billy Graham drawing record crowds, and polls indicating the a majority of Americans believed that religion was not only important to daily life but also growing in influence in the culture at large.[6] If switching membership from one Protestant group to another undermined denominational loyalty, it also buttressed a spirit of cooperation and ecumenical activity. Denominational mergers and agencies such as the National Council of Churches sent signals to Americans that one denomination was just as good as another, that particulars of belief—never central to white Protestant male spirituality and models of the Christian man—were increasingly unimportant. Just having a religious label made one a moral, trustworthy citizen. After all, the cold war pitted presumably "godless communism" against "God-fearing democracy," Soviet totalitarianism against American liberty. The addition of the now controversial phrase "under God" to the Pledge of Allegiance in 1954 and the legislation extending inclusion of "In God We Trust" to all U.S. coinage and currency underscored the tacit religious base presumed to buttress the American way. How that religious support for democracy played out in matters of personal faith and individual spirituality was of secondary importance.

Although jobs seemed plentiful for a time, the postwar economic boom was yielding to recession by the later 1950s, albeit not as severe a recession as that which barely two decades earlier had resulted in depression. At the same time, the heady excitement of building homes in suburbia and thereby carving out a niche for one's family where safety and security would prevail gave way to a sense that one deserved even greater satisfaction from the material well-being that had raised living standards to new heights. But much of this search for happiness was a facade that obscured lingering problems. In retrospect, the 1950s were also a time of anomie and ever greater rootlessness. The threat of a Communist menace lurking everywhere led to the witch hunts associated with U.S. Senator Joseph McCarthy and with seemingly constant investigations conducted by the House Un-American Activities Committee. Playwright Arthur Miller powerfully captured this menace in his rendering of the seventeenth-century Salem witch trials in *The Crucible*. As the cold war replaced World War II and the Korean War, potential enemies to the American way of life that mainline Protestantism had so profoundly shaped lay hidden beneath the veneer of a nation returning to the ideals and mores of a day already past.

In the mid-1950s, sociologist and seminary professor Will Herberg, a one-time labor organizer, wrestled with the impact of all these shifts in American self-understanding. As he surveyed American culture, he concluded that for most Americans it no longer mattered whether one identified as a Protestant, a Roman Catholic, or a Jew so long as one had some religious identification, however superficial it might be.[7] One religious label was as good as another, for all the major religious traditions presumably inculcated basic moral values that made good citizens. This popular understanding—what for a later age Nancy Ammerman would call "Golden Rule Christianity"[8]—lacked the rigor of vital commitment and the critique of culture inherent in biblical faith. Yet it not only supported a patriotism that helped sustain national cohesion in the years after the war but also sustained a commitment to consumerism and materialism in an almost desperate effort to demonstrate to the world that the American fusion of democracy and capitalism brought unbounded success, comfort, and happiness. From a theological perspective, Herberg bemoaned these developments, but he believed he had accurately captured the pulse of mainstream American life in his day.

The corporate culture that undergirded this "religion of the American way of life" to a large extent was a natural outgrowth of the business and industrial surge that had buttressed the spirituality of the white Christian man as efficient businessman. Bruce Barton, whose writings captured the essence and the irony of that spirituality, harbored reservations about an unrestrained capitalism, for the Jesus who epitomized the efficient businessman was also one whose personality exuded broad compassion.

Others who offered clusters of images to white American men that brought together spirituality and the world of work, however, more readily embraced the consumerism and love of materialism of the day, although a few voices urged caution. David Riesman, for example, demonstrated how the other-directed personality, when properly cultivated, could issue in material success, but the other-directed man might still be part of a "lonely crowd" without the sense of psychological wholeness that presumably should accompany such success.[9] Others highlighted both the possibilities and the dangers inherent in becoming an "organization man," who emerged in popular consciousness as a symbol of one caught in a rat race that finally led nowhere.[10] Playwright Arthur Miller again captured the dilemma in the character of Willy Loman, the central figure in *Death of a Salesman,* which opened on Broadway in February 1949. Consumed by dreams of material success, Loman watches his own life crumble; a hollow core replaces a spiritual center for this salesman who can never visualize himself as achieving the ideals inculcated by society.

Nevertheless, there were those who offered a new cluster of images for white Protestant men who sought a spiritual foundation for their lives as the Depression gave way to wartime and wartime in turn yielded to relative peace. Those spiritual images also were tied to those that went before, drawing especially on the tradition of self-help that echoed through the Gospel of Wealth, the fiction of Horatio Alger, the optimism of Russell Conwell, and even the fusion of advertising genius and spirituality in the religious writings of Bruce Barton. An appropriate label for this cluster comes from the familiar phrase in the title of a book that dominated the best-seller list for more than two years in the early 1950s, *The Power of Positive Thinking.*[11] The image of the positive thinker had a profound impact on how white American Protestant men received clues about spiritual formation from the middle third of the twentieth century almost until the century's close. In its classic form, it had links to some traditional forms of Christian piety and devotion, such as prayer and diligent reading of Scripture. Real men pray.

Other manifestations of the positive thinker had less obvious ties to the disciplines associated with spirituality. For some, the emphasis on how individuals could muster a sense of spiritual wholeness by tapping into a seemingly boundless reservoir of inner strength seemed almost devoid of overt religious substance, although the role played by this exercise of looking within and harnessing a sense of a unified self and an integrated outlook on life still retained religious dimensions.

At the same time, most of those who developed and advanced the spiritual image of the positive thinker had little to say about how this spirituality was connected to such arenas of life as a man's identity as a husband and father, arenas central to some earlier expressions of white male spirituality and models of the Christian man, such as that of the dutiful patriarch. Most simply assumed that a man who was a positive thinker would be attentive to his social duties and obligations and eager to carry them out in a responsible fashion. But like virtually all other expressions of white male spirituality, the cluster of ideas identified with the positive thinker was oriented to a man's relationships with others. Here, however, those to whom a man related tended to be employers, others who had authority in the workplace, and one's fellow workers, not to one's family, household, or close friends.

Winning and Influencing Friends

When Bruce Barton was concentrating more on politics and running an advertising agency than on religious writing targeted primarily to a white Protestant male audience, Dale Carnegie was helping to transform the image of the efficient businessman into that of the positive thinker as one barometer for male spirituality and what it meant to be a Christian man. Born in Missouri in 1888 with the surname Carnagey, Dale Carnegie initially embarked on a career in business as a salesman.[12] Not achieving the success as a salesman that he thought he deserved, Carnegie relocated to New York City, changing his name to reflect that of Carnegie Hall, where he rented office space.

From his teenage years, Carnegie had a flair for public speaking, and in New York, he turned his attention to studying the habits of men who had attained the pinnacle of success in business, combining his understanding of those habits with techniques of speech and theatrical presentation in classes he offered through the YMCA beginning in 1912. His aim was to train young men who were intent on business careers with a style of personal presentation, emphasizing both manner and speech, that would assure success. Although it may seem that Carnegie's approach was essentially secular, it presumed an appreciation of mainstream Protestant values that infused the religious world of the Midwest from which he came and that undergirded the program of the YMCA in his day.

Carnegie first systematized his approach in a series of pamphlets that he collected together in a work clearly aimed at white Protestant men whose identities were shaped by the world of business. He titled its first edition *Public Speaking: A Practical Course for the Businessman* when it appeared in 1926, although it was better known by its later title, *Public Speaking and Influencing Men in Business.*[13] Like all clusters of images promoting white male spirituality, those in Carnegie's system were intended to be practical, to have direct benefits in the realm of human relations. It did not promote an otherworldly devotionalism or have much to do with the particulars of belief and doctrine. In a nutshell, to influence men in business was to tap into a realm of power that would bring positive results to the man who had that ability, results that could be concretely measured in terms of material success. Individual men who associated that power with the God of Protestant Christianity could effectively link their faith and their spirituality to their success in business.

In what Donald Meyer has called "one of those pulse points in modern American popular culture,"[14] Carnegie transformed his program almost to the level of sacred writ when he published *How to Win Friends and Influence People,* a book that sold more than thirty million copies before Carnegie's death in 1955 and remains in print in the twenty-first century.[15] Meyer recognized that ethical principles drawn from mainstream Protestantism lay at the heart of Carnegie's approach when he summarized it as an "ethic of cooperation."[16] But Meyer suggests that there was also an element of deception in what Carnegie taught, a substratum that would seem to undermine its promoting a constellation of values and practices consonant with white Protestant male spirituality and notions of the ideal Christian man. To understand Meyer's critique and to modify it, one must first understand exactly what Carnegie tried to instill in his readers, in his audiences on the lecture tours that followed publication of *How to Win Friends and Influence People,* and in the thousands—mostly men—who took courses at the hundreds of branches of the Dale Carnegie Institute for Effective Speaking and Human Relations that were established in metropolitan areas across the United States and in numerous other countries.

At the core of Carnegie's message was the conviction that every man possessed an inner reservoir of strength that he could tap to create a persona exuding success. A man who called on that inner strength could transform not only his self-image but also the perception that others had of him. The use of masculine pronouns here is deliberate. In theory, Carnegie's approach is gender neutral; women could "win friends and influence people" as much as men. But when one scrutinizes Carnegie's text, it becomes apparent that Carnegie assumes that it is primarily men who will benefit from the scheme he presents. Most of Carnegie's illustrations, for example, were men. Salesmen appeared with regularity, selling not only a product but themselves. And they were selling themselves not only to others, ranging from potential employers to potential customers, but more important, they were selling themselves to themselves. Much of what Carnegie offered is similar to any version of what has become popularly known as "self-help." Yet there was more to Carnegie's method than self-help; there was a way of understanding human nature and how the world works that gave his strategy spiritual force.

Carnegie recognized that all men would like to seem important and that such a sensibility was practically impossible without a sense of self-worth. The basic practical step that he urged men to take to gain this self-worth was almost too simple. All one had to do was learn to smile at others. A man did not smile because he was in a good mood or pleased about circumstances; rather, he smiled because of the results it got. A man who smiled made others feel good about themselves and, conversely, about the man himself. The downside is that there is a fairly negative appraisal of human nature behind this technique, for it implies that men are fundamentally egocentric or that they like signals of their own importance from others. In turn, one's response to the individual who smiles is positive. The effect continues because that positive response likewise signals that the man who is smiling is himself a person of worth and deserving of acknowledgment.

Donald Meyer claims that Carnegie thus makes insincerity the basic ingredient in human relations.[17] He notes that Carnegie does not affirm the classic but simplistic liberal Protestant moralism of loving others simply because they are also creatures fashioned by God or because altruism is perceived as a Christian virtue. The insincerity comes in the motivation for treating others beneficently. A man smiles not because he wants to but because others like receiving smiles. There is a two-sided aspect of self-interest at play here, although Meyer emphasizes only one of them. The first is the self-interest of the person receiving the smiles of another. Meyer stresses that an almost Hobbesian understanding of human nature undergirds Carnegie's approach at this point, insisting that the man who smiles actually becomes more vulnerable to the power of others by pandering to their sense of self-importance.[18]

Self-interest of a different sort is also at work. A man smiles at someone whose power can work for his own advantage. Therefore he smiles in anticipation of the good that will come to him because of the gesture. Either way, self-interest, not the common good or postulates about the importance of loving all men, motivates the man who would "win friends and influence people." Yet even Meyer admits there is more to this program, for he notes that Carnegie made being insincere into a way of living that was itself sincere. A man could be genuinely sincere about trying to please others, to disarm them, and to cooperate with them. It may not have mattered that in an empirical sense a man still remained vulnerable and was also disarming himself in the process.

Precisely here, however, is where a spiritual dimension enters, allowing us to include the images presented by Carnegie among the constellation of symbols promoting the distinctive white male spirituality associated with the Christian man as positive thinker. Other voices will articulate that spiritual dimension more forcefully, but it is here in embryonic form. If one role of spirituality is to provide a sense of wholeness to life, then the techniques advanced by Carnegie are spiritual ones. To cultivate a perception of the self as being a success is to make a commitment that embraces the whole of a man's being. It is as vital a commitment as that made by the Puritan dutiful patriarch to an understanding of male behavior as reflective of divine behavior. That commitment alone lifts up a spiritual aspect of the positive thinker. There is also as clear a link to work and action in the world with Carnegie's approach as there was with that of the Christian gentleman entrepreneur. After all, the man with a positive, constructive self-image saw himself as a success primarily in the world of work; the simple smile was only a tactic to achieve success or perhaps just the perception of success.

Carnegie did not offer explicit guidance in any of the traditional disciplines of spirituality, such as prayer and meditation, Bible reading, or other acts of devotion. However, it is clear that he himself understood that his approach had a spiritual anchor and provided images to nurture the spiritual life of American men. Decades later when Norman Vincent Peale promulgated a more patently religious style in his wildly popular *The Power of Positive Thinking*, he acknowledged the similarities between his idea of the positive thinker and Carnegie's notion of the man who could win friends and influence people. Peale also called attention to a personal spirituality that sustained Carnegie as an individual. In his own discussion of how men could develop techniques of relaxation that would in turn provide a context for easing stress and promoting better use of time, Peale observed that it was Dale Carnegie's custom, when he was under tremendous pressure and consumed by inner tension, to go "to a church near his New York City office to spend a quarter-hour in prayerful meditation. He says he leaves his office for this when busiest."[19]

Neither Peale nor Carnegie commented on what went into that prayerful meditation or even whether Carnegie had a formal affiliation with this particular church. Neither is important in the context of most Protestant images of white male spirituality or models of the ideal Christian man, for none emphasizes the specifics of belief, matters of doctrine, or the content of exercises like meditation. What matters is what results in the arena of self-awareness and how a dynamic understanding of the self carries over into relationships with associates in the world of work and business. Real men pray.

Carnegie's work appeared when the nation was still in the grips of economic depression. In one sense, if one measured success simply in terms of actual wealth, there would be fewer and fewer men who would be acclaimed as successes. Even the efficient businessman epitomized by Bruce Barton could not be assured of continued economic gain, given the precariousness of the global economy. Part of the attractiveness of Carnegie's image of the man who sees himself as a success and smiles to break down the power of others stems from the economic uncertainties of the Great Depression.

As unemployment soared and wages plummeted, men whose sense of self-worth was inextricably tied to work and the status provided by a job were confronted with the challenge of affirming a positive identity despite the conditions that surrounded them. By calling on men to muster and master a positive self-image, to present themselves—indeed, to sell themselves—as men who were successful was to provide a positive spiritual counterpoint to the deleterious effects of economic depression and collapse. In the end, it made little difference that Carnegie devoted almost no attention to the phenomenon of friendship; what did matter was that he taught a strategy for promoting a viable self-image that drew on the inner strength, the inner spirit, of American men.

In an earlier age, as we have noted, many men buttressed their spiritual sensibility through involvement in fraternal orders and lodges where, through rituals and through associations with other men, they received reinforcement of what it meant for a man to be a spiritual being, often drawing on the images associated with the spirituality of the Christian man as gentleman entrepreneur or courageous adventurer. Membership in such associations declined rather significantly in the 1930s, just as Carnegie was promoting an alternative vision. One reason for that decline may be that in an age of economic depression, fewer and fewer men could afford the dues and membership fees that went with membership in a lodge or fraternal group.

Here, too, emerge other grounds for the plausibility of Carnegie's far more individualistic approach. In Carnegie's scheme, one did not need the reinforcement that came from association with others to have a viable way of affirming self-worth. The man who set out to "win friends and influence people" needed only himself and the force of his own spiritual strength to develop and sustain a sense of self-worth. From the perspective of institutional religion, even the mainline Protestantism that shaped Carnegie's world, that individualistic emphasis likewise meant that a man of spiritual strength might not find membership in a congregation essential to maintaining a sense of meaning and purpose in life.

The Quest for Peace, Happiness, and Success

The practical dimensions of spirituality basic to Carnegie's kind of individualism had obvious links to the heritage of self-help implicit in the spirituality of the Christian man as courageous adventurer. That pragmatic emphasis took fresh shape in the years immediately after the close of World War II, finding its most popular expression in the writings of Norman Vincent Peale that concentrated on the "power of positive thinking." Peale's book by that title topped the best-seller lists for nearly three years after it appeared in 1952, the same year that Dwight Eisenhower was first elected to the presidency. Yet even before 1952, there were other hints that practical results would dominate images of white male spirituality in the years after Allied victory in Europe and the Pacific became reality. The end of war suggested that peace had returned to the world, but the ominous threat of communism and cold war, together with the social transformations that swept through an American society attempting to reintegrate millions of military personnel into the civilian work force, meant that millions found a different kind of peace missing from their lives, an inner peace that went well beyond contentment.

Among the first voices to probe a spirituality that made this kind of peace its focus was that of a Jewish rabbi, Joshua Loth Liebman, from Boston's Temple Israel. Liebman's best-known work, however, found the bulk of its readership among Christians. Called simply *Peace of Mind*,[20] Liebman's book tapped deeply into Freudian psychology and some of the latent hostility to traditional theological constructions that Freud's thought embodied. Liebman was not intentionally addressing matters of spirituality, certainly not specifically those linked to white male spirituality. But his book, which went through thirty printings between its appearance in 1946 and the release of a paper cover edition in 1955, helped set the stage for those, like Norman Vincent Peale, who did pick up on such matters. Liebman also captured well the anxiety of the postwar years, with its concern for challenges to peace of mind brought by such social issues as the potential for global destruction symbolized by the atomic bomb as well as more personal matters such as marital happiness or satisfaction in one's work. Indeed, the broader net that Liebman cast no doubt extended the appeal of his work well beyond American Jews, for he touched on a human angst that seemed the daily fare for much humanity.

As Carnegie before him and Peale after him, Liebman addressed issues of self-worth, calling for his readers to accept themselves and to banish inferiority complexes in order to release the inner potential for love that would eliminate fear—whether such fears were the result of neuroses, hostility, or even economic conditions.[21] At least one aspect of Liebman's psychotheology did have ramifications for male spirituality, although its full force was perhaps not realized among white Protestant men for a generation or more. Liebman at one point called for a "new God" for America.[22] This proposal, which historian Martin E. Marty noted was "hardly modest,"[23] derived from both Freud's and Liebman's identification of judgmental father figures as negative forces in human life. Liebman believed that a dominant father figure signaled a repressive force that kept a man from realizing his full potential. The threat of judgment and punishment throttled individual achievement; it denied the force of inner strength by making impossible external standards the criteria for determining self-worth and thus for attaining peace of mind.

In place of such a father figure, Liebman offered a God who affirmed the worth of each individual and who thus blessed personal pursuits apart from absolute standards. Men should think of themselves, wrote Liebman, "as *responsible co-workers with God*" who would therefore find "Divinity not primarily through mystical surrender, but through practical moral activity."[24] The practical aspect stoked the fires of Peale's positive thinking.

Liebman's benevolent validater God also undermined some of the images associated with the dutiful patriarch that had long sustained male spirituality and self-understanding. Most obviously missing, for example, was the idea of the dominant Father/father, a concept Liebman believed out of step with the mood of postwar America. Later, however, the generation that advanced a constellation of new images associated with the spirituality of the Christian man as faithful leader would seek to recapture some of the religious authority capsuled in the idea of the dutiful patriarch. Those who did were convinced that Liebman's approach, with its concomitant understandings of more fluid male roles and a less-well-defined masculinity, had fostered a self-centeredness among American men that had deleterious results not only for men themselves but also for their families and for American society as a whole.

Nonetheless, Liebman's blending of psychology and theology helped cement a sense that whatever else spirituality might involve, it had a practical character that promoted a sense of personal well-being and happiness. Liebman was not alone in sensing that a practical, pragmatic tactic would receive a favorable hearing in the postwar religious climate. In 1949, three years after Liebman's book dazzled the American spiritual imagination, Roman Catholic Archbishop Fulton J. Sheen released his *Peace of Soul*.[25] As Liebman tapped an audience that extended well beyond the orbit of American Judaism, so too Sheen was a figure whose impact transcended his Catholic identity, which was always obvious since he wore traditional clerical garb in public. Sheen had extraordinary gifts of communication, first realized when he launched *The Catholic Hour* on the NBC radio network in 1930 and then continued in his two popular television series on ABC, *Life Is Worth Living* (1955–57) and *The Bishop Sheen Hour* (1961–68). *Peace of Soul*, however, was something of a veiled attack on the Freudian narcissism that Sheen and others criticized in Liebman's work.

Sheen and Liebman shared a common starting point, namely, that modern man wallowed in confusion, unhappiness, and failure. To be sure, if pressed, Sheen would have included modern woman in his appraisal, but a careful reading of his work reveals that males, unhappy at home and work and adrift in their sense of personal anxiety, are at the heart of his understanding. What postwar American men living in fear of atomic destruction and personal inadequacy needed was not simply inner peace or the peace of mind Rabbi Liebman touted. Rather, for Sheen, always a traditional Catholic theologian at base, the practical remedy came through a spirituality that still affirmed the necessity of belief in a supernatural force whose power and order brought enduring, not superficial, well-being—peace of soul, not simply peace of mind.

Sheen was careful not to dwell on the content of such belief or demonstrably claim that only within a Roman Catholic framework could a man find peace of soul. Donald Meyer has argued that the legitimacy and sufficiency of Catholic identification was fundamental to Sheen's position and that Sheen was intentionally not only promoting the viability of a Catholic identity but also encouraging his followers to abandon their Protestant allegiance for a Catholic one.[26] Sheen himself was never that direct; even when he wrote in the final chapter of *Peace of Soul* about the salutary benefits of conversion in bringing order and wholeness to a man's life, he talked about the effects of an abiding personal unity within a man's soul, not about Roman Catholicism per se. At the same time, the man who had peace of soul was an object of both envy and opposition, the latter reinforcing Meyer's conviction that Sheen was keenly aware of a residual anti-Catholicism in American culture.

However, what Sheen wrote also echoed the spirituality long nurtured by white American men, particularly Protestant men. The man who was converted, who had found peace of soul, would discover that his "friends will intuitively know that he no longer shares the spirit of the world, that he is now governed by Spirit, is lifted into a truly supernatural order, is united with Divinity in a special way, which is a challenge and reproach to those who would make the best of two worlds."[27]

Protestant thinkers were quick to offer their own contributions to a spirituality that offered results—peace, happiness, and success. On the surface, the most obvious cognate to Liebman's *Peace of Mind* and Sheen's *Peace of Soul* came from Baptist revivalist Billy Graham, who was just beginning to gain name recognition across the American religious spectrum when he published the first edition of his *Peace with God* in 1953.[28] Unabashedly evangelical in his approach, Graham insisted that no peace—whether peace of mind or peace of soul or even world peace—was possible without a prior peace with God that resulted only from a traditional conversion experience involving repentance and belief in Jesus Christ as savior.

If Graham intended to offer an evangelical Protestant counterpoint to Rabbi Liebman and Archbishop Sheen, he found his effort eclipsed by fellow Protestant Norman Vincent Peale. Peale also proclaimed a vision of spirituality that had white American men as its target audience and a practical, results-based system at its center. Indeed, Peale offered the classic argument for the spirituality of the white Christian man as positive thinker in a way that did not require the public expression of making a "decision for Christ" that capped the sermons of Graham.

Peale was already a significant personality on the American religious landscape when *The Power of Positive Thinking* brought even greater fame. His carefully honed, unaffected preaching style and his ability to promote his ministry had seen Methodist churches that he had pastored in Brooklyn and Syracuse, New York, experience stunning growth, when, in 1932, he accepted the pastorate of a struggling congregation affiliated with the Reformed Church in America, the Marble Collegiate Church in Manhattan. Shortly after beginning his work there, Peale began what became a long and rewarding association with psychiatrist Smiley Blanton, who became a major influence in prodding Peale to think through connections that tied together spirituality, religious faith, mental health, and personal well-being. Together, the two established the still flourishing Blanton-Peale Institute of Religion and Health, with several branches around the country, and wrote two books that really set out the themes that later would be associated almost exclusively with Peale.[29]

Like Sheen, Peale also was a figure in religious radio, in 1933 starting *The Art of Living* program that aired for forty years. Peale took its title for his first single-authored book in 1937, expanding on his lifelong conviction that Christian faith had practical benefits for everyday living. Two other books, *You Can Win* and *A Guide to Confident Living*, outlined his pragmatic spirituality before he submitted the draft of his most well known work to Prentice-Hall under the designation "The Power of Faith."[30] A deft editor suggested changing "faith" to "positive thinking," in part to increase the appeal of the book for those who did not already see themselves as religious. More than half a century later, *The Power of Positive Thinking* remains in print, a testimony to its impact on the spiritual life of all Americans, not just that of white American men.

On the surface, like the programs of Dale Carnegie and Joshua Loth Liebman, Peale's system does not come across as directed exclusively to men. Indeed, there is nothing in the strategies for positive thinking that Peale develops that is in any way necessarily restricted to men. But a close examination of what Peale has to say, particularly the examples on which he draws, suggests that Peale knew full well that his primary audience was male. A quick survey of the text of the 1952 edition of *The Power of Positive Thinking* reveals that of all the cases Peale cites of persons who had problems that were overcome through the techniques associated with positive thinking, more than 80 percent centered on men. Even in those cases in which the experience of a woman was the focus, very often the woman faced difficulty because of the behavior of a husband or son; hence men were not far removed even from these cases.

Even more, it is clear that Peale assumed that his audience had a broadly Protestant bent and consisted primarily of persons who had careers in business or the professions. In other words, upwardly mobile white-collar white Protestant men made up his target audience. One need note only the frequency with which Peale introduces an example drawn from life by noting that he had recently been talking with a businessman at a Rotary Club meeting or some such similar venue where the overwhelming bulk of those in attendance would come from the ranks of the urban, white Protestant middle class.[31]

In the opening chapter on the importance the positive thinker should attach to believing in himself, a construct reminiscent of Dale Carnegie, Peale notes, for example, that the ideas for the book came to him after he had spoken at an otherwise unidentified businessmen's convention. They coalesced in his mind as he reflected on his own rather unhappy boyhood when he felt inadequate both because he was extraordinarily shy and because he felt held to unfairly high standards of achievement and moral behavior as a "preacher's kid." As Peale unfolds his method on how every man can become a positive thinker and release enormous spiritual energy, he does make connections to more obvious religious practice.

In the fourth chapter, titled "Try Prayer Power," Peale summarizes his method in three steps. The positive thinker confronting any situation over which he wishes to have power and energetic control should first "prayerize" his dilemma and the desired outcome. Peale frequently exhorts the positive thinker to pray; real men pray. What he does not do is offer instruction in how to pray or how to nurture the spiritual discipline of prayer.

Second, the positive thinker should "picturize" the desired result, usually in terms of some success in work or business or an improvement in domestic relations. Later generations would talk about techniques of visualization. Peale meant much the same. A man should imagine or visualize a situation, assuming that all went well, and keep doing so for an extended period. Peale was not talking about the desired result's occurring as soon as a man had a mental picture of what he wanted. In some of the examples, individuals had to sustain such mental visualization over many weeks or months.

Finally, a man could then "actualize" that which was desired. The assumption was that over time conditions would become such that a man would almost be assured of attaining the goal. Peale recognized that this three-step approach did not have much specific theological content. Nor did it dwell on precisely what a man had to do in order to pray. In keeping with the business milieu, Peale noted that he advocated studying "prayer from the efficiency point of view." The results, not the doctrine or discipline, mattered in the spirituality of the white Christian man as positive thinker.

The practical thrust of positive thinking and the white male spirituality associated with it received reinforcement when Peale wrote about the power men possessed to solve personal problems. One might assume that personal problems referred primarily to issues such as flawed marriage relationships, a sense of individual unhappiness, or the malaise that accompanied a lack of focus and direction in life. But when *The Power of Positive Thinking* first led the best-seller lists, the examples that Dr. Peale offered when talking about personal problems had to do with success on the job.

Here, too, Peale's approach suggests that he believed that white-collar, professional or managerial Protestant men constituted his primary readership and that the personal problems they confronted were those that plagued middle- or upper-class white men in general, not those challenging factory workers or common laborers. The spiritual power inherent in the positive thinker was a force that could generate new ideas for the businessman. It pointed to a spiritual strength that paid off in concrete assets. His advice was direct and to the point: "Whenever you get a chance to talk to businessmen tell them that if they will take God as their partner in their business they will get more good ideas than they can ever use, and they can turn those ideas into assets."[32] In a subsequent chapter, Peale proclaimed that all men could think their way either to failure or to success, but that those committed to the values emerging from the spirituality of the positive thinker, those who had perfected "optimistic visualization," were possessed of a faith that could conquer all kinds of negativeness.[33] They were the ideal white Protestant Christian men.

Peale founded his popular *Guideposts* magazine to provide testimonies to the power of this pragmatic faith. In time, *Guideposts* offered many stories featuring women who turned to positive thinking, perhaps because women have long constituted the bulk of the readership of religiously oriented periodicals. In the inaugural edition of *The Power of Positive Thinking*, however, examples featuring women rather than Protestant businessmen were in the majority in only one chapter, that dealing with the connection between faith and physical healing.[34] Perhaps Peale was unwittingly endorsing the cultural image of the woman as nurse and caregiver to the sick, even though in the early 1950s most medical doctors were still men. Ironically, in this discussion of positive thinking and physical health, when Peale mustered medical authorities to buttress his claims about the practical power of faith to effect physical healing, the majority of physicians quoted or otherwise cited likewise were female. Otherwise, the positive thinker and the spirituality that it denoted were overwhelmingly part of the world of Protestant businessmen.

The spirituality of positive thinking remained linked with Peale until his death in 1993 and continued in the twenty-first century to be associated with the various publishing and counseling enterprises he established to carry on his work after his death. His brief foray into politics in the 1960 presidential campaign, when he endorsed Richard Nixon and questioned John F. Kennedy's ability to serve because of Kennedy's Roman Catholic affiliation, brought stinging criticism. Peale quickly abandoned political comment and returned to promoting positive thinking and its benefits. His later works, including *The Amazing Results of Positive Thinking, The Tough-Minded Optimist, You Can If You Think You Can*, and *Power of the Plus Factor*, simply repeated and rephrased the formula of prayerize, picturize, and actualize. Even Peale's *The True Joy of Positive Living: An Autobiography*, published when he was eighty-six, is a paean to his system.[35] But none enjoyed the success of *The Power of Positive Thinking*.

From the outset, though, Peale's version of the spirituality of the white Christian man as positive thinker attracted critics. Among the earliest was William Lee Miller, whose essay on "The Gospel of Norman Vincent Peale" was widely reprinted after it first appeared in 1955. Miller also devoted considerable attention to an analysis of positive thinking in his study of the casual connections between an unthinking patriotism and popular spirituality in *Piety Along the Potomac*.[36] Miller believed that Peale had too casually transformed Christian spirituality into a gospel of success, a mental process that presumed the innate goodness of all men and therefore avoided the deeper theological issues of sin and redemption. Spirituality in Peale's hands became a device to cope with times that were bad and times that were good and for maintaining a positive self-image even when one did not truly realize within himself the happiness that was presumed to accompany positive thinking and success. Instead of the gospel, Miller contended, Peale proclaimed a strategy for successful living.

Yet herein also lay the genius of the spirituality of the white Christian man as positive thinker. Like the images for white male spirituality and models of the Christian man from the dutiful patriarch to the courageous adventurer, the image of the positive thinker resonated with American Protestant men precisely because it was devoid of heavy theological content. To wed the spirituality of the positive thinker to particulars of belief or creed would have been to divorce it from the practical results that Peale and those before him wanted from a program for Protestant men that would give a sense of spiritual fulfillment and virtually guarantee that life would have a sense of order and enduring meaning. At the same time, Peale's strategy was particularly suited for the 1950s, when American men were seeking a way to give life meaning now that the decades of Depression and war were presumably over. But the spirituality of the positive thinker proved less wedded to time than others; in the hands of some whom Peale influenced, it took on new facets that gave it increased viability for decades after.

From Positive Thinking to Possibility Thinking

Some writers who attempted to craft spiritual images for the American reading public, male and female alike, were more obviously overt in using the language of popular psychology, but without necessarily drawing on that psychology as the basis for their programs of spiritual uplift. Charles L. Allen, for example, had a distinguished career as a pastor of large churches in Atlanta, Georgia, and then in Houston, Texas. To the casual observer, his book *God's Psychiatry,* which appeared in 1953, the year after Peale's *The Power of Positive Thinking* first dominated the best-seller list, would seem a simple amalgam of religious faith and self-help, as would his later work, *Roads to Radiant Living.*[37] But Allen made a bolder claim, that a traditional, commonsense understanding of Scripture made it manifest that all the principles associated with psychiatry were already available to the man of faith through the pages of the Bible.

Allen acknowledged the fascination with Peale and with positive thinking, yet he was hesitant to equate positive thinking with divine approbation. The man of faith, in Allen's reckoning, did not simply seek a self-gratifying peace of mind, for he might well encounter divine judgment in the process. Allen was reluctant to equate feeling good about one's self with authentic faith and spirituality. Sometimes a spiritual man would be uncomfortable with himself and with the world. Yet, like Peale, Allen drew most of his examples from the world of men, a move indicating that he, too, was concerned about advocating a posture that would resonate with the lived experience of middle-class and upper-class white Protestant men.

The one who took up where Peale left off and reshaped the spirituality of the positive thinker to render it viable for the next generation of American men was another clergyman affiliated with the Reformed Church in America, Robert Schuller, whose life will provide the case study for the spirituality of the positive thinker. Called to start a new church for the denomination, Schuller arrived in Orange County, California, in the mid-1950s, just as the Los Angeles area and much of southern California were entering a tremendous period of population growth and economic prosperity. Capitalizing on what he perceived as the more casual style of California life, Schuller took to preaching in a drive-in movie theater, where his congregation could remain in their cars, relaxed and carefree, rather than stifling in pews attired in "Sunday clothes."

The response was astounding, and Schuller continued to develop an approach that he had started as pastor of a struggling Reformed Church in America congregation outside Chicago after his graduation from seminary. Rather than adhering to the doctrinally based preaching in which he had been trained as a seminary student, he sought to address "real life" situations with a practical faith that brought results, especially for persons who regarded themselves as not having any particular religious affiliation.

Later acknowledging his debt to both Dale Carnegie and Norman Vincent Peale for the core of his approach to spirituality, and to Bishop Sheen for his understanding of communications,[38] Schuller labeled his method "possibility thinking." He captured its essence in what he called the "Possibility Creed":

> When faced with a mountain,
> I WILL NOT QUIT!
> I will keep striving until I climb over,
> Find a pass through,
> Tunnel underneath,
> Or simply stay
> And turn the mountain into a gold mine,
> With God's help![39]

Repeatedly, Schuller called on his listeners and readers to drop the word "impossible" from their vocabulary, for it fostered negative thinking that destroyed self-esteem and thwarted achieving both personal goals and what

God planned for their lives. To dwell on problems that might stand in the way of success was, for Schuller, to guarantee failure and assure that one would wallow in wrong decisions. In his autobiography, Schuller noted that from adolescence on he knew he was going "somewhere" if he heeded his own admonition: "Never let possible problems defeat your decisions."[40]

Clearly echoing Carnegie and Peale, Schuller advanced a technique that drew on both visualization and expectations of being regarded by others as a success. For example, he offered another capsule of possibility thinking by taking each letter of the word "strive" and attaching it to what was for him a spiritual principle:

> *S*tart small.
> *T*hink possibilities.
> *R*each beyond your known abilities.
> *I*nvest all you have in your dreams.
> *V*isualize miracles.
> *E*xpect to experience success.[41]

Spirituality for Schuller thus centered on a message of hope, not a message of condemning lost sinners or even one of doctrine and creed. "I was called to be a preacher, and I was called to preach hope, nothing more and nothing less," he observed as he prepared to hand over much of the day-to-day leadership of his still expanding ministry to his son, Robert A. Schuller, after he turned seventy-five.[42]

In his writing and preaching, Schuller was far more careful than Dale Carnegie or Norman Vincent Peale in his choice of language and examples. His wife, Arvella DeHaan, for example, as music director and then producer of Schuller's *Hour of Power* television program when it debuted in 1970, not only selected hymns but edited them to eliminate gender-specific language. At times she even paraphrased biblical texts to avoid what could be perceived as negative by the "unchurched" people who were the targets of Schuller's ministry.[43] Yet Schuller also took pains to direct much of his possibility thinking to men. For example, when Schuller began to invite successful people to tell their own stories as part of the *Hour of Power* services and telecasts, the vast majority of those who appeared were men, and, as with Carnegie and Peale, success was measured in terms of occupation and career. Among those who have appeared are political figures such as former president Gerald Ford and former vice president Al Gore, military figures such as Colin Powell (before he became secretary of state) and Norman Schwarzkopf, entertainment figures such as Gregory Peck and Charlton Heston, well-known psychologists such as William Glasser and Viktor

THE POSITIVE THINKER   163

Frankl, and business leaders such as MacDonald's founder Ray Croc. Most of the women, other than entertainers such as Mary Martin, have been individuals who overcame various kinds of hardship, personal tragedy, or other challenges (e.g., Rosa Parks, June Scobee Rogers, Coretta Scott King).

As with Carnegie and Peale, so with Schuller: the primary benchmark of vital spirituality for white Protestant Christian men is success in one's line of work, and the payoff for real success is happiness and the same sort of inner peace that Rabbi Joshua Loth Liebman had touted at the close of World War II. Schuller made the connection explicit in the title of one of his later works: *Peace of Mind through Possibility Thinking*.[44]

Schuller's "possibility thinking" had specific ramifications for how men understood their roles as husbands and fathers in ways that represent a natural extension of some of the familial concerns central to the spirituality of the white Christian man as dutiful patriarch. In looking at a man's role within the family, Schuller moved well beyond Carnegie and Peale. In *Power Ideas for a Happy Family*, first published in 1971 as *Power Ideas for Successful Families* and reprinted many times since 1972 under the newer title, Schuller compares the family with a benevolent autocracy, in which the husband is king who "holds court from time to time to confer what is best for all his subjects," including the queen (his wife) and all the princes (sons) and princesses (daughters). "Here is a government where every citizen has a hot line to the head of state."[45]

The spirituality of the possibility thinker does not mean that men are dictators or that men who seek to shape their lives through a vital faith are hoping to exercise unbridled power over their wives and children. Schuller provides eight guidelines for men as husbands and fathers: think positively, try positively, touch tenderly, talk positively, tune in positively, train children in positive morality, tackle problems positively, and trust positively.[46] The last is the one most directly related to male spirituality. Schuller begins his discussion of what it means to trust positively: "Now move ahead through life with a vital, happy, positive religious faith. Believe in God and be an inspiring father. Find faith. Live that faith. Practice that faith. Let that faith color your whole personality and you'll be a successful husband and father."[47]

What Schuller does not do is define exactly what faith is, what belief in God entails, how one practices faith, or even how one finds faith. In his spiritual autobiography, Schuller talked about his own commitment to prayer; real men did pray. But prayer was often a means of eliminating negative thoughts, looking within to imagine possibilities, and a conviction that God—however defined in a theological sense—wanted men to find success. Repeatedly, Schuller urged himself and those he counseled to make room in their dreams for God's plan. What he does not do is offer instruction in how to pray, how to nurture and cultivate what for many would be a traditional spiritual discipline.[48]

Regardless, for men with families, Schuller is convinced that his guidelines will not only produce the possibility and reality of happiness but also generate the self-esteem that Schuller sees at the center of the Christian gospel.[49] Although self-esteem is as vital to women as to men, it is essential to male spiritual images associated with the positive thinker. Without self-esteem, a man has no spiritual identity. With self-esteem, all things are possible, for self-esteem represents the unleashing of a vast reservoir of divine power within the self.

Reflections

For men whose hopes of success in business were dashed by global depression and for men whose lives were dramatically reoriented by military service in World War II, the spirituality of the positive thinker had much to offer. It provided for Protestant males who saw themselves as Christian men a way to gain the respect of others, both in the family and in the workplace. It promised a peace of mind and contentment that were hard to find in depression and war and then in cold war. It posited an inner strength that could transform dreams into reality and virtually assure achievement—material achievement—in the suburban culture of the postwar decades.

But there were subtle shifts in how the positive thinker took his rightful place in the world of home and business, shifts that resound through the writings of Dale Carnegie, Norman Vincent Peale, and Robert H. Schuller. For Carnegie, the primary thrust of positive thinking was outward-directed. It involved the creation of a persona that would receive the respect of others, usually those already at the pinnacles of success and influence in business, by tapping inner power, confidence, and self-assurance. In other words, the object of positive thinking was a change in the perception others had of a man determined by how that man projected himself on their consciousness. As with so many other expressions of white male spirituality, relationships with others were a primary focus and a practical result the most significant aim. Here the relationships were with those who were poised to help the individual man become a success in his own eyes and in the eyes of others, and the practical result came in the happiness and self-satisfaction that followed once success was attained.

None of that disappears in the construction of the spirituality of the white Christian man as positive thinker that emerges in the thought of Norman Vincent Peale, but there is a new twist. For Peale, positive thinking is not concerned only with how others view the individual man based on his own self-image. Peale pushes the psychological aspect of positive thinking more than Carnegie, for he promotes a technique for conquering inner fears, self-doubt, and misgivings about one's own abilities that brings a happiness and contentment transcending material success.

What made Peale's approach especially effective was the way in which it offered white American men a positive self-concept even if they were not dazzlingly successful in business or even if they were successful but did not believe they had attained the happiness that was presumed an automatic accompaniment of success. Peale's positive thinker is making a greater turn inward than the positive thinker based on Dale Carnegie's strategy.

That turning inward reaches its pinnacle in the possibility thinking of Robert Schuller and in his version of the spirituality of the positive thinker. By making self-esteem the heart of the gospel message, Schuller came close to leaving behind the pervasive presence of external relationships that propelled Carnegie's strategy. Schuller insisted that self-esteem, the power to transform every problem into a possibility, and the strength to recast every obstacle as an opportunity lay at the heart of vital faith. His version of the positive thinker may carry the danger of becoming a kind of egocentrism and self-centeredness. To be sure, Schuller himself avoided that trap by repeatedly emphasizing that self-esteem is the power of God in Christ within the individual and that the possibilities emerging from problems are linked to a divine plan, not merely self-aggrandizement. But the danger remains.

Such dangers did not confront only white American Protestant men whose spirituality was shaped by images of the positive thinker. In the decades after Peale dominated the best-seller lists, the United States and its religious culture underwent cataclysms that no one expected. From the civil rights movement to protesting the U.S. military engagement in Southeast Asia, from calls for women's liberation to controversy over issues such as homosexuality that still divide Americans, the larger society witnessed a burgeoning interest in all kinds of self-esteem. Ethnic groups again found a corporate dignity in celebrating their unique heritages. Women in the home and workplace shattered conceptions of patriarchy by asserting their own self-esteem apart from roles subordinate to men. Spirituality became ever more a privatized journey to an unknown destination.[50] The constellation of images associated with the spirituality of the white Christian man as positive thinker did seem to yield a self-centered narcissism. In time, another layer of images would be added to those of the positive thinker, the complex of spiritual ideas linked to the faithful leader.

In Focus
Robert H. Schuller: Preacher and Positive Thinker

In his autobiography, Robert Schuller repeatedly referred to his childhood as the son of a Dutch American farming family in northwestern Iowa. Even at the seeming pinnacle of success as a world-renowned preacher and writer, he was still fond of pointing out that a dead-end dirt road that had no formal name led to the farm and home where he was raised. It was a street without a name that led to nowhere.[51] At time of his birth to Anthony and Jennie Beltman Schuller on August 16, 1926, the youngest of their three daughters and two sons, Schuller was known by his middle name, Harold. When an uncle who was a missionary visited the family, Schuller determined that one day he would be a preacher, although he had not yet started school. Decades later, his father would tell him that he had hoped from the time of his last child's birth that the boy would become a preacher. But the image of the preacher held up by the Schuller family was something rather different from what Robert Harold Schuller became.

Within the enclave of Dutch American immigrants, the Reformed Church in America held sway. Tracing its American roots to 1628 and the Dutch colonial settlement on New York's Manhattan Island, the Dutch Reformed Church had a well-deserved reputation for adhering to a rather stringent understanding of Calvinist Reformed theology, with its emphasis on human depravity and sinfulness. The Dominee or preacher was consequently a rather austere figure, whose sermons explicated the nuances of Reformed doctrinal construction, intent on preserving the purity of the faith and maintaining proper order in the congregation.

Preaching in the pastures and sometimes having rows of corn for a congregation, Schuller envisioned himself promulgating the pure Reformed doctrine of his childhood church. Respect went with the role of preacher, but not always self-esteem. As a child, Schuller was rather pudgy and also awkward when it came to strenuous physical activity, even the basic chores that went with a farm boyhood. More than half a century later, when he wrote his autobiography, he could still recall some moments of despair and feelings of a total lack of self-worth as a child. Particularly vivid were occasions when, at the one-room schoolhouse where his aunt taught all eight grades, teams would be chosen for games during recess. It seemed that young Harold was always the last to be chosen, and even as a grade-school child he became keenly aware of how this sign of rejection by classmates and peers harbored within himself a sense of worthlessness and despair. Nonetheless, he remained convinced that somehow someday he would leave behind that nameless road that went nowhere for an unknown "somewhere" where he would have a positive sense of self-worth.

After graduation from high school at the age of sixteen, Harold headed to Holland, Michigan, another center of Dutch American Reformed life, where he enrolled first at Hope College, a denominational school, and then the Reformed Church's Western Theological Seminary, also in Holland. As a student, Robert—for that was the name by which he was now known—distinguished himself for his dedication and diligence, somehow finding time to organize a traveling quartet that toured the country. Mishaps that came to the young men while on the road, such as flat tires or mechanical problems with the dilapidated car that they were using, became occasions when Robert emerged as a voice of hope. No obstacle should or could stand in the way of these college boys if indeed they were doing the work of God. Problems were only possibilities in disguise.

While a seminary student, Schuller had become acquainted with the ministry of Norman Vincent Peale, whose Marble Collegiate Church in New York City was the oldest congregation of the Reformed Church in America. At the time, however, he did not realize that "Peale was my future."[52] Schuller and his fellow seminarians were also familiar with the techniques promoted by Dale Carnegie, although Carnegie was regarded with disdain and dismissed as a shallow thinker by theological students for whom the intricacies of doctrinal disputation represented not only true learning but also the stuff of preaching necessary to sustain the faith. Schuller already had a reputation for skill as a preacher, winning awards as a seminary student for the quality and substance of his sermons.

After graduation from seminary in 1950, Schuller accepted a call to become pastor of a struggling and deeply divided thirty-five-member congregation in Riverdale, Illinois. Within a few weeks, he was ordained to the ministry of the Reformed Church and married to Arvella DeHaan, the sister of one of his friends from adolescence. Although Schuller was following all that he had learned in seminary, for several months he seemed to make little headway in healing the internal rifts within his congregation or in stimulating the growth that would assure its future. It did not take him long to realize that the negativity that surrounded him was deleterious to his ministry and that his focus on doctrine in preaching, although based on patterns he had mastered as a student, had little relevance even for the few faithful folks who came to church Sunday after Sunday. He began to reevaluate what he had once so casually dismissed, namely, the strategies proposed by Dale Carnegie in *How to Win Friends and Influence People* and by Norman Vincent Peale in the book that was about to top the best-seller lists, *The Power of Positive Thinking*.

Schuller concluded that both Carnegie and Peale—and thus the spirituality centered around the white Christian man as positive thinker—offered a practical understanding of Christian faith that related to real life situations in a way that stiff doctrinal discourses did not. Years later, he would write that the "effect of Peale's and Carnegie's theories on my theology and methodology of church work would prove nothing short of amazing."[53] The secret of success for Christian ministry lay not in outworn formulas but in finding a need that ordinary people had and setting out to fill it.

As he began to refocus his preaching and his pastoral ministry, emphasizing positive thinking and transforming problems into possibilities, the Ivanhoe Reformed Church began to grow. By the time Schuller, his wife, and two children (Sheila was born in 1951 and Robert Anthony in 1954) left Illinois, the congregation had grown more than tenfold and the young pastor was gaining a reputation within Reformed Church circles as someone with extraordinary gifts and skills. Positive thinking paid off in practical results. Not only was the congregation healthy, but its pastor was a success, finding fulfillment in overcoming whatever challenges came his way.

The Possibilities of a California Ministry

On March 27, 1955, Robert Schuller preached his first sermon in a drive-in movie theater in Orange County, California. Called to start a new church in an area where the population was growing rapidly and where there were few persons of the ethnic backgrounds that had stocked the Reformed Church in generations past, Schuller was confronted with what seemed an impossibility: finding a location where he could hold services. Positive thinking and prayer brought results. After all, real men pray.

Although conducting services in a drive-in theater was a new venture, it represented another instance of turning an obstacle into an opportunity, of finding a possibility in a problem. Then as throughout much of his career, Schuller had his own understanding of prayer. For him, prayer was not so much petition or even thanksgiving but a seeking for strength not to stand in the way of what God envisioned. In this case, if God wanted a Reformed

Church congregation to establish itself in Orange County, then God would unfold the possibilities to allow a congregation to emerge.

The story of Schuller's drive-in enterprise is well known, for the new tactic met with almost instant success. Soon there was need for land for a building. Securing adequate funding seemed impossible. Once again positive thinking yielded results. Then and in countless other cases throughout Schuller's ministry, when money—sometimes a million dollars or more—was needed to launch a new venture or deadlines for signing documents, making payments, or entering formal legal agreements were near without the necessary money having been secured, an unsolicited check in the precise amount required (or often more) would appear. When all, including at times Schuller himself, were ready to give up hope, the possibilities for success suddenly and unexpectedly appeared. Over the years, Schuller developed a quiet confidence that if he could banish negativity and step aside from interfering in God's making divine dreams come true, opportunities for ministry would always emerge.

When Schuller and architects prepared plans for the Tower of Hope on what was to become a new and ever-expanding campus, codes restricting the height of buildings seemed to thwart the majestic structure that Schuller saw in his dreams. But a new design topped by a ninety-two-foot cross met both the codes and the dream. Positive thinking brought results. More than a decade later, when the Crystal Cathedral, basically an all-glass structure, was in the design stages, the problems that threatened to doom the project were not only monetary. Because of the dangers that could result from earthquake damage to a glass structure, new building codes about to go into effect would have scuttled Schuller's dream permanently. Yet again the problem was transformed into possibility when the design for the structure was approved by local authorities just days before the new codes would have prohibited its construction. Positive thinking had concrete, practical results. Faith was not abstract doctrine but a conviction that all things were indeed possible if one believed they were possible.

Although Schuller has reached millions through his televised *Hour of Power* service, which debuted on a California station in February 1970, he has also been a best-selling author, sharing the spirituality of the white Christian man as positive thinker with millions more. In the early 1980s, for example, he published two wildly popular books, *Tough Times Never Last, but Tough People Do* (his first to make the *New York Times* best-seller list) and then *Tough-Minded Faith for Tender-Hearted People*. For a time in 1983, both were on the *New York Times* list of top-selling books in the nation. His 1982 book *Self-Esteem: The New Reformation* achieved extraordinary circulation after a business tycoon, impressed with the practical results of positive thinking as conveyed in Schuller's possibility thinking, purchased and then distributed a quarter of a million copies to clergy across the country. Schuller himself regarded *Self-Esteem: The New Reformation* as one of his more important theological contributions, for he believed that he would not be taken seriously by Protestant theologians until he produced a work that carried some sort of endorsement from leading Protestant scholars. With some satisfaction, Schuller saw another possibility become reality when University of Chicago church historian Martin E. Marty agreed to read and critique the manuscript of *Self-Esteem* prior to its publication.

Self-Esteem and the Spiritual Life

Those who have analyzed Schuller's thought and ministry recognize that there is considerable value in his strategy of positive/possibility thinking and the spirituality that revolves around it. Dennis Voskuil, for example, believes Schuller's approach is important because it affirms the pivotal role self-esteem plays in human life. It provides a viable alternative to the negative theology that has plagued much of American Protestant evangelicalism with its emphasis on sin and human weakness. It also gives a central role to the Christian gospel as the foundation for self-esteem.[54] At the same time, Schuller reorients traditional teaching about sin, striving to deemphasize its negative connotations. He recasts sin and even the Reformed doctrine of human depravity into an inability to grasp one's essential self-worth as part of a divine creation and a failure to link latent inner potential to divine power. In sum, Schuller's message represents a valiant effort to render Christian spirituality plausible for the generation of men who came of age surrounded by memories of depression and war, haunted by threats of nuclear destruction, and burdened by the increasing complexities of the social order in the last half of the twentieth century.

Like his preaching, after he abandoned rigorous doctrinal discourse for the practical spirituality of positive thinking, Schuller's books speak in simple, straightforward language to ordinary folks who are looking for some anchor in their lives. The spirituality of the white Christian man as positive thinker provides a toughness, a resilient power, that enables one to withstand and even rise above the vicissitudes of life. Toughness here is not callous disregard for others through wanton use or misuse of power, but a rugged and stalwart perseverance, a refusal to give in to problems and difficulties, a conviction that new life emerges from every potential defeat.

Here, too, is where Schuller's possibility thinking as a fulcrum for personal spirituality embraces not just white Protestant men. More than most Protestant writers of the 1970s and 1980s, Schuller was particularly careful to avoid sexism in his language construction, although he did continue to use male referents for God. Although more of his examples of public success are male, examples of those who achieved triumph in their personal lives through the spirituality of positive thinking include both females and males. Schuller's work as pastor and counselor reinforced his conviction that self-esteem was a need for women, just as it was for men.

Positive thinking had implications not only for Schuller's theology. Its import went deeper even than a ministry that ultimately included a counseling center, an institute for church growth, a weekly television program aired throughout the world, various mission endeavors, and scores of activities involving the ten thousand–plus members of the Garden Grove Community Church, the first of the megachurches in later-twentieth-century U.S. religious life. Possibility thinking had very personal dimensions.

Between the fall of 1975, when plans to construct the Crystal Cathedral got underway, and September 1980, when the first services were conducted in the new structure (albeit with severe acoustical problems yet to be resolved), Schuller and his family confronted several personal crises. After moving to California, Schuller and his wife had three more children, all daughters: Jeanne Anne (1957), Carol Lynn (1964), and Gretchen Joy (1967). When she was a teenager, Carol suffered severe injuries in a motorcycle accident. One leg was amputated below the knee, but not too long after, more of the leg had to be removed. The experience was devastating to Schuller, especially in the first days after the accident, when the prospects for his daughter's future were unclear.

Even as a teenager, Carol revealed that she had imbibed the possibility thinking of her father. While recovering, she announced her conviction that this challenge had come her way so that she in turn could become an advocate and inspiration for others who might let physical limitations destroy their self-worth and impede their attaining their dreams. Not only did Carol survive, but she was soon engaged in serious athletic training. Her skill was such that she was close to becoming a world-class skier. Schuller had visualized the miracle of his daughter's recovery; the family expected that dream to become reality, and it did.

Then, even before the Crystal Cathedral opened its doors, physicians diagnosed Arvella Schuller with breast cancer that required a mastectomy if she were to survive. The Schullers had nurtured a particularly close relationship within the family and had shared in the expanding ministry. Arvella had served as music director of the ministry for many years after the move to California and was the producer of the *Hour of Power* from its inception. Once again, despite the ravages of disease, the spirituality of the positive thinker yielded practical results. Arvella not only survived surgery and treatment, but more than twenty years later she was still flourishing.

Both experiences, but especially his daughter's triumph over physical disability, provided some of the personal backdrop for the two best-selling works, *Tough Times Never Last, but Tough People Do* and *Tough-Minded Faith for Tender-Hearted People*. Schuller and his family could offer themselves as prime examples of tough people who made it through tough times because of their tough-minded faith, rooted in the spirituality of the positive thinker.

Other personal challenges would follow, but every potential personal tragedy became transformed into a possibility. Robert Anthony Schuller, the only son in the family, had followed his father into the ministry, but he saw his own orderly life crumble in the early 1980s as he went through a divorce from his first wife. Both father and son held marriage in such high regard that the younger son at first believed he would have to abandon professional ministry altogether once his divorce was final. Positive thinking enabled the son and ultimately the entire family to transform what could have been a negative event, one that could have destroyed a career, into an opportunity for new growth. The younger Schuller found that his congregation rallied around him, enabling him to continue his ministry. In time, he joined his father at the Crystal Cathedral, and by 2002 he was poised to take over primary leadership of the entire operation.

For Schuller himself, a major personal challenge that had the potential to become a disaster occurred in 1991. On a trip to Europe that was to include a personal audience with Pope John Paul II, Schuller hit his head while getting into an automobile shortly after he arrived in the Netherlands. The resulting headache proved far more serious than Schuller expected. After he was found unconscious, he underwent emergency brain surgery in Amsterdam. For the master of possibility thinking, even this personal trauma became a triumph. When he regained consciousness after the surgery, the first words he struggled to write were, "How sweet it is to stand on the edge of tomorrow." Another mountain had become a gold mine. In 1996, when Schuller underwent angioplasty that involved inserting a stent to keep an artery open, he was still standing on the edge of tomorrow.

Schuller turned seventy-five in 2001 but remained at the helm of the ever-expanding ministries centered around the Crystal Cathedral campus. The following year, however, he announced plans to shift more responsibilities to his son, although he indicated that he intended to remain active at least until 2005, when the ministry launched by his preaching from the roof of the snack bar at a drive-in movie theater would celebrate its fiftieth anniversary.[55] As the title of one of his books put it, Schuller, through his commitment to the spirituality of the positive thinker, had found "God's way to the good life." He had discovered what it meant to be a Christian man.

Does Possibility Thinking Always Work?

At the same time, however, Schuller and the strategies he has so vigorously advocated have reaped criticism.[56] One of the most frequent is a charge leveled against Peale before him and even against Carnegie, namely, that mental power alone may not conquer every challenge. One may visualize, but not every dream becomes empirical reality. Schuller himself dealt with such concerns more effectively when material issues, not personal ones, were at stake. For example, had pledges not come in to support launching the *Hour of Power* telecasts in 1970, Schuller believed that God simply did not intend for his ministry to take on that component at that time, not that there was a potential failure that would have negative consequences. However, individuals who visualize good health or an end to tension within the home may have greater difficulty remaining oriented to the spirituality of the positive thinker if their hopes do not become realities.

Then, too, Schuller may downplay what are unavoidable negative experiences that come to every human being in the course of life. In contrast to Schuller's efforts to avoid dealing head-on with negative experiences stands the posture of Rabbi Harold Kushner, who was also a best-selling author. For Kushner, positive thinking was inadequate. So too was the peace of mind approach of his co-religionist, Rabbi Joshua Loth Liebman. Rather, Kushner, whose son had a condition that brought rapid aging and death at an early age, argued that what was central to a vital spirituality was confronting negative situations directly and recognizing their negativity. In his popular work, *When Bad Things Happen to Good People*, Kushner insisted that trying to determine why negative situations occurred was futile.[57] Where he may approach the optimism of the positive thinker like Schuller is in his conviction that how one responds to negativity determines whether life remains charged with the potential for meaning.

Finally, Schuller often seems to equate the practical results of his version of the spirituality of the positive thinker with economic gain and wealth. After all, so many of the cases that thrust obstacles in the way of Schuller's ministry had to do with money: a million dollars needed for the purchase of land, a million dollars needed to begin construction, hundreds of thousands of dollars needed to launch a television ministry. And in almost every case, a wealthy businessman would provide the needed resources, usually just in time to avoid disaster. So Schuller often seems to make the practical results of positive thinking synonymous with individual economic and material success. But in doing so, he is surely in harmony with other constellations of images influencing Protestant male spirituality and concepts of the Christian man over the centuries.

In keeping with other clusters of images advancing white Protestant male spirituality, the Christian man as positive thinker or possibility thinker promoted by Schuller is one who has very little interest in specific beliefs or doctrines. He has intentionally cast a wide net, hoping to bring into the fellowship of the church those who were previously "unchurched." He no doubt recognized that adding significant doctrine or sets of belief to his approach would alienate precisely those whom he hoped to reach. Dennis Voskuil has pointed out, however, that consistent with the broad American Protestant evangelical heritage, Schuller has repeatedly urged those who read his books, watch his programs, or hear him in person to develop a personal relationship with Christ. But just how to do that and just what such a relationship entails are left to the individual, whether male or female, rather than being carefully explicated.

In his later years, Schuller was more inclined to speak in the first person about his ministry and approach than he was earlier in his professional career. He seemed more willing to take personal credit for developing the array of programs associated with the Crystal Cathedral, rather than attributing the range of ministries to God's vision. But such self-confidence and self-assurance are also marks of the ideal Christian man whose spirituality is shaped by positive/possibility thinking.

CHAPTER 7

✝ ✝ ✝

The Faithful Leader

Even as the constellation of images associated with the spirituality of the white Christian man as positive thinker was taking root in the 1950s, forces were at work to make other aspects of white male spirituality come to the fore. The notion of the positive thinker may have helped white American Protestant men come to terms with the business climate of suburbanizing America in the decades after World War II, but much in the larger culture suggested that positive thinking, even if it brought peace of mind and peace of soul, would not necessary yield peace on Earth. On the heels of victory over Hitler and the Nazis came the menace of Stalin and Mao and an aggressively expanding communism. Communism seemed doubly dangerous, for in the popular mind it represented the antithesis of both democracy and an economic system grounded in free enterprise and capitalism. It also stood for an atheism that mocked Christian spirituality and the life of faith, however it was expressed.

From the Korean War, which erupted even before the nation had adjusted to the end of the Second World War, to the American military engagement in Vietnam, which so divided the American people during much of the 1960s and 1970s, Asia seemed the arena where it was vital to halt the advance of communism. In turn, Asia would also have a profound impact on the spirituality of white Americans, men and women alike. Many in the military received exposure to Asian religious practice first-hand. Some, from World War II on, brought home spouses who sought to continue their native religious practice in their adopted land. All the military engagements brought displacement to thousands of Asians. Thousands sought refuge in the United States, a matter that was eased considerably after Congress adopted significant changes in immigration laws in 1965. The intrigue with Asia also received a boost from writers of the "beat generation" who, in the 1950s, promoted various adaptations of Zen Buddhism and other Asian-based alternatives to the standard expressions of American religiosity that seemed increasingly wedded to a morally bankrupt culture. By the 1960s, American devotees of groups such as Hare Krishna (International Society for Krishna Consciousness) were common sights across the nation, with devotees chanting on the streets of larger cities and college towns or selling copies of the Bhagavad Gita to passersby there and in airports.[1]

I shall not here explore in depth the contours of this Asian spirituality or the ways it dovetailed with the fascination for things New Age a couple of decades later. For the moment, it must suffice to note that one attraction of Asian religions was an emphasis on looking inward, of finding the truth within, that resonated with those who understood the constellation of images that went with the spirituality of the white Protestant Christian man as positive thinker. They, too, looked within for sources of strength and self-affirmation. It was not a large step to move from a Christian-based positive thinking to an Asian-based meditative approach.

Concern with communism and the dangers it presumably presented to American political, economic, and religious values was not the only social movement in the last third of the twentieth century that had an impact on white American Protestant male spirituality and models of the Protestant Christian man. In 1954, the U.S. Supreme Court, in *Brown v. Board of Education*, struck down the principle of "separate but equal" that had since the end of the nineteenth century provided the legal buttress of the racism that cascaded through American society. The following year, African Americans began a sustained boycott of the Montgomery, Alabama, bus system to protest practices of racial segregation. The civil rights movement had begun.[2]

When leaders across the American religious spectrum appeared in the news marching in demonstrations, whether calling for civil rights for all Americans or for an end to U.S. military involvement in Southeast Asia, rank and file Americans were confronted with the need to take a harder look at religious institutions and the expressions of spirituality the popular mind associated with them. Whatever unquestioned authority most folks had once ceded to faith traditions and their leaders was jettisoned. But here, too, there is consonance with the prevailing spiritual image of the positive thinker, for the one who found self-worth within, the one who was in control of his own life, was not dependent on religious institutions or its functionaries for a spirituality that gave coherence to life. America's Catholics, who by and large lie outside the parameters of this study, were caught in the same vortex, but with the added disarray that came to church structures and ways of operating as a result of the Second Vatican Council, which met from 1962–65.

Not only African Americans, however, found in calls for liberation from operative social patterns the spurs to activism. Especially significant for white American Protestant male spirituality were the religious implications of second-wave feminism, for a time popularly called the women's liberation movement. Although some of the earliest voices articulating a spirituality and a theology grounded in the experience of women as women came from Roman Catholic thinkers such as Mary Daly and Rosemary Radford Ruether, Protestant women quickly began to develop and explore forms of spirituality that included embracing pre-Christian fertility rituals (retooled for a postmodern age) and celebrating rites of passage unique to women from menarche to menopause. They readily challenged male dominance in the clergy and all ranks of church leadership and unabashedly mined the Christian tradition for language and symbols that spoke to women.

Many of these efforts presumed that all Christian spirituality had been cast in patriarchal terms, although in the American setting at least traditional forms of spirituality, from prayer and cognate devotional expressions to reading sacred texts and participating in worship, had long been primarily the domain of women. But the construction of feminist theology and the push to formulate new expressions of spirituality directly connected to female experience had ramifications for male spirituality and what it meant for Protestant males to be Christian men. The most obvious came in the challenge to patriarchal notions, especially the cluster of images identified with the dutiful patriarch. Feminist-based spirituality also undermined the viability of approaches to spirituality centered on the Christian man as gentleman entrepreneur, courageous adventurer, and efficient businessman. After all, the liberated woman was herself an entrepreneur who relished adventure and epitomized efficiency in her business success. If such images were no longer the province of white Protestant Christian men who sought to mold their lives after a spiritual ideal, were there new images on which men could draw in cultivating their spiritual lives?

Add to this maelstrom the increasing visibility of homosexual men in American culture, another of the consequences of the larger movement to secure civil rights for all Americans and to affirm the self-worth and value of one's identity (whether based on gender, ethnicity, sexuality, or some combination thereof). As with spiritual and theological issues surrounding women, a literature too vast to explore here has emerged to address what it means to be a homosexual and a Christian. Scores of works probe how to think spiritually and theologically when one is sexually attracted to persons of the same gender and how to use homosexuality itself as a basis for building and nurturing an approach to Christian spirituality.

Although the voices advancing a spirituality and a theology reflective of a homosexual identity come from virtually every religious community in the nation, American Protestants remain deeply divided over how their religious institutions as such should respond to such matters as whether homosexuals, whether gay men or lesbian women, should be ordained to the professional ministry and whether they should serve in positions of lay leadership within their congregations and denominations. Controversy surrounds any consideration of whether committed relationships between persons of the same gender should receive the same religious blessing as marriage between a man and a woman, a matter that received fresh import when Vermont granted legal recognition to same-gender unions and when in 2003 Massachusetts courts ruled that denying same-gender couples the right to marry was illegal. Others debated whether the very presence of homosexuals within a community of faith represented a threat because of convictions that homosexual practice (as perhaps distinguished from homosexual identity) is totally at odds with Christian belief.

For some, the visibility of homosexuals raised awkward questions about understanding masculinity itself. Homosexuals often became an "other." They functioned as a foil against which heterosexual men could describe, if not define, what it meant to be male simply by way of contrast and consequent rejection. If the cultural transformations underway in the second half of the twentieth century made neatly defining masculinity problematic, at least some white American Protestant men could do so by affirming that they were not homosexual men.

For men and women alike, spirituality in the second half of the twentieth century thus took shape in a world marked by uncertainty. Robert Wuthnow astutely identified the transformation and uncertainty that marked spirituality in those decades when he contrasted a spirituality that functioned like a dwelling, providing security and a clear center around which meaning in life revolved, and a spirituality that was a journey, movement toward a destination that was itself unknown.[3] Some of Wuthnow's concern received amplification in a larger cultural concern for spiritual for-

THE FAITHFUL LEADER   179

mation, a term that suggests a process that is underway rather than one that is completed. Perhaps under the sway of the image of the positive thinker with its own style of self-reliance, Americans increasingly took idiosyncratic spiritual paths. They mixed together dimensions of Asian spirituality with more traditional Christian expressions and with ideas that came from one's personal experience as a man or a woman. Some added notions that came from a wide range of sources to create a way of being religious that worked. The key was to find a center for one's life and to endow empirical reality with some overarching meaning.

As a consequence, white American Protestant men gradually began to ask whether there were in their own experiences as men materials from which to craft a viable spirituality, whether there was something unique to men as men that could provide the basis for spirituality. Were there norms or standards that could provide a foundation on which to build a spirituality that spoke to white Protestant male experience the way, for example, that recasting some rituals centered on the goddess established a foundation for a spirituality that spoke to female experience? American culture had long taken for granted what being male was all about and what masculinity entailed in some absolute sense. The currents prevailing in the later twentieth century stripped those assumptions of their absolute character and thrust men into a vortex where the start of the spiritual journey required coming to grips with what it meant to be male. Men had to figure out what it meant to experience human life as a male and what it meant to use masculinity—however defined—as a springboard for giving order and significance to life.

In the midst of this uncertainty, especially among evangelically inclined Protestants, there emerged a regrouping of some images for male spirituality into a cluster centering around the Christian man as faithful leader. No doubt some of the motivation for articulating a clear set of ideas and images stemmed from a desire to provide something specific around which men could organize their spiritual pursuits in an age when authority had sustained challenges on every front. Popular writer Susan Faludi spoke of a male backlash, a reaction against not only women's liberation and, for our purposes, the efforts of women to craft a spirituality rooted in their life experiences as women, but also other forces that subverted longstanding stereotypes of masculinity and male identity.[4]

When Faludi began to look more closely at the position and posture of men within American society at the turn of the millennium, however, she modified her stance somewhat, concluding in a subsequent study that many of the changes in American life that had bolstered the status of women and enriched women's sense of self-worth and personal identity had the unin-tended result of sabotaging male self-worth and personal identity.[5] The shattering of gender stereotypes necessary to producing the context for a viable female spirituality had left a void for men instead of opening up new strategies for male spirituality. The spirituality of the faithful leader was designed to fill that void, albeit probably not in ways that Faludi and others committed to more strident feminist approaches welcomed.

I'll Do the Leading and You Do the Following

In many respects, the image of the faithful leader as a basis for male spiri-tuality and the model for the white Protestant Christian man echoes that of the dutiful patriarch, for it begins with an assumption, namely, that the male by nature and divine design has authority over women. For many Protestants, that authority is rooted in the order of creation. The narrative in the second chapter of Genesis that describes the unfolding of creation has God creating man prior to creating woman and then fashioning woman from the man.

Where the spirituality of the faithful leader differs from that of the duti-ful patriarch, and thus betrays its postmodern origins, is in its refusal to connect this authority to an innate superiority or supremacy. There is a dif-ference in the order of creation, but difference does not necessarily require seeing one as superior and one as inferior. In other words, the spirituality of the white Christian man as faithful leader struggles to take into account many of the cultural issues of inequality and discrimination raised by women who forged a feminist spirituality, grounded in their experience as women. At the same time, it gives credence to the assertion of Michael Kimmel that men, when thinking themselves threatened by social change, often resort to arguments based on natural distinctions between men and women.[6]

One of the more conservative constructions of a white male spirituality oriented around the image of the Christian man as faithful leader claimed that Christianity was from the start a man's religion. Rueben Herring asserted that this male focus stemmed not only from Christianity's having a male, Jesus, as its founder but also because it was rooted in the patriarchal traditions of Judaism.[7] But, claimed Herring, men had abandoned the spir-itual life because they felt they did not need it and because much of organ-ized Protestantism in the United States did not recognize the particular needs of men as men, beginning with the religious instruction offered by women to males when they were boys. It would be a challenge, Herring felt, to recapture that male center in order to fashion a dynamic spirituality that affirmed the unique character of boys and adult men as males.

One alternative was suggested by Patrick Arnold.[8] Arnold insisted that it was possible to find resources within the Christian tradition and its sacred text, the Bible, that would resonate with the distinctive characteristics, gifts, and archetypes of the male spirit. Drawing on Jungian psychology,[9] he argued that a competitive temper, orientation toward independence and autonomy, a particular kind of vulnerability that tended to draw men toward healing, and an abiding sense of responsibility and accountability were essential to the masculine spirit and to male spirituality.[10]

These characteristics are likewise fundamental to the white male spirituality centered on the image of the Christian man as faithful leader. All of these qualities he found exemplified in various characters in the Bible (among them are Abraham, Moses, Solomon, Elijah, Elisha, Jeremiah, and Jonah from the Hebrew tradition) but epitomized most fully in the kind of leadership offered by Jesus. Jesus, for Arnold, was a "man's man" in that he was a shamanic healer, a trickster who managed to outsmart his opponents (the competitive dimension), and an authoritative patriarch when it came to dealing with his disciples.

Jesus was thus a viable model for a white male spirituality that would affirm what masculinity was all about and thus set the standard for what it meant for white Protestant males to be Christian men. A faithful leader must seize the competitive edge, exert authority, yet offer healing. The last may be the most obvious indication of how the spirituality of the faithful leader shows the influence of the women's movement and its demolishing of some gender stereotypes. Healing and the kind of care that the healer demonstrates were long thought to be inherent in women and not in men, despite the male domination of the medical profession until well into the twentieth century.

Central as well to the spirituality of the faithful leader is the role of the man as biological father, an idea that to some extent echoes the image of the dutiful patriarch as one who assumes the role and prerogatives of God the Father within the human family. Later-twentieth-century efforts to bring the idea of fatherhood within the orbit of spirituality likewise had to take into account the difficulties in using gender-specific language and concepts for the divine, issues raised by countless women religious writers. By the later twentieth century, identifying the Protestant Christian man whose spirituality was informed by the notion of the faithful leader in the role of father no longer entailed asserting supremacy of the male over the female.

Some claimed, for example, that although the possibility of becoming a mother was biologically determined, becoming a father—apart from the simple act of procreation—was a responsibility that was culturally acquired.[11] Once could argue, of course, that mothering is a responsibility distinct from child-bearing and is therefore also one that is culturally acquired. For men, at least, the notion of God as Father provided a mechanism for understanding a viable male role within the family as caring parent and teacher devoid of the more authoritarian aspects of the dutiful patriarch. To be sure, those particular roles were not exclusively the domain of men as fathers, but in the minds of some were essential to the process of allowing children to acquire an individual identity distinct from that of the mother, from whose body they had literally emerged.

Trying to understand the spiritual dimensions of the faithful leader as father raises a host of complicated biological issues and has led others to conclude that biblical conceptions of God as Father may not, after all, be that appropriate for men of the twenty-first century as the starting point for a white male spirituality. Philip Culbertson, for example, begins his exploration of male spirituality with the recognition that at the moment of conception, all fetuses start as female. Those that develop as males do so as part of an involved, subsequent process. For Culbertson, one consequence is modern culture's seemingly extraordinary emphasis on how males, more than females, must struggle to separate themselves from their mothers in order to acquire a viable gender identity. He acknowledges that in this necessary operation some unintended repercussions have resulted that have trapped men in unfortunate gender stereotypes. One is making rough and rugged individualism essential to male identity.[12] Especially problematic are biblical representations of God as an absent Father, one who wields power but rarely demonstrates compassion. Such representations do little to foster male spiritual development.

Culbertson does find many clues in the biblical narratives that provide a more positive basis for white male spirituality and models for the Protestant Christian man. For example, he looks at the story of David and Jonathan as representative of how male friendship can bolster spiritual identity. Unlike some who recoil at this story because of its possible sexual overtones, Culbertson insists that the spiritual man as faithful leader can and must have relationships with other men based on a shared gender identity, not on homosexual attraction. Here, too, the biblical depictions of Jesus become models for the faithful leader. The Jesus of the Gospels is fully masculine in his demonstrations of courage and power, stereotypical qualities assigned to men by the larger culture. Yet this Jesus is not afraid of male friendship, or even male touch, and not averse to manifesting some characteristics that modern American culture classifies as feminine, such as humility and compassion.

Culbertson's view of a man as faithful leader is one that comes closer to touching on traditional spiritual disciplines than some others. For Culbertson, real men pray. The man who would be a faithful leader is first and foremost a man of prayer, despite the longstanding association of prayer as primarily part of women's lives. The faithful leader must also reject the often unstated belief that resorting to prayer is a sign of weakness, an indication that an individual man is not in control of a particular situation and therefore has not really developed a workable male identity.[13] But like so many other writers who discuss aspects of male spirituality, Culbertson does not offer instruction in the discipline of prayer. He finally echoes the same refrain that cuts through all the other images of white male spirituality and the ideal Protestant Christian man: Men as men can understand only prayer that gets results. Prayer must be practical, not purely adorational or devotional. Prayer that signifies a letting go of concerns seems to the faithful leader an abandonment of responsibility, and prayer that might expose personal weakness and vulnerability comes across as a refusal to confront life's realities with a countervailing authority.

The spirituality of the white Christian man as faithful leader also has ramifications for how men understand their role as husbands. Without necessarily subjugating the wife to a position of inferior deference, the man who would be a faithful leader is one who, as a reflection of the order of creation, takes the initial authority in his relationship with his wife. Authority in this context does not signify brute power that could readily become abusive, but a prevailing influence. In evangelical Protestant circles, women have themselves often—but not always—acknowledged the role of husband as leader.

Among twentieth-century Protestant evangelists, few are more widely known than Billy Graham, whose global crusades often took him away from his family and, it would seem, from active involvement within the family as husband and father. But Ruth Bell Graham even before their marriage acknowledged his role as faithful leader. The daughter of missionary parents, Ruth Bell believed that she, too, was called to the mission field. Her eyes were fixed on going to Tibet as an unmarried female missionary. But after she met Billy Graham while both were students at Wheaton College, she had second thoughts that Graham himself encouraged when he argued that her role was to be wife and mother, not an unmarried missionary. At the time, Ruth Bell Graham recalled later, it seemed to her that

Graham was a "little bossy."[14] He did not hesitate to exert authority. "He told Ruth what to eat and sat across from her until she complied. He insisted that she get more exercise and personally put her through a rigorous program of calisthenics."[15]

After nearly fifty-nine years of marriage to Graham, Ruth Bell Graham reflected a bit differently. In an interview published in May 2002, she recalled her desire to be a missionary in Tibet, but also Graham's asking her if she believed that God had brought them together. "I had to admit that I was convinced He had. Then Bill said, 'Well, then, I'll do the leading, and you do the following.' I've been doing the following ever since."[16] After second-wave feminism, such strident assertions of authority might have been rarer, but a sense of authority remained a hallmark of the spirituality centered on the faithful leader as the ideal of the white Protestant Christian man.

The Faithful Leader as Competitor

Dealing with competition is an implicit component of most of the constellations of images promoting male spirituality that have emerged within American Protestantism. It is reflected especially in the fascination with sports that marked the notion of the faithful leader as it developed in the later twentieth century. Linking sports to male spirituality was not new in itself. The earlier muscular Christianity movement had looked at sports as a means to draw men into the churches and had sparked a movement particularly among larger urban Protestant churches to build gymnasia as part of their complex of buildings to provide a morally positive place where men could engage in sports and other athletic activities. As second-wave feminism brought increasing attention to the participation of women in sports, highlighting their athletic prowess and the same sort of competitiveness that marks male athletic endeavors, it became more difficult to view sports as an arena for cultivating only male spirituality. But those who promoted various images of the faithful leader as the model for white male spirituality and the Protestant Christian man did not hesitate to draw on sports and stress the physical side of athletic activity as central to any effective male spirituality.[17]

As early as the mid-1970s, for example, Michael Novak extolled the role of sports in exemplifying the American spirit.[18] Although personally informed by the Roman Catholic heritage, Novak by no means addressed his paean to sports only to Catholics. But he did address it virtually exclusively to men, for his text completely ignored women's sports and the increasing prominence of women in both collegiate and professional athletics. When

Novak recounted the virtues of sports, he noted that all of them were male virtues and that women athletes who demonstrated those same virtues suffered from "split personalities."[19]

Sport, for Novak, was itself a kind of godliness, integrating the male body, mind, and spirit together through ritual play as well as through a common language. Sports venues became sacred places, and times of formal play became sacred time. Both were set apart from the mundane world of empirical reality. Here heroes were created and bonds forged between team members that transcended a private individualism. Those who played the same sport shared a liturgical brotherhood that nonetheless fostered development of the self-confidence essential to the spirituality of the Christian man as both positive thinker and faithful leader.

For Novak, the way sports promoted healthy competition was also central to their moral value for men. Although he intentionally shunned what he called the "culture of the Christian athlete," he emphasized the way sports urged individuals to compete with themselves, in the sense of always striving to perform better in the next athletic contest, as well as the way sports had a near eschatological dimension, foreshadowing the final confrontation between good and evil, albeit in a carefully orchestrated ritual fashion.[20] Unlike that theological battle, however, sport remained play, but play that brought a critical self-discovery to participants that gave an abiding sense of identity. In this sense, then, for Novak the athlete becomes a paragon of the spirituality of the faithful leader and a model for the Christian man.

Others recognized that the increased plausibility of an evangelical style within American Protestantism in the last quarter of the twentieth century also brought a fresh emphasis on sports and the physicality associated with athletics as a basis for white male spirituality and models of the Christian man. As we have seen, evangelicals once regarded sports with disdain because athletes were thought to epitomize what was morally disreputable and exhibit a hostility to the spiritual life. As the evangelical mind tied together masculinity and athletic prowess, sports became sanctified. Traditional evangelical discussion of spirituality as involving a yielding of control over one's life to God in Christ was seen as alienating men for it emasculated them. Popular writer Carol Flake suggested that the language of traditional spirituality was too humbling for men as men, but that the star athlete, who represented physical success and leadership, could be a model for a moral manhood, for the ideal Protestant Christian man.[21] The athlete symbolized one who was in control and who never gave up control over his life.

The athlete as a model for male spirituality signaled a conscious desire to dispel the idea that Protestant Christian men were somehow "sissies" or less than real men.[22] Physical strength became an analogue of spiritual strength, leadership in sports a sign of faithful leadership in all aspects of life. The revival of muscular Christianity represented a male battle to conquer those forces that thwarted spirituality, embodied in almost caricature form in phenomena like John Jacobs, who broke out of metal chains in front of an audience in order to demonstrate how the spiritual man could break out of the chains of sin, or the Power Team, a group of male body builders whose strength performances were the center of gospel crusades in the early 1990s.

As with other forms of white male spirituality, specific doctrine and belief remained pretty much in the background, but the faithful leadership of the muscular athlete was demonstrated in observable behavior. As one commentator noted, "A real man takes his family to church, leads his family in prayer and devotion, and otherwise ensures that the lives of his wife and children conform to Christian doctrine."[23] The same could be said of the Protestant Christian man whose spirituality was shaped by images of the dutiful patriarch prominent among New England Protestants in the seventeenth and eighteenth centuries. By the end of the twentieth century, however, there was a much wider range in choice of churches to attend and considerably more variation in formulation of Christian doctrine. Little was said, however, about what went into the prayer and devotion that should be central to family life, and little direct guidance offered to men who affirmed the spirituality of the faithful leader for themselves. But real men did pray.

At the same time, when individual athletes became models of the spiritual life, often their success as athletes seemed more important than the particulars of their belief. When pressed, many seemed to have become more oriented to spirituality as their professional careers waned and the athletic achievements that had brought recognition were no longer as effective in giving life purpose. Where competition and victory had once provided a framework of meaning for life, a vacuum now loomed. For many athletes, inspiration seemed more likely to come from the spirituality of the Christian man as positive thinker. The emphasis there on self-confidence, self-worth, and inner strength provided a motivation that translated into success in the sports arena, or at least into a stamina that sustained an individual man in the heat of straining physical exertion.[24]

Then, too, by the end of the twentieth century, women exhibited as much "sanctified sweat" as men,[25] undermining the viability of sports as symbols of the physical achievement, competitiveness, and authority of the faithful leader. But in the 1990s, however, the world of sports provided another range of metaphors for the faithful leader when well-known football coach Bill McCartney launched a movement to spur male spirituality, emphasizing how the faithful leader remained true to his word and to the covenants he made. The faithful leader was also a "promise keeper."

The Faithful Leader and His Obligations

When Bill McCartney drew some forty-two hundred men in 1991 to a rally held in the basketball arena at the University of Colorado, the school where he coached football and had led a team to a national championship, he launched a movement promoting the distinctive male spirituality of the Christian man as faithful leader. Like the Men and Religion Forward Movement of the early twentieth century, McCartney's Promise Keepers had as their goal bringing the millions of American men who remained outside the nation's churches into the ranks of those committed to the spiritual life and reclaiming for men the role of leader within the family unit.[26] The prevailing image that recurred in Promise Keepers literature and that was ultimately taken up by some of the more evangelically inclined Protestant denominations to highlight concerns of male spirituality was that of the "servant leader," in many respects synonymous with what I have here termed the faithful leader.

The phrase "servant leader" in late-twentieth-century usage had roots that were not exclusively religious, and the term itself was not always used in the context of male spirituality. As early as 1970, management researcher Robert K. Greenleaf, who founded an institute for management leadership bearing his name, wrote a provocative essay called "The Servant as Leader."[27] After a distinguished career in management research with AT&T and faculty positions at MIT and the Harvard Business School, among others, Greenleaf devoted his retirement to promoting the model of the servant leader as the most viable symbol for effective leaders, including not only business executives but also trustees of all sorts of organizations.

In addition, Greenleaf sought to apply the concept of the servant as leader to agencies and institutions as diverse as businesses, religious congregations, and even theological seminaries. A practicing Quaker, Greenleaf infused his understanding of servant leadership with a spiritual dimension, some of which carried over when the phrase was popularized in American Protestant Christian circles by folks who may or may not have known of Greenleaf's earlier work.

Greenleaf repeatedly acknowledged that what inspired him to think of the servant as leader was his reading of Hermann Hesse's well-known novel, *Journey to the East*. In that novel, a key figure is a character named

Leo, who for much of the story is traveling with a group of men in the capacity of a servant. But it is clear that what Leo actually does for the group extends well beyond his appointed tasks. His spirited personality and his gift of song unwittingly become forces that give the group cohesion and direction. Hence, Leo is much more than a servant; he is the de facto leader of the group. But it is only after Leo disappears and the group disintegrates that it becomes apparent that the servant was indeed the real leader.

When Greenleaf applied this notion to the dynamics of effective leadership, he insisted that all real leaders were servants first. But what did he mean by servant? As Greenleaf developed the idea, the first characteristic of the servant is an ability to listen to the needs and concerns of others. In this instance, listening is not merely a gesture, but a genuine hearing, a recognition of the legitimacy and validity of whatever issues others bring forward. This active listening leads to empathy, an entering into the situations of others and taking them on in one's own life. From this empathetic listening come first a healing, not only in the sense of individual psychological wholeness but also in the relationships that one has with others, and then an awareness, an almost intuitive "feel" for possible ways to deal with problematic situations and resolve them creatively.

In Greenleaf's construction, the servant as leader possesses an ability to conceptualize and articulate what others are experiencing but may not be able to express. The servant as leader is thus able to persuade others that this understanding will help build community, sustain personal growth for all involved, and reflect responsible stewardship along the way. Emphasizing matters of power and authority, in Greenleaf's view, destroys servant leadership. Although power and authority are what the larger culture sees as fundamental to leadership, they actually undermine the wholeness and defusing of anxiety that mark the leader who puts serving before acquisition of power.

In outlining this approach to servant leadership, Greenleaf rarely draws directly on spiritual imagery, although there is a deep spiritual undercurrent in his emphasis on healing and wholeness. He becomes more explicitly spiritual, however, when he claims that servant leadership is always a matter of faith, although he refrains from defining precisely what goes into such faith beyond vague assertions that a servant leader has a sense of the unknowable and an art for foreseeing the unforeseeable.[28] But Greenleaf does insist that this faith has a practical result in that it sustains a healthy self-confidence, albeit a self-confidence grounded in the servant leader's willingness to listen and ability to empathize. Faith therefore enables the servant leader to persevere, regardless of obstacles in the way of achieving one's goals. In connecting faith with practical results, Greenleaf provides a link with a host of other images shaping white male spirituality in American Protestant life that in the final analysis are also practical and result-oriented, especially the images of the positive thinker and the efficient businessman. Other thinkers, though, sought to make more direct associations with Christianity, particularly with the style of leadership found in the New Testament accounts of the figure of Jesus.[29]

Bill McCartney and the Promise Keepers transformed this tool to describe effective management into a spiritual cliché for the millions of men who were involved in some fashion with the Promise Keepers movement that flourished in the last half of the final decade of the twentieth century. Much of what influenced the approach taken by McCartney and his associates represented ramifications of the women's movement of the 1960s and 1970s and the conviction, stretching back into the first half of the nineteenth century, that spirituality and things religious were the natural, if not almost exclusive, domain of women. Since World War II, the proportion of women working outside the home had steadily increased. By the time Promise Keepers came to the fore, one could no longer assume that the husband/father was the sole wage earner for the family. Yet most analysts insisted that women still bore primary responsibility for tasks within the home, including the religious nurture of children, and that men, more than women, defined their worth through their employment.

At the same time, figures reported by Protestant religious groups indicated that women still continued to outnumber men, usually by a margin of two or three to one, on the membership rolls of local congregations. Hence, it was easy to conclude that a deep spirituality was not central to the lives of most men, particularly not to those who were trapped by the world of work, those who, to borrow the title of one of McCartney's popular autobiographical books, had "sold out" to success.[30]

Like the Men and Religion Forward Movement, the Promise Keepers hoped to spark a religious awakening among men and bring millions of men into the fellowship of local congregations. Unlike the Men and Religion Forward Movement, however, Promise Keepers at first worked primarily outside the churches. If churches were already alien territory, few men would be attracted even to new programs that they offered. Capturing the spirit of muscular Christianity, McCartney and his associates sought to use sports venues, usually large football stadiums, for mass rallies and to appropriate the same techniques of building crowd enthusiasm among the thousands attending them that sports teams, cheerleaders, and the like used to excite fans at an athletic event. Like those who promoted muscular Christianity, Promise Keepers organizers saw athletics as the natural domain of men, just as the home was perceived the natural domain of women.

Another underlying conviction propelling Promise Keepers centered on regaining for men what even for the dutiful patriarch of the colonial era was seen as central to white male spirituality, namely, taking on responsibility for the spiritual life of the family. The man who would be a faithful disciple of Jesus Christ had the duty to provide spiritual leadership. If men had abdicated that role to women, as spiritual images of the dutiful patriarch blended into those of the gentleman entrepreneur, the courageous adventurer, the efficient businessman, and then the positive thinker, it was time for Christian men to take back responsibility for the spiritual life of the family. Writing in *Seven Promises of a Promise Keeper,* a handbook for the movement, Tony Evans proclaimed:

> The first thing you do is sit down with your wife and say something like this: "Honey, I've made a terrible mistake. I've given you my role. I gave up leading this family, and I forced you to take my place. Now I must reclaim my role."
>
> Don't misunderstand what I'm saying here. I'm not suggesting that you ask for your role back. I'm urging you to *take it back.* . . .
>
> . . . Unfortunately, however, there can be no compromises here. If you're going to lead you must lead. Be sensitive. Listen. Treat the lady gently and lovingly. But lead![31]

For some, the language of Promise Keepers and its advocacy of male spiritual leadership seemed a retreat to a patriarchy that defied gender equality and harkened back to a day long past in American culture. Michael Kimmel called it "a kinder, gentler patriarchy" than what had once marked Western civilization, while Reformed evangelical feminist Mary Stewart Van Leeuwen mused whether Promise Keepers was promoting a "soft patriarchy."[32]

Sometimes the rhetoric and writing of the movement suggested that the spiritual image of the faithful leader promoted by Promise Keepers mirrored the servant leader concept advanced by Robert Greenleaf. Male spiritual leadership was not dictatorial. One of the seven promises that lay at the ideological center of Promise Keepers was the vow to build strong marriages and families. That task was not an easy one but required the kind of listening, empathy, and use of persuasion that Greenleaf highlighted. Faithful leadership was not tyrannical but relational, concentrating on healing and advancing the wholeness of every member of the family. As Jon Bloch has pointed out, such faithful leadership could easily involve having men cultivate in themselves personality traits that an earlier age saw as feminine, such as an openness to emotional expression, nurture, cooperation, and a sense of equality between husband and wife within the marriage covenant.[33] So the faithful leader did not exercise power and authority for their own sake but sought to serve and thereby empower others within the family to find wholeness.

Nonetheless, when some Promise Keepers promoters spoke of servant leadership or faithful leadership as the spiritual ideal for Christian men, they used language that seemed aggressive, echoing more the competitive world of business where their commitment to entrepreneurship, adventure, and efficiency might assure success. Michael Kimmel, reporting on a Promise Keepers rally that attracted some thirty-five thousand men to New York City's Shea Stadium in September 1996, noted how at least one speaker construed faithful, servant leadership as a kind of competition between husband and wife, as "'spiritual warfare,' a test of masculine strength to do more at home than his wife does. 'I'm never gonna let no woman outserve me,' [Wellington Boone] shouts to thunderous applause."[34]

But just how could a man transform himself from an efficient businessman or a positive thinker into a faithful leader? How could he enter into a right relationship with his wife and children, no more the absentee husband and father but one exercising what McCartney and Promise Keepers saw as his rightful spiritual role? As with those who wrote about other constellations of images promoting white Protestant male spirituality, those who have addressed Promise Keepers rallies have spoken in very general theological terms. After all, the thousands who have attended rallies have come from a range of religious backgrounds. To be narrow and specific when it came to doctrine and belief would have revealed significant differences among participants rather than promoting male friendship, racial reconciliation, and the restoration of strong marriage and family relationships that Promise Keepers proclaimed as its goals.

Nonetheless, Promise Keepers, more than many others who have advanced male spirituality, have lifted up some traditional spiritual disciplines as fundamental to exercising faithful leadership. There was something deeper that went beyond the media presentations of men clustered together, sometimes with arms linked, in highly emotional prayer as they stand together in football stadiums. But real men did pray.

The Promise Keepers movement has produced a vast literature to promote its image of the spirituality of the faithful leader, the servant leader. Such works range from the handbook-like *Seven Promises of a Promise Keeper* to a periodical called *New Man*. There and elsewhere, as in the autobiographical writings of founder Bill McCartney that will be discussed later, men who wish to live committed Christian lives, who wish to shape their spirituality around the image of the faithful leader, must discipline themselves (much as athletes discipline themselves in training) through prayer and regular reading of Scripture. What is not discussed in detail, however, is how one goes about the business of praying and how one cultivates a meaningful prayer life. But real men did pray.

Perhaps the most intensive efforts to advance more traditional forms of spirituality in the model of the Christian man as faithful leader came at the local level. At its peak the Promise Keepers movement hired regional coordinators, whose tasks included helping men in various local communities to establish groups for mutual support and accountability.[35] Usually having some time for prayer and Scripture reading, these groups were loosely structured around discussion of materials produced by Promise Keepers or some similar agency like the Christian Men's Network.[36] They always provided opportunities for the men to share with each other personal concerns about their faithful leadership, their shortcomings in trying to live up to the ideals of servant leadership, and their hopes for continued spiritual growth.

Underlying these small groups was another of the fundamental assumptions of Promise Keepers, namely, that men in turn-of-the-millennium American culture had difficulty in forming and maintaining close personal friendships with other men. Perhaps since the decline of the lodge and fraternal order movement more than half a century earlier, the culture had provided men with few opportunities for interaction that did not also include the participation of women. If part of the challenge to faithful leadership stemmed from dysfunctional relationships between men and women, it seemed plausible to Promise Keepers that a "men only" environment that fostered bonding among men might empower men to look at all human relationships from a fresh perspective.

Complicating the matter, however, was the popular perception that construed same-gender friendships, especially among men, in sexual terms. Promise Keepers literature and speakers, including Coach McCartney, have repeatedly condemned homosexual activity. McCartney and his associates consider homosexuality a sin that thwarts genuine spirituality, but they also want to reassure men who identified with Promise Keepers that males could have close-knit, emotionally charged relationships with other men without adding a sexual component to them.

Promise Keepers, and the spirituality of the faithful leader that it promoted, received tremendous publicity and within five years after the first gathering counted those attending events in a single year in the millions. By the dawn of the twenty-first century, the movement was less conspicuous. Other voices had picked up on some of the ideas promoted by the movement and given them a different twist.

The stadium rallies had set as one goal of the movement the eradication of racism in American life. African American speakers appeared at most of them, yet relatively few African Americans attended. Critics suggested that few African Americans could afford the relatively steep entrance fees charged for the weekend events. When fees were lowered, income plummeted, and the movement was faced with serious cutbacks. By 2003, Promise Keepers was no longer front-page news and fewer regional and local events carried its name. Perhaps the image of the Christian man as faithful leader was giving way to new expressions of spirituality for American Protestant men. Or perhaps the patriarchal aspects of faithful servant leadership were not as soft as they first appeared.

But in 1998, when the movement was cresting, another challenge appeared. It came in the form of a resolution adopted by delegates attending the Southern Baptist Convention (SBC), the annual meeting of representatives from the nation's largest Protestant denomination and one that for two decades had become increasingly vocal in proclaiming its evangelical, if not fundamentalist, cast and increasingly strident in its statements on issues such as gender roles, the family, and limiting the pastoral office to men. On June 9, 1998, with more than eight thousand delegates voting, the SBC adopted a resolution that affirmed the headship of the husband in marriage and that called on wives to "submit graciously" to that headship.[37]

Even though some Southern Baptist pastors and officials talked about headship in terms of faithful servant leadership, the language itself echoed what historian of religion in America Margaret Lamberts Bendroth called "last gasp patriarchy."[38] Confirmation that headship reflected a greater passion for power and authority than Greenleaf or the Promise Keepers attached to the spirituality of the servant leader came two years later when the delegates or messengers attending the convention voted to restrict the pastoral office to men, reaffirming what had been the practice among most churches affiliated with the SBC.[39] It mattered not whether male headship in marriage mirrored the lived reality of Southern Baptist men and women or whether even within Southern Baptist families, a complementarity or even a mutuality more in keeping with the deeper sense of faithful servant leadership prevailed.[40] The posture of the convention seemed to strip the spirituality of the faithful leader of all the characteristics Greenleaf had decades earlier given to the servant leader. Instead, it made leadership an exercise of brute power.

At the same time, however, there were voices that gave both implicit and explicit support to the kind of image of the Protestant Christian man associated with the Promise Keepers notion of the faithful servant leader. Some of those actually preceded the formation of Promise Keepers, although none reaped the national publicity that came to a movement started by a nationally known university football coach. At its peak in the 1980s, the ministry to men of Edwin Louis Cole provides one example. Cole was an evangelical Protestant of distinct Pentecostal leanings who founded an outfit called Manhood, Inc. Working largely through weekend retreats for men that attracted a few hundred rather than the thousands that later flocked to Promise Keepers rallies as well as through numerous published books, Cole demonstrated how the various images for male spirituality and models of the Christian man often fused together.[41] In his discussion of what he called "maximized manhood," he not only tried to speak in a colloquial way that he believed would appeal to men because "God is no semantic masseur. He talks a man's language."[42] But he also insisted that "God made man to be a leader and a steward" and proclaimed that "men must take charge."[43] Here he presents a model for male spirituality and the ideal Christian man that points to images associated with the faithful leader.

In a work that seems a late-twentieth-century instance of the advice books for young men that promoted the spirituality of the Christian man as gentleman entrepreneur in the early nineteenth century, Cole described the young man of courage. Such a one would become a champion like the positive thinker and courageous adventurer, who was willing to take responsibility for his life and live his dreams.[44] If earlier notions of the Christian man as gentleman entrepreneur and efficient businessman especially emphasized how male spirituality was linked to career and work, Cole proclaimed that "the workplace is where a man's unique desire is basically satisfied" because, he believed, man was created that way, while woman was created to be beautiful, desired, and loved.[45] Like those in the early nineteenth century who warned men who would be Christian to avoid sexual impropriety, Cole in many of his writings identified sex and sexual conduct as the arena that presented the greatest challenge to cultivating a spiritual life. In *Maximized Manhood,* for example, he discussed five elements common to the lives of most men that thwarted their achieving their potential as Christians—lust, idolatry, fornication, tempting Christ, and murmuring—and two of them (fornication primarily, but also lust) were linked to sex. Repeatedly, he called on men attending his retreats to confess their sexual misconduct. In his books, he offered countless examples about how inappropriate sexual behavior or desires on the part of husbands impeded loving relationships with wives.

Cole brought together facets of the Christian man as dutiful patriarch and faithful leader when he described women as objects of love and beauty, implying a status distinct from but not necessarily inferior to the place men held in the order of creation sketched in the second chapter of Genesis.

Since he insisted that men carried a role analogous to that of a priest, he did grant the husband a position akin to how the dutiful patriarch ideally functioned within the Puritan family. But just as the Christian man as faithful leader did not in theory hold authority over his wife through the exercise of sheer force and power, so Cole also contended that men should see their wives as joint heirs even as they assumed headship of the family.[46]

At the same time, in keeping with virtually all the images of white male spirituality and the ideal Protestant Christian man, Cole included an emphasis on prayer but gave little instruction in what went into prayer and how one could sustain a disciplined life of prayer. He also minimized the particulars of doctrine yet called on men to believe. Like those who promoted the spirituality associated with the white Christian man as positive thinker, he urged men to believe in God "for great things" and then to receive these great things from God, but he did not detail what went into belief.[47] As others, Cole's model for white male spirituality and the ideal Christian man was grounded in the practical and workable, assuming that men would understand what went into belief and what constituted the prayer and other spiritual components that would allow men to achieve their divinely intended potential.

Reflections

It may seem that the popularity of the spirituality of the white Protestant Christian man as faithful leader at the close of the twentieth century signaled that American Protestantism had come full circle, returning to a cluster of images for male spirituality not all that distinct from those that predominated in the Puritan culture of the seventeenth and eighteenth centuries. But many expressions of the constellation of ideas making up the spirituality of the faithful leader rejected the patriarchal authority and power that lurked beneath that earlier approach. By emphasizing sensitivity, emotional expression, listening, use of persuasion, and the like, the faithful leader was more inclined to support mutuality or at least complementarity than power or patriarchy.

To be sure, some expressions of male spirituality, such as those implicit in the Southern Baptist 1998 statement on marriage and the family, remained based on power and authority, albeit a power and authority thought to be built into the divine order of creation. For the most part, however, it was impossible for advocates of a renewed emphasis on male spirituality to cast aside the cultural gains achieved by women in the second half of the twentieth century and to talk in terms of female subordination and male headship. Bringing in the idea of the faithful leader as servant gave quite a different nuance to any discussion of power and authority.

As with earlier manifestations of images of white male spirituality, that of the faithful leader thus reflected the larger cultural context in which some Christian thinkers sought to promote commitment and dedication on the part of American Protestant men. Here, too, a key feature remained the relationship men had with others, another pointing outward rather than looking inward. The primary relationship, beyond the fundamental but vaguely defined relationship with God, was the one a man had with his wife and children.

This orientation to the family was different from that which undergirded earlier images of male spirituality and models of the Protestant Christian man. The family focus stemmed from the conviction that as men had over several generations devoted themselves more and more to their work and vocations, they had abandoned a healthy relationship with their wives and children. For the dutiful patriarch of the Puritan era, there was no such sense of prior abandonment, but only of playing the role in the human realm that was analogous to that of God. Yet as the image of the dutiful patriarch merged into those of the gentleman entrepreneur, the courageous adventurer, the efficient businessman, and the positive thinker, male spirituality carried with it a direct link to work and vocation and a concomitant forsaking of faithful leadership within the family itself.

Some, however, did not want to construe the faithful servant leader only in male terms and argued that committed Christian women could also find in servant leadership a viable model for their own spiritual lives.[48] Even so, there was a difference, for popular perception had long seen the wife and mother in the role of servant. Hence, discussions about servant leadership exercised by women tended to focus not on the family and a woman's relationship with her husband and children. Instead, they looked at the leadership roles of women within local congregations or cognate venues. Serving in the home remained a given.

The spirituality of the faithful leader did move men to look at their inner lives, at traditional things of the spirit, more forcefully than had other approaches. By promoting conventional spiritual disciplines such as prayer, fasting, study of Scripture, and meditation, the spirituality of the faithful leader began to nudge men to look inward, even if relationships with others were the primary arena where the results of spirituality revealed themselves. By the dawn of the twenty-first century, a spate of resources, from printed pamphlets and books to video presentations, sought to guide men who wished to cultivate a more inner-oriented spirituality that complemented that of the faithful leader. Many of these also attempted to nurture the associations of men with other men, often not in as dramatic ways as the mass rallies in football stadiums. Several promoted small groups as more likely venues to guide men in spiritual formation and in the specifics of spiritual disciplines such as prayer. Reliance on small groups was likewise a reflection of larger cultural trends, for American Protestantism in the last third of the twentieth century increasingly appropriated the small group as the most viable mechanism for promoting and sustaining religious commitment.[49] Perhaps the increasing focus on the inner life would add another tier to the constellation of images offered by white American Protestantism to inform male spirituality. Real men did pray.

In Focus
Bill McCartney: Coach and Faithful Leader

Few men at the dawn of the twenty-first century better illustrated in their own lives the layering of various images of male spirituality and the struggles to become a faithful leader than did Bill McCartney.[50] For millions of American men, McCartney had instant name recognition outside the realm of male spirituality. For more than a decade, he was the head football coach at the University of Colorado, spurring the team to a national championship after the University of Colorado Buffaloes beat Notre Dame in the Orange Bowl on New Year's Day 1991. After resigning as head coach at Colorado following the 1994 regular season, McCartney remained in the public mind for another reason. In 1991, he and some like-minded associates had started a spiritual movement for men called Promise Keepers. By 1996, Promise Keepers was drawing a total of more than one million men to events it sponsored across the nation. How did a coach become a promise keeper? How did one who admittedly for more than three decades was "sold out" to athletic endeavors become a faithful leader?

From Michigan to Missouri and Back

The man later known to thousands as "Coach Mac" was born August 22, 1940, to William Patrick McCartney, then forty-one years old, and his wife, Ruth Lloyd McCartney. Bill was the middle of three sons born to the couple. Tom, the oldest, was two years older than Bill, and Richard was nine years younger. McCartney's mother had a daughter, from a previous marriage, who was a teenager when Bill was born. This half-sister married at the

age of seventeen and did not figure prominently in the McCartney household when Bill was growing up. The family were devout Catholics, although
because McCartney's mother had been divorced and the church did not recognize divorce and remarriage, they traveled to Trenton, Michigan, a short
distance from their home, for worship each Sunday. Parishioners there were
unfamiliar with the details of Mrs. McCartney's earlier life.

Looking back, McCartney remembered that for his father, who worked
in the automotive industry for Chrysler Corporation, meaning in life revolved around his commitment to the Catholic Church, the Democratic
Party, and the U.S. Marine Corps, in which he had served. The commitment to Roman Catholicism carried over in the education provided for the
McCartney children. McCartney was sent to a parochial school in Trenton
to begin his schooling. Later, at Detroit's Riverview High School, from
which he was graduated in 1958, he distinguished himself as an athlete,
playing football, baseball, and basketball. Even then his devotion to sports
evidenced signs of what others might call an addictive personality. There
was never any halfway commitment to any of those athletic endeavors. As
an adolescent Bill gave each sport a near total dedication, although football
was clearly his favorite.

A high school senior class trip to New York City introduced McCartney
to another phenomenon that was to be a major ingredient of his life for
many years. He and some of his friends brought beer back to their hotel.
This experimentation with alcohol was an exercise in overindulgence. The
summer after graduation, McCartney tried hard liquor for the first time,
finding that he so enjoyed the sensation of being "high" that he rarely knew
when to stop drinking once he started. At the same time, however, he
remained absorbed in the ways of the Catholic Church. Receiving his first
communion at the age of six, McCartney later developed the habit of
attending Mass each morning. At one point, he went for ten years without
missing daily communion.[51] Here, too, was another portent of things to
come, for his dedication to Catholic practice signaled an interest in spirituality that would one day supersede his attachment to sports.

A football scholarship took McCartney to the University of Missouri,
where he was both a center and linebacker for the Missouri Tigers for four
years under the coaching of Dan Devine. He was not a particularly distinguished player, although he earned three letters in football. But coaches and
teammates alike recognized that McCartney had an almost instinctive feel
for the technical side of football and a level of commitment to excelling that
few others could match. McCartney continued to party rather heavily off
season but avoided drinking during the regular season. One episode of

overindulgence became imprinted in his mind. In December 1961 on one of his first dates with Lyndi Taussig, whom he married on December 29, 1962, a drunk McCartney hit a parked police car while taking his future wife back to her Stephens College dormitory and made such a spectacle of himself that he was ordered not to return to the Stephens campus.[52]

McCartney's first job after graduation was teaching school in St. Charles, Missouri, where he was also an assistant coach. Another assistant's position in Joplin, Missouri, followed. In 1965, now a father, McCartney returned to Detroit, where he was basketball coach and assistant football coach, working with his older brother at Holy Redeemer High School. But when he became both football and basketball coach at Divine Child High School in Dearborn, he began to make a name for himself in the world of secondary school coaching when in the same year his two teams won statewide championship titles. Dedication and hard work became marks of McCartney's leadership. In retrospect, however, he realized he was neglecting his wife and growing family. Although it was rare for a highly respected university sports program to hire a secondary school coach, the University of Michigan, where the legendary Bo Schembechler was head coach, named McCartney an assistant coach in 1974, promoting him to defensive coordinator three years later.

The move to Ann Arbor not only represented a recognition of McCartney's skills as a football coach but also brought him into contact with Athletes in Action, a branch of the evangelically oriented Campus Crusade for Christ that had a ministry targeted to student athletes. While attending an Athletes in Action meeting with a Michigan football player in 1974, McCartney had a religious experience that changed his life. He realized that although he had long been religious in terms of attending religious services and accepting basic Christian belief, he did not have a personal realization of the reality of faith. As he put it in *Sold Out*, a volume of memoirs, he realized he knew a lot about Jesus Christ but did not know Jesus Christ.[53] The kind of personal commitment that he brought to football had been lacking in his spiritual life. Now, for the first time, he felt a spiritual power. It was still not the kind of power that Robert Greenleaf identified with the servant leader. It was a power that enhanced control.

Now, like the dutiful patriarch, McCartney tried to lead family devotions a couple of times a week. Real men prayed. He also started to read about men of faith, such as John Wesley. His overarching commitment to coaching and success, which went well beyond that associated even with the efficient businessman, meant that there remained little time for nurturing the spiritual life through such traditional spiritual activities as reading the Scriptures. It was as if prayer had become a key to power and success. McCartney prayed for guidance in determining winning plays as a coach, convinced that success was a now a sign of divine favor.

With the zeal of a new convert, though still a devout Catholic, McCartney talked freely of his faith experience to co-workers, student athletes, and his family. All of them remained somewhat mystified. McCartney still had occasional problems with excessive drinking. He also had too little time to be actively involved in raising three sons and a daughter, who were primarily Lyndi McCartney's responsibility.

From Rebuilding to a National Championship

When McCartney interviewed for the job as head football coach at the University of Colorado in Boulder, he knew that his candidacy was a long shot. He insisted to university officials, who were looking for someone to take a losing program and bring it national recognition, that football was a distant "third" in his life. His commitment to God was first, and his wife and family came second. The time he gave to coaching, however, suggested otherwise. But in part because McCartney suggested that his deep spiritual commitment gave him an integrity that he could transfer to an ailing program and bring it the success university officials and thousands of fans wanted, he was offered the job. That the move to Colorado was also in keeping with McCartney's professed spirituality came when two persons he did not know contacted him in Missouri with messages that they claimed to have received from God indicating that McCartney was to be God's "rock in Boulder."[54]

McCartney recalled that he privately consecrated the Colorado football program to Jesus Christ on his arrival in Boulder in 1982. At the time, however, such consecration was more a conviction that because he was a public Christian, God would bring the success that McCartney craved for his coaching endeavors. By now, McCartney had given up alcohol, but he was still so absorbed in coaching and in public professions of his faith that there was little time remaining for his wife and family, and Lyndi McCartney, who had herself undergone a spiritual transformation in 1975, was becoming increasingly resentful and depressed.

The distance between McCartney and his family grew, since providing the authoritative, power-based leadership to transform a losing team into a national powerhouse consumed more time and energy that even McCartney had imagined when he first went to Colorado. Only much later would McCartney come to believe that his devotion to football or at least to success as a football coach was a form of idolatry, not an exercise in the faithful leadership of a spiritual man.[55] Life was compartmentalized: Spirituality was in one compartment, coaching in another, wife and family in a third.

Still a devoted Catholic when he moved to Colorado, McCartney was also becoming more inclined to dimensions of Pentecostal expression. The roots went back to Ann Arbor, where he had for a time been involved with the Word of God community at a time when Ann Arbor itself boasted an enclave of charismatically oriented Catholics. In June 1988, he made a more decisive move in the direction of a Protestant evangelical style when he and the family began attending the Boulder Valley Vineyard Church, which was affiliated with the Vineyard Christian Fellowship founded by John Wimber. Wimber's charismatic foundation led him to proclaim that miraculous "signs and wonders" always resulted from authentic faith and ministry. It was hard for McCartney not to see the dramatic success that started coming to the Colorado Buffaloes from 1988 on, culminating in a national championship, as just such "signs and wonders." In that national championship year, coaching awards were also heaped on McCartney. Success had come to this leader of men. Or had it?

A Shifting of Priorities

Before that 1990–91 national championship, McCartney had been pondering ways to be even more public about his Christian profession. With friends who were involved with the Fellowship of Christian Athletes, McCartney determined to launch some sort of ministry that would target men in order to convince them that "a man's man is a Godly man."[56] The first gathering of what became Promise Keepers came during the summer of 1991, when 4,200 men met together in Boulder. The following summer, some 22,500 massed in the university's Folsom Stadium.

Soon McCartney was devoting almost all his time not consumed by football coaching and recruiting to spearheading a movement to kindle male spirituality among American Christian men. From the start, the rhetoric of the movement called for men to take an active role in family life and transform their marriage vows from words to lived realities. But for the McCartney family, Promise Keepers for a time became yet another entity that took the husband and father away from home and family.

One clear signal should have come during 1988–89, when McCartney's daughter Kristy learned she was pregnant, with the father being the Colorado Buffaloes quarterback. Kristy decided not only to have the baby—the family were still practicing Catholics who accepted without question the church's teaching prohibiting abortion—but to remain in Boulder. So the pregnancy generated a fair amount of publicity. When the baby's father, Sal Aunese, was diagnosed with cancer and then died a few months after McCartney's first grandson was born, much of the criticism turned to sympathy. Kristy had a second son in November 1993, this one also fathered by a Colorado football player. McCartney supported his daughter during these difficult times but admitted that he began to wonder about his own parenting skills when she had what he regarded as serious lapses of moral judgment. McCartney did not condemn or judge. He knew too well that he struggled with his own moral dilemmas, ranging from his earlier problems with alcohol abuse to continuing difficulties in controlling his temper and his neglect of his wife, Lyndi.

Nevertheless, McCartney continued to proclaim in public his unyielding commitment to his wife and family. Difficulties with Lyndi began to surface more directly when the McCartneys were on a coaches' cruise in 1990. Lyndi McCartney later recognized that a large part of the problem was that her husband had been raised to assume that men exerted a leadership based on authority and power, not one that looked upon wives as members of a team.[57] When Promise Keepers began to consume most of what little spare time McCartney had for his family, Lyndi McCartney remained optimistic at first but gradually grew resentful. She noted that she was enthusiastic about how Promise Keepers urged men to stop abdicating responsibility for their families to their wives in the hopes that her husband would heed the rhetoric and change his own behavior. She applauded the use of the image of the servant leader to describe the faithful husband and father. "My favorite teaching," she wrote, "was on the subject of servant-leadership. PK taught, 'A leader is a servant who enables those he leads to be all they can be.'"[58] But as McCartney spent more and more time with coaching and the Promise Keepers movement, there was less and less time for wife and family.

By 1994, Lyndi McCartney had gone into clinical depression and lost eighty pounds. Her husband, the voice but not yet the model of the faithful leader, began to listen. And listening with empathy was a hallmark of the servant leader in Robert Greenleaf's paradigm. The McCartneys sought professional counseling to save their marriage, with the coach admitting for the first time that he was not a good listener but simply assumed that his wife and family would automatically follow his leading and be happy doing so.

Almost as soon as healing began, the 1994 football season got underway, and McCartney was once again the absentee husband and father, inspired by visions of another national championship. Part of him knew that if his life were to reflect his spirituality, then listening had to be a daily matter, not something confined to off season. Being a husband and a father required faithful leadership in fact, not just in proclamations made before thousands of men at Promise Keepers rallies in football stadiums around the country. Yet once football season started, it was almost impossible to listen, to empathize, or to exhibit any of the other qualities of the faithful leader in his personal life.

Promise Keepers had used the phrase "Men of Integrity" as a slogan, but McCartney began to doubt that he could be described as such because of the gap he perceived between his public persona and the private reality that he lived. For once, he looked inward and felt himself exposed as a fraud—not to the world or to Buffaloes fans but to his inner self, his spiritual self.[59] He also realized that even when he engaged in traditional acts of devotion, such as prayer, much was self-oriented or at least based on success he hoped to achieve—usually a football victory. Real men prayed. But McCartney's prayers were hollow.

McCartney felt that he had betrayed all that he had sought to symbolize. His own marriage was in disarray again, to the point that he wondered whether it was terminal. Lyndi McCartney, however, never saw divorce as an option—such would have been counter to her own religious convictions—but she did want a marriage in the sense of a dynamic relationship between two partners each committed to the other. McCartney, after much personal reflection and meditation, decided that he would resign as head coach at Colorado, although for the moment he did not rule out accepting another coaching position. Even before he had made his announcement, there were rumors that Michigan State would invite him to become head coach, a position that could be tempting because it would take McCartney back to his home state, back to his roots.

When McCartney formally announced his resignation on November 19, 1994, detractors and many in the media were more suspicious than supportive. They were used to a Bill McCartney who cherished the limelight, not a Bill McCartney who had made a renewed spiritual commitment and was now determined that he would embody the spirituality of the white Christian man as faithful leader in his life as well as in his rhetoric. Some went so far as to denounce McCartney as being un-American for abandoning his team and profession and for letting down the thousands of Buffaloes fans who were anticipating another national championship.[60]

At the same time, Lyndi McCartney was apprehensive that her husband would harbor resentment against her, thinking she had forced him to give up his career and the meaning in life it provided. Even though she had resented the time that coaching and Promise Keepers had taken from her marriage and family, she feared that McCartney would experience a more stinging bitterness if he felt that he had forsaken everything for which he had struggled on her account.[61] Both insisted, though, that Bill McCartney, like any spiritually committed faithful leader, needed to be a "godly and devoted husband and father."[62] In this case, that meant retiring from coaching. Circumstances could differ for others.

In retirement, McCartney would not be tempted by other professional coaching positions. Some days after he first discussed his impending retirement with Promise Keepers president Randy Phillips, Phillips came to him and shared his own conviction that had emerged from Phillips's own practice of prayer: God did not want McCartney to coach anywhere. Long before there were rumors about Michigan State, McCartney had extended conversations with Southern Methodist University, then under football's "death penalty" and thus prohibited from competing for two years, about trying to restart the program there. For a moment, the position had been appealing because McCartney thought that the historic religious affiliation of that university meant that the athletic environment was more open to his public religious style than that of a state university such as Colorado. But at the time, he had discerned that God had not wanted him to break his contract, to break his promise to stay at Colorado. Now in retirement, he would focus on the promises made to Lyndi McCartney.

McCartney soon realized that cultivating the spirituality epitomized by the Christian man as faithful leader required much the same sort of discipline that he had endeavored to instill in his players over the years. If he had lived much of his spiritual life expecting forgiveness, since "nobody's perfect," and if he had strained to forgive players for their shortcomings and even some of his family for behavior that did not match their spiritual proclamations,[63] McCartney now embarked on a more regular schedule of spiritual discipline. For him, that included prayer, silence and meditation, simplicity, intense study of Scripture, and even the traditional regimen of fasting (sometimes for up to forty days) in order to nurture the clear-mindedness, self-control, and persuasive, empathetic listening that were hallmarks of the faithful leader. Real men prayed. But now McCartney's prayers centered not on himself but on God.

McCartney's commitment to training himself to be a faithful, servant leader was buttressed by a curious event. He attended the funeral of a friend, a man who was widely respected and held in great admiration. The officiant at the service extolled many virtues manifested in the life of the deceased man but, much to McCartney's amazement, made no mention at all of the man's spirituality. It was as if his friend's spiritual life had been divorced from the lived reality of daily existence. McCartney was determined that the spirituality of the faithful leader would not be pigeonholed in a place hidden from view in his own life. There was a new dimension of accountability—to God, to himself, to his wife—that was part of the spirituality of the Christian man as faithful leader incarnate in Bill McCartney.

McCartney closed his second volume of autobiographical meditations with reflections on the October 1997 Promise Keepers "Stand in the Gap" rally, held in Washington and something of an echo of the earlier Million Man March that had targeted African American men. The phrase "Stand in the Gap" was chosen with care. Men would stand, as did the ancient Israelites at the Hebrew solemn assemblies when the people recommitted themselves to the way of Yahweh, and in doing so fill the gap caused by their having ceded spiritual leadership in their homes and families to their wives. Like McCartney, millions, it was hoped, would become accountable and commit themselves to the faithful leadership necessary for the nation as a whole to regain a moral vision which McCartney and his associates believed had also dissipated. Men were the ones responsible for this perceived moral decay. As McCartney was fond of noting, more men than women were likely to break their marriage vows, more men than women were lured into sexual immorality of all sorts (from cyberpornography to homosexuality), more self-avowed Christian men than Christian women reported behavior to pollsters that was virtually no different from the behavior reported by those who made no profession of a spiritual life, much less to the life of a faithful leader.[64]

As the twenty-first century dawned, Promise Keepers had less visibility than it had enjoyed a decade earlier. Efforts to reach out across racial lines, one of the foundations of the movement, had resulted in lowering and sometimes dropping fees to participate in rallies. The resulting loss of income meant that the overall ministry had to scale down its programs. McCartney, after a decade of retirement from coaching, was also less in public view, more content to pursue the spiritual life of the faithful leader, not yet perfect by any means but closer to being the man of integrity that he had long seen himself to be. Whatever else went into the spirituality of the Christian man as faithful leader for Bill McCartney, constant vigilance remained paramount to assure that he remained on track.

By 2003, McCartney had even pulled back from the top ranks of leadership of the Promise Keepers movement he had founded. His wife had developed health challenges. It was time for the faithful leader to become servant healer in a different way. It was time for wife and family fully and finally to be the sole human focus of Bill McCartney's spirituality.

CHAPTER 8

✛ ✛ ✛

Male Spirituality in White Protestant America

Different images of the Christian man and of a spirituality that speaks to white male experience have run through American
Protestant life from the arrival of European settlers in the seventeen century to the twenty-first century. These images represent more a layering of
ideas and understandings rather than separate, unrelated approaches. Each
image builds on what went before, often highlighting particular dimensions
of what it meant for a man to call himself a Christian and seek to live a
Christian life. All reflect developments in the larger culture in which American Protestantism found its home.

Evaluating Images of White Male Spirituality

The dutiful patriarch, a symbol more dominant in the colonial period, was
a man who accepted a serious responsibility for maintaining order and
authority in his household, taking on a role that was analogous to the role
of God the Creator/Father in the universe. Such responsibility was not to
be taken lightly. Rather, it pushed the spiritual man to become ever aware
of the depth of his own shortcomings, even as he sought to instruct children and others in the household in the rudiments of Protestant belief and
practice. There was a sense of deference to the dutiful patriarch, but it too

was analogous to the deference all humanity owed to God. At the same time, such deference, properly understood and lived, also yielded great meaning and direction to life when a man was able to fulfill his duty.

As the label suggests, this image did contribute to the dominance of white men in American society. In the religious sector, men continued to control the various institutions of the church, in part because as patriarchs they restricted the clergy and leadership to men. As well, white men exercised near total control of social and political structures, seeing their public roles as extensions of their familial standing as dutiful patriarchs. Although there were challenges to that male control in the nineteenth century, not until the ratification of the Nineteenth Amendment to the U.S. Constitution in 1920 did women gain the right to vote and thus have the legal standing to question even more profoundly their exclusion from the ranks of social and political leadership.

At the same time, however, the image of the dutiful patriarch and the principle of deference that sustained it helped bring a stability to family structure in white America. In turn, that fostered social stability at all levels. Nonetheless, the dutiful patriarch perpetuated much injustice based on race and gender, even though the ideas behind that image sparked resistance to tyranny that issued in American independence.

As the nation gradually became more oriented to towns and villages and to factories and shops, changes in how the family operated modified the image of the dutiful patriarch. Other aspects of the white Christian man came to the fore. Ethical behavior, particularly in a man's relationship with his employer, became a hallmark of the Christian man, the gentleman entrepreneur. Careful in his choice of friends as well as in his choice of a wife, the gentleman entrepreneur demonstrated honesty and integrity, steadfastness and a persistence in self-education. The practical result came in gaining a reputation that brought respect and opportunities for achievement in a man's career that would allow him to have an impact not only on his family but also on the society around him.

The values associated with the gentleman entrepreneur no doubt enabled a capitalist economy to establish itself firmly in American life. In the nineteenth century, at least, another result was that the United States became more self-sufficient as a nation. Economic self-sufficiency in turn strengthened the experiment with republican democracy in the political sector. However, much of the economic gain until the time of the Civil War depended on maintaining a system of chattel slavery. Most whose spirituality was shaped by images of the gentleman entrepreneur were reluctant at best and slow at worst to condemn slavery.

The Christian man as gentleman entrepreneur also reflected the numerical standing of Protestantism in the United States in the first half of the nineteenth century. This numerical strength virtually guaranteed that the upper echelons of political and economic leadership would remain in white Protestant male hands in disproportionate numbers for generations to come.

By the end of the nineteenth century, immigration, urbanization, and industrialization were transforming the character of the nation. Added on to the traits of the dutiful patriarch and the gentleman entrepreneur as models for the Christian man and male spirituality came those associated with the courageous adventurer. If a man were to survive in the city, he would need both moral and physical muscle. A muscular Christianity that elevated the athlete to the paragon of the ideal man was the order of the day. The hard work that characterized the gentleman entrepreneur, along with his commitment to high moral standards, remained intact. The Christian man was still theoretically the dutiful patriarch within the home, although the home had become more a privatized space permeated by female influence. But the spiritual life for a man was akin to a battle that required daring and courage. Those same qualities were needed not only in places like foreign mission fields, where all sorts of unknown dangers awaited the man who battled for the souls of the heathen, but also in the factories of the cities. Those immigrants whose religious ways were alien to Protestantism and whose moral style was rather different threatened to undermine commitment to a spiritual life. To be a Christian man was to embark on an adventure that demanded courage to meet challenges of all sorts.

The courageous adventurer helped move the American nation from isolation to the center of world affairs. Political action, missions, and trade alike brought contact with other nations and peoples. Unfortunately, the white male whose spirituality revolved around the image of the courageous adventurer rarely appreciated the diversity of these peoples and their cultures. Instead, they often simplistically assumed the superiority of both the American way of doing things and of white American Protestantism.

In many arenas, the courageous adventurer contributed to a spirit of inquiry and exploration that, when combined with some of the positive features of the efficient businessman, yielded stunning gains in medical science, technology, and other areas that had benefit for all humanity. The spirit of the courageous adventurer also influenced the Progressive movement in politics, with its trust busting, efforts at government regulation of working conditions, and efforts to improve living conditions and sanitation in the nation's cities.

In industrializing America, however, Protestant Christian men could assure their success and thus position themselves to carry out their responsibilities as dutiful patriarchs if they were dynamic leaders. Moving to the top ranks of leadership in business would bring wealth and power that could be used not just for the benefits of a man's family, but for the improvement of the whole of society. Individual initiative, rooted in the same discipline and hard work that had marked the gentleman entrepreneur, meant that the dedicated white Christian man could move quite literally from rags to riches. Diligence and determination had their own reward that most often could be measured in monetary terms. If the white Christian man looked to the church for support, he expected the same standards of organization and efficiency to prevail there as he did in his business, for the church was a business as much as it was a place of devotion and center for worship.

The efficient businessman was one catalyst in transforming the United States from an agrarian to an industrial nation. Yet the turn to industry also meant that the white Protestant man whose spiritual identity drew on the ideal of the efficient businessman was often too willing to exploit immigrant workers for personal advantage. He was likewise prone to accept the prevalence of racism and sexism in American life, since he believed he owed his place of privilege to the pervasive influence of a white male Protestant style.

In the years after the Depression and World War II, when many of the values thought inherent in American society seemed under constant attack from ideologies associated with everything from godless communism to second-wave feminism, the social supports that buttressed earlier images of the white Christian man and male spirituality also seemed more shaky and tenuous. But the notion of the Christian man as positive thinker helped give Protestant male spirituality a fresh foundation. Building on the individual initiative associated with the earlier idea of the Christian man as courageous adventurer, the positive thinker was a man who looked not only to God but also to a reservoir of inner strength to project a perception of himself that would denote security, certainty, and success.

The positive thinker cultivated the skill to envision the results he wanted, whether in terms of personal happiness or achievement in the world of business, and to focus on that vision until it became empirical reality. By transforming possibilities into realities, the positive thinker could banish inner fears, solidify a sense of strong self-worth, and thus assure his own peace and happiness. On a larger scale, the positive thinker saw no potential obstacle as too daunting to thwart moving ahead. One wonders whether the gains in human knowledge resulting from exploration in space, nuclear physics, and other cognate fields would have come when they did if what previous generations saw as absolute limits had not become possibilities to be actualized for the positive thinker.

Much more self-oriented than the idea of the Christian man as dutiful patriarch, the one for whom obligations to the household and society were paramount, the positive thinker represented an almost extreme form of individualism. At times, it seemed to promote a self-centered egotism where personal satisfaction became the highest goal. There was thus a narcissistic side to the positive thinker. But the spirituality of the positive thinker gave white American Protestant men a direction for their lives in a cultural context where all the rules had changed and where forces over which it appeared that an individual man had little control jeopardized the hope for inner contentment and wholeness.

The individualism that went with the Christian man as positive thinker extracted a heavy price in the minds of a succeeding generation that offered the image of the faithful leader as the epitome of the white Christian man. Challenges to traditional understandings of masculinity that were rampant in American life in the last third of the twentieth century raised anew questions of what it meant to be a man, not just what it meant for a man to be a Christian. Once again a man's relationships to his household, especially to his wife and children, became a focal point of the spiritual life, for, like the dutiful patriarch, the faithful leader was perceived to be the head of the household.

In the wake of changes that had altered gender roles in the larger culture, the faithful leader could not exert his authority as a dictator but as a servant. A servant was one who listened and responded with empathy, thus healing breaches between members of the family and then between members of the larger society by persuading others to follow a course of action that was consonant with shared religious values. Like the courageous adventurer, the faithful leader understood the spiritual life in terms of athletic competition, but now a man competed with himself and sought to develop his inner potential to the maximum, whether in a sports contest or in spiritual pursuits.

At the same time, it is not yet clear that the faithful leader has mastered the virtues promoted by that image of the white Christian man. Barriers between races have yet to be demolished. New prejudices directed against Hispanic Americans and Asian Americans seem to highlight ethnic divisions in American society. The faithful leader faces walls of ethnic suspicion awaiting demolition, along with those that have to do with homophobia.

As well, there is little evidence to suggest that the faithful leader as husband and father has succeeded in becoming an empathetic listener when one looks at the statistics on divorce and the number of single-parent households headed by women in the United States. The faithful leader may be more open to expressing feelings and emotions, including acute pain when his marriage ends in divorce, but he has a long way to go before he is an agent of healing and wholeness in the home or in society. Genuine mutuality across lines of race, gender, and sexual orientation remains an elusive goal.

The various constellations of images promoting white male spirituality and the models for the white Christian man discussed here are by no means all of those that American Protestants have offered over the centuries. What is captured in the dutiful patriarch, the gentleman entrepreneur, the courageous adventurer, the efficient businessman, the positive thinker, and the faithful leader reflects only some of the dominant notions that mark white Protestant efforts to describe what it means for a man to identify himself as a Christian and structure his life around that identity. These six clusters are therefore more representative than exhaustive. However, in looking at them together, there emerge several themes that have shaped prevalent concepts of the ideal Christian man and endeavors to provide a guide to the spiritual life for white American Protestant men.

Action More than Contemplation

White Protestant male spirituality in America historically has centered more on action than on the inner life or spiritual disciplines such as contemplation. For the Puritans, for example, the Christian man who looked to the dutiful patriarch as the model for the spiritual life was one who accepted a host of obligations in terms of responsibility for others. Those obligations, ranging from organizing daily devotions each morning and evening for the household to examining children about the state of their souls, all required that the Christian man take action. For some, from the colonial period to the present, that obligation also entailed public leadership, usually in holding governmental office.

The gentleman entrepreneur added to those obligations action especially with regard first to his employer and then, when one actually became an entrepreneur in his own right, toward his employees. Such action at times might become indirect, expressed through support for agencies like the YMCA, but the white Christian man had a clear responsibility that was manifested through action. For the courageous adventurer, action was likewise central, whether in the lure of the mission field, the attraction of "muscular Christianity" and sports, or the call to social service in a society that was rapidly becoming urban and industrial rather than rural and agrarian. Action remained the key to Christian spirituality for Protestant men.

The world of business that dominated much writing geared toward men in the early twentieth century demanded particular styles of action. Efficiency, the ability to manage, providing leadership for workers—all reflected the ethos of action that went into an understanding of male spirituality. Simply put, the spiritual man was the one who acted like Jesus in crafting a dynamic religion from the yearnings of a handful of disparate disciples. For the positive thinker, action was more mental, though its results were again usually seen in the world of business and successful careers. A man had to visualize what results he wanted in order for vision to become empirical reality. The faithful leader, too, was a man of action, the loving servant who once again assumed leadership of his family and set the tone for their common life.

The emphasis on action that undergirds the dominant images of male spirituality and what it means to be a Christian man in white Protestant America helps explain the significance attached to what is practical in each of those images. The efficient businessman wanted results. His spirituality had to be practical, not theoretical, in order to guarantee those results. The positive thinker was not given just to arbitrary psychologizing. Thinking about the possibilities in life and calling on an inner reservoir of strength to transform those possibilities into realities meant that religion—spirituality—had to be practical. It was "how to" that mattered more than anything else. The practical dimension echoes through the nineteenth-century advice books for young men as well as in their late-twentieth-century counterparts in many of the writings of someone such as Edwin Louis Cole. Spirituality had to provide a blueprint, a set of directions, for accomplishment or it was worthless.

Mere speculation had no place in white American Protestant male spirituality. The discipline and training of the athlete that resounded in some of the understandings of the Christian man, such as the courageous adventurer, likewise accented the importance of what was practical. What was the purpose of training for the athlete if not to assure results that came in victory in competition? Action demanded a practical spirituality, not "pie in the sky" piety that had no cash value in the real world of work and play.

Morals More than Doctrine

Perhaps because of its focus on action, white male spirituality has emphasized moral behavior more than the particulars of belief. Although sociologist Nancy Ammerman was writing more about lived religion in late-twentieth-century American Protestant circles when she suggested that "Golden Rule Christianity" was more pervasive than doctrine or creed, her argument applies as well to the images white Protestants have provided for men in terms of what it means to be a Christian and to live a spiritual life.[1] For the most part, those addressing an audience primarily of men or writing about what being a Christian man was all about have simply assumed the basics of belief, without ever examining core theological doctrines or exploring particular constructs. Few have looked at something as fundamental to the Christian tradition as the nature of God and the person of Jesus Christ. In the host of guidebooks for young men that helped give shape to the model of the gentleman entrepreneur for the Christian man, for example, many writers talked about the importance of belief in God. Virtually none probed just what that belief entailed or how different concepts of God might have very different ramifications for how one became a man of action in the larger society.

The popular understanding of the Puritans as Protestants who were consumed by matters of right doctrine unravels a bit when one looks, for example, at the diary of Samuel Sewall, who represented the paragon of the dutiful patriarch. Sewall did make a public statement of his belief in order to join in the church covenant, but he waited until social circumstances made it prudent. He often commented about the challenges in carrying out his religious obligations within the household and noted frequently in his diary that he took time for personal meditation and reflection—itself something of an anomaly. But he rarely wrote about his personal religious beliefs. The closest he came to delving into matters of doctrine came in his expressions of unworthiness when he was about to present one of his children for baptism and his hope that his own sin would not be imputed to the child and thereby hinder the child's hope of election to salvation. Right belief was assumed more than it was articulated, for the constellation of images that went into constructing the model of the dutiful patriarch did see the biblical notions of God as father and God as an authority figure as analogues for the committed Puritan man.

In lifting up moral values such as honesty and integrity as the key to success, the spiritual images associated with the gentleman entrepreneur and the efficient businessman likewise illustrate how images of white male spirituality and the ideal Protestant Christian man downplay matters of belief. Bruce Barton could craft a portrait of Jesus as the model for the efficient businessman without going into any extended christological discussion or even raising the host of thorny issues surrounding what it meant for the Christian tradition to claim that Jesus was both divine and human, God and man.

As well, the spirituality linked to the idea of the positive thinker avoids specifics of belief. Dale Carnegie, Norman Vincent Peale, and Robert

Schuller might all insist that divine power was essential to the process of positive thinking and somehow responsible for what happened when the hopes and aspirations of the man of faith became reality. That power likewise enabled the positive thinker to tap an inner reservoir of strength. But little was said about the nature of the God behind that power or about how to resolve the theological dilemma that might result if two men had opposing goals but each fit the model of the positive thinker.

Even the model for white male spirituality and the Christian man presented in the courageous adventurer is one that sidesteps details of doctrine. Far more important was the willingness of a man to give himself over to a righteous cause, to persevere in service to others regardless of the personal cost or consequences. The faithful leader likewise emerges as one for whom the minutiae of right belief become buried under the greater need to reassert some sort of symbolic spiritual authority. Drawing men from a range of theological traditions to their rallies, Promise Keepers, for example, would have reached millions fewer if it had made doctrinal agreement basic to its understanding of spirituality and reconciliation between husbands and wives or between men of different racial and ethnic backgrounds. The differences in belief stemming from the nuanced interpretation of various doctrines from one denomination to another would have undercut the hopes for any reconciliation by stressing what divided men, not what united them.

Hence, the way American Protestant men live out their spirituality, because of its focus on action, has not stressed creed and doctrine. Instead, it has offered a practical approach to morality and ethics that would support the man of action in the larger society. The minimizing of doctrine and belief is another dimension of the practical thrust that undergirds white Protestant male spirituality. Doing theology is a speculative enterprise, an abstract endeavor that may or may not have any direct connection to how one deals with an employer or how one demonstrates his worth on the job. In theory, ethics may be have its roots in theology, but those connections are of little import in the presentation of spiritual images and models of the Christian man for American Protestant men. Ethical principles have value primarily because living by them and working by them brings practical results. Morals have a payoff; the payoff is success, whether as a gentleman entrepreneur, courageous adventurer, efficient businessman, or positive thinker.

External Relations More than Internal Musing

If the exercises and disciplines commonly associated with traditional approaches to spirituality highlight the inner life or what a man does with his solitude, those exercises and disciplines form only minor elements in the dominant images offered to white American Protestant men who have sought to lead a spiritual life. Rather than looking inward, those images have emphasized external relationships. Even the positive thinker who exercises the mind and taps into a personal power does so because of the practical results that will ensue in dealing with other men, most often in the world of career and work. The dutiful patriarch and the faithful leader both place striking importance on a man's relationships with his wife and children and, in the case of the dutiful patriarch, with others who make up the household. There are obligations and responsibilities attached to the life of faith that involve not only the man himself but also those persons who are in close relationship with him. For many, those relations extended into the larger society. The dutiful patriarch was also a godly magistrate.

Several of the clusters of spiritual images extended to white American Protestant men in their efforts to discern what being a Christian man is all about have to do with the relationships one had with other men, usually with one's employers or co-workers but sometimes just with one's male friends. Part of the rationale for the establishment of the YMCA, an agency that helped foster the image of the gentleman entrepreneur, was to provide an environment in which working men could be associated with other working men of high moral and spiritual character. William Alcott, Sylvester Graham, and the many others who drafted handbooks of practical advice for young working men highlighted the importance attached to a man's relationships with other men and the centrality of being associated only with those who also adhered to principles of integrity and honesty, those who shared the same moral values as the gentleman entrepreneur. The Jesus of Bruce Barton, the model for the efficient businessman, was known primarily as a leader of men. In other words, he was known by his relationships in guiding an inchoate group of unlettered fishermen into a cadre of workers who provided the labor force that made Christianity a success. He was remembered because of his relationships with others.

The inward aspect of spirituality did not completely vanish. Every model for the ideal Christian man presumed that the spiritual man, for example, was a man of prayer. But as I have repeatedly noted, all of those models also presumed that men knew what prayer was all about and how its practice could be incorporated into a life of action. Samuel Sewall suggested in his diaries that he sometimes removed himself from the society around him, whether of the society of household or of work, for a time of personal prayer and meditation, but he never indicated just what he did on those occasions. One infers that there was a sense in which they strength-

MALE SPIRITUALITY IN WHITE PROTESTANT AMERICA   217

ened his resolve to return to the multitude of external relationships where others could discern his steadfastness in carrying out his obligations, his commitment to spirituality and to being a Christian man, through his behavior.

The businessmen's revival of the late 1850s, which represented one of the high points in the development of the cluster of images associated with the gentleman entrepreneur, likewise had prayer as a significant component, for the noontime prayer meetings of the faithful were vital to sustaining the revival. Yet much of those meetings was given over to testimony of the practical results that came from being a Christian man, whether in terms of abandoning a wanton life of immorality for the integrity and purity that employers favored or for the fortitude that positioned a man to be a "good" husband and father. Those testimonies often attributed the transformation that came to a man who embarked on the path to being a devoted gentleman entrepreneur to the prayers of women, usually the prayers of a devout and long-suffering wife or mother. Even when prayer was critical to buttressing male spirituality, therefore, its function was to enable a man to be more appropriately positioned in his relationships with others.

Prayer has also marked some of the festivities associated with Promise Keepers rallies held in football stadiums and hence is not absent altogether from the image of the white Christian man as the faithful leader and from the spirituality clustered around that image. However, many of these prayers resemble the cheers of sports fans, the usual crowd in these venues, more than they do the sustained discipline of personal prayer. Even when small groups of men gather together for directed prayer, the result looks more like the huddle before a play at a football game than a group of the devout in humble meditation. And the group dimension reinforces the emphasis on external relationships that has run through most notions of male spirituality in Protestant America.

Finding Space for Men to Be Spiritual

Repeatedly the gender imbalance in the membership of Protestant churches and in attendance at worship services has informed this discussion of the Christian man and male spirituality. Particularly since the early nineteenth century, when American culture first began to fix gender roles that would remain in place for nearly two centuries, religious institutions such as Protestant churches were seen as feminine and the practice of religion, spirituality, located primarily in the domain of women. One result is that many of the subsequent ideas of what it meant for a white Protestant male to be a Christian and of how he went about demonstrating that Christian identity in a life oriented toward spirituality minimized the necessity of being formally connected with a religious body such as a church. By the end of the nineteenth century, belonging to a church—with a few notable exceptions—became identified as a feminine trait. Even at the dawn of the twenty-first century, studies that attempted to measure spirituality or religiousness tended to identify men whose spirituality included church membership as evidencing feminine traits. For some, the rule of thumb was that a male whose responses to questions about self-identity marked him as evidencing more feminine personality traits than masculine ones was also likely to be more religious.[2]

Most of the advice books for young men that helped shaped the image of the gentleman entrepreneur made little reference to formal church membership, although some assumed that a white Christian man would be affiliated with a congregation. Instead, the venues for developing a spiritual life were shifted more in the directions of groups like the YMCA that were exclusively male in their constituency. Noontime prayer meetings in the businessmen's revival, while having a smattering of women in attendance, were also attempts to seize space where men could express their spirituality and affirm a Christian identity apart from the presence of women that was numerically or even symbolically overwhelming. So too are gatherings of groups such as the Full Gospel Businessmen's Fellowship International efforts to provide space for men to be religious with other men.

Even the emphasis on work and gainful employment that undergirded especially the images of the gentleman entrepreneur, the courageous adventurer, and the efficient businessman signified an attempt to have a psychological space where men could interact with other men in a predominantly male environment. To some extent, the developing factories were for laboring men what the churches were to the women, the symbolic center of a male world where there were few women present. They were thus places were men could celebrate their identities as men and discover, in relationship with other men, what it meant to be a Christian and to live a spiritual life.

As the image of the gentleman entrepreneur yielded to that of the courageous adventurer, the sense that men would more likely affirm a Christian identity outside of religious institutions and in contexts that were restricted to men or at least almost exclusively male gained momentum. One way to account for the attractiveness of all-male fraternal orders and lodges, with their reliance on religious language and rituals, is to see them as providing space that was not feminized and therefore space where males could be "real men." Although church leaders often regarded lodges and fraternal groups as dangerous competition that drew men away from the churches, the men were not in the churches anyway. Rather, these groups were complementary to the churches, providing an environment where men could be both males and spiritual beings. They functioned as religious groups simply because it was through them that millions of men gained a sense of direction and purpose for their lives. They nurtured a spiritual sensibility.

The emphasis on locating and protecting a distinctive male space fed into the approach of muscular Christianity and its efforts to cultivate the religious lives of men, particularly in the way this movement influenced congregations to build gymnasia, organize sports teams, and hold athletic events. Without consciously affirming that traditional churches were part of the domain of women, advocates of muscular Christianity instinctively looked for space apart from anything associated with women or with feminine personality traits to promote ways men could be religious.

The popular notion of the crass masculinity of professional athletes helped inspire the theatrics of evangelist Billy Sunday, a former baseball player who consciously sought to emulate the crudeness of male language in his preaching style. If ordained Protestant clergy were feminized men to the core, Sunday would demonstrate that one could be a real man and still pray. One could express spiritual concerns in colloquial language, aspire to be the paragon of masculinity, and still be a Christian man, a courageous adventurer. Sunday's meetings for men only predated Promise Keepers by more than three-quarters of a century, yet both were propelled by the conviction that traditional churches were so feminized that they were not good locations for men to affirm a Christian identity and build a viable spirituality.

For white American Protestant men, then, a Christian identity and the development of spiritual life were likely to occur in venues other than traditional religious institutions. In some cases, the workplace, or at least the associations a man formed with co-workers, whether on the job or in a residence like the YMCA, provided a place that functioned almost as a religious incubator to shape a Christian identity and spur a spiritual life. In others, separate organizations and structures developed, ranging from fraternal orders that met in lodge halls to Promise Keepers rallies that packed men into sports stadiums. But under certain conditions, these places likewise took on religious dimensions and became sacred spaces for men much in the way that the church and home were long sacred spaces for women. The Men and Religion Forward Movement, in promoting the image of the courageous adventurer, did have some lectures that were open only to men in church buildings, but many were in other auditoriums.

For yet others, a white male Christian identity was forged and a distinctive spirituality maintained on a more individual basis, but usually in some kind of association with other men. Hence, the positive thinker set out to impress other men with his skills and potential. The efficient businessman exuded a dynamic leadership over other men, modeled after that of Jesus. Neither required a traditional religious institution or an obviously religious space in order to function. The links to other men might be more implicit than explicit. They were such for the dutiful patriarch, whose private commitments recorded in letters and diaries were intensely personal, but who expected that his fellow men would witness the example he sought to live in part because they were engaged in the same pursuits.

Real Men Pray

So much of the writing directed to white Protestant men and so many programs designed to attract men to the Christian life presume that the ideals of the Christian man and the character that sustains those ideals in a spiritual life will be primarily practical rather than theoretical. They must center on morals rather than on doctrines or beliefs, emerge from relationships with others (external orientation) more than from quiet contemplation (internal orientation), and receive undergirding from institutions and networks other than traditional religious organizations. These qualities allow distinctive elements to weave through the tapestry of white male spirituality in America. These dimensions give less emphasis to traditional spiritual disciplines and ways of being religious, such as prayer and meditation. They orient white male spirituality more to the results that can be seen in an individual man's life in terms of success on the job or productive relationships with others, from wives and children to employers and subordinate workers.

Is there a distinctive white male spirituality? Is being a white Christian man in Protestant America something fundamentally different than being a white Christian woman in Protestant America? In other words, is there something in the biology of being male and the psychology of being male that leads men to shun doctrine for ethics, traditional devotion for the results of practical action, membership in a religious community for affiliation with a lodge or labor union or some other entity that is or was part of a "male only" environment? No ready answer emerges even now.

Menarche and menopause have frequently served as biological markers for those who have sought to craft a spirituality and religious identity unique to women, markers that have a ready tie to the rhythms of life that undergird all existence and that are more likely addressed directly in some forms of Goddess worship. Also propelling a passion for constructing a way of being religious that emerges from women's experience was the sense that religious institutions, like churches and congregations, were part of a male world even if women made up the majority of members. That conviction logically followed from social patterns that once restricted professional ministry to men and limited opportunities for women to exercise leadership at the top ranks of religious organizations. Women were a majority that remained a minority, given assumptions about gender roles that spilled over from the larger culture into the arena of Protestant Christianity.

The obverse does not seem to hold. That is, what some have called semenarche, a contrived term to denote the experience of puberty for men, and a gradual change in sexual desire and perhaps ability to function sexually as men age have not had carried the same obvious religious significance for men. There are simply less obvious links to the natural rhythms of birth and death in the male experience, although they are surely there. Instead, cultural markers for male identity have revolved around work and roles played in association with others. These markers have had an impact on all the images of the Christian man and male spirituality examined here, from the dutiful patriarch to the faithful leader.

The one common element that crosses gender lines, one that emerged only gradually in American religious life, is the felt need to construct religious identity and buttress spirituality in contexts that are generally restricted to persons of the same gender. It may be that the religious impact of second-wave feminism spurred more women to seek ways of being religious in all-female contexts. But second-wave feminism also came to the fore as Protestant religious institutions were opening the ranks of the clergy and other leadership positions to women, unwittingly cementing even more the cultural equation of that which is generally accepted as religious as being feminine rather than masculine. At the beginning of the twenty-first century, white churches were still religious institutions where women outnumbered men. Men still sought to sustain a Christian identity in other venues.

Yet most of the images of the Christian man that have developed within white American Protestantism have assumed that real men pray. If the dutiful patriarch and the faithful leader carried out their obligations to be the spiritual heads of their households, doing so involved prayer, whether in family devotions or in a man's personal life. The positive thinker could pray as a means to summon divine power to sustain the inner strength to transform visions into reality, to render dreams and hopes tangible. The gentleman entrepreneur was exhorted to look to prayer to undergird a life committed to morality and purity. Every image of the white Christian man presumed, however, that men knew what prayer was all about and knew how to pray. That assumption is flawed because men have not sought out the religious institutions and agencies that could help them understand prayer as a spiritual discipline or cultivate the spiritual traits where prayer became natural rather than contrived.

White American Protestantism has offered males a host of images of what it means to be a Christian man and a host of images linking spirituality to the lived experience of men. But white American Protestantism by and large has not offered the resources that would allow men to bind those images to the spiritual disciplines, like prayer, that have been part of the substructure of the Protestant Christian tradition.

For many men whose spirituality is shaped by white American Protestant notions of the Christian man, one hears echoes of the first-century disciples in their request, "Lord, teach us to pray." The challenge to white American Protestantism in the twenty-first century, then, is to offer a model of the Christian man and an understanding of male spirituality that will bring together the spiritual disciplines and habits that have emerged within the Christian tradition with the lived experience of men as males. If white American Protestantism can succeed in this effort, more men might pray.

Notes

Preface

1. Betty A. DeBerg, *Ungodly Women: Gender and the First Wave of American Fundamentalism* (Minneapolis: Fortress, 1990).
2. Donald Capps, *Men and Their Religion: Honor, Hope, and Humor* (Harrisburg, Pa.: Trinity Press International, 2002).

Chapter 1

1. Several studies are pertinent: Robert N. Bellah, William M. Sullivan, Ann Swidler, and Steven M. Tipton, *Habits of the Heart: Individualism and Commitment in American Life* (Berkeley: Univ. of California Press, 1985); Benton Johnson, Donald A. Luidens, and Dean R. Hoge, *Vanishing Boundaries: The Religion of Mainline Protestant Baby Boomers* (Louisville, Ky.: Westminster John Knox, 1994); Wade Clark Roof, *A Generation of Seekers: The Spiritual Journeys of the Baby Boomer Generation* (San Francisco: Harper, 1994); Wade Clark Roof, *Spiritual Marketplace: Baby Boomers and the Remaking of American Religion* (Princeton, N.J.: Princeton Univ. Press, 1999); and Robert Wuthnow, *After Heaven: Spirituality in America Since the 1950s* (Berkeley: Univ. of California Press, 1998).
2. See Charles H. Lippy, *Pluralism Comes of Age: American Religious Culture in the Twentieth Century* (Armonk, N.Y.: M. E. Sharpe, 2000), esp. chap. 2. For a complementary study told from the vantage of intellectual history, see Amanda Porterfield, *The Transformation of American Religion: The Story of a Late Twentieth Century Awakening* (New York: Oxford Univ. Press, 2001).
3. Some studies have demonstrated that congregations may remain vital; see Carl Dudley and David Roozen, eds., *Faith Communities Today (FACT): A Report on Religion in the United States Today* (Hartford, Conn.: Hartford Institute for Religion Research of the Hartford Seminary Foundation, 2001).
4. See Roof, *Generation of Seekers;* Roof, *Spiritual Marketplace;* and Wuthnow, *After Heaven.*
5. See "Religion and the Brain: In the New Field of 'Neurotheology,' Scientists Seek the Biological Basis of Spirituality," *Newsweek,* May 17, 2001, 50–57; "Tracing the Synapses of Our Spirituality: Researchers Examine the Relationship between the Brain and Religion," *Washington Post,* June 17, 2001, p. A1; and Sharon Bagley, "Searching

for the God Within: The Way Our Brains Are Wired May Explain the Origin and Power of Religious Beliefs," *Newsweek,* Jan. 29, 2001, 59.

6. Here again the work of Capps, *Men and Their Religion,* is instructive, particularly his claim that the real dynamic of Protestant male spirituality is "invisible" sometimes even to men themselves.

7. See, for example, Starhawk, *The Spiral Dance* (San Francisco: Harper, 1979); Z[suszana] Budapest, *Grandmother Moon* (San Francisco: Harper, 1991); Z[suszana] Budapest, *The Grandmother of Time: A Woman's Book of Celebrations, Spells, and Sacred Objects for Every Month of the Year* (San Francisco: Harper, 1989); and Z[suszana] Budapest, *The Holy Book of Women's Mysteries* (Oakland, Calif.: Wingbow, 1989). Robert Orsi has examined aspects of the spirituality of Roman Catholic women oriented to St. Jude in his provocative *Thank You, St. Jude: Women's Devotion to the Patron Saint of Lost Causes* (New Haven, Conn.: Yale Univ. Press, 1996). Contemporary Jewish women are also developing ritual resources to reflect their spiritual experiences as women; see Susan Grossman, "Finding Comfort after a Miscarriage," in *Daughters of the King,* ed. Susan Grossman and Rivka Haupt (Philadelphia: Jewish Publication Society of America, 1992), 285–90.

8. Jon Butler argued that the colonial population needed to be "Christianized" because such a small proportion were actually church members; see his *Awash in a Sea of Faith: Christianizing the American People* (Cambridge: Harvard Univ. Press, 1990). For one account of the story, see Roger Finke and Rodney Stark, *The Churching of America, 1776–1990: Winners and Losers in Our Religious Economy* (New Brunswick, N.J.: Rutgers Univ. Press, 1992).

9. See Cedric B. Cowing, "Sex and Preaching in the Great Awakening," *American Quarterly* 20, no. 3 (Fall 1968): 624–44; and Herbert Moller, "Sex Composition and Correlated Culture Patterns in Colonial America," *William and Mary Quarterly,* 3d ser., 2 (1945): 113–53.

10. That the perception prevails receives confirmation in the opening two sentences of John Dart, "Men Behaving Badly: Gender and Churchgoing," *Christian Century* 117, no. 32 (Nov. 15, 2000): 1174–75: "'Women are more religious than men.' That's a long-standing generalization made by pastors surveying their pews and by social scientists surveying the public."

11. This is implicit in Capps, *Men and Their Religion.*

12. Barbara Welter's classic essay "The Feminization of Religion in America, 1800–1860" is reprinted in her *Dimity Convictions: The American Woman in the Nineteenth Century* (Athens: Ohio Univ. Press, 1992), 83–102.

13. The classic study is Philip Greven, *The Protestant Temperament: Patterns of Child-Rearing, Religious Experience, and the Self in Early America* (New York: Knopf, 1977).

14. See Colleen McDannell, *The Christian Home in Victorian America, 1840–1900* (Bloomington: Indiana Univ. Press, 1986).

15. Jonathan Edwards, *A Treatise Concerning Religious Affections in Three Parts,* ed. John E. Smith, in *The Works of Jonathan Edwards,* vol. 2 (New Haven, Conn.: Yale Univ. Press, 1959). The work was first published in 1746.

16. Ann Douglas, *The Feminization of American Culture* (New York: Knopf, 1977); Welter's work is cited in note 12 above. I shall return to Welter's and Douglas's work in chapter 3.

17. Harriet Beecher Stowe, *The Minister's Wooing*, with a new introduction by Sandra R. Duguid (1859; reprint, Hartford, Conn.: Harriet Beecher Stowe Center, 1978).

18. Barbara Epstein, *The Politics of Domesticity: Women, Evangelism and Temperance in Nineteenth-Century America* (Middletown, Conn.: Wesleyan Univ. Press, 1981). See the counterargument in Susan Juster, "'In a Different Voice': Male and Female Narratives of Religious Conversion in Post-Revolutionary America," *American Quarterly* 41 (Mar. 1989): 34–62.

19. See the discussion of the businessmen's revival in chapter 3.

20. See the discussion in chapter 4.

21. Although his approach is very different from mine, Donald Capps also reaches this conclusion in his *Men and Their Religion*.

22. Mary Beth Norton, *Founding Mothers and Fathers: Gendered Power and the Forming of American Society* (New York: Knopf, 1996), argues forcefully that the Puritan understanding of society as hierarchical, patriarchal, and familial derived from the political philosophy set forth by Sir Robert Filmer.

Chapter 2

1. Edmund S. Morgan, *The Puritan Family: Religion and Domestic Religion in Seventeenth-Century New England*, rev. ed. (New York: Harper & Row, 1966), 14.

2. John Demos, *A Little Commonwealth: Family Life in Plymouth Colony* (New York: Oxford Univ. Press, 1970), also emphasizes this point.

3. Lisa Wilson, *Ye Heart of a Man: The Domestic Life of Men in Colonial New England* (New Haven, Conn.: Yale Univ. Press, 1999).

4. Judith S. Graham, *Puritan Family Life: The Diary of Samuel Sewall* (Boston: Northeastern Univ. Press, 2000).

5. Benjamin Wadsworth, *The Well-Ordered Family; or, Relative Duties*, 2d ed. (Boston: S. Kneeland for Nicholas Buttolph, 1715. No complete copy of the 1712 original edition has been found.

6. Cotton Mather, *A Family Well-Ordered, Or an Essay to Render Parents and Children Happy in One Another* (Boston: B. Green and J. Allen for Michael Perry, 1699), 3–4.

7. William Gouge, *Of Domesticall Duties: Eight Treatises* (London: John Haviland, 1622).

8. See David Hackett Fischer's magisterial study, *Albion's Seed: Four British Folkways in America* (New York: Oxford Univ. Press, 1989).

9. Norton, *Founding Mothers and Fathers*.

10. See Norton, *Founding Mothers and Fathers*, 38.

11. Ibid., 35–41.

12. Morgan, *Puritan Family*, chap. 2. See also Demos, *Little Commonwealth*, 104–6.

13. Wadsworth, *Well-Ordered Family*, 25.

14. There is an enormous literature on Puritan child-rearing practices that evidences considerable disagreement among recent historians regarding them. Such lie beyond the purview of this discussion, although it is worth noting that most disagreement concerns whether such practices were overly severe and whether until near the end

of the eighteenth century dutiful patriarchs would have seen their offspring as sinful, miniature adults rather than as children per se. It seems to me, from reading numerous diaries, letters, and sermons, that they theory comes across as far more rigid and severe than the actual practice. Both Wilson, *Ye Heart of a Man*, and Graham, *Puritan Family Life*, summarize a good deal of this literature. The most comprehensive study, although its conclusions have been challenged, is Greven, *Protestant Temperament*.

15. Mather, *Family Well-Ordered*, 22.

16. Michael Zuckerman, *Peaceable Kingdoms: New England Towns in the Eighteenth Century* (New York: Knopf, 1970), 73, is among those who insists that Puritan fathers regarded offspring as miniature adults and thus denied them a real childhood because they were thought to be infected by original sin. In my estimation, Zuckerman overstates the case. To be sure, children, as all humans, were thought to be tainted by original sin, but such did not mean that their status as children was denied. Why would Puritan parents have gone to such efforts to educate and instruct children if not to help children learn what being a responsible adult was all about? Cotton Mather, in his *Parental Wishes and Charges, Or, The Enjoyment of a Glorious Christ* (Boston: T. Green, 1705), 23, noted that parents are well aware of how original sin infects their children; he then urges parents who wish their children to enjoy Christ to guide their children by their counsel and their own conduct so that they will learn how to avoid evil.

17. Cotton Mather, *The Diary of Cotton Mather, 1681–1724*, ed. Worthington Chauncey Ford, *Collections of the Massachusetts Historical Society*, 7th ser., vols. 7–8 (Boston: Massachusetts Historical Society, 1911–12); reprinted in 2 vols. (New York: F. Ungar [1957]), 2:127. See also Elizabeth Bancroft Schlesinger, "Cotton Mather and His Children," *William and Mary Quarterly*, 3d ser., 10 (Apr. 1953): 181–89.

18. John C. Miller, *The First Frontier: Life in Colonial America* (New York: Laurel, 1966), 215–16.

19. Mather, *Diary*, 2:485.

20. See Kenneth Silverman, ed., *Selected Letters of Cotton Mather* (Baton Rouge: Louisiana State Univ. Press, 1971), xii.

21. See the discussion in Anne S. Brown and David D. Hall, "Family Strategies and Religious Practice: Baptism and the Lord's Supper in Early New England," in *Lived Religion in America: Toward a History of Practice*, ed. David D. Hall (Princeton, N.J.: Princeton Univ. Press, 1997), 41–68.

22. Cotton Mather, *Right Thoughts in Sad Hours, Representing the Comforts and Duties of Good Men under all their Afflictions, And Particularly, That One, the Untimely Death of Children* (London: L. B. Seeley and Sons, 1689).

23. Wadsworth, *Well-Ordered Family*, 51–58. See also Demos, *Little Commonwealth*, 104–5.

24. Cotton Mather, *Bonifacius: An Essay upon the Good, That Is to Be Devised and Designed by Those Who desire to Answer the Great End of Life, and to Do Good While They Live* (Boston: B. Green for Samuel Gerrish, 1710).

25. Cotton Mather, *Optanda. Good Men Described, and Good Things Propounded* (Boston: Benjamin Harris, 1692).

26. See, for example, Steven Mintz and Susan Kellogg, *Domestic Revolutions: A Social History of American Family Life* (New York: Free Press, 1988), chap. 1.

27. Kenneth A. Lockridge, *A New England Town: The First Hundred Years* (New York: W. W. Norton, 1970), long ago pointed out this problem. The way shortage of

land to distribute to sons undermined a father's authority in all areas of life is also emphasized by Mintz and Kellogg, *Domestic Revolutions,* 18.

28. Thomas Shepard, *Works of Thomas Shepard,* ed. John Albro, 3 vols. (Boston: Doctrinal Tract and Book Society, 1853), 3:263, quoted in Morgan, *Puritan Family,* 7.

29. Wadsworth, *Well-Ordered Family,* 59, 103–12.

30. Cotton Mather outlines the standard pattern for family devotions led by the father in *A Family Sacrifice: A Brief Essay to Direct and Excite Family Religion* (Boston: B. Green and J. Allen, 1703), 30–38.

31. Alice Morse Earle, *Home Life in Colonial Days* (1898; reprint, Middle Village, N.Y.: Jonathan David, 1975), 379–80, provides a classic description of Sabbath keeping in the Cotton household, although she does not identify her sources.

32. Arthur Cole, "The Tempo of Mercantile Life in Colonial America," *Business History Review* 33 (1959): 277–99. He notes (290) the extraordinarily high degree of both religious and civic involvement of Puritan men based on his examination of diaries.

33. Mather, *Family Sacrifice;* Cotton Mather, *Family Religion Excited and Assisted,* 2d impression (Boston: B. Green, 1707); and Cotton Mather, *Family Religion Urged* (Boston: B. Green, 1709). See also Richard F. Lovelace, *The American Pietism of Cotton Mather: Origins of American Evangelicalism* (Grand Rapids, Mich.: Christian Univ. Press, 1979), 126.

34. Mather, *Diary,* 1:520, entry for July 27, 1705.

35. Mather, *Family Religion Urged,* 5.

36. Increase Mather, *The Duty of Parents to Pray for Their Children Open and Applyed in a Sermon, Preached May 19, 1703* (Boston: B. Green and J. Allen, 1703).

37. See Mather, *Diary,* 2:25, entry for Feb. 3, 1710.

38. Cotton Mather, *Pastoral Desires* (Boston: B. Green for Nicholas Boone, 1712), 82–83. Mather notes the importance of baptism in ibid., 31.

39. Wadsworth, *Well-Ordered Family,* 64–65.

40. Ibid., 81.

41. Mather, *Diary,* 1:239–40.

42. Ibid., 2:485, entry for Sept. 7, 1717.

43. Mather, *Pastoral Desires,* 82–83.

44. David Stannard, *The Puritan Way of Death: A Study in Religion, Culture, and Social Change* (New York: Oxford Univ. Press, 1977), 69–71.

45. Morgan, *Puritan Family,* 88.

46. An example of a discourse presented to a religious society of young men is the first of the sermons appearing in Cotton Mather, *Piety and Equity United* (Boston: J. Allen for Robert Starke, 1717).

47. Mather, *Diary,* 1:177–78, 1:322, 1:370, 1:399, 1:419, 1:480, 1:545, 2:275.

48. Wilson, *Ye Heart of a Man,* 129–30.

49. Historians have recognized this gender disparity for generations. See, for example, Moller, "Sex Composition," 113–53; Maurice W. Armstrong, "Religious Enthusiasm and Separatism in Colonial New England," *Harvard Theological Review* 38 (1945): 111–40; and Cowing, "Sex and Preaching," 624–44.

50. Cotton Mather, *Ornaments for the Daughters of Zion* (1692; reprint, Delmar, N.Y.: Scholars' Facsimiles and Reprints, 1978), 48–49.

51. Cotton Mather, *A Good Character* (Boston: B. Green, 1723), 10.

52. Timothy H. Breen, *The Character of the Good Ruler: Puritan Political Ideas in New England, 1630–1730* (New Haven, Conn.: Yale Univ. Press, 1970), remains the classic study.

53. Mather, *Optanda*, 4.

54. Mather, *Right Thoughts*.

55. My understanding of Sewall is based primarily on his diary and his letters: *The Diary of Samuel Sewall*, ed. M. Halsey Thomas, 2 vols. (New York: Farrar, Straus and Giroux, 1973), and *The Letter-Book of Samuel Sewall*, 2 vols., *Collections of the Massachusetts Historical Society*, 6th ser. (Boston: Massachusetts Historical Society, 1886–18), vols. 1–2. I have also relied especially on Graham, *Puritan Family Life;* David D. Hall, "The Mental World of Samuel Sewall," in *Worlds of Wonder, Days of Judgment: Popular Belief in Early New England*, by David D. Hall (New York: Knopf, 1989), 213–38; Ola Elizabeth Winslow, *Samuel Sewall of Boston* (New York: Macmillan, 1964); and Charles G. Steffen, "The Sewall Children in Colonial New England," *New England Historical and Genealogical Register* 131 (1977): 163–72. But see also N. H. Chamberlain, *Samuel Sewall and the World He Lived In* (1897; reprint, New York: Russell and Russell, 1967), and T. B. Strandness, *Samuel Sewall: A Puritan Portrait* (East Lansing: Michigan State Univ. Press, 1967). I have converted all dates to New Style.

56. Hall, "Mental World of Samuel Sewall," is particularly helpful here.

57. Sewall, *Diary*, 1:35.

58. See Sewall, *Diary*, 1:35–40.

59. Hall, "Mental World of Samuel Sewall."

60. Ibid.

61. Sewall, *Diary*, 1:589, entry for Feb. 9, 1708.

62. Ibid., 1:265, entry for Aug. 24, 1690. This Judith died six weeks after her baptism.

63. See, for example, the entry for Jan. 6, 1696, in Sewall, *Diary*, 1:344.

64. Sewall, *Diary*, 1:76 n. 25.

65. Ibid., 1:543, entry for Mar. 27, 1706.

66. Ibid., 1:346, entry for Feb. 1, 1696.

67. Charles E. Hambrick-Stowe, *The Practice of Piety: Puritan Devotional Discipline in Seventeenth-Century New England* (Chapel Hill: Univ. of North Carolina Press, 1982), 9–13.

68. See especially diary material for May 18–23, 1696, in Sewall, *Diary*, 1:350.

69. See, for example, scattered entries in Sewall, *Diary*, 1:345–49.

70. My discussion here is based on numerous entries in Sewall's diary from November 1691 to the spring of 1696.

71. Trouble between the couple is first noted in the diary entry for Feb. 12, 1713 (Sewall, *Diary*, 2:705), and continued for some five years or more.

72. Sewall, *Diary*, 2:706, entry for Dec. 20, 1716.

73. Ibid., 2:705 n. 4.

74. Ibid., 1:179, 545.

75. Ibid., 1:499, entry for Mar. 29, 1704.

76. Ibid., see editor's note inserted after the entry for Mar. 31, 1714, 2:746–47. See also *Diary of Samuel Sewall*, vol. 6 of *Collections of the Massachusetts Historical Society*, 5th ser. (Boston: Massachusetts Historical Society, 1878–82), 427–28.

77. Sewall, *Diary*, 2:864, entry for Oct. 19, 1717.

78. Ibid., 2:882, entry for Feb. 6, 1718.

79. See the Genealogical Appendix in Sewall, *Diary*, 2:1077–78.

Chapter 3

1. See Louis B. Wright, *The First Gentlemen of Virginia: Intellectual Qualities of the Early Colonial Ruling Class* (San Marino, Calif.: Huntington Library, 1940).

2. Among the more recent studies are Edwin S. Gaustad, *Sworn on the Altar of God: A Religious Biography of Thomas Jefferson*, Library of Religious Biography, ed. Mark A. Noll, Nathan S. Hatch, and Alan C. Guelzo (Grand Rapids, Mich.: Eerdmans, 1996); and Kerry S. Walters, *Benjamin Franklin and His Gods* (Urbana: Univ. of Illinois Press, 1999).

3. The appeal of evangelicalism to women is a theme in both Christine Leigh Heyrman, *Southern Cross: The Beginnings of the Bible Belt* (New York: Alfred A. Knopf, 1997); and Cynthia Lynn Lyerly, *Methodism and the Southern Mind, 1770–1810* (New York: Oxford Univ. Press, 1998).

4. The tension between evangelical wives and husbands who wished to reinvigorate the Episcopal Church is an underlying theme of Richard Rankin, *Ambivalent Churchmen and Evangelical Churchwomen: The Religion of the Episcopal Elite in North Carolina, 1800–1860* (Columbia: Univ. of South Carolina Press, 1993).

5. See Charles Reagan Wilson, *Baptized in Blood: The Religion of the Lost Cause, 1865–1920* (Athens: Univ. of Georgia Press, 1980).

6. Mary P. Ryan, *Cradle of the Middle Class: The Family in Oneida County, New York, 1790–1865* (New York: Cambridge Univ. Press, 1981).

7. Helpful here is Paul Johnson, *A Shopkeeper's Millennium: Society and Revivals in Rochester, New York, 1815–1837* (New York: Hill and Wang, 1978), esp. 43–47.

8. Juster, "In a Different Voice," 34–62.

9. Epstein, *Politics of Domesticity.*

10. One of the early classic statements of this argument is Barbara Welter, "The Cult of True Womanhood: 1800–1860," reprinted in *Dimity Convictions: The American Woman in the Nineteenth Century,* by Barbara Welter (Athens: Ohio Univ. Press, 1976), 21–41. The most forceful statement that links this interpretation to currents of Romanticism is Douglas, *Feminization of American Culture,* esp. chaps. 2 and 3.

11. E. Anthony Rotundo, "Learning about Manhood: Gender Ideals and the Middle-Class Family in Nineteenth Century America," in *Manliness and Morality: Middle-Class Masculinity in Britain and America, 1800–1940,* ed. J. A. Mangan and James Walvin (New York: St. Martin's, 1987), 36.

12. John S. Gilkeson Jr., *Middle-Class Providence, 1820–1940* (Princeton, N.J.: Princeton Univ. Press, 1986), 41.

13. See the excerpt in Milton Powell, ed., *The Voluntary Church: American Religious Life Seen through the Eyes of European Visitors* (New York: Macmillan, 1967), 115–16, 125–26.

14. Ibid., 125.

15. From Trollope, *The Domestic Manners of Americans,* in Powell, *Voluntary Church,* 68–69; quotation from 69.

16. Of those read for this study, the only one published in the twentieth century was Albert J. Beveridge, *The Young Man and the World* (New York: Appleton, 1905), which was originally a series of articles appearing in the *Saturday Evening Post.*

17. William A. Alcott, *Gift Book for Young Men: or, Familiar Letters on Self-knowledge, Self-Education, Female Society, Marriage, &c.* (Auburn, N.Y.: Miller, Orton, and Mulligan, 1854), 3. I was not able to examine Alcott's *Young Man's Guide,* but I did locate a copy of its sequel, *Familiar Letters to Young Men on Various Subjects* (1849; reprint, Auburn, N.Y.: Miller, Orton, and Mulligan, 1854).

18. Timothy Shay Arthur, *Advice to Young Men on Their Duties and Conduct in Life* (1847; reprint, Boston: N.C. Barton, 1849).

19. Sylvester Graham, *A Lecture to Young Men, on Chastity,* 2d ed. (1837; reprint, Boston: C. H. Peirce, 1848). The first edition appeared in 1834.

20. Rev. Daniel Wise, *The Young Man's Counselor; or, Sketches and Illustrations of the Duties and Dangers of Young Men,* 31st ed. (New York: Phillips and Hunt, 1850).

21. Arthur, *Advice to Young Men,* chap 2. This chapter is titled "Man—His Origin, Nature and Destiny." Chapter 3 moves to what characterizes "The Age of Responsibility."

22. Ibid., 136.

23. Ibid., 135–42.

24. Graham, *Lecture to Young Men,* 64, 67–68.

25. Wise, *Young Men's Counselor,* 29.

26. Alcott, *Gift Book,* chaps. 32 and 33.

27. Ibid., chap. 4.

28. Ibid., chap. 7, but see also chaps. 5 and 6.

29. Ibid., chap. 10.

30. Wise, *Young Man's Counselor,* in a discussion of intelligence in chapter 4, suggested that religion would propel the intellect in the right direction, including the study of the Bible.

31. Alcott, *Gift Book,* chap. 21. See also Arthur, *Advice to Young Men,* chaps. 6 and 7.

32. Arthur, *Advice to Young Men,* 166–67.

33. See, for example, Alcott, *Gift Book,* chap. 9.

34. Ibid., chap. 19.

35. Wise, *Young Man's Counselor,* chap. 3.

36. Ibid., 33–35.

37. Ibid., chap. 11.

38. Allan Horlick, *Country Boys and Merchant Princes: The Social Control of Young Men in New York* (Lewisburg, Pa.: Bucknell Univ. Press, 1975), 231.

39. Ibid., 235.

40. Although now dated, the standard history of the YMCA movement is C. Howard Hopkins, *History of the Y.M.C.A. in North America* (New York: Association Press, 1951).

41. Horlick, *Country Boys,* 231, emphasizes how the YMCA functioned as a surrogate family.

42. See Ronald Formisano and Kathleen Smith Kutlowski, "Antimasonry and Masonry: The Genesis of Protest, 1826–1827," *American Quarterly* 29 (Summer 1977): 139–65; and Lynn Dumenil, *Freemasonry and American Culture, 1880–1939* (Princeton, N.J.: Princeton Univ. Press, 1984), 7.

43. Dumenil, *Freemasonry and American Culture, 1880–1939*, although concentrating on a later period than I am discussing here, notes (25) that there was much more than escape from the sphere of women to the attraction of fraternal societies for men.

44. Ibid., 32.

45. Dorothy Ann Lipson, *Freemasonry in Federalist Connecticut, 1789–1835* (Princeton, N.J.: Princeton Univ. Press, 1977), 1–45.

46. Ibid., 187–97, 329–38; Dumenil, *Freemasonry and American Culture*, 25.

47. Donald Yacovone, "Abolitionists and the 'Language of Fraternal Love,'" in *Meanings for Manhood: Constructions of Masculinity in Victorian America*, ed. Mark C. Carnes and Clyde Griffen (Chicago: Univ. of Chicago Press, 1990), 85–95.

48. Alcott, *Gift Book*, chaps. 30 and 31.

49. Wise, *Young Man's Counselor*, chap. 12.

50. Ibid., 247.

51. Arthur, *Advice to Young Men*, 168–69.

52. William A. Alcott, *The Young Husband; or, Duties of Man in the Marriage Relation* (1837; reprint of 5th ed. [1841], New York: Arno, 1972).

53. Ibid., chap. 4.

54. See the description of the Tuesday meetings in Richard Wheatley, *The Life and Letters of Mrs. Phoebe Palmer* (1876; reprint, New York: Garland, 1984), 238–57.

55. The best analysis is Kathryn Teresa Long, *The Revival of 1857–58: Interpreting an American Religious Awakening* (New York: Oxford Univ. Press, 1998).

56. Samuel Irenaeus Prime, an indefatigable contemporary chronicler of the revival, emphasized that the noontime gatherings were led by laymen, not clergy. See his commentary in *The Power of Prayer, Illustrated in the Wonderful Displays of Divine Grace at the Fulton Street and Other Meetings* (New York: Scribner's, 1858), 57.

57. Ibid., 14.

58. In addition to Prime's *Power of Prayer*, already noted, see Samuel Irenaeus Prime, *Fifteen Years of Prayer in the Fulton Street Meeting* (New York: Scribner's, 1872); James W. Alexander, *The Revival and Its Lessons* (New York: American Tract Society, 1858); James W. Alexander, ed., *The New York Pulpit in the Revival of 1858: A Memorial Volume of Sermons* (New York: Sheldon, Blakeman, 1858); and William C. Conant, *Narratives of Remarkable Conversions and Revival Incidents* (New York: Derby and Jackson, 1858). The last work also treats earlier revivals and accounts of conversion, but does devote considerable space to the revival of 1857–58. See also Russell E. Francis, "The Religious Revival of 1858 in Philadelphia," *Pennsylvania Magazine of History and Biography* 70 (1946): 52–77; and Richard Carwardine, "The Religious Revival of 1857–58 in the United States," in *Religious Motivation: Biographical and Sociological Problems for the Church Historian*, ed. Derek Baker (Oxford: Blackwell, 1978), 393–406.

59. Prime, *Power of Prayer*, 178.

60. Prime, *Fifteen Years of Prayer*, 147.

61. Alexander, *Revival and Its Lessons*, esp. chap. 12.

62. Long, *Revival of 1857–58*, 87, 89.

63. Ibid., 87.

64. James O. Henry, "The United States Christian Commission in the Civil War," *Civil War History* 6 (1960): 374–88.

65. Drew Gilpin Faust, "Christian Soldiers: The Meaning of Revivalism in the Confederate Army," *Journal of Southern History* 58 (Feb. 1987): 63–90.

66. I take the phrase from Margaret L. Bendroth, "Horace Bushnell's Christian

Nurture," in *The Child in Christian Thought*, ed. Marcia J. Bunge (Grand Rapids, Mich.: Eerdmans, 2001), 350–64.

67. My understanding of Dodge comes primarily from the appreciative tribute compiled by his son, D. Stuart Dodge, *Memorials of William E. Dodge* (New York: Randolph, 1887); the well-known lecture presented by Dodge in his later years, *Old New York: A Lecture* (New York: Dodd, Mead, 1880); numerous references to Dodge by Theodore L. Cuyler in his *Recollections of a Long Life* (New York: Baker and Taylor, 1902); the laudatory biography by Carlos Martyn, *William E. Dodge: The Christian Merchant, American Reformers Series* (New York: Funk and Wagnalls, 1890); Richard Lowitt's study of Dodge as a businessman, *A Merchant Prince of the Nineteenth Century: William E. Dodge* (New York: Columbia Univ. Press, 1954); and Horlick, *Country Boys*, chap. 3.

68. Dodge, *Memorials*, 11.

69. Cuyler, *Recollections*, 56.

70. Dodge was among those who, in 1828, had persuaded Charles Grandison Finney to come to New York City for a revival campaign the following year. When Finney and his wife arrived in New York in 1829, they resided with Dodge's in-laws, Anson and Elizabeth Phelps.

71. Dodge, *Memorials*, 42.

72. Cuyler, *Recollections*, 56.

73. William E. Dodge, *Old New York*, 59. See also Dodge, *Memorials*, chap. 16.

74. Martyn, *William E. Dodge*, 124.

75. See Lowitt, *Merchant Prince*, 196–98.

76. See Dodge, *Memorials*, chap. 18, and Martyn, *William E. Dodge*, 295.

77. Martyn, *William E. Dodge*, 298.

78. Ibid., 300–309, provides a detailed discussion of the golden wedding anniversary celebration.

79. See Horlick, *Country Boys*, chap. 3.

80. The episode is recounted in Lowitt, *Merchant Prince*, 174–78.

81. Ibid., 177–78.

82. Ibid., 335.

Chapter 4

1. Ted Ownby, *Subduing Satan: Religion, Recreation and Manhood in the Rural South, 1865–1910* (Chapel Hill: Univ. of North Carolina Press, 1990), 6–11.

2. Beveridge, *Young Man and the World*.

3. Josiah Strong, *The Times and Young Men* (New York: Baker and Taylor, 1901). Strong sets out his basic argument in chapters 5 to 7 and then applies the laws of service, self-giving, and love to such specific matters as how one uses one's time and how one spends one's money in the chapters that follow.

4. Ibid., chaps. 10 and 11.

5. Frederick A. Atkins, *Moral Muscle, and How to Use It: A Brotherly Chat with Young Men* (London: James Nisbet, 1890); quotation from 62.

6. Susan Curtis, "The Son of Man and God the Father: The Social Gospel and

Victorian Masculinity," in *Meanings for Manhood: Constructions of Masculinity in Victorian America*, ed. Mark C. Carnes and Clyde Griffen (Chicago: Univ. of Chicago Press, 1990), 67-78; quotations from 72. Curtis amplified her thesis considerably in *A Consuming Faith: The Social Gospel and Modern American Culture* (Baltimore: Johns Hopkins Univ. Press, 1991).

7. Walter Rauschenbusch, quoted in Curtis, "Son of Man," 72-73.

8. Henry Ward Beecher, *Addresses to Young Men* (Philadelphia: Henry Altemus, 1895). This work was published in many earlier editions, the first as early as 1844, under the title *Lectures to Young Men on Various Important Subjects.*

9. Strong, *Times and Young Men,* 179-80.

10. F. W. Dupee, *Henry James: His Life and Writings* (New York: William Sloane Associates, 1951), 9 and 14, offers these quotations form Henry James Sr. but does not identify the source.

11. Beveridge, *Young Man and the World,* chap. 4.

12. The way Victorian gender roles enhanced the status of women by exalting motherhood is stressed by Daniel Walker Howe in his "Victorian Culture in America," the essay that opens his edited collection, *Victorian America* (Philadelphia: Univ. of Pennsylvania Press, 1976).

13. Mark C. Carnes, *Secret Ritual and Manhood in Victorian America* (New Haven, Conn.: Yale Univ. Press, 1989), 1-3, and Mark C. Carnes, "Iron John in the Gilded Age," *American Heritage* 44, no. 5 (Sept. 1993): 37-45. See also Mary Ann Clawson, *Constructing Brotherhood: Class, Gender, and Fraternalism* (Princeton, N.J.: Princeton Univ. Press, 1989).

14. Carnes, *Secret Ritual,* 76-77.

15. This is the major argument of Thekla Ellen Joiner Caldwell, "Women, Men, and Revival: The Third Awakening in Chicago" (Ph.D. diss., Univ. of Illinois at Chicago, 1991).

16. Ibid., 24.

17. Ibid., 108-9.

18. Gamaliel Bradford, *D. L. Moody: A Worker in Souls* (New York: George H. Doran, 1927), 291-92.

19. Ibid., 208-9.

20. See Caldwell, "Women, Men, and Revival," 124-25, and Bradford, *D. L. Moody,* 292.

21. Caldwell, "Women, Men, and Revival," 257. My understanding of Sunday has been shaped largely by Robert F. Martin, *Hero of the Heartland: Billy Sunday and the Transformation of American Society, 1862-1935* (Bloomington: Indiana Univ. Press, 2002); Lyle W. Dorsett, *Billy Sunday and the Redemption of Urban America,* Library of Religious Biography, ed. Mark A. Noll and Nathan O. Hatch (Grand Rapids, Mich.: Eerdmans, 1991); William G. McLoughlin, *Billy Sunday Was His Real Name* (Chicago: Univ. of Chicago Press, 1955); Roger Bruns, *Preacher: Billy Sunday and Big-Time American Evangelism* (New York: W. W. Norton, 1992); and relevant sections of Douglas W. Frank, *Less than Conquerors: How Evangelicals Entered the Twentieth Century* (Grand Rapids, Mich.: Eerdmans, 1986).

22. See Robert F. Martin, "Billy Sunday and Christian Manliness," *Historian* 58, no. 4 (Summer 1996): 811-23.

23. The text of this sermon is included in Dorsett, *Billy Sunday,* 181-207.

24. Bruns, *Preacher*, 15–16.

25. Michael Kimmel, *Manhood in America: A Cultural History* (New York: Free Press, 1996, 179.

26. Sunday is thus quoted in McLoughlin, *Billy Sunday Was His Real Name*, 141, 179. See also Kimmel, *Manhood in America*, 179.

27. On the Men and Religion Forward Movement, see Gail Bederman, "'The Women Have Had Charge of the Church Work Long Enough': The Men and Religion Forward Movement of 1911–1912 and the Masculinization of Middle-Class Protestantism," *American Quarterly* 41, no. 3 (Sept. 1989): 432–65; Gary Scott Smith, "The Men and Religion Forward Movement of 1911–1912: New Perspectives on Evangelical Social Concerns and the Relationship between Christianity and Progressivism," *Westminster Theological Journal* 49, no. 1 (Spring 1987): 91–118; and Charles H. Lippy, "Miles to Go: Promise Keepers in Historical and Cultural Context," *Soundings: An Interdisciplinary Journal* 80, nos. 2–3 (Summer/Fall 1997): 289–304. See also Gail Bederman, *Manliness and Civilization: A Cultural History of Gender and Race in the United States, 1880–1917* (Chicago: Univ. of Chicago Press, 1995).

28. "For Men," *Christian Advocate* 86 (Aug. 1911): 1026.

29. Men and Religion Forward Movement, *The Program of Work* (New York: Association Press, 1911), 6. This organizational manual was prepared for use by local committees.

30. Walter Rauschenbusch, *Christianizing the Social Order* (1912; reprint, New York: Macmillan, 1926), 19–20.

31. See Bederman, "Women Have Had Charge."

32. C. Howard Hopkins, *The Rise of the Social Gospel in American Protestantism, 1865–1915* (1940; reprint, New Haven: Yale Univ. Press, 1967), 297; Martin E. Marty, *Modern American Religion*, vol. 1, *The Irony of It All* (Chicago: Univ. of Chicago Press, 1986), 279.

33. *Messages of the Men and Religion Movement*, 6 vols. (New York: Association Press, 1912).

34. William D. Murray, "The Bible and the Individual Man," in *Messages of the Men and Religion Movement*, vol. 3, *Bible Study, Evangelism* (New York: Association Press, 1912), 44–55.

35. George W. Robinson, "The Bible and the Home," in *Messages of the Men and Religion Movement*, vol. 3, *Bible Study, Evangelism* (New York: Association Press, 1912), esp. 60–63.

36. See part 5 of *Messages of the Men and Religion Movement*, vol. 4, *Christian Unity, Missions* (New York: Association Press, 1912), 212–27.

37. The tag was, of course, also the title of a journal founded in the closing years of the nineteenth century that, by the dawn of the twenty-first century, still retained the name but put the word "century" in a much larger typeface, almost obscuring the "Christian" designation.

38. Some mission boards would accept only women already married to men who were being sent as missionaries. Some would accept single women but expect them to remain unmarried while on the mission field. Regardless, in virtually every case, until well into the twentieth century when the approach to missions had changed, men were responsible for overseeing mission work. Even when women might head schools or other training programs that targeted a female constituency, they were expected to be subordinate to the men. However, it is also clear that the realities of mission work meant

that many women had the opportunity to engage in religious activities, even preaching, that were often denied to them at home because of the gender role expectations that prevailed there. See Wayne Flynt, *Taking Christianity to China: Alabama Missionaries in the Middle Kingdom, 1850–1950* (Tuscaloosa: Univ. of Alabama Press, 1997).

39. Especially helpful on American developments are Clifford Putney, *Muscular Christianity: Manhood and Sports in Protestant America, 1880–1920* (Cambridge: Harvard Univ. Press, 2001); and Tony Ladd and James A. Mathisen, *Muscular Christianity: Evangelical Protestants and the Development of American Sport* (Grand Rapids, Mich.: Baker Book House, 1999).

40. Ladd and Mathisen, *Muscular Christianity,* 57.

41. Ibid., 70–71.

42. See Ownby, *Subduing Satan.*

43. As prominent as Speer became in Presbyterian and ecumenical circles, there are only a handful of secondary works about him. During his life, he discouraged those who wished to write his story; his family reluctantly consented to allow a one-time colleague, W. Reginald Wheeler, to draft an appreciative memoir after Speer's death. Wheeler book, *A Man Sent from God: A Biography of Robert E. Speer,* with an introduction by John A. Mackay (Westwood, N.J.: Fleming H. Revell, 1956), remained the only full-length study until the publication of John F. Piper Jr., *Robert E. Speer: Prophet of the American Church* (Louisville, Ky.: Geneva Press, 2000), a magisterial and appreciative work. Speer's legacy included some sixty-seven books he wrote, countless addresses given at places like the Hill School and at college and university chapels across the nation, a large number of presentations to groups of missionaries as he toured various sites, sermons preached in many churches, and speeches offered to the General Assembly of the (then northern) Presbyterian Church and to various ecumenical bodies in the United States and Europe. My discussion draws heavily from the generous extracts from letters in Wheeler's book and from those of Speer's published books cited in the bibliography.

44. Wheeler, *Man Sent from God,* 32.

45. Helpful for context as well as for its appraisal of Speer's work is Leon Glen Rosenthal, "Christian Statesmanship in the First Missionary-Ecumenical Generation" (Ph.D. diss., Univ. of Chicago, 1989).

46. Wheeler, *Man Sent from God,* 104, notes visits to mission sites in South America in 1909; to Thailand (then Siam), the Philippines, China, Korea, and Japan in 1915; to India, Iran (then Persia), and China in 1921 and 1922; to Brazil, Argentina, Uruguay, and Chile in addition to attending a conference in Montevideo in 1925; to China, Korea, and Japan in 1926; to sites in the Near East as well as an international conference in Jerusalem in 1928; to a conference in Panama in 1916; to a Student Volunteer Movement gathering in Keswick, England, in 1894; to a British Student Volunteer Movement conference in London in 1900; and to the important World Missionary Conference in Edinburgh in 1910. In addition, Speer and his wife took a personal trip in 1939 to England to visit their daughter and her family who lived there.

47. Ibid., 106.

48. Emma Bailey Speer to her mother, Nov. 27, 1896, reprinted in Wheeler, *Men Sent from God,* 108.

49. Wheeler, *Men Sent from God,* 109.

50. Robert E. Speer, *The Stuff of Manhood: Some Needed Notes in American Character* (New York: Fleming H. Revell, 1917), esp. 11, 30–31.

51. Robert E. Speer, *The Marks of a Man; or, the Essentials of Christian Character* (Cincinnati: Jennings and Graham, 1907). Speer devoted a lecture (and chapter) to each of these qualities.

52. Robert E. Speer, *Some Great Leaders of the World Movement* (1911; reprint, Freeport, N.Y.: Books for Libraries, 1967).

53. Ibid., 165.

54. Robert E. Speer, *Studies of the Man Christ Jesus* (New York: Fleming H. Revell, 1896).

55. Ibid., 29.

56. Ibid., 37.

57. Ibid., chap. 3.

58. Robert E. Speer, *The Meaning of Christ to Me* (New York: Fleming H. Revell, 1936). In this work, Speer wrote of his personal beliefs, tackling such topics as the significance of the person, death, resurrection, and second coming of Christ. However, he also expressed his frustration with those who made a single interpretation or understanding of each of these topics a requirement of Christian identity, calling such endeavors "misdirected."

59. Robert E. Speer, quoted in Wheeler, *Man Sent from God,* 210.

60. Galen Fisher, quoted in Wheeler, *Man Sent from God,* 224.

61. John Timothy Stone, quoted in Wheeler, *Man Sent from God,* 273.

62. Wheeler, *Man Sent from God,* 89.

63. Ibid., 100, 101.

64. The connection between missionary work and ecumenical activity is the central theme of Rosenthal, "Christian Statesmanship."

65. See Rosenthal, "Christian Statesmanship," chap. 16.

66. Speer, *Stuff of Manhood,* 30−31.

Chapter 5

1. Carnegie wrote an autobiography: *The Autobiography of Andrew Carnegie,* with a new foreword by Cecelia Tichi (Boston: Northeastern Univ. Press, 1986). For many years, the standard biography was Louis Hanks, ed., *The Life of Andrew Carnegie,* 2 vols. (New York: Harper and Row, 1949). But see also James T. Baker, *Andrew Carnegie: Robber Baron as American Hero* (Belmont, Calif.: Wadsworth, 2003).

2. See the centennial collection: David P. Demarest Jr., gen. ed., *"The River Ran Red": Homestead 1892* (Pittsburgh: Univ. of Pittsburgh Press, 1992).

3. The best edition is in Andrew Carnegie, *The Gospel of Wealth, and Other Timely Essays,* ed. Edward C. Kirtland (Cambridge, Mass.: Belknap Press of Harvard Univ. Press, 1962).

4. Lawrence's most forceful statement of his understanding of the Gospel of Wealth is his "The Relation of Wealth to Morals." See the reprint in *Democracy and the Gospel of Wealth,* ed. Gail Kennedy (Boston: D. C. Heath, 1949), 68−76. See also William Lawrence, *Memories of a Happy Life* (Boston: Houghton Mifflin, 1926), 47−49, where Lawrence appears somewhat more open to dealing with the poor, but in a very patronizing manner.

5. Helpful to me have been the biographical and analytical studies of Gary Scharnhorst: *Horatio Alger, Jr.,* Twayne's United States Authors Series, ed. David J. Nordloh (Boston: Twayne, 1980) and, with Jack Bales, *The Lost Life of Horatio Alger, Jr.* (Bloomington: Indiana Univ. Press, 1985). Ralph D. Gardner, *Horatio Alger, or the American Hero Era* (1964; reprint, New York: Arco, 1978), retains value for its bibliographical material, 355–495. See also William R. Hutchison, *Religious Pluralism in America: The Contentious History of a Founding Ideal* (New Haven, Conn.: Yale Univ. Press, 2003), 90–93.

6. Horatio Alger Jr., *Bound to Rise; or, Harry Walton's Motto* (Boston: Loring, 1873), and *Risen from the Ranks; or, Harry Walton's Success* (Boston: Loring, 1874). There can be little doubt that the model for Harry Walton was the young Benjamin Franklin, or at least the young Franklin that Franklin created in his autobiography, particularly when it comes to efficient use of time. Walton, for example, at one point writes some articles for a periodical using the pseudonym Frank Lynn.

7. Horatio Alger Jr., *The Young Outlaw; or, Adrift in the Streets* (Boston: Loring, 1875) and *Sam's Chance; and How He Improved It* (Boston: Loring, 1876).

8. See Scharnhorst, *Horatio Alger, Jr.,* 99.

9. Ibid., 94.

10. Horatio Alger Jr., *Ragged Dick; or, Street Life in New York* (Boston: Loring, 1868). See also John Cawelti, *Apostles of the Self-Made Man* (Chicago: Univ. of Chicago Press, 1965), 110.

11. Frederick Lewis Allen, *The Big Change: America Transforms Itself, 1900–1950* (New York: Harper, 1952), 50.

12. On Conwell, see Daniel W. Bjork, *The Victorian Flight: Russell H. Conwell and the Crisis of Individualism* (Washington: Univ. Press of America, 1979); Agnes Rush Burr, *Russell H. Conwell and His Work* (1926; reprint, Philadelphia: Winston, 1943); and Albert Hatcher Smith, *The Life of Russell H. Conwell* (Boston: Silver, Burdette, 1899). A helpful guide to Conwell's writings is Maurice F. Tauber, *Russell Herman Conwell, 1843–1925: A Bibliography* (Philadelphia: Temple Univ. Library, 1935). Emphasizing the way Conwell's approach highlighted the spirituality of the efficient businessman, although not using that label, are Clyde K. Nelson, "Russell H. Conwell and the 'Gospel of Wealth,'" *Foundations* 5 (Jan. 1962): 39–51; and Thane Wilson, "Russell H. Conwell: Who Has Helped 3,000 Young Men to Succeed," *American Magazine* 81 (Apr. 1916): 15. A scathing critique of Conwell's position, published shortly after his death, is W. C. Crosby, "Acres of Diamonds," *American Mercury* 14 (May 1928): 104–13. See also Hutchison, *Religious Pluralism,* 93–96.

13. Martin E. Marty, *Modern American Religion,* vol. 2, *The Noise of Conflict, 1919–1941* (Chicago: Univ. of Chicago Press, 1991), 43.

14. John R. Wimmer, "Russell H. Conwell," in *Twentieth-Century Shapers of American Popular Religion,* ed. Charles H. Lippy (Westport, Conn.: Greenwood, 1989), 83.

15. Marty, *Noise of Conflict,* 44.

16. Roger Babson, *Religion and Business* (New York: Macmillan, 1921); and Roger Babson, *New Tasks for Old Churches* (New York: Macmillan, 1922).

17. Babson, *Religion and Business,* 8.

18. Albert Schweitzer, *The Quest for the Historical Jesus: A Critical Study of Its Progress from Reimarus to Wrede,* translated by W. Montgomery (1906; reprint, New York: Macmillan, 1964), demonstrated how hopeless were all efforts to craft a biography of

Jesus, at least in terms of the models prevalent at the dawn of the twentieth century. On the intellectual climate surrounding biblical criticism, see Charles H. Lippy, "The Rise of Biblical Criticism and Challenges to Religious Authority," in *Encyclopedia of American Cultural and Intellectual History,* ed. Mary Kupiec Cayton and Peter W. Williams, 3 vols. (New York: Scribner's, 2001), 1:581–88.

19. McDannell, *Christian Home in Victorian America,* discusses both paternal and maternal models of religious leadership within Protestant and Roman Catholic families.

20. See Erika Doss, "Making a 'Virile, Manly Christ': The Cultural Origins and Meanings of Warner Sallman's Religious Imagery," in *Icons of American Protestantism: The Art of Warner Sallman,* ed. David Morgan (New Haven, Conn.: Yale Univ. Press, 1996), 61–94.

21. See the discussion in Charles H. Lippy, *Being Religious, American Style: A History of Popular Religiosity in the United Sates* (Westport, Conn.: Greenwood, 1994), 150–51; Lee Scott Thiesen, "'My God, Did I Set All This in Motion?' General Lew Wallace and *Ben Hur,*" *Journal of Popular Culture* 18, no. 2 (1984): 33–41; Frank Luther Mott, *Golden Multitudes: The Story of Bestsellers in the United States* (New York: R. R. Bowker, 1947), 172–74; and Henry Herx, "Religion and Film," in *Encyclopedia of the American Religious Experience,* ed. Charles H. Lippy and Peter W. Williams, 3 vols. (New York: Scribners, 1988), 3:1345, 1349.

22. Kimmel, *Manhood in America,* 177–79, takes this approach.

23. Harry Emerson Fosdick, *The Manhood of the Master* (New York: Association Press, 1913); and Harry Emerson Fosdick, *The Man from Nazareth: As He Was Seen by the People of His Time* (New York: Harper, 1949). There were earlier titles by other writers that reflected similar concerns. Among them are Thomas Hughes, *The Manliness of Christ* (Boston: Houghton Mifflin, 1880), and R. W. Conant, *The Manly Christ: A New View* (Chicago: n.p., 1904). The last was reprinted in 1915 under the title *The Virility of Christ: A New View.*

24. Jason Noble Pierce, *The Masculine Power of Christ; or, Christ Measured as a Man* (Boston: Pilgrim Press, 1912); and Kenneth Wayne, *Building the Young Man* (Chicago: A. C. McClurg, 1912).

25. Wayne, *Building the Young Man,* esp. 168–69.

26. Kimmel, *Manhood in America,* 177.

27. Bouck White, *The Call of the Carpenter* (New York: Doubleday, 1913), esp. 135–36, 168–69, 333–34.

28. Bruce Barton, *The Man Nobody Knows* (1925; reprint, Indianapolis, Bobbs-Merrill, 1962), 12–13. On Barton, see also Edrene S. Montgomery, "Bruce Barton's *The Man Nobody Knows:* A Popular Advertising Illusion," *Journal of Popular Culture* 19, no. 3 (Winter 1985): 21–34, based on her "Bruce Barton and the Twentieth Century Menace of Unreality" (Ph.D. diss., Univ. of Arkansas, 1984); Richard M. Huber, *The American Idea of Success* (New York: McGraw-Hill, 1971), 196–209; James A. Nuechterlein, "Bruce Barton and the Business Ethos of the 1920's," *South Atlantic Quarterly* 76 (1977): 293–308; and Leo P. Ribuffo, "Jesus Christ as Business Statesman: Bruce Barton and the Selling of Corporate Capitalism," *American Quarterly* 33 (1981): 206–31. See also Hutchison, *Religious Pluralism,* 154–58.

29. Barton, *Man Nobody Knows,* 24–25.

30. Ibid., 26–27.

31. Ibid., 29–30.

32. Ibid., 71.

33. Ibid., 93–97.

34. Ibid., 104.

35. Ibid., 31.

36. Ibid., 19.

37. Among the earliest studies of this phenomenon is Ben Primer, *Protestants and American Business Methods*, Studies in American History and Culture, No. 7 (Ann Arbor, Mich.: UMI Research Press, 1979).

38. Ibid., 8.

39. Shailer Mathews, *Scientific Management in the Churches* (Chicago: Univ. of Chicago Press, 1912). Some historians have seen a passion for efficiency as one characteristic of the larger Progressive movement; see, for example, Samuel Haber, *Efficiency and Uplift: Scientific Management in the Progressive Era, 1890–1920* (Chicago: Univ. of Chicago Press, 1964).

40. William T. Ellis, "A Movement: A Message: A Method," *Independent* 72 (May 9, 1912): 984–88.

41. See Primer, *Protestants and American Business Methods*, esp. 74–76. For contemporary examples, see Henry F. Cope, *Efficiency in the Sunday School* (New York: George H. Doran, 1912); and Jesse L. Hurlbut, *Organizing and Building Up the Sunday School* (New York: Eaton and Mains, 1910).

42. Meredith Nicholson, "Should Smith Go to Church?" *Atlantic* 109 (June 1916): 721–33.

43. Henry F. Cope, *The Efficient Layman, or the Religious Training of Men* (Philadelphia: Griffith and Rowland, 1911).

44. Lynn Harold Hough, *The Man of Power: A Series of Studies in Christian Efficiency* (New York: Abingdon, 1916).

45. Harry Emerson Fosdick, "What Is the Matter with Preaching," *Harper's* 157 (June 1928): 133–41. Quote from 141.

46. James Brett Kenna, "Minister or Business Executive," *Harper's* 157 (June 1928): 38–44.

47. Russell Niese, *The Newspaper and Religious Publicity* (Nashville: Sunday School Board of the Southern Baptist Convention, 1925), 15–16.

48. See Primer, *Protestants and American Business Methods*, chaps. 8 and 9 for discussion of both perspectives.

49. For a brief discussion, see Marty, *Noise of Conflict*, 132–34.

50. There is little literature on FGBMFI. See Demos Shakarian, "FGBMFI Struggles toward the Future," *Charisma* 13 (Mar. 1988): 24; B. Bird, "The Legacy of Demos Shakarian," *Charisma* 11 (June 1986): 20–25; and B. Bird, "FGBMFI: Facing Frustrations and the Future," *Charisma* 11 (June 1986): 25, 26, 28. FGBMFI spawned a group for women called Women's Aglow that has received scholarly analysis in R. Marie Griffith, *God's Daughters: Evangelical Women and the Power of Submission* (Berkeley and Los Angeles: Univ. of California Press, 1997); and Meredith B. McGuire with Debra Kantor, *Ritual Healing in Suburban America* (New Brunswick, N.J.: Rutgers Univ. Press, 1988).

51. There is relatively little published appraisal of Barton's life and career, although there are brief entries in most standard compilations such as the *Dictionary of American Biography*. Besides Barton's own writings, I have in the discussion above relied primarily

on Robert S. Bishop, "Bruce Barton: Presidential Stage Manager," *Journalism Quarterly* 43 (1966): 85–89; James M. Ferreira, "Only Yesterday and the Two Christs of the Twenties," *South Atlantic Quarterly* 81 (1981): 77–83; Edrene Stephens Montgomery, "Bruce Barton and the Twentieth Century Menace of Unreality" (Ph.D. diss., Univ. of Arkansas, 1984); James A. Nuechterlein, "Bruce Barton and the Business Ethos of the 1920's," *South Atlantic Quarterly* 76 (1977): 293–308; Ribuffo, "Jesus Christ as Business Statesman," 206–31; Gerald L. Sittser, "Bruce Barton," in *Twentieth-Century Shapers of American Popular Religion,* ed. Charles H. Lippy (Westport, Conn.: Greenwood, 1989), 20–29; and Warren Susman, "Piety, Profits, and Play: The 1920s," in *Men, Women, and Issues in American History,* vol. 2, ed. Howard H. Quint and Milton Cantor (Homewood, Ill.: Dorsey, 1980), 191–216. See also Hutchison, *Religious Pluralism,* 154–58.

52. Bruce Barton, *More Power to You: Fifty Editorials from Every Week* (New York: Century, 1917).

53. Ibid., chap. 13.

54. Ibid., esp. chap. 6. But see also chaps. 7, 8, 17, 30, and 34.

55. Ibid., chaps. 24 and 26.

56. Ibid., chap. 29.

57. Bruce Barton, *What Can a Man Believe?* (Indianapolis: Bobbs-Merrill for Grossett and Dunlap, 1927).

58. Ibid., chap. 4.

59. Ibid., 153.

60. Ibid., chap. 5, esp. 204–8.

61. Bruce Barton, *He Upset the World* (Indianapolis: Bobbs-Merrill, 1931).

62. This tendency is most apparent in Bruce Barton, *The Book Nobody Knows* (Indianapolis: Grossett and Dunlap in cooperation with Bobbs-Merrill, 1926).

63. Barton, *He Upset the World,* 20–26.

64. Ibid., 101, 109.

65. Ibid., 103.

66. Ibid., esp. chap. 3.

67. Ibid., 177.

Chapter 6

1. Robert T. Handy, "The American Religious Depression, 1925–1935," *Church History* 29 (1960): 3–16. See also Robert T. Handy, *A Christian America: Protestant Hopes and Historical Realities,* 2d ed. (New York: Oxford Univ. Press, 1984), chap. 7.

2. Charles Fiske, *The Confessions of a Troubled Parson* (New York: Charles Scribner's Sons, 1928), 14.

3. Winthrop S. Hudson, *The Great Tradition of the American Churches* (New York: Harper & Bros., 1953), 196.

4. Walter M. Horton, *Theism and the Modern Mood* (New York: Harper & Bros., 1930), 6.

5. I have discussed all these matters in greater depth in chapter 2 of *Pluralism Comes of Age: American Religious Culture in the Twentieth Century* (Armonk, N.Y.: M. E. Sharpe, 2000).

6. See the overview provided in James Hudnut-Buemler, *Looking for God in the Suburbs: The Religion of the American Dream and Its Critics, 1945–1965* (New Brunswick, N.J.: Rutgers Univ. Press, 1994).

7. See Herberg's classic study, *Protestant, Catholic, Jew: An Essay in American Religious Sociology* (Garden City, N.Y.: Doubleday, 1955).

8. Nancy T. Ammerman, "Golden Rule Christianity: Lived Religion in the American Mainstream," in *Lived Religion in America: Toward a History of Practice*, ed. David D. Hall (Princeton, N.J.: Princeton Univ. Press, 1997), 196–216.

9. Riesman's classic study, written with Nathan Glazer and Reuel Denney, is still worth careful scrutiny: *The Lonely Crowd* (New Haven, Conn.: Yale Univ. Press, 1950).

10. The classic study is William H. Whyte Jr., *The Organization Man* (Garden City, N.Y.: Doubleday Anchor, 1956).

11. Norman Vincent Peale, *The Power of Positive Thinking* (New York: Prentice-Hall, 1952).

12. Precious little has been written about Dale Carnegie. But see Giles Kemp, *The Man Who Influenced Millions* (New York: St. Martin's 1989); and Donald Meyer, *The Positive Thinkers: Popular Religious Psychology from Mary Baker Eddy to Norman Vincent Peale and Ronald Reagan*, rev. ed. (Middletown, Conn.: Wesleyan Univ. Press, 1988), chap. 14.

13. Dale Carnegie, *Public Speaking and Influencing Men in Business* (New York: Association Press, 1932). I was unable to secure a copy of this work under its original title.

14. Meyer, *Positive Thinkers*, 180.

15. Dale Carnegie, *How to Win Friends and Influence People* (New York: Simon and Schuster, 1936).

16. Meyer, *Positive Thinkers*, 180–81.

17. Ibid., 181.

18. Ibid., 185–86.

19. Peale, *Power of Positive Thinking*, 228.

20. Joshua Loth Liebman, *Peace of Mind* (New York: Simon and Schuster, 1946).

21. Ibid., esp. chaps. 3, 4, and 5.

22. Ibid., 159–62.

23. Martin E. Marty, *Modern American Religion*, vol. 3, *Under God, Indivisible, 1941–1960* (Chicago: Univ. of Chicago Press, 1996), 315.

24. Liebman, *Peace of Mind*, 161.

25. Fulton J. Sheen, *Peace of Soul* (New York: McGraw-Hill, 1949). For many years, the only studies of Sheen, who died in 1979, were James C. G. Conniff, *The Bishop Sheen Story* (Greenwich, Conn.: Fawcett, 1953), and two studies by Daniel P. Noonan: *Missionary with a Mike: The Bishop Sheen Story* (New York: Pageant Press, 1968) and *The Passion of Fulton Sheen* (New York: Dodd, Mead, 1972). Sheen did publish an autobiography, initially released the year after his death by Doubleday: *Treasure in Clay: The Autobiography of Fulton J. Sheen* (San Francisco: Ignatius Press, 1993). In recent years, there have been both appreciative and critical analyses. Among them are Christopher Owen Lynch, *Selling Catholicism: Bishop Sheen and the Power of Television* (Lexington: Univ. Press of Kentucky, 1998); Myles P. Murphy, *The Life and Times of Archbishop Fulton J. Sheen* (New York: Alba House, 2000); and Thomas C. Reeves, *America's Bishop: The Life and Times of Fulton J. Sheen* (San Francisco: Encounter Books, 2001).

26. Meyer, *Positive Thinkers*, 333.

27. Sheen, *Peace of Soul,* 289–90.

28. Billy Graham, *Peace with God* (Garden City, N.Y.: Doubleday, 1953). A revised and expanded edition, virtually devoid of gender-specific language, was published by Word Books in 1984.

29. Norman Vincent Peale and Smiley Blanton, *Faith Is the Answer* (Englewood Cliffs, N.J.: Prentice-Hall, 1940); and Peale and Blanton, *The Art of Real Happiness* (New York: Prentice-Hall, 1950).

30. Norman Vincent Peale, *The Art of Living* (New York: Abingdon-Cokesbury, 1937); Peale, *You Can Win* (New York: Abingdon, 1938); Peale, and *A Guide to Confident Living* (New York: Macmillan, 1948). My understanding of Peale draws as well on Allan R. Broadhurst, *He Speaks the Word of God: A Study of the Sermons of Norman Vincent Peale* (Englewood Cliffs, N.J.: Prentice-Hall, 1963); Carol V. R. George, *God's Salesman: Norman Vincent Peale and the Power of Positive Thinking* (New York: Oxford Univ. Press, 1993); Arthur Gordon, *Norman Vincent Peale: Minister to Millions* (Englewood Cliffs, N.J.: Prentice-Hall, 1958; reprint, Greenwich, Conn.: Fawcett, 1964); and Mrs. Norman Vincent Peale (Ruth Stafford), *The Adventure of Being a Wife* (Englewood Cliffs, N.J.: Prentice-Hall, 1971). See also the discussion in Meyer, *Positive Thinkers,* esp. chap. 21.

31. I make no claim to having a definitive count, but my own estimates are that Peale referred to some 123 men, some identified by name but most anonymous, and just 28 women for his case studies. My informal count, using the 1952 edition of *The Power of Positive Thinking,* did not include other authorities who were mentioned by name for purposes of quotation only.

32. Peale, *Power of Positive Thinking,* 162.

33. Ibid., chap. 13 ("Inflow of New Thoughts Can Remake You.")

34. Ibid., chap. 11 ("How to Use Faith in Healing").

35. Norman Vincent Peale, *The Amazing Results of Positive Thinking* (Englewood Cliffs, N.J.: Prentice-Hall, 1959); Peale, *The Tough-Minded Optimist* (Englewood Cliffs, N.J.: Prentice-Hall, 1961); Peale, *You Can If You Think You Can* (Greenwich, Conn.: Fawcett, 1974); Peale, *Power of the Plus Factor* (Old Tappan, N.J.: Fleming H. Revell, 1987); and Peale, *The True Joy of Positive Living: An Autobiography* (Pawling, N.Y.: Foundation for Christian Living, 1984).

36. William Lee Miller, "The Gospel of Norman Vincent Peale," *Union Seminary Quarterly Review* 10 (Jan. 1955): 15–22; and Miller, *Piety Along the Potomac* (Boston: Houghton Mifflin, 1964), esp. 125–43.

37. Charles L. Allen, *God's Psychiatry* (Old Tappan, N.J.: Fleming H. Revell, 1953); and Allen, *Roads to Radiant Living* (Old Tappan, N.J.: Fleming H. Revell, 1968). Allen also produced an autobiography: *What I Have Lived By: An Autobiography* (Old Tappan, N.J.: Fleming H. Revell, 1976).

38. See Schuller's recent autobiography, *My Journey: From an Iowa Farm to a Cathedral of Dreams* (San Francisco: HarperSanFrancisco, 2001), 141–42, 169–71, 261–62. Schuller has written nearly three dozen books; those I have read in preparation for this discussion will be documented fully in the epilogue to this chapter.

39. Ibid., 238.

40. Ibid., 115.

41. Ibid., 350.

42. Ibid., 282. On the transfer of leadership, see John Dart, "Schuller's Glass Act," *Christian Century* 119, no. 8 (Apr. 10–17, 2002): 24.

43. Schuller, *My Journey*, 306.
44. Robert H. Schuller, *Peace of Mind through Possibility Thinking* (Garden City, N.Y.: Doubleday, 1977).
45. Robert H. Schuller, *Power Ideas for a Happy Family* (Old Tappan, N.J.: Fleming H. Revell, 1972), 15.
46. Ibid., chap. 4.
47. Ibid., 77.
48. Robert H. Schuller, *Prayer, My Soul's Adventure with God: A Spiritual Autobiography* (Nashville: Thomas Nelson, 1995).
49. What Schuller regarded as his keystone book, *Move Ahead with Possibility Thinking* (Old Tappan, N.J.: Spire Books, 1967), did not attract the attention that had come to Norman Vincent Peale with the appearance of *The Power of Positive Thinking.* Rather, it was Schuller's *Self-Esteem: The New Reformation* (Waco, Tex.: Word Books, 1982) that first brought a significant readership, thanks largely to a wealthy businessman who ordered 250,000 copies and had them sent to clergy throughout the United States. As a result, both of Schuller's next two books achieved recognition by being on the *New York Times* best seller list.
50. See Wuthnow, *After Heaven;* Roof, *Generation of Seekers;* and Roof, *Spiritual Marketplace.*
51. My understanding of Schuller is based primarily on the two autobiographical works he has published, along with selected other books from among the nearly three dozen that have appeared under his name. The two autobiographical pieces are Schuller's *My Journey* and *Prayer, My Soul's Adventure with God.* I studied Schuller's understanding of the spirituality of the positive thinker by reading the following, all by Robert H. Schuller: *The Be Happy Attitudes: Eight Positive Attitudes that Can Transform Your Life* (Waco, Tex.: Word, 1985); *Be Happy You Are Loved* (1986; Boston: G. K. Hall, 1988); *Believe in the God Who Believes in You* (Nashville: Thomas Nelson, 1989); *God's Way to the Good Life* (Grand Rapids, Mich.: William B. Eerdmans, 1963; reprint, New Canaan, Conn.: Keats, 1974); *Move Ahead with Possibility Thinking; Peace of Mind through Possibility Thinking; The Peak to Peek Principle* (Garden City, N.Y.: Doubleday, 1980); *Power Ideas for a Happy Family; Power Thoughts* (New York: HarperCollins, 1993); *Self-Esteem: The New Reformation; Self-Love: The Dynamic Force of Success* (New York: Hawthorn, 1969); *Success Is Never Ending, Failure Is Never Final* (Nashville: Thomas Nelson, 1988); *Tough Times Never Last, but Tough People Do* (Nashville: Thomas Nelson, 1983); and *Tough-Minded Faith for Tender-Hearted People* (Nashville: Thomas Nelson, 1983). I also consulted Robert A. Schuller, ed., *Robert Schuller's Life Changers* (Old Tappan, N.J.: Fleming H. Revell, 1981), a collection of meditations. There is relatively little sustained secondary analysis of Schuller and his career. Two persons associated with his staff, Michael Nason and Donna Nason, two decades ago provided a laudatory study, *Robert Schuller: The Inside Story* (Waco, Tex.: Word Books, 1983). The most comprehensive work, both analytical and appreciative, is Dennis Voskuil, *Mountains into Goldmines: Robert Schuller and the Gospel of Success* (Grand Rapids, Mich.: William B. Eerdmans, 1983), but that, too, is now outdated.
52. Schuller, *My Journey*, 142.
53. Ibid., 170.
54. Voskuil, *Mountains into Goldmines*, 144–45.
55. Dart, "Schuller's Glass Act," 24.
56. Some of that criticism is summarized in Voskuil, *Mountains into Goldmines,*

155–58, and in Dennis N. Voskuil, "Robert Schuller," in *Twentieth-Century Shapers of American Popular Religion*, ed. Charles H. Lippy (Westport, Conn.: Greenwood, 1989), 369–70.

57. Harold S. Kushner, *When Bad Things Happen to Good People* (New York: Schocken Books, 1981).

Chapter 7

1. Many of the trends discussed here receive fuller treatment in the following complementary studies: Diana Eck, *A New Religious America: How a "Christian Country" Has Become the World's Most Religiously Diverse Nation* (San Francisco: HarperSanFrancisco, 2001); Lippy, *Pluralism Comes of Age;* and Porterfield, *Transformation of American Religion.*

2. Among the better studies are Taylor Branch, *Parting the Waters: America in the King Years, 1954–63* (New York: Simon and Schuster, 1988); Branch, *Pillar of Fire: America in the King Years, 1963–65* (New York: Simon and Schuster, 1998); and David J. Garrow, *Bearing the Cross: Martin Luther King, Jr., and the Southern Christian Leadership Conference* (New York: Random House, 1986).

3. See Wuthnow, *After Heaven.* Similar interpretations have been advanced in Roof, *Generation of Seekers;* and Roof, *Spiritual Marketplace.*

4. Susan Faludi, *Backlash: The Undeclared War against American Women* (New York: Crown Books, 1991).

5. Susan Faludi, *Stiffed: The Betrayal of the American Man* (New York: William Morrow, 1999). See also a perceptive review of *Stiffed:* Mary Stewart Van Leeuwen, "Why Men Get Anxious," *Christian Century* 116, no. 33 (Dec. 1 1999): 1166–68.

6. Kimmel, *Manhood in America*, 53.

7. Rueben Herring, *Men Are Like That* (Nashville: Broadman Press, 1967), esp. the final chapter.

8. Patrick M. Arnold, *Wildmen, Warriors, and Kings: Masculine Spirituality and the Bible* (New York: Crossroad, 1991).

9. Jung was among the first to explore differences between the male psyche and the female psyche, although he did not necessarily claim that one was superior to the other. One of the most rigorous contemporary approaches to male spirituality that builds on a Jungian foundation is Robert A. Johnson, *Understanding Masculine Psychology* (San Francisco: Harper and Row, 1974), reissued in 1983 as *He! Understanding Masculine Psychology.*

10. Arnold, *Wildmen, Warriors, and Kings,* chap. 2.

11. This idea informs much of John W. Miller, *Biblical Faith and Fathering: Why We Call God "Father"* (New York: Paulist Press, 1990).

12. Philip Culbertson, *New Adam: The Future of Masculine Spirituality* (Philadelphia: Fortress Press, 1992).

13. Ibid., esp. chaps. 7–9.

14. Ruth Bell Graham, quoted in Marshall Frady, *Billy Graham: A Parable of American Righteousness* (Boston: Little, Brown, 1979), 142.

15. William C. Martin, *A Prophet with Honor: The Billy Graham Story* (New York: William Morrow, 1991), 82–83.

16. Jim Dailey, "A Conversation with Ruth Bell Graham," *Decision* 43, no. 4 (May 2002): 15. No doubt Ruth Bell Graham had a vivid memory of this conversation; she had told the same story several years earlier to her biographer. See Patricia Daniels Cornwell, *A Time for Remembering: The Ruth Bell Graham Story* (San Francisco: Harper and Row, 1983), 26.

17. Tim Bayley, "Going for the Men," *Faith and Renewal* 15, no. 1 (July–Aug. 1990): 18–22, stressed how men like to get physical, thus making sports activities a good device for increasing the involvement of men in local congregations.

18. Michael Novak, *The Joy of Sports: End Zones, Bases, Baskets, Balls, and the Consecration of the American Spirit* (New York: Basic Books, 1976).

19. Ibid., 192.

20. Ibid., 152, 213–17.

21. Carol Flake, *Redemptorama: Culture, Politics, and the New Evangelism* (New York: Viking, 1984), esp. chap 4 ("The Spirit of Winning: Sports and the Total Man").

22. Sharon Mazer, "The Power Team: Muscular Christianity and the Spectacle of Conversion," *Drama Review* 38, no. 4 (Winter 1994): 169.

23. Ibid., 170–71.

24. See Flake, *Redemptorama*, 102.

25. The phrase comes in Flake, *Redemptorama*, 98.

26. Much has now been written about McCartney and the Promise Keepers phenomenon. A personal testimony comes in John T. Trent and Charles W. Colson, eds., *Go the Distance: The Making of a Promise Keeper* (Colorado Springs, Colo.: Focus on the Family Publishing, 1996). Helpful are three collections of essays: Dane S. Claussen, ed., *Standing on the Promises: The Promise Keepers and the Revival of Manhood* (Cleveland: Pilgrim Press, 1999); Claussen, ed., *The Promise Keepers: Essays on Masculinity and Christianity* (Jefferson, N.C.: McFarland, 1999); and Rhys H. Williams, ed., *Promise Keepers and the New Masculinity: Private Lives and Public Morality* (Lanham, Md.: Lexington Books, 2001). Especially perceptive is Mary Stewart Van Leeuwen, "Servanthood or Soft Patriarchy? A Christian Feminist Looks at the Promise Keepers Movement," *Journal of Men's Studies* 5, no. 3 (Feb. 1997): 233–61, also in *Priscilla Papers* 11, no. 2 (1997): 28–40. See also Edward Gilbreath, "Manhood's Great Awakening," *Christianity Today* 39, no. 2 (Feb. 6, 1995): 20–28; Lippy, "Miles to Go," 289–304; Donna Minkowitz, "In the Name of the Father," *Ms.* 6, no. 3 (Nov.–Dec. 1995): 64–71; Jeff Wagenheim, "Among the Promise Keepers," *Utne Reader* 73 (Jan.–Feb. 1996): 74–77; and Brett Webb-Mitchell, "And a Football Coach Shall Lead Them: A Theological Critique of *Seven Promises of a Promise Keeper*," *Soundings: An Interdisciplinary Journal* 80, nos. 2–3 (Summer/Fall 1997): 305–26. In addition, Susan Faludi devoted chapter 5 ("Where Am I in the Kingdom? A Christian Quest for Manhood") of *Stiffed* to the Promise Keepers, looking at primarily at local support groups rather than the mass rallies.

27. I have not seen a copy of the 1970 version. The essay has been reprinted in both pamphlet and article form. See Robert K. Greenleaf, "The Servant as Leader," *Journal of Religion and Applied Behavioral Science* (Winter 1982): 3, 7–10; and *The Servant as Leader* (Indianapolis: Greenleaf Center, 1991). Greenleaf, who died in 1990, expanded his ideas in several other books and essays, some of which were published posthumously. See, for example, Greenleaf's *Servant Leadership: A Journey into the Nature of Legitimate Power and Greatness* (New York: Paulist Press, 1977); *On Becoming a Servant Leader*, ed. Don M. Frick and Larry C. Spears (San Francisco: Jossey-Bass, 1996); and *The Power*

of Servant Leadership, ed. Larry C. Spears (San Francisco: Barrett-Koehle, 1998). The last, primarily essays that were also published independently by the Greenleaf Center in Indianapolis, also includes an extensive bibliography of Greenleaf's writings. See also Larry C. Spears, *Insights on Leadership: Service, Stewardship, Spirit, and Servant Leadership* (New York: Wiley, 1998).

28. Greenleaf, *Servant Leadership,* 25.

29. See, for example, Alan Geoffrey Palmer, *The Servant-Leader: An Examination of the New Testament Concept of Leadership* (Ottawa: National Library of Canada, 1985); Cecil McSparron, *The Servant Leader in the New Testament: An Exposition with Special Reference to the Works of Robert K. Greenleaf* (Ottawa: National Library of Canada, 1987); and C. Gene Wilkes, *Jesus on Leadership: Becoming a Servant Leader* (Nashville: LifeWay, 1996). The last, produced under Southern Baptist auspices, has cognate study and leader guides.

30. Bill McCartney with David Halbrook and Lyndi McCartney, *Sold Out: Becoming Man Enough to Make a Difference* (Nashville: Word Books, 1997).

31. Tony Evans, "Spiritual Purity," in *The Seven Promises of a Promise Keeper,* ed. Tony Evans (Colorado Springs, Colo.: Focus on the Family, 1994), 79–80.

32. Michael S. Kimmel, "Patriarchy's Second Coming as Masculine Renewal," in Claussen, *Standing on the Promises,* 114; and Mary Stewart Van Leeuwen, "Servanthood or Soft Patriarchy."

33. Jon P. Bloch, "The New and Improved Clint Eastwood: Change and Persistence in Promise Keepers Self-Help Literature," in Williams, *Promise Keepers and the New Masculinity,* 24.

34. Kimmel, "Patriarchy's Second Coming," 115.

35. Susan Faludi, in chapter 5 of *Stiffed,* recounts her perception of the dynamics of one of these local support groups that she observed over several months.

36. See, for example, Daryl G. Donovan, *Men Mentoring Men: Men's Discipleship Course, an Interactive One-on-One or Small Group Christian Growth Manual for Men* (Lima, Ohio: CSS Publishing, 1998).

37. See "SBC Approves Family Statement," *Christian Century* 115 (June 17–24, 1998): 602–3; and Gustav Niebuhr, "SBC Declares Wife Should 'Submit' to Her Husband," *New York Times,* June 10, 1998.

38. Margaret Lamberts Bendroth, "Last Gap Patriarchy: Women and Men in Conservative American Protestantism," *Muslim World* 9, nos. 1–2 (Spring 2002): 45–54.

39. "SBC Moves to Limit Office of Pastor to Men," *Christian Century* 117 (June 7–14, 2000): 641.

40. See the discussion in Marie Griffith and Paul Harvey, "Wifely Submission: The SBC Resolution," *Christian Century* 115 (July 1–8, 1998): 636–38.

41. Of Edwin Louis Cole's many books, I was able to read for this study just four: *Communication, Sex and Money* (Tulsa, Okla.: Honor Books, 1987); *Courage: A Book for Champions* (Tulsa, Okla.: Honor Books, a Division of Harrison House, 1985); *Maximized Manhood: A Guide to Family Survival* (Springdale, Pa.: Whitaker House, 1982); and *The Potential Principle: Living Life to Its Maximum* (Springdale, Pa.: Whitaker House, 1984). Cole died in 2002 while I was writing this book.

42. Cole, *Maximized Manhood,* 33.

43. The first quotation is from Cole, *Maximized Manhood,* 85; the second is the title of chapter 10 of that work.

44. Cole makes the point repeatedly in *Courage*.

45. Cole, *Communication, Sex and Money*, 23.

46. Cole, *Maximized Manhood*, 75, 90.

47. See Cole, *Potential Principle*, 72.

48. See, for example, Daisy Hepburn, *Look, You're a Leader! A New Look at Servant Leadership for Women* (Ventura, Calif.: Regal Books, 1985).

49. See Robert Wuthnow, ed., *"I Come Away Stronger": How Small Groups Are Shaping American Religion* (Grand Rapids, Mich.: Eerdmans, 1994). Curiously, none of the groups that contributors analyze in this collection is oriented exclusively to men.

50. I have gleaned most of the factual information from the two works by McCartney that offer a "message to Christian men" along with autobiographical reminiscences: Bill McCartney with Dave Diles, *From Ashes to Glory*, rev. ed. (Nashville: Thomas Nelson, 1995); and McCartney with Halbrook and McCartney, *Sold Out*. The phrase quoted is from *Sold Out*, xi.

51. McCartney with Halbrook and McCartney, *Sold Out*, chap. 8.

52. Ibid., chap. 1.

53. McCartney discusses this experience at great length in *Sold Out*, chaps. 9 and 10.

54. McCartney, *From Ashes to Glory*, chap. 9.

55. McCartney with Halbrook and McCartney, *Sold Out*, chap. 25.

56. Such is the title of chapter 20 of McCartney with Halbrook and McCartney, *Sold Out*.

57. McCartney writes about the cruise in *Sold Out*, chapter 19, and Lyndi McCartney's comments are included in an aside within that chapter.

58. From observations offered by Lyndi McCartney in *Sold Out*, 188.

59. McCartney with Halbrook and McCartney, *Sold Out*, chap. 28.

60. Richard Hoffer and Shelley Smith, "Putting His House in Order," *Sports Illustrated*, Jan. 16, 1995, 27–32.

61. See Lyndi McCartney's observations in *Sold Out*, chap. 31.

62. Ibid., 269.

63. McCartney took the title that coauthor Dave Diles had given to one of his own books, *Nobody's Perfect*, as the title for chapter 7 of *From Ashes to Glory*.

64. See McCartney with Halbrook and McCartney, *Sold Out*, chap. 35.

Chapter 8

1. Ammerman, "Golden Rule Christianity," 196–216.

2. For example, see the discussion in Edward H. Thompson Jr. and Kathryn R. Remmes, "Does Masculinity Thwart Being Religious? An Examination of Older Men's Religiousness," *Journal for the Scientific Study of Religion* 41, no. 3 (Sept. 2002): 521–32.

Bibliography

Alcott, William A. *Familiar Letters to Young Men on Various Subjects.* 1849. Reprint, Auburn, N.Y.: Miller, Orton and Mulligan, 1854.

———. *Gift Book for Young Men: Or, Familiar Letters on Self-Knowledge, Self-Education, Female Society, Marriage, &c.* Auburn, N.Y.: Miller, Orton and Mulligan, 1854.

———. *The Young Husband; or, Duties of Man in the Marriage Relation.* 1837. Reprint of 5th ed. [1841]. New York: Arno, 1972.

Alexander, James W. *The Revival and Its Lessons: A Collection of Fugitive Papers, Having Reference to the Great Awakening.* New York: American Tract Society, 1858.

———, ed. *The New York Pulpit in the Revival of 1858: A Memorial Volume of Sermons.* New York: Sheldon, Blakeman, 1858.

Alger, Horatio, Jr. *Bound to Rise; or, Harry Walton's Motto.* Boston: Loring, 1873.

———. *Ragged Dick; or, Street Life in New York.* Boston: Loring, 1868.

———. *Risen from the Ranks; or, Harry Walton's Success.* Boston: Loring, 1874.

———. *Sam's Chance; and How He Improved It.* Boston: Loring, 1876.

———. *The Young Outlaw; or, Adrift in the Streets.* Boston: Loring, 1875.

Allen, Charles L. *God's Psychiatry.* Old Tappan, N.J.: Fleming H. Revell, 1953.

———. *Roads to Radiant Living.* Old Tappan, N.J.: Fleming H. Revell, 1968.

———. *What I Have Lived By: An Autobiography.* Old Tappan, N.J.: Fleming H. Revell, 1976.

Allen, Frederick Lewis. *The Big Change: America Transforms Itself, 1900–1950.* New York: Harper, 1952.

Ammerman, Nancy T. "Golden Rule Christianity: Lived Religion in the American Mainstream." In *Lived Religion in America: Toward a History of Practice,* edited by David D. Hall, 196–216. Princeton, N.J.: Princeton Univ. Press, 1997.

Armstrong, Maurice W. "Religious Enthusiasm and Separatism in Colonial New England." *Harvard Theological Review* 38 (1945): 111–40.

Arnold, Patrick M. *Wildmen, Warriors, and Kings: Masculine Spirituality and the Bible.* New York: Crossroad, 1991.

Arthur, Timothy Shay. *Advice to Young Men on Their Duties and Conduct in Society.* 1847. Reprint, Boston: N. C. Barton, 1849.

Arthur, William. *The Successful Merchant: Sketches of the Life of Mr. Samuel Budgett.* Rev. by Thomas O. Summers. Nashville: E. Stevenson and J. E. Evans, 1856.

Atkins, Frederick A. *Moral Muscle, and How to Use It: A Brotherly Chat with Young Men.* London: James Nesbit, 1890.

Babson, Roger. *New Tasks for Old Churches.* New York: Macmillan, 1922.

———. *Religion and Business.* New York: Macmillan, 1921.

Bagley, Sharon. "Searching for the God Within: The Way Our Brains Are Wired May Explain the Origin and Power of Religious Beliefs." *Newsweek,* Jan. 29, 2001, 59.

Baker, Derek, ed. *Religious Motivation: Biographical and Sociological Problems for the Church Historian.* Oxford: Blackwell, 1978.

Baker, James T. *Andrew Carnegie: Robber Baron as American Hero.* Belmont, Calif.: Wadsworth, 2003.

Barton, Bruce. *The Book Nobody Knows.* Indianapolis: Grosset and Dunlap in cooperation with Bobbs-Merrill, 1926.

———. *He Upset the World.* Indianapolis: Bobbs-Merrill, 1931.

———. *The Man Nobody Knows.* 1925. Reprint, Indianapolis: Bobbs-Merrill, 1962.

———. *More Power to You: Fifty Editorials from Every Week.* New York: Century, 1917.

———. *What Can a Man Believe.* Indianapolis: Bobbs-Merrill for Grosset and Dunlap, 1927.

Batson, C. Daniel, P. A. Schoenrade, and W. Larry Ventis. *The Religious Experience: A Social-Psychological Perspective.* New York: Oxford Univ. Press, 1993.

Bayley, Tim. "Going for the Men." *Faith and Renewal* 15, no. 1 (July–Aug. 1990): 18–22.

Bederman, Gail. *Manliness and Civilization: A Cultural History of Gender and Race in the United States, 1880–1917.* Chicago: Univ. of Chicago Press, 1995.

———. "'The Women Have Had Charge of the Church Work Long Enough': The Men and Religion Forward Movement of 1911–1912 and the Masculinization of Middle-Class Protestantism." *American Quarterly* 41, no. 3 (Sept. 1989): 432–65.

Beecher, Henry Ward. *Addresses to Young Men.* Philadelphia: Henry Altemus, 1895. Also published in various earlier editions as *Lectures to Young Men on Various Important Subjects.*

Beecher, Lyman. *The Autobiography of Lyman Beecher.* Edited by Barbara M. Cross. 2 vols. Cambridge: Belknap Press of Harvard Univ. Press, 1961.

Bellah, Robert N., William M. Sullivan, Ann Swidler, and Steven M. Tipton. *Habits of the Heart: Individualism and Commitment in American Life.* Berkeley and Los Angeles: Univ. of California Press, 1985.

Bendroth, Margaret L. *Fundamentalism and Gender: 1875 to the Present.* New Haven, Conn.: Yale Univ. Press, 1992.

———. "Horace Bushnell's Christian Nurture." In *The Child in Christian Thought,* edited by Marcia J. Bunge, 350–64. Grand Rapids, Mich.: Eerdmans, 2001.

———. "Last Gasp Patriarchy: Women and Men in Conservative American Protestantism." *Muslim World* 9, nos. 1–2 (Spring 2001): 45–54.

Beveridge, Albert J. *The Young Man and the World.* New York: D. Appleton, 1905.

Bird, B. "FGBMFI: Facing Frustrations and the Future." *Charisma* 11 (June 1986): 25, 26, 28.

———. "The Legacy of Demos Shakarian." *Charisma* 11 (June 1986): 20–25.

Bishop, Robert S. "Bruce Barton: Presidential Stage Manager." *Journalism Quarterly* 43 (1966): 77–83.

Bjork, Daniel W. *The Victorian Flight: Russell H. Conwell and the Crisis of Individualism.* Washington, D.C.: Univ. Press of America, 1979.

Bloch, Jon P. "The New and Improved Clint Eastwood: Change and Persistence in Promise Keepers Self-Help Literature." In *Promise Keepers and the New Masculinity,* edited by Rhys H. Williams, 11–31. Lanham, Md.: Lexington Books, 2001.

Bradford, Gamaliel. *D. L. Moody: A Worker in Souls.* New York: George H. Doran, 1927.

Branch, Taylor. *Parting the Waters: America in the King Years, 1954–63.* New York: Simon and Schuster, 1988.

———. *Pillar of Fire: America in the King Years, 1963–65.* New York: Simon and Schuster, 1998.

Breen, Timothy H. *The Character of the Good Ruler: Puritan Political Ideas in New England, 1630–1730.* New Haven, Conn.: Yale Univ. Press, 1970.

Bridgeman, Howard Allen. "Have We a Religion for Men?" *Andover Review* 13 (1890): 388–96.

Broadhurst, Allan R. *He Speaks the Word of God: A Study of the Sermons of Norman Vincent Peale.* Englewood Cliffs, N.J.: Prentice-Hall, 1963.

Brod, Harry, ed. *A Mensch Among Men: Explorations in Jewish Masculinity.* Freedom, Calif.: Crossing Press, 1988.

Brown, Anne S., and David D. Hall. "Family Strategies and Religious Practice: Baptism and the Lord's Supper in Early New England." In *Lived Religion in America: Toward a History of Practice,* edited by David D. Hall, 41–68. Princeton N.J.: Princeton Univ. Press, 1997.

Bruns, Roger. *Preacher: Billy Sunday and Big-Time American Evangelism.* New York: W. W. Norton, 1992.

Budapest, Z[suzsana]. *The Grandmother of Time: A Women's Book of Celebrations, Spells, and Sacred Objects for Every Month of the Year.* San Francisco: Harper, 1988.

———. *Grandmother Moon.* San Francisco: Harper, 1991.

———. *The Holy Book of Women's Mysteries.* Oakland, Calif.: Wingbow, 1989.

Bunge, Marcia J., ed. *The Child in Christian Thought.* Grand Rapids, Mich.: Eerdmans, 2001.

Burr, Agnes Rush. *Russell H. Conwell and His Work.* 1926. Reprint, Philadelphia: Winston, 1943.

Buther, Willis H. "What Men Like: Three Things That Stir Enthusiasm." *Congregationalist and Christian World,* Sept. 23, 1911, 411.

Butler, Jon. *Awash in a Sea of Faith: Christianizing the American People.* Cambridge: Harvard Univ. Press, 1990.

Cabot, Richard C. *What Men Live By: Work, Play, Love, Worship.* Boston: Houghton Mifflin, 1914.

Caldwell, Thekla Ellen Joiner. "Women, Men and Revival: The Third Awakening in Chicago." Ph.D. diss., Univ. of Illinois at Chicago, 1991.

Capps, Donald. *Men and Their Religion: Honor, Hope, and Humor.* Harrisburg, Pa.: Trinity Press International, 2002.

Carmody, John. *Toward a Male Spirituality.* Mystic, Conn.: Twenty-third Publications, 1990.

Carnegie, Andrew. *The Autobiography of Andrew Carnegie.* With a new foreword by Cecelia Tichi. Boston: Northeastern Univ. Press, 1986.

———. *The Gospel of Wealth, and Other Timely Essays.* Edited by Edward C. Kirtland. Cambridge: Belknap Press of Harvard Univ. Press, 1962.

Carnegie, Dale. *How to Win Friends and Influence People.* New York: Simon and Schuster, 1936.

———. *Public Speaking and Influencing Men in Business.* New York: Association Press, 1932.

Carnes, Mark C. "Iron John in the Gilded Age." *American Heritage* 44, no. 5 (Sept. 1993): 37–45.

———. *Secret Ritual and Manhood in Victorian America.* New Haven, Conn.: Yale Univ. Press, 1989.

Carnes, Mark C., and Clyde G. Griffen, eds. *Meanings for Manhood: Constructions of Masculinity in Victorian America.* Chicago: Univ. of Chicago Press, 1990.

Cawardine, Richard. "The Religious Revival of 1857–58 in the United States." In *Religious Motivation: Biographical and Sociological Problems for the Church Historian,* edited by Derek Baker, 393–406. Oxford: Blackwell, 1978.

———. *Transatlantic Revivalism: Popular Evangelicalism in Britain and America, 1790–1865.* Westport, Conn.: Greenwood, 1978.

Cawelti, John. *Apostles of the Self-Made Man.* Chicago: Univ. of Chicago Press, 1965.

Chamberlain, N. H. *Samuel Sewall and the World He Lived In.* 1897. Reprint, New York: Russell and Russell, 1967.

Chambers, Talbot W. *The Noon Prayer Meeting of the North Dutch Church.* New York: Board of Publication of the Reformed Dutch Protestant Church, 1858.

Christ, Carol. "Victorian Masculinity and the Angel in the House." In *A Widening Sphere: Changing Roles of Victorian Women,* edited by Martha Vicinus, 146–62. Bloomington: Indiana Univ. Press, 1977.

Claussen, Dane S., ed. *The Promise Keepers: Essays on Masculinity and Christianity.* Jefferson, N.C.: McFarland, 1999.

———, ed. *Standing on the Promises: The Promise Keepers and the Revival of Manhood.* Cleveland: Pilgrim Press, 1999.

Clawson, Mary Ann. *Constructing Brotherhood: Class, Gender, and Fraternalism.* Princeton, N.J.: Princeton Univ. Press, 1989.

Cole, Arthur. "The Tempo of Mercantile Life in Colonial America." *Business History Review* 33 (1959): 277–99.

Cole, Edwin Louis. *Communication, Sex and Money.* Tulsa, Okla.: Honor Books, 1987.

———. *Courage: A Book for Champions.* Tulsa, Okla.: Honor Books, a Division of Harrison House, 1985.

———. *Maximized Manhood: A Guide to Family Survival.* Springdale, Pa.: Whitaker House, 1982.

———. *The Potential Principle: Living Life to Its Maximum.* Springdale, Pa.: Whitaker House, 1984.

Conant, R. W. *The Manly Christ: A New View.* Chicago: n.p., 1904. Reprinted in 1915 as *The Virility of Christ: A New View.*

Conant, William C. *Narratives of Remarkable Conversions and Revival Incidents.* New York: Derby and Jackson, 1858.

Conniff, James C. G. *The Bishop Sheen Story.* Greenwich, Conn.: Fawcett, 1953.

Cope, Henry F. *Efficiency in the Sunday School.* New York: George H. Doran, 1912.

———. *The Efficient Layman, or the Religious Training of Men.* Philadelphia: Griffith and Rowland, 1911.

Cornwell, Patricia Daniels. *A Time for Remembering: The Ruth Bell Graham Story.* San Francisco: Harper and Row, 1983.

Cowing, Cedric B. "Sex and Preaching in the Great Awakening." *American Quarterly* 20 (Fall 1968): 624–44.

Crosby, W. C. "Acres of Diamonds." *American Mercury* 14 (May 1928): 104–13.

Crunden, Robert M. *Ministers of Reform: The Progressives' Achievement in American Civilization, 1889–1920*. New York: Basic Books, 1982.

Culbertson, Philip. *New Adam: The Future of Masculine Spirituality*. Philadelphia: Fortress, 1992.

Curtis, Susan. *A Consuming Faith: The Social Gospel and Modern American Culture*. Baltimore: Johns Hopkins Univ. Press, 1991.

———. "The Son of Man and God the Father: The Social Gospel and Victorian Masculinity." In *Meanings for Manhood: Constructions of Masculinity in Victorian America*, edited by Mark C. Carnes and Clyde Griffen, 67–78. Chicago: Univ. of Chicago Press, 1990.

Cuyler, Theodore L. *Recollections of a Long Life*. New York: Baker and Taylor, 1902.

Dailey, Jim. "A Conversation with Ruth Bell Graham." *Decision* 43, no. 5 (May 2002): 12–15.

Dart, John. "Men Behaving Badly: Gender and Churchgoing." *Christian Century* 117, no. 32 (Nov. 15, 2000): 1174–75.

———. "Schuller's Glass Act." *Christian Century* 119, no. 8 (Apr. 10–17, 2002): 24.

Dawson, William. *Threshold of Manhood*. New York: Fleming H. Revell, 1909.

DeBerg, Betty A. *Ungodly Women: Gender and the First Wave of American Fundamentalism*. Minneapolis: Fortress, 1990.

Demarest, David P., Jr., gen. ed. *"The River Ran Red": Homestead 1892*. Pittsburgh: Univ. of Pittsburgh Press, 1992.

Demos, John. *A Little Commonwealth: Family Life in Plymouth Colony*. New York: Oxford Univ. Press, 1970.

deVaus, D., and I. McAllister. "Gender Differences in Religion: A Test of the Structural Location Theory." *American Sociological Review* 51 (1987): 472–81.

Dittes, James. "A Men's Movement for the Church." *Christian Century*, May 29–June 5, 1991, 588–90.

Dobson, James. *Straight Talk to Men and Their Wives*. New York: Tyndale House, 1975.

Dodge, D. Stuart. *Memorials of William E. Dodge*. New York: Randolph, 1887.

Dodge, William E. *Old New York: A Lecture*. New York: Dodd, Mead, 1880.

Donovan, Daryl G. *Men Mentoring Men: Men's Discipleship Course, an Interactive One-on-One or Small Group Christian Growth Manual for Men*. Lima, Ohio: CSS Publishing, 1998.

Dorsett, Lyle W. *Billy Sunday and the Redemption of Urban America*. Edited by Mark A. Noll and Nathan W. Hatch. Library of Religious Biography. Grand Rapids, Mich.: Eerdmans, 1991.

Doss, Erika. "Making a 'Virile, Manly Christ': The Cultural Origins and Meanings of Warner Sallman's Religious Imagery." In *Icons of American Protestantism: The Art of Warner Sallman*, edited by David Morgan, 61–94. New Haven, Conn.: Yale Univ. Press, 1996.

Douglas, Ann. *The Feminization of American Culture*. New York: Knopf, 1977.

Dudley, Carl, and David Roozen, eds. *Faith Communities Today (FACT): A Report on Religion in the United States Today*. Hartford, Conn.: Hartford Institute for Religion Research of the Hartford Seminary Foundation, 2001.

Dumenil, Lynn. *Freemasonry and American Culture, 1880–1939*. Princeton, N.J.: Princeton Univ. Press, 1984.

Dupee, F. W. *Henry James: His Life and Writings*. New York: William Sloane Associates, 1951.

Earle, Alice Morse. *Home Life in Colonial Days.* 1898. Reprint, Middle Village, N.Y.: Jonathan David, 1975.

Eck, Diana. *A New Religious America: How a "Christian Country" Has Become the World's Most Religiously Diverse Nation.* San Francisco: HarperSanFrancisco, 2001.

Edwards, Jonathan. *A Treatise Concerning Religious Affections in Three Parts.* 1746. Reprinted as vol. 2 of *The Works of Jonathan Edwards,* edited by John E. Smith. New Haven, Conn.: Yale Univ. Press, 1959.

Ellis, William T. "A Movement: A Message: A Method." *Independent* 72 (May 9, 1912): 984–88.

Epstein, Barbara. *The Politics of Domesticity: Women, Evangelism, and Temperance in Nineteenth-Century America.* Middletown, Conn.: Wesleyan Univ. Press, 1981.

Evans, Tony. "Spiritual Purity." In *The Seven Promises of a Promise Keeper,* edited by Tony Evans, 75–80. Colorado Springs, Colo.: Focus on the Family, 1994.

Faludi, Susan. *Backlash: The Undeclared War against American Women.* New York: Crown Books, 1991.

———. *Stiffed: The Betrayal of the American Man.* New York: William Morrow, 1999.

Faust, Drew Gilpin. "Christian Soldiers: The Meaning of Revivalism in the Confederate Army." *Journal of Southern History* 58 (Feb. 1987): 63–90.

Feltey, K. M., and M. M. Poloma. "From Sex Differences to Gender Role Beliefs: Exploring Effects on Six Dimensions of Religiosity." *Sex Roles* 25 (1991): 181–93.

Ferreira, James M. "Only Yesterday and the Two Christs of the Twenties." *South Atlantic Quarterly* 81 (1981): 77–83.

Finke, Roger, and Rodney Stark. *The Churching of America, 1776–1990: Winners and Losers in Our Spiritual Economy.* New Brunswick, N.J.: Rutgers Univ. Press, 1992.

Finney, Charles G. *Memoirs of Charles G. Finney: The Complete Restored Text.* Edited by Garth M. Rosell and Richard A. G. Dupuis. Grand Rapids, Mich.: Academie Books of Zondervan, 1989.

Fischer, David Hackett. *Albion's Seed: Four British Folkways in America.* New York: Oxford Univ. Press, 1989.

Fish, Henry Clay. *Primitive Piety Revived, or The Aggressive Power of the Christian Church.* Boston: Congregational Board of Publication, 1855.

Fiske, Charles. *The Confessions of a Troubled Parson.* New York: Charles Scribner's Sons, 1928.

FitzGerald, Frances. *Cities on a Hill.* New York: Simon and Schuster, 1986.

Flake, Carol. *Redemptorama: Culture, Politics, and the New Evangelism.* New York: Viking, 1984.

Flynt, J. Wayne. *Taking Christianity to China: Alabama Missionaries in the Middle Kingdom, 1850–1950.* Tuscaloosa: Univ. of Alabama Press, 1997.

"For Men." *Christian Advocate* 86 (1911): 1026.

Formisano, Ronald, and Kathleen Smith Kutolowski. "Antimasonry and Masonry: The Genesis of Protest, 1826–1827." *American Quarterly* 29 (Summer 1977): 139–65.

Fosdick, Harry Emerson. *The Man from Nazareth: As He Was Seen by the People of His Time.* New York: Harper, 1949.

———. *The Manhood of the Master.* New York: Association Press, 1913.

———. "What Is the Matter with Preaching." *Harpers* 157 (June 1928): 133–41.

Frady, Marshall. *Billy Graham: A Parable of American Righteousness.* Boston: Little, Brown, 1979.

Francis, Russell E. "The Religious Revival of 1858 in Philadelphia." *Pennsylvania Magazine of History and Biography* 70 (1946): 52–77.

Frank, Douglas W. *Less than Conquerors: How Evangelicalism Entered the Twentieth Century.* Grand Rapids, Mich.: Eerdmans, 1986.

Friedman Edwin H. *Generation to Generation: Family Process in Church and Synagogue.* New York: Guilford Press, 1985.

Gardner, Ralph D. *Horatio Alger, or the American Hero Era.* 1964. Reprint, New York: Arco, 1978.

Garrow, David J. *Bearing the Cross: Martin Luther King, Jr., and the Southern Christian Leadership Conference.* New York: Random House, 1986.

Gaustad, Edwin S. *Sworn on the Altar of God: A Religious Biography of Thomas Jefferson.* Edited by Mark A. Noll, Nathan S. Hatch, and Alan C. Guelzo. Library of Religious Biography. Grand Rapids, Mich.: Eerdmans, 1996.

George, Carol V. R. *God's Salesman: Norman Vincent Peale and the Power of Positive Thinking.* New York: Oxford Univ. Press, 1993.

Gilbreath, Edward. "Manhood's Great Awakening." *Christianity Today* 39, no. 2 (Feb. 6, 1995): 20–28.

Gilkeson, John S., Jr. *Middle-Class Providence, 1829–1940.* Princeton, N.J.: Princeton Univ. Press, 1986.

Gilman, Charlotte Perkins. *His Religion and Hers.* New York: Century, 1923.

Gladden, Washington. *The Church and Modern Life.* Boston: Houghton Mifflin, 1908.

———. *Social Salvation.* Boston: Houghton Mifflin, 1902.

———. *Tools and the Man.* Boston: Houghton Mifflin, 1893.

Gordon, Arthur. *Norman Vincent Peale: Minister to Millions.* Englewood Cliffs, N.J.: Prentice-Hall, 1958. Reprint, Greenwich, Conn.: Fawcett, 1964.

Gouge, William. *Of Domesticall Duties: Eight Treatises.* London: John Haviland, 1622.

Graham, Billy. *Peace with God.* Garden City, N.Y.: Doubleday, 1953. Rev. ed., Waco, Tex.: Word Books, 1984.

Graham, Judith S. *Puritan Family Life: The Diary of Samuel Sewall.* Boston: Northeastern Univ. Press, 2000.

Graham, Sylvester. *A Lecture to Young Men, on Chastity.* 2d ed. Boston: C. H. Peirce, 1837.

Greenleaf, Robert K. *On Becoming a Servant Leader.* Edited by Don M. Frick and Larry C. Spears. San Francisco: Jossey-Bass, 1996.

———. *The Power of Servant Leadership: Essays.* Edited by Larry C. Spears. San Francisco: Barrett-Koehler, 1998.

———. *The Servant as Leader.* Indianapolis: Greenleaf Center, 1991. First published in 1970.

———. "The Servant as Leader." *Journal of Religion and Applied Behavioral Science* (Winter 1982): 3, 7–10.

———. *Servant Leadership: A Journey into the Nature of Legitimate Power and Greatness.* New York: Paulist Press, 1977.

Greven, Philip. *The Protestant Temperament: Patterns of Child-Rearing, Religious Experience, and the Self in Early America.* New York: Knopf, 1977.

Griffith, R. Marie. *God's Daughters: Evangelical Women and the Power of Submission.* Berkeley and Los Angeles: Univ. of California Press, 1997.

Griffith, R. Marie, and Paul Harvey. "Wifely Submission: The SBC Resolution." *Christian Century* 115 (June 17–24, 1998): 636–38.

Griswold, Robert L. *Fatherhood in America: A History.* New York: Basic Books, 1993.

Grossman, Susan. "Finding Comfort after a Miscarriage." In *Daughters of the King,* edited by Susan Grossman and Rivka Haupt, 285–90. Philadelphia: Jewish Publication Society of America, 1992.

Haber, Samuel. *Efficiency and Uplift: Scientific Management in the Progressive Era, 1890–1920.* Chicago: Univ. of Chicago Press, 1964.

Hacker, Louis, ed. *The Life of Andrew Carnegie.* 2 vols. New York: Harper and Row, 1949.

Hackett, David G. "Gender and Religion in American Culture, 1879–1930." *Religion and American Culture* 5, no. 2 (Summer 1995): 127–57.

Hall, David. D. *Worlds of Wonder, Days of Judgment: Popular Religious Belief in Early New England.* New York: Knopf, 1989.

———, ed. *Lived Religion in America: Toward a History of Practice.* Princeton, N.J.: Princeton Univ. Press, 1997.

Hambrick-Stowe, Charles E. *The Practice of Piety: Puritan Devotional Discipline in Seventeenth-Century New England.* Chapel Hill: Univ. of North Carolina Press, 1982.

Handy, Robert T. "The American Religious Depression, 1925–1935." *Church History* 29 (1960): 3–16.

———. *A Christian America: Protestant Hopes and Historical Realities.* 2d ed. New York: Oxford Univ. Press, 1984.

Hearn, Thomas K., Jr. "Jesus Was a Sissy After All." *Christian Century* 87, no. 40 (Oct. 1970): 1191–94.

Henry, James O. "The United States Christian Commission in the Civil War." *Civil War History* 6 (1960): 374–88.

Hepburn, Daisy. *Look, You're a Leader! A New Look at Servant Leadership for Women.* Ventura, Calif.: Regal Books, 1985.

Herberg, Will. *Protestant, Catholic, Jew: An Essay in American Religious Sociology.* Garden City, N.Y.: Doubleday, 1955.

Herring, Reuben. *Men Are Like That.* Nashville: Broadman Press, 1967.

Herx, Henry. "Religion and Film." In *Encyclopedia of the American Religious Experience,* edited by Charles H. Lippy and Peter W. Williams, 3:1341–58. 3 vols. New York: Scribner's, 1988.

Heyrman, Christine Leigh. *Southern Cross: The Beginnings of the Bible Belt.* New York: Alfred A. Knopf, 1997.

Hoffer, Richard, and Shelley Smith. "Getting His House in Order." *Sports Illustrated,* Jan. 16, 1995, 27–32.

Hoge, Dean R., Benton Johnson, and Donald A. Luidens. *Vanishing Boundaries: The Religion of Mainline Protestant Baby Boomers.* Louisville, Ky.: Westminster/John Knox, 1994.

Hopkins, C. Howard. *History of the Y.M.C.A. in North America.* New York: Association Press, 1951.

———. *The Rise of the Social Gospel in American Protestantism, 1865–1915.* 1940. Reprint, New Haven: Yale Univ. Press, 1967.

Horlick, Allan. *Country Boys and Merchant Princes: The Social Control of Young Men in New York.* Lewisburg, Pa.: Bucknell Univ. Press, 1975.

Horton, Walter M. *Theism and the Modern Mood.* New York: Harper & Bros., 1928.

Hough, Lynn Harold. *The Man of Power: A Series of Studies in Christian Efficiency.* New York: Abingdon, 1916.

Howe, Daniel Walker. "Victorian Culture in America." In *Victorian America*, edited by Daniel Walker Howe, 3–28. Philadelphia: Univ. of Pennsylvania Press, 1976.

Huber, Richard M. *The American Idea of Success*. New York: McGraw-Hill, 1971.

Hudnut-Buemler, James. *Looking for God in the Suburbs: The Religion of the American Dream and Its Critics, 1945–1965*. New Brunswick, N.J.: Rutgers Univ. Press, 1994.

Hudson, Winthrop S. *The Great Tradition of the American Churches*. New York: Harper & Bros., 1953.

Hughes, Thomas. *The Manliness of Christ*. Boston: Houghton Mifflin, 1880.

Hurlbut, Jesse L. *Organizing and Building Up the Sunday School*. New York: Eaton and Mains, 1910.

Hutchison, William R. *Religious Pluralism in America: The Contentious History of a Founding Ideal*. New Haven, Conn.: Yale Univ. Press, 2003.

Hyde, William DeWitt, ed. *Vocations*. 10 vols. Boston: Hyde, 1911.

"In Search of the Hero: Masculine Spirituality and Liberal Christianity." *America* 161 (Oct. 7, 1989): 206–10.

Johnson, Curtis D. *Redeeming America: Evangelicals and the Road to Civil War*. Chicago: Ivan R. Dee, 1993.

Johnson, Paul. *A Shopkeeper's Millennium: Society and Revivals in Rochester, New York, 1815–1837*. New York: Hill and Wang, 1978.

Johnson, Robert A. *Understanding Masculine Psychology*. San Francisco: Harper and Row, 1974. Reissued in 1983 as *He! Understanding Masculine Psychology*.

Juster, Susan. "'In a Different Voice': Male and Female Narratives of Religious Conversion in Post-Revolutionary America." *American Quarterly* 41 (Mar. 1989): 34–62.

Kemp, Giles. *The Man Who Influenced Millions*. New York: St. Martin's, 1989.

Kenna, James Brett. "Minister or Business Executive." *Harpers* 157 (June 1928): 38–44.

Kennedy, Gail, ed. *Democracy and the Gospel of Wealth*. Boston: D. C. Heath, 1949.

Kimmel, Michael. *Manhood in America: A Cultural History*. New York: Free Press, 1996.

———. "Patriarchy's Second Coming as Masculine Renewal." In *Standing on the Promises: Promise Keepers and the Revival of Manhood*, edited by Dane S. Claussen, 111–20. Cleveland: Pilgrim Press, 1999.

Kushner, Harold S. *When Bad Things Happen to Good People*. New York: Schocken Books, 1981.

Ladd, Tony, and James A. Mathisen. *Muscular Christianity: Evangelical Protestants and the Development of American Sport*. Grand Rapids, MI: Baker Book House, 1999.

Lawrence, William. *Memories of a Happy Life*. Boston: Houghton Mifflin, 1926.

———. "The Relation of Wealth to Morals." In *Democracy and the Gospel of Wealth*, 68–76. Edited by Gail Kennedy. Boston: D.C. Heath, 1949.

Liebman, Joshua Loth. *Peace of Mind*. New York: Simon and Schuster, 1946.

Lippy, Charles H. *Being Religious, American Style: A History of Popular Religiosity in the United States*. Westport, Conn.: Greenwood, 1994.

———. "Miles to Go: Promise Keepers in Historical and Cultural Context." *Soundings: An Interdisciplinary Journal* 80, nos. 2–3 (Fall/Summer 1997): 289–304.

———. *Pluralism Comes of Age: American Religious Culture in the Twentieth Century*. Armonk, N.Y.: M. E. Sharpe, 2000.

————. "The Rise of Biblical Criticism and Challenges to Religious Authority." In *Encyclopedia of American Cultural and Intellectual History,* edited by Mary Kupiec Cayton and Peter W. Williams, 1:581–88. 3 vols. New York: Scribner's, 2001.

————, ed. *Twentieth-Century Shapers of American Popular Religion.* Westport, Conn.: Greenwood, 1989.

Lipson, Dorothy Ann. *Freemasonry in Federalist Connecticut, 1789–1835.* Princeton, N.J.: Princeton Univ. Press, 1977.

Lockridge, Kenneth A. *A New England Town: The First Hundred Years.* New York: W. W. Norton, 1970.

Lombard, Anne Spencer. "Playing the Man: Conceptions of Masculinity in Anglo-American New England, 1675 to 1765." Ph.D. diss., Univ. of California at Los Angeles, 1998.

Long, Kathryn Teresa. *The Revival of 1857–58: Interpreting an American Religious Awakening.* New York: Oxford Univ. Press, 1998.

Lovelace, Richard F. *The American Pietism of Cotton Mather: Origins of American Evangelicalism.* Grand Rapids Mich.: Christian Univ. Press, 1979.

Lowitt, Richard. *A Merchant Prince of the Nineteenth Century: William E. Dodge.* New York: Columbia Univ. Press, 1954.

Luckmann, Thomas. *The Invisible Religion: The Problem of Religion in Modern Society.* New York: Macmillan, 1967.

Lyerly, Cynthia Lynn. *Methodism and the Southern Mind, 1770–1810.* New York: Oxford Univ. Press, 1998.

Lynch, Christopher Owen. *Selling Catholicism: Bishop Sheen and the Power of Television.* Lexington: Univ. Press of Kentucky, 1998.

Mahalik, J. R., and H. D. Lagan. "Examining Masculine Gender Role Conflict and Stress in Relation to Religious Orientation and Spiritual Well-Being." *Psychology of Men and Masculinity* 2 (2001): 24–33.

Mangan, J. A., and James Walvin, eds. *Manliness and Morality: Middle-Class Masculinity in Britain and America, 1800–1940.* New York: St. Martin's, 1987.

Martin, Robert F. "Billy Sunday and Christian Manliness." *Historian* 58, no. 4 (Summer 1996): 811–23.

————. *Hero of the Heartland: Billy Sunday and the Transformation of American Society, 1862–1935.* Bloomington: Indiana Univ. Press, 2002.

Martin, William C. *A Prophet with Honor: The Billy Graham Story.* New York: William Morrow, 1991.

Marty, Martin E. *Modern American Religion.* Vol. 1, *The Irony of It All.* Chicago: Univ. of Chicago Press, 1986.

————. *Modern American Religion.* Vol. 2, *The Noise of Conflict, 1919–1941.* Chicago: Univ. of Chicago Press, 1991.

————. *Modern American Religion.* Vol. 3, *Under God, Indivisible, 1941–1960.* Chicago: Univ. of Chicago Press, 1996.

Martyn, Carlos. *William E. Dodge: The Christian Merchant.* New York: Funk and Wagnalls, 1890.

Mather, Cotton. *Bonifacius: An Essay upon the Good, That Is to Be Devised and Designed by Those Who Desire to Answer the Great End of Life, and to Do Good While They Live.* Boston: B. Green for Samuel Gerrish, 1710.

————. *Brethren Dwelling Together in Unity.* Boston: S. Gerrish, 1718.

———. *Diary of Cotton Mather, 1681–1724*. 2 vols. Edited by Worthington Chauncey Ford. Collections of the Massachusetts Historical Society. 7th ser., vols. 7–8. Boston: Massachusetts Historical Society, 1911–12. Reprint, New York: F. Ungar [1957].

———. *Family Religion Excited and Assisted*. 2d impression. Boston: B. Green, 1707.

———. *Family Religion Urged*. Boston: B. Green, 1709.

———. *A Family Sacrifice: A Brief Essay to Direct and Excite Family Religion*. Boston: B. Green and J. Allen, 1703.

———. *A Family Well-Ordered, Or an Essay to Render Parents and Children Happy in One Another*. Boston: B. Green and J. Allen for Michael Perry, 1699.

———. *A Good Character*. Boston: B. Green, 1723.

———. *Magnalia Christi Americana*. 2 vols. in 1. Edited by Kenneth B. Murdock and Elizabeth W. Miller. Cambridge: Harvard Univ. Press, 1977.

———. *Malachi: Or, The Everlasting Gospel, Preached Unto the Nations, and Those Maxims of Piety*. Boston: T. Crump for Robert Starke, 1717.

———. *Optanda. Good Men Described, and Good Things Propounded*. Boston: Benjamin Harris, 1692.

———. *Ornaments for the Daughters of Zion*. Boston: B. Green for Samuel Phillips, 1692. Reprint, Delmar N.Y.: Scholars' Facsimiles and Reprints, 1978.

———. *Parental Wishes and Charges; Or, The Enjoyment of a Glorious Christ*. Boston: T. Green, 1705.

———. *Pastoral Desires*. Boston: B. Green for Nicholas Boone, 1712.

———. *Piety and Equity, United*. Boston: J. Allen for Robert Starke, 1717.

———. *Right Thoughts in Sad Hours, Representing the Comforts and Duties of Good Men under all their Afflictions, And Particularly, That One, the Untimely Death of Children*. London: L. B. Seeley and Sons, 1689.

———. *Selected Letters of Cotton Mather*. Edited by Kenneth Silverman. Baton Rouge: Louisiana State Univ. Press, 1971.

———. *Small Offerings Towards the Service of the Tabernacle in the Wilderness*. Boston: R. Pierce, 1689.

———. *A Soul Well-Anchored*. Boston: B. Green, 1712.

Mather, Increase. *The Duty of Parents to Pray for Their Children, Open and Applyed in a Sermon, Preached May 19, 1703*. Boston: B. Green and J. Allen, 1703.

Mathews, Shailer. *The Message of Jesus to Our Modern Life*. Chicago: Univ. of Chicago Press, 1915.

———. *Scientific Management in the Churches*. Chicago: Univ. of Chicago Press, 1912.

———. *What Religion Does for Personality*. Chicago: American Institute for Sacred Literature, 1932.

Mathisen, James A. "From Muscular Jesus to Jocks for Jesus." *Christian Century*, Jan. 1–8, 1992, 11–15.

Mazer, Sharon. "The Power Team: Muscular Christianity and the Spectacle of Conversion." *Drama Review* 38, no. 4 (Winter 1994): 162–88.

McCartney, Bill, with Dave Diles and Lyndi McCartney. *From Ashes to Glory*. Rev. ed. Nashville: Thomas Nelson, 1995.

McCartney, Bill, with David Halbrook and Lyndi McCartney. *Sold Out: Becoming Man Enough to Make a Difference*. Nashville: Word Publishing, 1997.

McDannell, Colleen. *The Christian Home in Victorian America, 1840–1900.* Bloomington: Indiana Univ. Press, 1986.

———. "'True Men as We Need Them': Catholicism and the Irish-American Male." *American Studies* 26, no. 2 (Fall 1986): 19–36.

McGuire, Meredith B., with Debra Kantor. *Ritual Healing in Suburban America.* New Brunswick, N.J.: Rutgers Univ. Press, 1988.

McLaren, Angus. *The Trials of Masculinity: Policing Sexual Boundaries, 1870–1930.* Chicago: Univ. of Chicago Press, 1997.

McLoughlin, William G. *Billy Sunday Was His Real Name.* Chicago: Univ. of Chicago Press, 1955.

McSparron, Cecil. *The Servant Leader in the New Testament: An Exposition with Special Reference to the Works of Robert K. Greenleaf.* Ottawa: National Library of Canada, 1987.

Men and Religion Forward Movement. *The Program of Work.* New York: Association Press, 1911.

Messages of the Men and Religion Movement. 7 vols. New York: Association Press, 1912.

Meyer, Donald. *The Positive Thinkers: Popular Religious Psychology from Mary Baker Eddy to Norman Vincent Peale and Ronald Reagan.* Rev. ed. Middletown, Conn.: Wesleyan Univ. Press, 1988.

Middlekauff, Robert. *The Mathers: Three Generations of Puritan Intellectuals, 1596–1728.* New York: Oxford Univ. Press, 1971.

Miller, John C. *The First Frontier: Life in Colonial America.* New York: Laurel, 1966.

Miller, John W. *Biblical Faith and Fathering: Why We Call God "Father."* New York and Mahwah, N.J.: Paulist Press, 1990.

Miller, William Lee. "The Gospel of Norman Vincent Peale." *Union Seminary Quarterly Review* 10 (Jan. 1955): 15–22.

———. *Piety Along the Potomac.* Boston: Houghton Mifflin, 1964.

Minkowitz, Donna. "In the Name of the Father." *Ms.* 6, no. 3 (Nov.–Dec. 1995): 64–71.

Mintz, Steven, and Susan Kellogg. *Domestic Revolutions: A Social History of American Family Life.* New York: Free Press, 1988.

Moller, Herbert. "Sex Composition and Correlated Culture Patterns in Colonial New England." *William and Mary Quarterly,* 3d ser., 2 (1945): 113–53.

Monick, Eugene. *Phallos: Sacred Image of the Masculine.* Toronto: Inner City Books, 1987.

Montgomery, Edrene Stephens. "Bruce Barton and the Twentieth Century Menace of Unreality." Ph.D. diss., Univ. of Arkansas, 1984.

———. "Bruce Barton's *The Man Nobody Knows:* A Popular Advertising Illusion." *Journal of Popular Culture* 19, no. 3 (Winter 1985): 21–34.

Moorhead, James H. "Presbyterians and the Mystique of Organizational Efficiency, 1870–1936." In *Reimagining Denominationalism: Interpretive Essays,* edited by Robert Bruce Mullin and Russell E. Richey, 264–87. New York: Oxford Univ. Press, 1994.

Morgan, David, ed. *Icons of American Protestantism: The Art of Warner Sallman.* New Haven, Conn.: Yale Univ. Press, 1996.

Morgan, Edmund S. *The Puritan Family: Religion and Domestic Relations in Seventeenth-Century New England.* 1944. Reprint, New York: Harper and Row, 1966.

Morley, Patrick M. *The Man in the Mirror: Solving the 24 Problems Men Face.* Nashville: Thomas Nelson, 1992.

Mott, Frank Luther. *Golden Multitudes: The Story of Bestsellers in the United States.* New York: R. R. Bowker, 1947.

Mullin, Robert Bruce, and Russell E. Richey, eds. *Reimagining Denominationalism: Interpretive Essays.* New York: Oxford Univ. Press, 1994.

Murphy, Myles P. *The Life and Times of Archbishop Fulton J. Sheen.* New York: Alba House, 2000.

Murray, William D. "The Bible and the Individual Man." In *Messages of the Men and Religion Movement,* vol. 3, *Bible Study, Evangelism,* 44–55. New York: Association Press, 1912.

Nason, Michael, and Donna Nason. *Robert Schuller: The Inside Story.* Waco, Tex.: Word Books, 1983.

Nelson, Clyde K. "Russell H. Conwell and the 'Gospel of Wealth.'" *Foundations* 5 (Jan. 1962): 39–51.

Nelson, James B. *The Intimate Connection: Male Sexuality, Male Spirituality.* Philadelphia: Westminster, 1988.

Nicholson, Meredith. "Should Smith Go to Church?" *Atlantic* 109 (June 1916): 721–33.

Niebuhr, Gustav. "SBC Declares Wife Should 'Submit' to Her Husband." *New York Times,* June 10, 1998, p. A1.

Niese, Russell. *The Newspaper and Religious Publicity.* Nashville: Sunday School Board of the Southern Baptist Convention, 1925.

Noonan, Daniel P. *Missionary with a Mike: The Bishop Sheen Story.* New York: Pageant Press, 1972.

———. *The Passion of Fulton Sheen.* New York: Dodd, Mead, 1972.

Norton, Mary Beth. *Founding Mothers and Fathers: Gendered Power and the Forming of American Society.* New York: Knopf, 1996.

Novak, Michael. *The Joy of Sports: End Zones, Bases, Baskets, Balls, and the Consecration of the American Spirit.* New York: Basic Books, 1976.

Nuechterlein, James A. "Bruce Barton and the Business Ethos of the 1920's." *South Atlantic Quarterly* 76 (1977): 293–308.

Orsi, Robert. *Thank You, St. Jude: Women's Devotion to the Patron Saint of Lost Causes.* New Haven, Conn.: Yale Univ. Press, 1996.

Ownby, Ted. *Subduing Satan: Religion, Recreation and Manhood in the Rural South, 1865–1910.* Chapel Hill: Univ. of North Carolina Press, 1990.

Palmer, Alan Geoffrey. *The Servant-Leader: An Examination of the New Testament Concept of Leadership.* Ottawa: National Library of Canada, 1985.

Peale, Norman Vincent. *The Amazing Results of Positive Thinking.* Englewood Cliffs, N.J.: Prentice-Hall, 1959.

———. *The Art of Living.* New York: Abingdon-Cokesbury, 1937.

———. *A Guide to Confident Living.* New York: Macmillan, 1948.

———. *Power of the Plus Factor.* Old Tappan, N.J.: Fleming H. Revell, 1987.

———. *The Power of Positive Thinking.* New York: Prentice-Hall, 1952.

———. *The Tough-Minded Optimist.* Englewood Cliffs, N.J.: Prentice-Hall, 1961.

———. *The True Joy of Positive Living: An Autobiography.* Pawling, N.Y.: Foundation for Christian Living, 1984.

————. *You Can If You Think You Can.* Greenwich, Conn.: Fawcett, 1974.

Peale, Norman Vincent, and Smiley Blanton. *The Art of Real Success.* New York: Prentice-Hall, 1950.

————. *Faith Is the Answer.* Englewood Cliffs, N.J.: Prentice-Hall, 1940.

Peale, Mrs. Norman Vincent (Ruth Stafford). *The Adventure of Being a Wife.* Englewood Cliffs, N.J.: Prentice-Hall, 1971.

Pierce, Jason Noble. *The Masculine Power of Christ; or, Christ Measured as a Man.* Boston: Pilgrim Press, 1912.

Piper, John F., Jr. *Robert E. Speer: Prophet of the American Church.* Louisville, Ky.: Geneva Press, 2000.

Pleck, Elizabeth, and Joseph H. Pleck, eds. *The American Man.* Englewood Cliffs, N.J.: Prentice-Hall, 1980.

Pleck, Joseph H. *The Myth of Masculinity.* Cambridge: MIT Press, 1981.

Porterfield, Amanda. *The Transformation of American Religion: The Story of a Late Twentieth-Century Awakening.* New York: Oxford Univ. Press, 2001.

Powell, Milton, ed. *The Voluntary Church: American Religious Life Seen through the Eyes of European Visitors.* New York: Macmillan, 1967.

Prime, Samuel Irenaeus. *Fifteen Years of Prayer in the Fulton Street Meeting.* New York: Scribner, Armstrong, 1872.

————. *The Power of Prayer, Illustrated in the Wonderful Displays of Divine Grace at the Fulton Street and Other Meetings.* New York: Scribner's, 1858.

Primer, Ben. *Protestants and American Business Methods.* Studies in History and Culture, No. 7. Ann Arbor, Mich.: UMI Research Press, 1979.

Putney, Clifford. *Muscular Christianity: Manhood and Sports in Protestant America, 1880–1920.* Cambridge: Harvard Univ. Press, 2001.

Quint, Howard H., and Milton Cantor, eds. *Men, Women, and Issues in American History.* 2 vols. Homewood, Ill.: Dorsey, 1980.

Rankin, Richard. *Ambivalent Churchmen and Evangelical Churchwomen: The Religion of the Episcopal Elite in North Carolina, 1800–1860.* Columbia: Univ. of South Carolina Press, 1993.

Rauschenbusch, Walter. *Christianizing the Social Order.* 1912. Reprint, New York: Macmillan, 1926.

Reeves, Thomas C. *America's Bishop: The Life and Times of Fulton J. Sheen.* San Francisco: Encounter Books, 2001.

"Religion and the Brain: In the New Field of 'Neurotheology,' Scientists Seek the Biological Basis of Spirituality." *Newsweek,* May 17, 2001, 50–57.

Ribuffo, Leo. "Jesus Christ as Business Statesman: Bruce Barton and the Selling of Corporate Capitalism." *American Quarterly* 33 (1981): 206–31.

Riesman, David, with Nathan Glazer and Reuel Denney. *The Lonely Crowd.* New Haven, Conn.: Yale Univ. Press, 1950.

Robinson, George W. "The Bible and the Home." In *Messages of the Men and Religion Movement,* vol. 3, *Bible Study, Evangelism,* 56–63. New York: Association Press, 1912.

Rohr, Richard, and Joseph Martos. "The Two Journeys in Men's Spiritual Development." *Studies in Formative Spirituality* 12, no. 2 (May 1991): 159–67.

Roof, Wade Clark. *Community and Commitment.* New York: Elsevier, 1978.

————. *A Generation of Seekers: The Spiritual Journeys of the Baby Boomer Generation.* San Francisco: Harper, 1994.

———. *Spiritual Marketplace: Baby Boomers and the Remaking of American Religion*. Princeton, N.J.: Princeton Univ. Press, 1999.

Rosenberg, Charles. "Sexuality, Class and Role in Nineteenth-Century America." In *The American Man*, edited by Elizabeth Pleck and Joseph H. Pleck, 219–54. Englewood Cliffs, N.J.: Prentice-Hall, 1980.

Rosenthal, Leon Glen. "Christian Statesmanship in the First Missionary-Ecumenical Generation." Ph.D. diss., Univ. of Chicago, 1989.

Rotundo, E. Anthony. *American Manhood: Transformations in Masculinity from the Revolution to the Modern Era*. New York: Basic Books, 1993.

———. "Learning about Manhood: Gender Ideals and the Middle-Class Family in Nineteenth Century America." In *Manliness and Morality: Middle-Class Masculinity in Britain and America, 1800–1940*, edited by J. A. Mangan and James Walvin, 35–51. New York: St. Martin's, 1987.

———. "Romantic Friendship: Male Intimacy and Middle-Class Youth in the Northern United States, 1800–1900." *Journal of Southern History* 23 (Fall 1989): 1–25.

Rugoff, Milton. *The Beechers: An American Family in the Nineteenth Century*. New York: Harper and Row, 1981.

Ryan, Mary P. *Cradle of the Middle Class: The Family in Oneida County, New York, 1790–1865*. New York: Cambridge Univ. Press, 1981.

"SBC Approves Family Statement." *Christian Century* 115 (June 17–24, 1998): 602–3.

"SBC Moves to Limit Office of Pastor to Men." *Christian Century* 117 (June 7–14, 2000): 641.

Scharnhorst, Gary. *Horatio Alger, Jr*. Twayne's United States Authors Series. Edited by David J. Nordloh. Boston: Twayne, 1980.

Scharnhorst, Gary, with Jack Bales. *The Lost Life of Horatio Alger, Jr*. Bloomington: Indiana Univ. Press, 1985.

Schlesinger, Elizabeth Bancroft. "Cotton Mather and His Children." *William and Mary Quarterly* 3d ser., 10 (Apr. 1953): 181–89.

Schuller, Robert A., ed. *Robert Schuller's Life Changers*. Old Tappan, N.J.: Fleming H. Revell, 1981.

Schuller, Robert H. *The Be Happy Attitudes: Eight Positive Attitudes that Can Transform Your Life*. Waco, Tex.: Word, 1985.

———. *Be Happy You Are Loved*. 1986. Reprint, Boston: G. K. Hall, 1988.

———. *Believe in the God Who Believes in You*. Nashville: Thomas Nelson, 1989.

———. *God's Way to the Good Life*. Grand Rapids, Mich.: William B. Eerdmans, 1963. Reprint, New Canaan, Conn.: Keats, 1974.

———. *Move Ahead with Possibility Thinking*. Old Tappan, N.J.: Spire Books, 1967.

———. *My Journey: From an Iowa Farm to a Cathedral of Dreams*. San Francisco: HarperSanFrancisco, 2001.

———. *Peace of Mind through Possibility Thinking*. Garden City, N.Y.: Doubleday, 1977.

———. *The Peak to Peek Principle*. Garden City, N.Y.: Doubleday, 1980.

———. *Power Ideas for a Happy Family*. Old Tappan, N.J.: Fleming H. Revell, 1972.

———. *Power Thoughts*. New York: HarperCollins, 1993.

———. *Prayer, My Soul's Adventure with God: A Spiritual Autobiography*. Nashville: Thomas Nelson, 1995.

———. *Self-Esteem: The New Reformation*. Waco, Tex.: Word Books, 1982.

———. *Self-Love: The Dynamic Force of Success*. New York: Hawthorn, 1969.

————. *Success Is Never Ending, Failure Is Never Final.* Nashville: Thomas Nelson, 1988.

————. *Tough-Minded Faith for Tender-Hearted People.* Nashville: Thomas Nelson, 1983.

————. *Tough Times Never Last, but Tough People Do.* Nashville: Thomas Nelson, 1983.

Schweitzer, Albert. *The Quest for the Historical Jesus: A Critical Study of Its Progress from Reimarus to Wrede.* Translated by W. Montgomery. 1906. Reprint, New York: Macmillan, 1964.

Seven Promises of a Promise Keeper. Colorado Springs, Colo.: Focus on the Family, 1994.

Sewall, Samuel. *The Diary of Samuel Sewall.* 2 vols. Edited by M. Halsey Thomas. New York: Farrar, Straus and Giroux, 1973.

————. *The Diary of Samuel Sewall.* Vols. 5–7 of *Collections of the Massachusetts Historical Society.* 5th ser. Boston: Massachusetts Historical Society, 1878–82.

————. *The Letter-Book of Samuel Sewall.* Vols. 1–2 of *Collections of the Massachusetts Historical Society.* 6th ser. Boston: Massachusetts Historical Society, 1886–88.

Shakarian, Demos. "FGBMFI Struggles toward the Future." *Charisma* 13 (Mar. 1988): 24.

Sheen, Fulton J. *Peace of Soul.* New York: McGraw-Hill, 1949.

————. *Treasure in Clay: The Autobiography of Fulton J. Sheen.* Reprint, San Francisco: Ignatius Press, 1993.

Shepard, Thomas. *Works of Thomas Shepard.* Edited by John Albro. 3 vols. Boston: Doctrinal Tract and Book Society, 1853.

Sittser, Gerald L. "Bruce Barton." In *Twentieth-Century Shapers of American Popular Religion,* edited by Charles H. Lippy, 20–29. Westport, Conn.: Greenwood, 1989.

Smith, Albert Hatcher. *The Life of Russell H. Conwell.* Boston: Silver, Burdette, 1899.

Smith, Gary Scott. "The Men and Religion Forward Movement of 1911–1912: New Perspectives on Evangelical Social Concerns and the Relationship between Christianity and Progressivism." *Westminster Theological Journal* 49, no. 1 (Spring 1987): 91–118.

Smith-Rosenberg, Carroll. *Disorderly Conduct: Visions of Gender in Victorian America.* New York: Oxford Univ. Press, 1985.

————. "The Female World or Love and Ritual: Relations between Women in Nineteenth-Century America." *Signs* 1 (1975): 1–29.

Spears, Larry C. *Insights on Leadership: Service, Stewardship, Spirit, and Servant-Leadership.* New York: Wiley, 1998.

Speer, Robert E. *The Christian Man, the Church, and the War.* New York: Macmillan, 1918.

————. *Jesus and Our Human Problems.* New York: Fleming H. Revell, 1946.

————. *The Marks of a Man; or, The Essentials of Christian Character.* Cincinnati: Jennings and Graham, 1907.

————. *The Meaning of Christ to Me.* New York: Fleming H. Revell, 1936.

————. *Some Great Leaders in the World Movement.* 1911. Reprint, Freeport, N.Y.: Books for Libraries, 1967.

————. *Studies of the Man Christ Jesus.* New York: Fleming H. Revell, 1896.

————. *The Stuff of Manhood: Some Needed Notes in American Character.* New York: Fleming H. Revell, 1917.

————. *Young Men Who Overcame.* 2d ed. New York: Fleming H. Revell, 1905.

Stannard, David E. *The Puritan Way of Death: A Study in Religion, Culture, and Social Change.* New York: Oxford Univ. Press, 1977.

Starhawk. *The Spiral Dance.* San Francisco: Harper, 1979.

Stark, Rodney. "Physiology and Faith: Addressing the 'Universal' Gender Difference in Religious Commitment." *Journal for the Scientific Study of Religion* 41 (2002): 495–507.

Steffen, Charles G. "The Sewall Children in Colonial New England." *New England Historical and Genealogical Register* 131 (1977): 163–72.

Stelzle, Charles. *Boys of the Street: How to Win Them.* New York: Fleming H. Revell, 1904.

———. *Gospel of Labor.* New York: Fleming H. Revell, 1912.

Stowe, Harriet Beecher. *The Minister's Wooing* (1859). Introduction by Sandra R. Duguid. Hartford, Conn.: Harriet Beecher Stowe Center, 1978.

Strandness, T. B. *Samuel Sewall: A Puritan Portrait.* East Lansing: Michigan State Univ. Press, 1967.

Strong, Josiah. *The Times and Young Men.* New York: Baker and Taylor, 1901.

Susman, Warren. "Piety, Profits, and Play: The 1920's." In *Men, Women, and Issues in American History,* edited by Howard H. Quint and Milton Cantor, 2:191–216. Homewood, Ill.: Dorsey, 1980.

Swidler, Leonard. "Jesus Was a Feminist." *Catholic World* 212 (Jan. 1971): 177–83.

Tauber, Maurice F. *Russell Herman Conwell, 1843–1925: A Bibliography.* Philadelphia: Temple Univ. Library, 1935.

Thiesen, Lee Scott. "'My God, Did I Set All This in Motion?' General Lew Wallace and *Ben Hur.*" *Journal of Popular Culture* 18, no. 2 (1984): 33–41.

Thompson, Edward H., Jr. "Beyond the Sex Difference: Gender Variations in Religiousness." *Journal for the Scientific Study of Religion* 30 (1991): 381–94.

Thompson, Edward H., Jr., and Kathryn R. Remmes. "Does Masculinity Thwart Being Religious? A Study of Older Men's Religiousness." *Journal for the Scientific Study of Religion* 41 (2002): 521–32

Thompson, William G. "Men and the Gospels." *Catholic World* 235 (May/June 1992): 104–10.

"Tracing the Synapses of Our Spirituality: Researchers Examine the Relationship between the Brain and Religion." *Washington Post,* June 17, 2001, p. A1.

Trent, John T., and Charles W. Colson, eds. *Go the Distance: The Making of a Promise Keeper.* Colorado Springs, Colo.: Focus on the Family, 1996.

Van Leeuwen, Mary Stewart. *My Brother's Keeper.* Downers Grove, Ill.: InterVarsity, 2002.

———. "Servanthood or Soft Patriarchy? A Christian Feminist Looks at the Promise Keepers Movement." *Journal of Men's Studies* 5, no. 3 (Feb. 1997): 233–61. Also in *Priscilla Papers* 11, no. 2 (1997): 28–40.

———. "Why Men Get Anxious." *Christian Century* 116, no. 33 (Dec. 1, 1999): 1166–68.

Voskuil, Dennis. *Mountains into Goldmines: Robert Schuller and the Gospel of Success.* Grand Rapids, Mich.: William B. Eerdmans, 1983.

———. "Robert Schuller." In *Twentieth-Century Shapers of American Popular Religion,* edited by Charles H. Lippy, 364–71. Westport, Conn.: Greenwood, 1989.

Wadsworth, Benjamin. *The Well-Ordered Family: or, Relative Duties.* 2d ed. Boston: S. Kneeland for Nicholas Buttolph, 1715.

Wagenheim, Jeff. "Among the Promise Keepers." *Utne Reader* 73 (Jan.–Feb. 1996): 74–77.

Wayne, Kenneth. *Building the Young Man.* Chicago: A. C. McClurg, 1912.

Webb-Mitchell, Brett. "And a Football Coach Shall Lead Them: A Theological Critique of *Seven Promises of a Promise Keeper.*" *Soundings: An Interdisciplinary Journal* 80, nos. 2–3 (Summer/Fall 1997): 305–26.

Weeks, Louis. "The Incorporation of American Religion: The Case of the Presbyterians." *Religion and American Culture* 1 (Winter 1991): 101–18.

Welter, Barbara. *Dimity Convictions: The American Woman in the Nineteenth Century.* Athens: Ohio Univ. Press, 1976.

Wheatley, Richard. *The Life and Letters of Mrs. Phoebe Palmer.* 1876. Reprint, New York: Garland, 1981.

Wheeler, W. Reginald. *A Man Sent from God: A Biography of Robert E. Speer.* Introduction by John A. Mackay. Westwood, N.J.: Fleming H. Revell, 1956.

White, Bouck. *The Call of the Carpenter.* New York: Doubleday, 1913.

Whyte, William H., Jr. *The Organization Man.* Garden City, N.Y.: Doubleday Anchor, 1956.

Wilkes, C. Gene. *Jesus on Leadership: Becoming a Servant Leader.* Nashville: LifeWay, 1996.

Williams, Rhys S., ed. *Promise Keepers and the New Masculinity: Private Lives and Public Morality.* Lanham, Md.: Lexington Books, 2001.

Wilson, Charles Reagan. *Baptized in Blood: The Religion of the Lost Cause, 1865–1920.* Athens: Univ. of Georgia Press, 1980.

Wilson, Lisa. *Ye Heart of a Man: The Domestic Life of Men in Colonial New England.* New Haven, Conn.: Yale Univ. Press, 1999.

Wilson, Thane. "Russell H. Conwell: Who Has Helped 3,000 Young Men to Succeed." *American Magazine* 81 (Apr. 1916): 15.

Wimmer, John R. "Russell H. Conwell." In *Twentieth-Century Shapers of American Popular Religion,* edited by Charles H. Lippy, 80–88. Westport, Conn.: Greenwood, 1989.

Winslow, Ola Elizabeth. *Samuel Sewall of Boston.* New York: Macmillan, 1964.

Wise, Rev. Daniel. *The Young Man's Counselor; or, Sketches and Illustrations of the Duties and Dangers of Young Men.* 31st ed. New York: Phillips & Hunt, 1850.

Wright, Louis B. *The First Gentlemen of Virginia: Intellectual Qualities of the Early Colonial Ruling Class.* San Marino, Calif.: Huntington Library, 1940.

Wuthnow, Robert. *After Heaven: Spirituality in America Since the 1950s.* Berkeley and Los Angeles: Univ. of California Press, 1998.

———, ed. *"I Come Away Stronger": How Small Groups Are Shaping American Religion.* Grand Rapids, Mich.: Eerdmans, 1994.

Yacovone, Donald. "Abolitionists and the 'Language of Fraternal Love.'" In *Meanings for Manhood: Constructions of Masculinity in Victorian America,* edited by Mark C. Carnes and Clyde Griffen, 85–95. Chicago: Univ. of Chicago Press, 1990.

Zuckerman, Michael. *Peaceable Kingdoms: New England Towns in the Eighteenth Century.* New York: Knopf, 1970.

Index

Do Real Men Pray? was designed and typeset on a Macintosh computer system using QuarkXPress software. The body text is set in 10.5/13 Adobe Caslon and display type is set in Berthold City. This book was designed by Preston Thomas and manufactured by Thomson-Shore, Inc.